ALL GOD'S BIBLE DREAMS

ALL GOD'S BIBLE DREAMS
GOD'S PLANS AND PURPOSE FOR EVERY DREAM

BRENDAN MCCAULEY

Copyright © 2022 by Brendan McCauley

All rights reserved.

No part of this book may be reproduced in any form or by any electronic or mechanical means, including information storage and retrieval systems, without written permission from the author, except for the use of brief quotations in a book review.

Most of the Scriptures quoted are from the NIV unless otherwise stated.

For Harry and Flo Ferguson

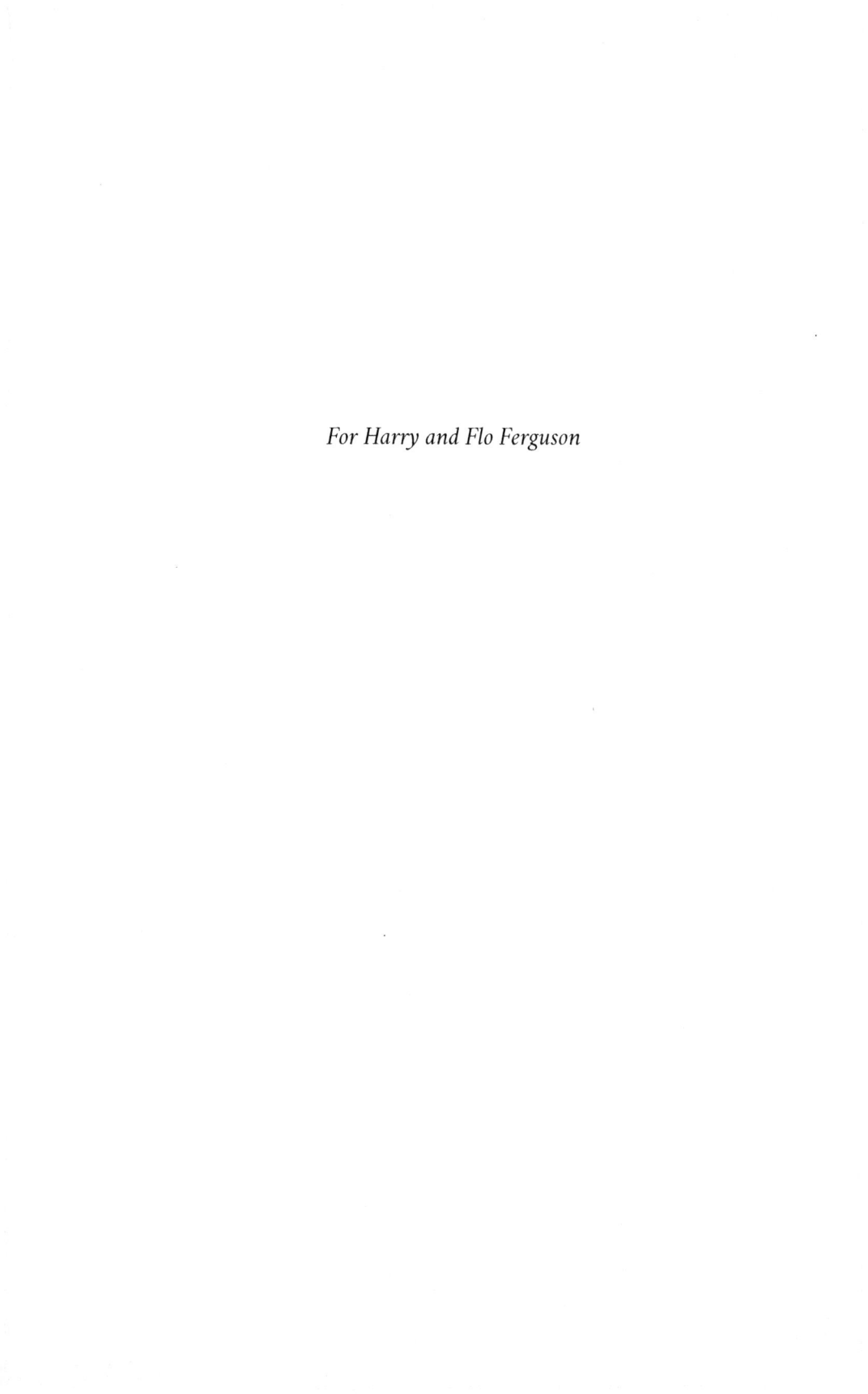

THE ETERNAL PURPOSE

All history is a record of Sovereign Almighty God fulfilling His eternal plans and purpose and the created angel Satan unsuccessfully trying to stop Him. The key word is purpose, not purposes, and that purpose is Jesus Christ.

Brendan McCauley

MCCAULEY BOOKS

Jesus Loves India!
Better Than Weapons Of War
A Man of Ethiopia
Staying Alive!
The Grapes Are Worth It!
A Little Child Shall Lead Them
All God's Bible Dreams

CONTENTS

The Eternal Purpose	vii
McCauley Books	1
God's Purpose	7
Jesus Interpreted A Dream	9
1. God's Holy Spirit Interprets God's Dreams	11
Biblical Dream Interpreters	13
2. Bible Dream Data	15
3. Bible Dream Statistics	17
4. God's Eternal Purpose For Dreams	19
5. The Danger Of Individualism	27
6. It's All About Jesus!	33
7. Satan Hates God's Dreams	41
8. My Purpose For This book	45
9. My Dream Qualifications	51
10. Bible Dreams And The Gods	57
11. God's Good Purposes For Sleep and Dreams	67
12. A Short History Of Dreams	75
13. God's Sovereign Purpose	83
14. God's Eternal Plans and Purpose	87
15. Satan's Hindering Purpose	93
16. The Angel Of The Lord	101
17. Angels In Bible Dreams	109
18. God And Jesus In Bible Dreams	111
19. Dream Purpose And Process	119
20. God's Overall Purpose For Bible Dreams	123
21. God's Purpose For Each Bible Dream	127
22. The Importance Of A Dreamer's Metron	137
23. God's Purpose For Each Dreamer's Metron	141
24. God's Purposes For Believer's Metrons	145
25. God's Purposes For Non Believer's Metrons	157
26. Definition Of A Dream	163
27. Four Kinds Of Bible Dreams	167

28. Where Dreams Come From	173
29. Dreams, Night Visions And Events Covered	179
30. The Bible's Symbolic Dreams	183
31. The Bible's Literal Dreams	185
32. The Timeline of Bible Dreams	187
33. How Jesus Interprets Dreams	193
34. The McCauley Dream Checklist	203
Old Testament Dreams	211
35. God's Purpose For Abraham	213
36. Abraham's Covenant Dream	221
37. King Abimelek's Dream	233
38. Jacob's Covenant Dream	241
39. Jacob's 'Goats and Go Back Home' Dream	251
40. Laban's 'Don't Harm Jacob' Dream	261
41. Jacob Wrestles With God and Man	269
42. The Era Of The Dream Interpreter	279
43. Joseph's 'Sheaves Of Grain' Dream	281
44. Joseph's 'Sun, Moon and Stars' Dream	291
45. Pharaoh's Cupbearer's Dream	301
46. Pharaoh's Baker's Dream	309
47. Pharaoh's Two Same 'Famine' Dreams	317
48. Jacob's 'Go Down To Egypt' Night Vision Dream	329
49. Balaam's 'Don't Curse Israel' Dream	337
50. Balaam's 'If They Call You' Dream	343
51. The Midianite's Dream for Gideon	351
52. Samuel's Night Vision Dream	361
53. Nathan's Dream For King David	371
54. David's Bedtime Prayer	379
55. Solomon's 'Discerning Heart' Dream	387
56. Solomon's 'The Bride's' Dream	395
57. Solomon's Warning Dream	409
58. Solomon 'Asks for Wisdom' Dream	419
59. Eliphaz's 'Demonic Nightmare' Dream	427
60. Job's Satanic Nightmares	435
61. Elihu's Dream Talk	441
62. Isaiah's Oracle On Dreams	451
63. Jeremiah's 'Israel Will Return' Dream	461
64. Nebuchadnezzar's 'Large Statue' Dream	475
65. Daniel's 'Mystery Revealed' Night Vision Dream	487

66. Nebuchadnezzar's 'Large Tree' Dream ... 497
67. Daniel's 'Four Beasts' Dream ... 511
68. Daniel's 'Ram, Goat and Little Horn' Dream ... 525
69. Zechariah's Dream Of Horses ... 537
70. Zechariah's Dream Of Horns And Craftsmen. ... 549
71. Zechariah's Dream Of The Measuring Line ... 559
72. Zechariah's Dream Of Joshua ... 567
73. Zechariah's Dream Of Lampstand and Trees ... 577
74. Zechariah's Dream Of The Flying Scroll ... 587
75. Zechariah's Dream Of The Woman in a Basket ... 597
76. Zechariah's Dream Of the Four Chariots ... 607
    New Testament Dreams ... 615
77. St. Joseph's 'Marry Mary' Dream ... 617
78. The Magi's Dream ... 625
79. St. Joseph's 'Escape To Egypt' Dream ... 631
80. St. Joseph's 'Back To Israel' Dream ... 637
81. St. Joseph's 'Go To Nazareth' Dream ... 643
82. Jesus' 'Tempted By Satan' Dream ... 649
83. Pilate's Wife's Dream ... 657
84. Peter Interpreting Pentecost ... 663
85. Saul's Vision On The Road to Damascus ... 669
86. Ananias' Vision About Paul ... 675
87. Paul's Trance ... 683
88. Cornelius' 'Send For Peter' Vision ... 691
89. Peter's 'Kill And Eat' Trance ... 699
90. Peter's Revelation At Cornelius's House ... 707
91. Paul's 'Man Of Macedonia' Night Vision Dream ... 715
92. Paul's 'Fear Not' Night Vision Dream ... 721
93. Paul's 'Angelic' Night Vision Dream ... 729
    Apocryphal Dreams ... 735
94. Egypt's 'Dreadful Dreams' ... 737
95. Esdras' Eagle And Lion' Dream ... 743
96. Esdras 'Man From The Sea' Dream ... 755
97. Mordecai's 'Two Great Dragons' Dream ... 765
98. Judas Maccabees' 'Golden Sword' Dream ... 773
99. The Primary Function Of God's dreams ... 781

Acknowledgments ... 783
Notes ... 785

GOD'S PURPOSE

God is working His purpose out
As year succeeds to year;
God is working His purpose out,
And the time is drawing near;
Nearer and nearer draws the time,
The time that shall surely be,
When the earth shall be filled
With the glory of God
As the waters cover the sea.

Arthur C Ainger (1894)

JESUS INTERPRETED A DREAM

"Interpreting dreams is God's business."

Genesis 40:8 (NLT)

Did you know Jesus interpreted a dream?

GOD'S HOLY SPIRIT INTERPRETS GOD'S DREAMS

A correct interpretation of a symbolic God given dream is a sovereign activity of God's Holy Spirit. All God's symbolic dreams are from the mind of God and as Paul reminds us,

> The Spirit searches all things, even the deep things of God. For who knows a person's thoughts except their own spirit within them? In the same way no one knows the thoughts of God except the Spirit of God.[1]

BIBLICAL DREAM INTERPRETERS

There are only three named people in Scripture who interpreted dreams.

Jacob interpreted Joseph's dream and rebuked his favourite son for sharing it.

Afterwards, Joseph interpreted four dreams and was made second in command of powerful Egypt as a result.

Later, Daniel interpreted a couple of dreams and was made ruler over the entire province of Babylon because of this gift.

An unnamed soldier interpreted a dream and was probably killed next day because of his accurate interpretation.

Joseph's brothers correctly interpreted Joseph's first dream and they hated him all the more because of it.

There were also four angels in Scripture who interpreted eleven dreams. One was Gabriel and another was Jesus as *The Angel of the Lord.*

Jesus' interpretation made Jacob rich and added no sorrow.[1]

BIBLE DREAM DATA

- Jesus interpreted a Bible dream.
- Jesus taught us how to interpret dreams.
- Did Satan tempt Jesus in a Bible dream?
- There are no Bible dreams about the past.
- Only one woman had a Bible dream.
- One unbeliever interpreted a Bible dream.
- God answered a prayer with a Bible dream.
- There are only two recorded satanic Bible dreams.
- No Bible dream ever came from the dreamer's self.
- Only one Bible dream was given for another person.
- 27 Bible dreams are literal.
- 21 Bible dreams are symbolic.
- All Bible dreams relate to the dreamer's metron.
- All Bible dreams destroyed Satan's work.
- All Bible dreams advanced God's plans and purpose.
- God's purpose is always Jesus Christ.

BIBLE DREAM STATISTICS

As regards the 53 Bible dreams examined in this book the statistics are,

In 62 % of Bible dreams God demonstrated His sovereign dominion over all the powers and principalities attacking His Covenant People and their seed line.

In 26% of Bible dreams God encouraged and guided His Covenant People with specific direction for their well-being and the safety of their seed line.

In 8% of Bible dreams God prevented kings and leaders from harming His Covenant People and their seed line and instead He caused them to bless His people.

In 4% of Bible dreams God helped and encouraged His New Testament Covenant People to carry out the Great Commission of Jesus Christ.

If we exclude the five Apocrypha dreams there are 48 dreams in most Bibles, which breaks down to 27 literal dreams and 21 symbolic dreams.

Of the 21 symbolic dreams, Zechariah is associated with eight of them, Joseph is associated with six, Daniel is associated with five,

Jacob is associated one and an unnamed Midianite soldier has the remaining one.

Because an angel interprets all of Zechariah's eight symbolic dreams the only named people who actually interpreted dreams in the Bible are Jacob, Joseph, Daniel. Jesus and the Midianite soldier also each interpreted a dream but more of that later.

Jacob interpreted the one dream he's linked with, Joseph interpreted four of the six dreams he's associated with, Daniel interpreted two of the five dreams he's related with and Jesus and the Midianite soldier each interpreted the one dream they were connected to.

So, if your main focus is on how to interpret dreams like Jacob, Joseph, Daniel, Jesus and the soldier then you need only concentrate on these nine dreams. In that case go to Chapter 31, *How Jesus Interprets Dreams* and learn about *The Symbol Replacement Method* of Christian Dream Interpretation.

If on the other hand you also want to know God's plans and purpose for all Bible dreams and how to interpret dreams like angels perhaps you better read all 53 dreams. You can of course start with chapter 29!

GOD'S ETERNAL PURPOSE FOR DREAMS

*A*ll history is a record of Sovereign Almighty God fulfilling His eternal plans and purpose and the created angel Satan unsuccessfully trying to stop Him. God sent His Bible dreams in order to advance His own Kingdom plans and purpose. The key word is *purpose*, not purposes and that purpose is Jesus Christ.

Paul says, God's eternal purpose is fully accomplished in Christ Jesus our Lord.[1] He also said, God,

> Has made known to us the mystery of His will
> according to His good pleasure, which He purposed
> in Christ as a plan for the fullness of time, to bring
> all things in heaven and on earth together in Christ.
> In Him we were also chosen as God's own, having been
> predestined according to the plan of Him who
> works out everything by the counsel of His will, in
> order that we, who were the first to hope in Christ,
> would be for the praise of His glory.[2]

All Bible dreams concern Jesus in one way or another and the three main characters are always God, Satan and the dreamer. There are only three types of spiritual beings and three sources of spiritual activity.

There is God and His faithful spirits who are always good and holy.

There is Satan and his rebellious spirits who are always bad and evil.

Then there is humanity whose spirit is either good or bad based on whether they are being influenced and ruled by God's Holy Spirit or Satan's evil spirit.

Our creator God is eternal from everlasting to everlasting.[3] He is always advancing His own sovereign eternal plans and purpose. Sometimes He uses dreams.

Satan slithered into the Bible in Genesis 3 and is thrown out again in Revelation 20. His sole purpose is to constantly attack and hinder God's plans and purpose.

The dreamers all have an opportunity to respond appropriately to their God given dreams and so play a positive part in furthering God's plans and purpose.

Before we slide each Bible dream under the microscope it's important to grasp something of the bigger picture of God's plans and purpose. Then, it's a whole lot easier to see how God uses dreams to advance His agenda.

God's dreams are always concerned with God's Eternal Purpose and God's Eternal Purpose is always Jesus Christ.

We must also remember after we've spent a couple of billion, trillion, gazillion years in eternity with Jesus we'll still only be getting to know Him and His Eternal purpose better.

Having said that, there is a golden cord running from Genesis 1 to Revelation 22 about redeemed mankind coming to reign with the enthroned Christ. This was always God's plan and three things God decided before the foundation of the world help us to grasp this better,

- God loved Jesus before time began.
- God created us to love Jesus before time began.
- God ordained Jesus to be our Saviour before time began.

Jesus said,

> I want those you have given me to be with me where I am, and to see my glory, the glory you have given me because you loved me before the creation of the world.[4]

God loved and delighted in Jesus long before creation. In fact, He delighted in Jesus so much He couldn't keep it all to Himself. So, He made mankind in His own image and likeness so we too could appreciate the wonder of Jesus. Paul says,

> For he chose us in him before the creation of the world to be holy and blameless in his sight. In love he predestined us for adoption to sonship through Jesus Christ, in accordance with his pleasure and will—to the praise of his glorious grace, which he has freely given us in the One he loves.[5]

God's primary purpose in creating us was to honour His Son. We're not here to do our own will or seek our own self-centred blessing. We were created to praise Jesus.

The third decision God made before the foundation of the world was that Jesus should redeem us. Peter said,

> For you know that it was not with perishable things such as silver or gold that you were redeemed from the empty way of life handed down to you from your ancestors, but with the precious blood of

Christ, a lamb without blemish or defect. He was chosen before the creation of the world, but was revealed in these last times for your sake. Through him you believe in God, who raised him from the dead and glorified him, and so your faith and hope are in God.[6]

Before the foundation of the world God decided to create and choose human beings made in God's likeness who'd be redeemed by Jesus and who'd love and praise Jesus forever.

The entire heavenly host in the unseen realm had to watch on as this drama unfolded over thousands of years. Satan and his army would always try to hinder God's purpose while God's holy angels would always help.

Without an understanding of the larger picture of God's eternal plans and purpose we could end up with a weak and limited understanding of God's intention for dreams. We could even end up thinking God's dreams were about our plans, purposes and destiny. That would be a big mistake.

All Bible dreams were sent to solve a problem. They all came in the midst of intense ongoing spiritual warfare. This sometimes made it seem as if God and man are stumbling from one spiritual crisis to another but that couldn't be further from the truth.

The reality is our sovereign God is always advancing His own eternal plans and purpose. Yet no prophet, priest or king in the Old Testament really knew God's purpose. Nor did any spiritual being in the unseen realm.

God's purpose was a total mystery to them. They had no knowledge of the Church of Christ, the Body of Christ or the Bride of Christ.

The word *mystery* describes something God has hidden for a period of time. Finally one day, God chose to reveal the mystery of His eternal purpose to Paul who wrote,

> Although I am less than the least of all the Lord's people, this grace was given me: to preach to the Gentiles the boundless riches of Christ, and to make plain to everyone the administration of this mystery, which for ages past was kept hidden in God, who created all things. His intent was that now, through the church, the manifold wisdom of God should be made known to the rulers and authorities in the heavenly realms, according to his eternal purpose that he accomplished in Christ Jesus our Lord. In him and through faith in him we may approach God with freedom and confidence.[7]

On one level God is putting on a show for the rulers and authorities in the heavenly realms and they don't really understand what's going on. Peter said, Even angels long to look into these things.[8] Paul similarly says,

> No, we speak of the mysterious and hidden wisdom of God, which He destined for our glory before time began. None of the rulers of this age understood it, for if they had, they would not have crucified the Lord of glory.[9]

Another image that helps us better understand God's plans and purpose is that of a wedding. At the heart of the Bible there's a *Divine Love Story* between Jesus and His beloved.

Genesis began with the wedding of Adam and Eve and Revelation ends with the eternal marriage between Jesus and His Church. Jesus's first miracle occurred at a wedding and Paul calls marriage a profound mystery similar to the relationship between Christ and the church.[10]

The marvellous truth is our Lord and Saviour Jesus Christ has always wanted a bride, a wife who will share all things with Him as He fulfils His will in the ages to come. Jesus specifically asked God for this. He prayed,

> My prayer is not for them alone. I pray also for those who will believe in me through their message, that all of them may be one, Father, just as you are in me and I am in you. May they also be in us so that the world may believe that you have sent me.
> I have given them the glory that you gave me, that they may be one as we are one— I in them and you in me —so that they may be brought to complete unity. Then the world will know that you sent me and have loved them even as you have loved me.
> "Father, I want those you have given me to be with me where I am, and to see my glory, the glory you have given me because you loved me before the creation of the world.[11]

God's covenant promise to Abraham that all nations would be blessed through him is still coming to pass as 200,000 new people from all over the word are daily being saved through the finished work of Jesus and are fast becoming part of His everlasting bride.

It hasn't yet been revealed what marvellous adventures Jesus has in store for us in eternity but you can be sure it'll be an amazing roller coaster ride in a never-ending love story.

The purpose of this short chapter is to remind us that God had plans and purpose from before the foundation of the world that He worked out in the Bible and that He is still working out today.

So when we slip a Bible dream under the microscope we should always remember this dream has been sent from God to a person for a specific purpose and it's not merely some random dream without a precise function.

Bible dreams were always sent to sort out a problem and to advance God's plans and purpose. Interestingly no Bible dream ever speaks about the past. Like the Four Living Creatures in Ezekiel they have one direction. Ezekiel said, Each one went straight ahead. Wherever the spirit would go, they would go, without turning as they went.[12]

THE DANGER OF INDIVIDUALISM

If you read and understand this book you'll know more than 99.99% of all Christians and all mankind about God's Bible dreams but please remember the main purpose is not to make you wiser and smarter so you can live a more self-centred life.

The main purpose for this book is to help Christians become very familiar with all of God's recorded Bible dreams and to equip us to better hear God's voice in our own dreams so we can better do God's will.

Psalm 105:1 says, O give thanks to the Lord, call on his name, make known his deeds among the peoples. It doesn't say make known my deeds or your deeds amongst the peoples. The focus is always on God.

God's dreams communicate God's thoughts and not man's thoughts. No Bible dream ever originated from the mind of the dreamer. No Bible dream ever came from man's consciousness, man's unconsciousness or Carl Jung's idea of the collective consciousness.

All God's Dreams come from a sovereign God who communicates directly to the dreamer in order to advance His Own kingdom purpose.

God's dreams are sent to fulfil God's specific sovereign plans and purpose and not to fulfil the dreamer's plans and purposes. The main focus for the dreamer should be on doing God's will and not on pursuing self interest or self-promotion.

In Scripture if the dreamer obeyed their dream they were blessed, if they disobeyed they were cursed. All Bible dreams came supernaturally from outside the dreamer.

One of the great strengths of the Pentecostal and Charismatic heritage of the last hundred years has been Christians coming to know and experience God in a personal way.

Millions of believers have been baptised in the Holy Spirit and have personally experienced Jesus through the gifts of the Holy Spirit and a renewed love of the Bible.

Unfortunately this strength of individual relationship and personal experience can also become a me-centred weakness. One of the nastiest demonic spirits invading the Western world nowadays is a spirit of individualism.

Today it's becoming increasingly okay to be self-centred. It certainly sells more products. After all you're worth it. This spirit of individualism has resulted in a 'me first' attitude resulting in millions of broken marriages and a billion worldwide abortions.

This selfish spirit also promotes independence and narcissism in people who so easily become self focused and isolated from others. This is particularly evident in economically developed nations where affluence tends towards self-reliance. Prosperous people can feel they don't need others!

Social media also leads to self-centredness as we strive to project our special presence to the world. Societies and cultures promoting celebrity, appearance, and narcissistic role models also fuel this increase in self-obsession.

Individualism has even penetrated some Pentecostal and Charismatic Churches moving them from being a caring community into individuals who make their own personal commitment without any sense of responsibility to the wider body of Christ.

Part of the problem is because we have been endlessly encouraged to pursue our own personal spiritual gifts and ministries. Then too often we begin to consider these heavenly endowments as personal possessions rather than God's tools to serve and equip the body of Christ to fulfil the Great Commission.

This individualisation of spiritual gifts can also be wrongly coupled with the erroneous teaching God wants us all to be happy, healthy, wealthy and wise. These desires are really the false aspirations of our western acquisitive materialistic society rather that God's plans and purpose for the body of Christ. Jesus said,

> If anyone comes to me and does not hate father and
> mother, wife and children, brothers and sisters—
> yes, even their own life—such a person cannot
> be my disciple. And whoever does not carry
> their cross and follow me cannot be my
> disciple.[1]

The Holy Spirit and His powerful gifts including dreams were not given for our personal use or for self-promotion. They were provided by Jesus to help us equip His Church to fulfil the Great Commission,

> Go therefore and make disciples of all the nations,
> baptising them in the name of the Father and of the
> Son and of the Holy Spirit, teaching them to
> observe all things that I have commanded you; and
> lo, I am with you always, even to the end of the age.
> Amen.[2]

God's purpose is always to equip the body of Christ to do God's will and not just to bless special individuals. Paul said,

> Instead, speaking the truth in love, we will grow to become in every respect the mature body of him who is the head, that is, Christ. From him the whole body, joined and held together by every supporting ligament, grows and builds itself up in love, as each part does its work.[3]

I recently read a book blurb about how to get more of God's power. It promised if you read this book your problems would transform into opportunities for success and you'd be helped to reach your dreams and goals with confidence, personal potential, wealth and communication.

And that's not all. The impossible would become possible, sorrow would become joy, defeat would become peace and doubt would become faith in God. Not a bad deal for $19.99.

Deliberately or not this blurb was appealing to the spirit of self-centredness in people. God's spiritual power was being peddled as something for our own personal blessing and problem solving.

There is no mention of being part of a corporate movement empowered by the Holy Spirit to go into the highways and byways and make disciples of all nations.

Unfortunately this 'me first' focus is also evident in the area of dreams, dream books and dream teaching. Too often the focus is on what's in it for the dreamer and not what's in it for God.

Blurbs selling dream books also make self-centred promises about unlocking the dreamer's destiny, the dreamer's ministry, the dreamer's success, the dreamer's direction and the dreamer's purpose.

This is all very dangerous and can lead to great disappointment and delusion. We need to remember God's true dreams are sent by God to fulfil God's specific sovereign plans and purpose.

The main focus is always 100% on doing God's will and not self-promotion for the dreamer.

It's never a case of, What's in it for me?

It's always a case of, What's in it for God? What does God want me to do? How does God want me to respond?

Jesus said similar,

> Very truly I tell you, the Son can do nothing by himself;
> he can do only what he sees his Father doing,
> because whatever the Father does the Son also
> does. For the Father loves the Son and shows him
> all he does.[4]

Jesus didn't come to earth to do His own thing, have His own ministry and take a Selfie. He only did what He saw the Father doing and what the Father showed him.

We too can do the same thing by being obedient to God's voice through dreams.

Like Jesus our focus must always be on God's will, plans and purpose.

The purpose of all spiritual gifts including dreams and visions is always on doing God's will, serving the Body of Christ and reaching the lost with the Gospel.

Recently I was talking to a longtime Pentecostal believer who has suffered much for his beliefs over the many years. He said he was dismayed at the selfishness and false promises of many Christian Holy Spirit books today. He also applied this to Christian dream books of which he'd read quite a few.

I told him I totally understood his position but I also said, I thank God for the many new Christian books on dreams and dreaming being written today.

I said I praised God for the obedience and sacrifice of those various authors and I reminded him of the porridge in *Goldilocks And The Three Bears*. Some of the porridge was too hot; some too cold and some just right.

Similarly some of the new Christian dream books are too shallow, some too deep, some too difficult, some too easy, some too boring, some too exciting, some too complicated, some too commercial, some too human, some too spiritual and of course some are just right.

My advice is, Eat what you can and spit out the bones and thank God dreams and dreaming are once again being taken seriously within the Body of Christ.

I'm a firm believer in Paul's advice to Timothy,

> Do your best to present yourself to God as one approved, a worker who does not need to be ashamed and who correctly handles the word of truth. [5]

I only wish these new dream books had been available forty years ago.

IT'S ALL ABOUT JESUS!

There's nothing new under the sun.

The question of whether a dream is from God, the devil or from the dreamer is still the big issue.

Sirach shows how Christians have struggled with this matter over the centuries. Catholics, Eastern Orthodox, and most Oriental Orthodox Christians all accept Sirach as part of the Canon of Scripture. In fact since 1564 the Catholic Church has threatened to excommunicate anyone who disagrees.

The Anglicans on the other hand, consider Sirach to be an apocryphal book, and read it 'for example of life and instruction of manners'. Listen to what Sirach says about dreams,

> Foolish people are deceived by vain hopes, and dreams get them all excited. A person who pays any attention at all to dreams is like someone who tries to catch shadows or chase the wind. What you see in a dream is no more real than the reflection of your face in a mirror. What is unreal can no more produce something real than what is dirty can

> produce something clean. Dreams, divination, and omens are all nonsense. You see in them only what you want to see.
>
> Unless the Most High has sent you the dream, pay no attention to it.
>
> Dreams have misled many people; they put their faith in them, only to be disappointed. The Law is complete without such falsehood. Wisdom, as spoken by the righteous, is also complete without it.[1]

Sirach only says one positive thing about dreams yet it's that one benefit that identifies the golden key to the whole issue. Sirach says,

> Unless the Most High has sent you the dream, pay no attention to it.

Here Sirach is really saying the creator of the universe might choose to communicate with us through a dream. Inadvertently he's actually saying, Pay careful attention to God's dreams.

Unfortunately Sirach never helps us understand what a God dream might look like. We're just left with a general negativity concerning dreams.

After all, who wants to become an excited foolish shadow catcher and wind chaser who is regularly deceived by vain hopes and dreams?

Yet wouldn't it be wonderful if there really was a reliable source that clearly explained what dreams from the Most High looked like?

Wouldn't it be marvellous if the Most High God had actually authored a book containing dozens of examples of His own true spiritual dreams?

Imagine that book also explained God's plans and purpose for all His divine dreams. Would you want to read a book like that?

Suppose you could get to know God better and also become so familiar with God's true dreams you become like an expert jeweller who instantly recognises the worth and value of any true diamond.

Imagine being a sheep who regularly hears his master's voice through dreams? Wouldn't that be something?

The truth is, as Christians we do have a book that supplies such a precious key. We have the Bible. The Bible is the only source book that accurately and consistently showcases and demonstrates what God's dreams look like. Every recorded dream in the Bible is from God except for a couple from Satan.

Prophetic people love dreams and visions and supernatural encounters and riddles and mysteries and dark speech. For us, It's the glory of God to conceal a matter; to search out a matter is the glory of kings.[2]

We love the flow of the Holy Spirit, the gifts of the Holy Spirit, the fruit of the Holy Spirit, prophecy, words of knowledge, healings, miracles, signs and wonders. It's our heady wine.

Yet we also know it's not just about the outpouring of the Holy Spirit. We know it's not just about the gifts and the fruit of the Holy Spirit. We know it's about Jesus!

We know it's all about Jesus! We know it's all about God's plans and purpose for Jesus!

We know dreams are only one way God communicates with His creation. We also know the reason we spend so much time being equipped in the word of God and the gifts of the Holy Spirit is so we can be effective in bringing the Gospel of Jesus Christ to all nations.

Then the end will come and Jesus shall return and see the travail of His soul and be satisfied.[3] It's all about Jesus! All Scripture is about Jesus.

This book is about Jesus. Jesus told the Jews, You study the Scriptures diligently because you think that in them you have eternal life. These are the very Scriptures that testify about me.[4]

Jesus opens eyes and minds. On the Road to Emmaus He told two doubting disciples,

> How foolish you are, and how slow to believe all that the prophets have spoken! Did not the Messiah have to suffer these things and then enter his glory? And beginning with Moses and all the Prophets, he explained to them what was said in all the Scriptures concerning himself. Then their eyes were opened and they recognised him.[5]

Later he appeared to the eleven and said, This is what I told you while I was still with you: Everything must be fulfilled that is written about me in the Law of Moses, the Prophets and the Psalms. Then he opened their minds so they could understand the Scriptures.[6]

The controlling theme of this book is of a Sovereign God who uses dreams to intervene in human history in order to carry out His own specific plans and purpose for Jesus. God's focus is always on Jesus. Paul called it, The Eternal Purpose.[7]

God does nothing without purpose. Every Bible dream contains a message from God. God's dreams are specific dreams sent for specific objectives.

Scripture is God's revelation about Who He is, Who we are, and How we should relate to Him. Without revelation we can't know God or the reason we exist.

God has a Master Plan for everything. As I previously mentioned, If you read this book you'll know more than 99.99% of all Christians about Bible dreams.

And perhaps you will have some great dream adventures with God. He might even choose you or one of your descendants to interpret a dream like Pharaoh's dream that changed world history.

The Israeli poet Yehuda Amachi said,

> Too many clocks, too little time.
> Too many oaths on the Bible.
> Too many roads,
> Too few ways for a man to really go:
> To his destiny.
> Too many hopes that fled their masters.
> Too many dreamers.
> Too few dreams
> Whose solution would change
> The history of the world
> Like Pharaoh's dream.[8]

We were born to know God. The purpose of all revelation is to know God better.[9] Dreams are a main way God reveals His plans and purpose. Yet after a zillion years, when Satan has been defeated and the kingdom of this world has become the kingdom of our Lord and of his Messiah,[10] our primary goal will still be to know Him better.

Paul told the Ephesians,

> I keep asking that the God of our Lord Jesus Christ, the glorious Father, may give you the Spirit of wisdom and revelation, so that you may know Him better. I pray that the eyes of your heart may be enlightened in order that you may know the hope to which He has called you, the riches of his glorious inheritance in His holy people, and His incomparably great power for us who believe.[11]

Worldly knowledge is limited. Paul said,

> The message of the cross is foolishness to those who are perishing, but to us who are being saved it is the

> power of God. For it is written: I will destroy the wisdom of the wise; the intelligence of the intelligent I will frustrate. Where is the wise person? Where is the teacher of the law? Where is the philosopher of this age?
>
> Has not God made foolish the wisdom of the world? For since in the wisdom of God the world through its wisdom did not know him, God was pleased through the foolishness of what was preached to save those who believe.
>
> Jews demand signs and Greeks look for wisdom, but we preach Christ crucified: a stumbling block to Jews and foolishness to Gentiles, but to those whom God has called, both Jews and Greeks, Christ the power of God and the wisdom of God. For the foolishness of God is wiser than human wisdom, and the weakness of God is stronger than human strength.[12]

The quality of our lives is the quality of our communication with God.

Hear God's voice and do God's will.

Jesus said, I have come down from heaven not to do my will but to do the will of him who sent me.[13] Jesus didn't come to fulfil His own plans and purposes. Jesus' priority was to please His Father and complete His Father's mission.

For Jesus it wasn't a case of my vision, my ministry, my dreams, my prophecies, my anointing, my power over Satan, my church, and so on. Jesus didn't come to take a selfie. He came to surrender to God's Sovereignty.

When we study Bible dreams we soon realise God's plans and God's purpose are paramount and our plans and purposes are secondary. It doesn't take long to realise if our plans and purposes are not aligned with God's plans and purpose then we're just wasting our time.

Scripture says, Unless the Lord builds the house, the builders labour in vain. Unless the Lord watches over the city, the guards stand watch in vain. In vain you rise early and stay up late, toiling for food to eat, for he grants sleep to those he loves.[14]

King Solomon, who wrote those words, started off as a great leader listening to God and being anointed in his dreams but ended up in disaster after he stopped obeying God's dream instructions.

We've all been given the opportunity of aligning our lives with God's plans and purpose and being blessed like Abraham. Or we can be like gifted and anointed Solomon who disobeyed God's revelation and was cursed.

God's dreams can place us right in the centre of God's will and enable us to fulfil our personal callings and bring God's blessings upon our families, our communities and our nations. Like Jesus we too can say, My food, is to do the will of him who sent me and to finish his work.[15]

The reason for every Bible dreams is to enable God's plans and purpose for the Messiah, Israel, and the Church to come to pass.

The only way we're going to know what God's dreams and plans and purpose look like is to study His Book; Your word is a lamp to my feet and a light to my path.[16]

Understanding our God given dreams helps us know God better and allows us to discover where we fit into God's greater plans and purpose.

The prophet Samuel was born in a time when dreams and visions were rare. Not so with us. We live in an era of tremendous opportunity when God's Holy Spirit is being poured out upon all people. We live in a day when dreams and visions and prophecy are freely available.

Believers and unbelievers can have dreams but only believers have visions.

When Jesus returned to heaven He said He'd send the Holy Spirit with power and Jesus always keeps His promises. Nowadays the whole earth is being filled with the knowledge of the glory of the Lord as the waters cover the sea.[17]

Christian dream interpreters require a good knowledge of how God uses dreams in Scripture. We can't apply truths we don't know. We need to understand how our dreams and the dreams we interpret compare with God's dreams. We should be as familiar with all the dreams and dreamers of the Bible as we are with the back of our hands.

One day my friend, the American prophet, John Paul Jackson said, If we want to understand our dreams we should study each dream in Scripture and look for patterns.

This book is my response to John Paul's advice. I believe it could save you years of study and propel you towards knowing God better and better and better.

SATAN HATES GOD'S DREAMS

Satan hates God's dreams because a successful interpretation and application of a God given dream always destroys his work.

Sixteen hundred years ago Satan released a powerful attack against dream interpretation within the Body of Christ. This assault has been very effective and has caused great confusion amongst Christians.

In 382 AD, Satan slipped some simple poison into a couple of verses of St. Jerome's Latin version of the Bible that slowly and surely created a potent spell.

Jerome's version better known as *The Vulgate* became the standard Latin Bible for the Western Latin-speaking Church until the mid 1960s.

The attack came through Jerome's mistranslation of a Hebrew four-letter word. That word was *anan*. Anan has negative spiritual connotations and can mean either *witchcraft* or *soothsaying*. Anan appears nine times in the Old Testament.

In his incredibility influential translation Jerome correctly interprets anan as *witchcraft* seven times but in Deuteronomy 18:10 and

Leviticus 19:26 he wrongly interprets it as *observing dreams* and consequently damaged Christian dream interpretation ever since.

The correct interpretation of Deuteronomy 18:10 should have been,

> There shall not be found among you anyone who makes his son or his daughter pass through the fire, one who uses divination, **one who practices witchcraft,** or one who interprets omens, or a sorcerer, or one who casts a spell, or a medium, or a spiritist, or one who calls up the dead. For whoever does these things is detestable to the Lord; and because of these detestable things the Lord your God will drive them out before you.[1]

Jerome's wrong interpretation was,

> There shall not be found among you anyone who makes his son or his daughter pass through the fire, one who uses divination, **one who observes dreams,** or one who interprets omens, or a sorcerer, or one who casts a spell, or a medium, or a spiritist, or one who calls up the dead. For whoever does these things is detestable to the Lord; and because of these detestable things the Lord your God will drive them out before you.[2]

Who would try to interpret their dreams after reading those lines if they believed Jerome's writings were a true translation of God's word?

The correct interpretation of Leviticus 19:26 should have been,

> You must not eat anything with blood still in it You must not practice **divination or sorcery**.

Jerome's wrong interpretation was,

> Do not eat any meat with the blood still in it.
> Do not **divine or observe dreams.**

Again, what sincere Christian would take dream interpretation seriously after reading that?

Some modern Catholic Bibles like the New Oxford and The New Jerusalem have restored the original and correct interpretation of *anan* but if you *Google* Leviticus 19:26 in the Catholic Douay-Rheims Bible you'll still read,

> You shall not eat with blood.
> **You shall not divine nor observe dreams**.

Sadly, Satan's strong poison from Jerome's mistranslation is still with the Christian Church even after all these years. The weeds from those wrong words have deep roots.

MY PURPOSE FOR THIS BOOK

I hope this book will enable Christians become very familiar with all of God's Bible dreams and better understand the purpose for which He sent them.

To this end, I have written on a number of issues that have personally helped me gain a deeper revelation of God, His dreams and the whole unseen realm they occur in.

I'm giving this study in the hope it'll save years of study and help move things forward in the Christian prophetic community, onto new levels, for ordinary people like you and me.

All the dreams of the Bible should be the foundation from which we build our understanding of dream interpretation. I also believe becoming very familiar with God's Bible dreams and His purpose for them makes us all better at dream interpretation. Our focus must also shift from our plans and purposes onto God's plans and purpose!

Appreciating the truth that God's dreams are always sent to advance God's plans and purpose is vital to our success in understanding and obeying God's dreams.

It's also important to realise all believers and non-believers have a specific metron for which they are responsible before God. Consequently having a good working understanding of the whole subject of metron is vital.

The reality is, God always sends His dreams to a person with the appropriate metron which allows them to implement the dream message.

Christians who regularly study God's dreams are also better at understanding and obeying their own God dreams. We ought to base our dream interpretation on the gold standard of Scripture.

We must also remember God's dreams and visions are not about our plans and purposes. They are about God's plans and purpose. In studying God's dreams we get to know God better and learn more about what's on His heart. We also learn to recognise and be obedient to His dreams.

My method in this book is to examine every dream in the Bible in detail but in so doing I'm aware what I'm really doing is exploring the nature and purpose of God concerning His covenant with Israel and His Church. That's what all Bible study is really about.

There are a number of lenses and a few viewpoints I use in this book for looking at God's dreams.

God's dreams are not just an eclectic jumble spread here and there throughout the Bible with no discernible pattern. Everything God does has purpose.

All of God's dreams were sent to advance His eternal purpose that the Bride of Christ, should occupy the heavenly realms vacated by Satan and the fallen angels.

The whole idea of purpose is one of the main lenses I use. I choose purpose over process because God does nothing without purpose.

Consequently many chapters have purpose in their title;

>My Purpose For This Book
>God's General Purposes For Sleep And Dreams

God's Sovereign Purpose
God's Eternal Plans And Purpose
God's Purpose For Abraham
God's Purpose For Each Bible Dream

When I approach a dream my first thought is, Is this a God dream? If it is, then I want to know God's purpose for sending it.

If it's not a God dream I also want to know if there is a purpose behind it. Sovereign God who knows the number of hairs on my head and who knows how the dice will fall[1] also knows about dreams not from Him. I just try not to waste a lot of time on dreams not from God.

The book starts with *Bible Dream Data* which shows God's four main areas of focus concerning all His dreams.

God's Eternal Purpose For Dreams focuses on Jesus.

In *The Danger of Individualism* I try to put the focus back on God's plans and purpose rather than on a self-centred focus on ourselves. Today our culture and society have placed man and not God at the centre of the universe. This must not be the case with us.

The next chapter *It's All About Jesus* reveals the core of the book and indeed of our lives.

Satan Hates God's Dreams shows how clever Satan has been at suppressing and sidelining dream study in Christianity.

Four Kinds of Bible Dreams looks at dreams from God, mankind and Satan.

My Purpose For This Book speaks of what I consider important for Christian dream interpretation.

My Dream Qualifications tells a little why I believe I'm qualified to do this study.

Bible Dreams And The God's reveals how God's dreams always come in the midst of spiritual opposition from the rebellious gods hell bent on hindering God's plans and purpose.

God's General Purposes For Sleep And Dreams looks at the wider importance and wonderful significance of sleep and dreams in our lives.

A Short History Of Dreams gives some sense of the spiritual battleground concerning dreams and visions over thousands of years.

God's Sovereign Purpose looks at how a proper understanding of God's sovereignty is necessary in order to correctly understand God's dreams

God's Eternal Plans And Purpose looks at the bigger picture of dreams and God's purpose.

Satan's Hindering Purpose highlights Satan's obstructing role concerning God's dreams.

Three other chapters are called T*he Angel Of The Lord, Angels in Bible Dreams* and *God And Jesus In Bible Dreams*. These short chapters show the reality that Jesus, Angels and God are everywhere in the Bible, often hidden in plain sight.

God's Overall Purpose For Bible Dreams recaps on the main issues again.

God's Main Purpose For Each Bible Dream identifies the reason for each Bible Dream.

The Importance Of A Dreamer's Metron highlights the fact God only sends His dreams to a person with the appropriate metron which allows them to implement the dream message.

God's Purpose For Each Dreamer's Metron shows the importance of understanding the role of metron in dream interpretation.

God's Purpose For Believer's Metrons describes the sphere of influence of each believing dreamer.

God's Purpose For Non Believer's Metrons describes the sphere of influence of each non believing dreamer.

Definition Of A Dream is interesting and might well open avenues that could revolutionise our present understanding of prophets and dreams.

Where Dreams Come From looks at the source of our dreams.

Dreams And Night Visions Covered looks at all the Bible dreams and a few important other incidents.

The Timeline Of Bible Dreams gives us a sense of where dreams fit into God's agenda.

McCauley's Dream Checklist is a worksheet I use in examining each Bible dream. This checklist gives a consistency and an accountability to the study.

God's Purpose For Abraham highlights the importance of God's covenant with Abraham and how all the believing dreamers in the Bible come from his seed line.

Overall, the main purpose is to help Christians become very familiar with God's true dreams.

Sometimes key concepts and key phrases are repeated in various chapters. This is done on purpose. I'm also well aware most people won't just read the book straight through, and that also accounts for some of the repetition of key ideas in different chapters.

Time and time again you will read some version of the words in the list below. I can't apologise for this because they are all actual versions of what is happening in and through the dreams,

- God is a Covenant Keeper and a Promise Keeper.
- God is keeping the Messiah's seed line on track
- God was still keeping His Covenant Promises to Abraham about the coming Messiah.
- God is advancing His Eternal plans and purpose as promised to Abraham.
- God is showing He is the Most High Sovereign over all earthly kingdoms and powers and principalities.
- God is keeping His promises to His enemy Satan and His friend Abraham.
- God is sending the Promised Seed who will crush Satan's head and bless all nations.
- God is working His purpose out.

When we study all God's Bible dreams we constantly see God being depicted as a covenant keeping and a promise keeping God. Time after time, He is always keeping His covenant promises to Abraham and His prophetic promises to Eve and Satan.

A study of Bible dreams clearly highlights the reality of God being 100% trustworthy. It also very quickly shifts our focus from my plans and purposes onto God's plans and purpose.

This book doesn't claim to be the last word on all the dreams of the Bible. In many ways it's merely an invitation to walk through a new door of understanding into a vast hall filled with the astonishing treasures of God's great plans and purpose. My hope is that others will press on in to discover and describe many of these treasures in greater detail and with greater revelation.

In some way I feel a bit like Peter and John who meet the lame man at the temple gate called Beautiful. When the man asked for money Peter said, Silver or gold I do not have, but what I do have I give you.

The truth is, we can only give what we have. Sometimes the person who receives is able to multiply what they have newly obtained. Afterwards they are sometimes able to feed a great multitude with the result. May it be so with you!

Please God, may some of the seeds you garner from this book become plantings of the Lord that will bring forth a great harvest of righteousness to Jesus Christ in the days to come.

MY DREAM QUALIFICATIONS

This book is not merely an academic exercise. I'm a dreamer of dreams and dream interpretation is part of my prophetic calling. I've never knowingly had an open vision nor have I ever received a long visionary oracle like Isaiah and Jeremiah.

But I've had plenty of dreams like Abraham, Abimelek, Joseph, Jacob, Laban, Pharaoh, Balaam, the Midianite soldier, Samuel, Nathan, Solomon, Eliphaz, Job, Nebuchadnezzar, Daniel, Zechariah, St Joseph, the Magi and Pilate's wife.

A few years ago God put it into my heart to write a book about all the dreams in the Bible in order to gain a better understanding of what dreams from God actually look like.

He also confirmed this in a dream.

I thought this was a wonderful idea. After all, the Bible is *God's Gold Standard* for everything spiritual. One scripture has become a touchstone for me in this assignment. This is Paul's words at the beginning of Ephesians,

> I keep asking that the God of our Lord Jesus Christ, the

> glorious Father, may give you the Spirit of wisdom
> and revelation, so that you may know him better. I
> pray that the eyes of your heart may be enlightened
> in order that you may know the hope to which he
> has called you, the riches of his glorious inheritance
> in his holy people, and his incomparably great
> power for us who believe.[1]

Here Paul is referring to us receiving revelation and wisdom that leads to us knowing God better and also knowing God's plans and purpose for His Church and our lives better. Paul is also praying for a growth in our understanding that we are also inheritors of God's blessings and power.

This reminds us of Jesus saying,

> You are my friends if you do what I command. I no
> longer call you servants, because a servant does not
> know his master's business. Instead, I have called
> you friends, for everything that I learned from my
> Father I have made known to you.[2]

I believe a study of God's true dreams and how He uses them helps release this spirit of wisdom and revelation Paul speaks about.

Dreams are a main way we get to know God better and a main way we come to understand our Father's business; how He conducts it and how we can become involved.

I've been dreaming and remembering dreams all of my life. My widowed mother, Mary, was a big dreamer. My childhood morning conversations were often peppered with her comments of, I had the strangest dream last night or I had a really through-other dream last night.

She'd then mention names of people and places and speak of

events that took place in her dreams. I'd listen but I hadn't a clue what her dreams meant.

Nor could I understand my own regular dreams though I can still remember childhood dreams about the end of the world in full living technicolor.

When I was twenty-eight I came to faith in Jesus as my Lord and Saviour. Soon afterwards I started attending a local Baptist Church and began reading the Bible. A couple of years later I was baptised in the Holy Spirit and started speaking in tongues and prophesying. I also started to flow in other gifts of the Holy Spirit.

Dreams continued to flow as usual but now with the benefit of the Bible I slowly began to understand how to interpret them.

I've never taken a dream interpretation course and my access to Christian dream books was very limited in those days. The few Christian dream books I did come across were overly influenced by the Swiss psychoanalyst Carl Jung.

I think dream interpretation is a gift from God but I'm not 100% sure. Maybe it's an offshoot of the gift of interpreting tongues or the word of wisdom. I'm a seer and when I prophesy I'm usually interpreting inner visions that I'm seeing at the time. I do much the same thing with dreams.

My gifting in this area has grown as I have continued to study the Bible and have pressed into knowing God better.

Over time I have prophetically ministered in over seventy nations regularly being accompanied by my wife. I'm seventy years old as I write this sentence and I've been in full time ministry for over thirty years.

Over those years I've interpreted lots of dreams. I've never charged for a dream interpretation and I've never gone out of my way to ask people to send me dreams.

Dream interpretation like any interaction with the unseen realm can be a tiring experience. I try to limit my dream interpretation to family and friends and to those God gives me dreams for and tells me to speak. Otherwise I'd be swamped by dream interpretation.

The same thing goes for prophecy and writing. I only try do what God tells me to do. Good enough for Jesus, good enough for me.

I've had plenty of experience of personal dreams that have come true. For example, I had a dream before the 1987 Stock Market Crash, the biggest one-day crash in history. That dream warned us to get out of the Stock Market and it saved our clients' monies.

I've also had dreams about how many children we should have. We ended up having fourteen children, all who at least have one degree from a leading UK University. I've also seen some my future grandchildren in dreams.

I've also dreamed the specific geographical locations of where we should live. Once I disregarded a dream that warned me not to go and live in a certain house. I suffered daily for nine months until I repented and went to the home God had originally planned for me.

Like Jesus, I too have learned obedience through the things I have suffered As Samuel said, to obey is better than sacrifice.

I've sometimes dreamed of what nations to travel to and minister in. I've also dreamed of who to travel with in ministry. I've also dreamed of people I would meet on the mission field.

I've been told what books to write and what books not to write in dreams. I've been told in dreams how to pray for my wife when she was healed from fourth stage colon cancer.

I've had dreams that directed Christians to go into politics and dreams that informed politicians of promotions. One even became the Prime Minister of a nation. I've had lots of dreams concerning my wife and children and our personal circumstances. I've also had dreams that empowered barren women to have children. I've also been warned about pending demonic attacks in dreams. Often I've been greatly encouraged by specific instruction and affirmation.

My wife Angela says I should write a book about all the dreams

God has given me but I remind her talking about one's personal dreams is a lot like speaking about your hospital operation. That which is important and vital to you can be very boring for the listener.

I'm only mentioning a few of my dreams in order to show that dreams have been a very important part of the Holy Spirit gift-mix God has given me. I appreciate and I take dreams and dreamers very seriously.

I believe the main reason for writing this book is that we should really get to know better and get to know what God's true dreams really look like. Then we can better do God's will.

I also believe there will be an acceleration in our understanding of the importance of God's dreams in the coming years. Great darkness is covering the earth through the increasing prying technology of power elites antagonistic to the Gospel. But thankfully God is always doing a new thing.[3] I believe God is presently helping us mature into a better understanding and appreciation of His dreams.

After all God made sure only His dreams were recorded in the Bible. He did that with purpose. God's dreams are sent for two main purposes,

1. Knowing and loving Jesus better and
2. Hearing His voice in order to do His will.

Paul highlights this first purpose when he writes,

> What is more, I consider everything a loss because of the surpassing worth of knowing Christ Jesus my Lord, for whose sake I have lost all things. I consider them garbage, that I may gain Christ.[4]

The second purpose is mentioned by Jesus who said,

If you love me you will obey what I command.[5]

My motto is,

>Hear God's Voice! Do God's Will!

BIBLE DREAMS AND THE GODS

Yahweh is not the only god.
The Bible is full of gods.
Our God is the Creator God.
The Psalms say,

- There is none like you among the gods, O Lord.[1]
- For great is the Lord, and greatly to be praised; he is to be revered above all gods.[2]
- Our Lord is above all gods.[3]
- Ascribe to Yahweh, you gods, ascribe to Yahweh glory and strength.[4]
- He is exalted above all gods.[5]
- For the Lord is the great God, the great King above all gods.[6]

Exodus said God would judge all the gods of Egypt[7] and Numbers confirmed how Yahweh executed judgments against Egypt's gods.[8]

The first commandment warns, You shall have no other gods

before me.[9] Later Israel is told not to covenant with or worship other gods.[10]

In Deuteronomy Moses warns Israel against idolatry. He says,

> And when you look up to the sky and see the sun, the moon and the stars—all the heavenly array—do not be enticed into bowing down to them and worshiping things the Lord your God has apportioned to all the nations under heaven. But as for you, the Lord took you and brought you out of the iron-smelting furnace, out of Egypt, to be the people of his inheritance, as you now are.[11]

In the above scripture Israel is warned never to worship other gods, not because other god's don't exist, but because God Almighty has 100% decided to take personal responsibility for ruling Israel Himself.

The other gods would rule the rest of the world's nations.

Moses said Israel's ability to live in the Promised Land was conditional on them remaining faithful to God. If they became involved in idol worship then God would remove them from the land and scatter them among the nations.[12]

This scattering amongst the nations is exactly what happened 550 years later during the Babylonian Exile of Judah. Solomon's dreams, Nebuchadnezzar's dreams, Jeremiah's dream, Daniel's dreams and Zechariah's dreams all relate to this tragic turn of events.

God's Bible dreams were always sent in the midst of ongoing conflict with the powers and principalities, the gods of other nations. The chief purpose of God's dreams is to advance God's divine agenda which includes destroying Satan's hindering plans.

The *Dream Statistics* show that 62 % of Bible dreams concern God directly exercising His dominion over the powers and principalities affecting His Covenant People and their seed line.

The first example occurs in *Abraham's Covenant Dream* where we learn the children of Israel will be slaves under the gods of Egypt for four hundred years until God intervenes and sets them free.

We also discover the sin of the Amorites who worshiped, the moon-god Sin, Amurru and other gods, would require those four hundred years before they were bad enough so God could judge them.

Josephs' dream about the sun, moon and stars bowing down to him on one level represents his family yet on another level represents the god's of Egypt and other nations bowing down before him. The Egyptians worshipped stars and aligned their pyramids with them.

As we look at all the dreams of the Bible we will be constantly aware of the constant background noise of the gods of the nations being totally subject to the God of Israel. At times they might appear to have defeated Israel but the truth is God only used them to punish and discipline His Covenant People. Nebuchadnezzar's and Daniel's dreams are good examples of this truth.

God is sovereign over all things in heaven and on earth. He has complete rulership over all powers and principalities, all spiritual beings and all angels and He shares that supremacy with His Son Jesus. Paul says,

> The Son is the image of the invisible God, the
> > firstborn over all creation. For in him all things
> > were created: things in heaven and on earth, visible
> > and invisible, whether thrones or powers or rulers
> > or authorities; all things have been created through
> > him and for him.
>
> He is before all things, and in him all things hold together.

> And he is the head of the body, the church; he is the beginning and the firstborn from among the dead, so that in everything he might have the supremacy.
> For God was pleased to have all his fullness dwell in him, and through him to reconcile to himself all things, whether things on earth or things in heaven, by making peace through his blood, shed on the cross.[13]

In Babylon, Satan's earthly headquarters at the time, God revealed the contents of *Nebuchadnezzar's 'Large Statue' Dream* to Daniel who immediately declared,

> Blessed be the name of God forever and ever,
> for wisdom and power belong to Him.
> He changes the times and seasons;
> He removes kings and establishes them.
> He gives wisdom to the wise
> and knowledge to the discerning.
> He reveals the deep and hidden things;
> He knows what lies in darkness,
> and light dwells with Him.[14]

Twenty two years later after God restored Nebuchadnezzar to sanity after his *Large Tree Dream* had come to pass the now humbled King of Babylon praised the God of Israel and said,

> How great are his signs,
> how mighty his wonders!
> His kingdom is an eternal kingdom;
> his dominion endures from generation to generation.[15]

In the midst of demonic Babylon with all the gods looking on Nebuchadnezzar also declared,

> His dominion is an eternal dominion;
> his kingdom endures from generation to generation.
> All the peoples of the earth
> are regarded as nothing.
> He does as he pleases
> with the powers of heaven
> and the peoples of the earth.
> No one can hold back his hand
> or say to him: "What have you done?"[16]

King Nebuchadnezzar's eyes were opened and he bowed the knee and proclaimed the God of Israel was sovereign. In Daniel's and Nebuchadnezzar's declarations we see many of God's attributes that regularly appear in Bible dreams.

God is all knowing and all powerful. He knows the future and often reveals it through dreams. He sets up kings and empires and destroys kings and empires. He is sovereign and supreme. The creator of all things.

His kingdom is an everlasting kingdom that continues from generation to generation. We often see this in Bible dreams as God constantly protects and cares for His Covenant People.

Through experience Nebuchadnezzar also realised God does what He pleases with the powers of heaven and the peoples of the earth. Whether they are obedient or rebellious God is still able to use kings and powers for His own sovereign plans and purpose. All creation is under God's authority and command.

The Bible spans a time period from before the creation of humanity until the final return of Jesus when as Habakkuk says, the earth will be filled with the knowledge of the glory of the Lord as the waters cover the sea.[17]

Before creation there'd been a great rebellion in heaven when a third of the Elohim, the gods, rebelled with Satan.

I believe there were three rebellions in Genesis.

From Psalm 82 we learn it was God's Sovereign Will to rule through a group of supernatural beings called a Divine Council. This Divine Council appears in *Nebuchadnezzar's 'Large Tree' Dream* and *Daniel's 'Four Beasts' Dream. It is* also evident in *Zechariah's Dream Of Joshua* when Joshua is told,

> 'If you walk in My ways and keep My instructions,
> then you will both govern My house and have
> charge of My courts; and I will give you a place
> among these standing here.'[18]

I also believe it was God's intention this council should include human representatives who'd meet together at Eden but this plan was hindered when a rebel from the divine council tempted Adam to sin with the resultant loss of mankind's access to this council.

I believe the second rebellion occurred when rebellious spiritual beings took on bodies and mated with human women to produce a race of giants, called the Nephilim.[19]

This evil coupling released such a great wickedness amongst men that God hit the reset button with Noah and the Flood, but four hundred years later the third rebellion occurred when Noah's descendants once again alienated themselves from God by worshipping the sun, moon, stars and signs of the Zodiac in the tower of Babel built by the Nephilim in the land of Shinar.

The entire heavenly realm kept watching while Satan tried his damnedest to scuttle God's plans.

After the third rebellion God gave the idolatrous nations into the custody of the gods of the Divine Council and He personally took complete responsibility for forming and looking after Israel Himself. Deuteronomy 32:8-9 says.

> When the Most High gave the nations their inheritance,
> when he divided all mankind,
> he set up boundaries for the peoples
> according to the number of the sons of Israel.
> For the Lord's portion is his people,
> Jacob his allotted inheritance.[20]

Not unsurprisingly the guardian god's of the other nations acted cruelly and unjustly so God had to judge them. We see this in Psalm 82 which says,

> God presides in the great assembly;
> he renders judgment among the "gods":
> "How long will you defend the unjust
> and show partiality to the wicked?
> Defend the weak and the fatherless;
> uphold the cause of the poor and the oppressed.
> Rescue the weak and the needy;
> deliver them from the hand of the wicked.
> "The 'gods' know nothing, they understand nothing.
> They walk about in darkness;
> all the foundations of the earth are shaken.
> "I said, 'You are "gods";
> you are all sons of the Most High.'
> But you will die like mere mortals;
> you will fall like every other ruler."
> Rise up, O God, judge the earth,
> for all the nations are your inheritance.[21]

Even though God specifically called Abraham for the purpose of creating a Covenant People for Himself there were still ongoing problems. Years later King Solomon disobeyed his God dreams and caused Abraham's descendants to do evil by worshiping the rebellious gods of the other nations. This resulted in God exiling Israel to Babylon, the very place where the Tower of Babel had been built.

But God already had a plan set in place. This plan was Jesus Christ, the Lamb slain from the creation of the world.[22]

There was also a great mystery hidden in God unknown to all the heavenly realm including the fallen powers and principalities. Paul said,

> This mystery is that through the gospel the Gentiles
> are heirs together with Israel, members together of
> one body, and sharers together in the promise in
> Christ Jesus.[23]

It was God's plan that Abraham's descendants would defeat the giant races inhabiting The Promised Land and one of them, Jesus Christ of Nazareth, would be the Saviour of the whole world. Then the great mystery hidden in God would be revealed.

This mystery was that through the Gospel the Gentiles could become heirs together with Israel, members together of one body, and sharers together in the promise in Christ Jesus.

Paul says God's main purposes was that through the church, God's manifold wisdom should be made known to the rulers and authorities in the heavenly realms, according to his eternal purpose that he accomplished in Christ Jesus our Lord.[24]

It was always God's plan the Church of Jesus Christ should fill the heavenly seats of authority vacated by the fallen Elohim.

Yet, the fallen powers and principalities were always ignorant of God's plans and purpose. Paul, calling them the rulers of this age, shows this when he says,

> Among the mature, however, we speak a message of
> wisdom—but not the wisdom of this age or of the

rulers of this age, who are coming to nothing. No, we speak of the mysterious and hidden wisdom of God, a wisdom which He destined for our glory before time began. None of the rulers of this age understood it. For if they had, they would not have crucified the Lord of glory.[25]

Without God's wisdom and revelation the fallen Elohim had no true understanding of spiritual things. They were totally ignorant of the implications of Jesus's death, His place in salvation and about God's hidden mystery.

They also didn't know how to interpret God's dreams. That's why neither they nor their devotees were able to interpret the dreams of Pharaoh or Nebuchadnezzar or the writing on Balthazar's wall.

As Daniel told Nebuchadnezzar,

> No wise man, enchanter, medium, or magician can explain to the king the mystery of which he inquires. But there is a God in heaven who reveals mysteries.[26]

Our Sovereign God knows all things.
He once told Jeremiah,

> Ask me, and I will tell you things that you don't know and can't find out.[27]

GOD'S GOOD PURPOSES FOR SLEEP AND DREAMS

God's purposes for sleep and dreams not only concern spiritual revelation. They also show His loving care because sleeping and dreaming are just as important for our lives as eating, drinking and breathing.

The quality of our sleeping and dreaming is as vital to our well-being as the quality of our food, water and air. The better the quality the better the life.

We are all born into a battle. Everyday is a struggle against the world, the flesh and the devil.[1]

Jesus said, Therefore do not worry about tomorrow, for tomorrow will worry about itself. Each day has enough trouble of its own.[2]

Nowadays, neuroscience is catching up with the Bible and discovering the importance of sleep and dreaming for our mental, emotional and physical health. They've found good quality peaceful sleep and dreams also aids our creativity and problem solving. The wrier of Proverbs knew this. He said,

> When you lie down, you will not be afraid; when you

lie down, your sleep will be sweet. Have no fear of sudden disaster or of the ruin that overtakes the wicked.[3]

Sleep is a daily necessity and God mercifully allows us all to sleep and dream. As Jesus said, He causes His sun to rise on the evil and the good, and sends rain on the righteous and the unrighteous.[4]

But Isaiah also warned there is no peace for the ungodly. He wrote,

> But the wicked are like the tossing sea,
> which cannot rest,
> whose waves cast up mire and mud.
> "There is no peace," says my God, "for the wicked."[5]

Perhaps that explains why nowadays insomnia has become a plague of biblical proportions and a leading cause of disease and death in developed nations. When our sleep is chronically disrupted we soon begin to experience ailments like mental health instability, reduced alertness, and impaired memory.

Sleep loss has been linked to numerous neurological and psychiatric conditions such as Alzheimer's disease, anxiety, depression, bipolar disorder, suicide, stroke, and chronic pain.

It's also been shown to negatively impact the body's physiological system causing disorders and diseases like cancer, diabetes, heart attacks, infertility, weight gain, obesity, and immune deficiency.

Many emotional and psychiatric problems occur because of sleep deprivation. If we regularly sleep less than eight hours a night our time to physical exhaustion drops by 10 to 30%, and our aerobic output is significantly reduced.

The new sobering maxim is, The shorter your sleep, the shorter your life.

There are many stages of sleep, which can be simplified into REM sleep and non-REM sleep.

REM is short for Rapid-eye-movement, a phase of sleep characterised by eye movements similar to those of wakefulness.

Non-REM sleep is a deep, slow-wave sleep, which facilitates a homeostatic recalibration of blood pressure which benefits cardiovascular health.

God given REM sleep on the other hand nightly recalibrates and fine-tunes the emotional circuits of our brains. Proper sleep and dreaming resets our mental and physical health.

REM sleep is vital for emotional well-being and also plays an important role in brain development and other functions including mood, dreaming, and memory. Most dreams occur during the REM stage of sleep.

Dreams can happen during any sleep stage but those experienced during REM sleep tend to be the most frequent and vivid.

Neuroscience is discovering human beings need more than seven hours of sleep each night in order to maintain premium cognitive performance. They say we also benefit from an afternoon nap of up to an hour.

This enhances our physical and mental well-being and improves our learning, mood and energy levels. It also regulates hormones, prevents cancer and diabetes and slows the effects of ageing.

It's also been shown to increase our creativity and improve the complex functions of the brain, including learning, memory, emotional stability, complex reasoning and decision-making.

Scripture has special promises for God's people concerning sleep and dreams. Psalm 127 says, He grants sleep to those he loves while Isaiah says the righteous have peace and rest on their beds.[6]

King David said, In peace I will lie down and sleep, for you alone, Lord, make me dwell in safety.[7]

Sleep is also a time when God can speak directly and give revelation to people in dreams. That's what this book is all about.

Sleep can also be an occasion when God gives wisdom and understanding about situations. Psalm 16 says, I bless the Lord who gives me counsel; in the night also my heart instructs me.[8]

Even in troubling times Christians are promised good sleep. David who was regularly in deadly trouble said, I lay down and slept; I woke again, for the Lord sustained me.[9]

Each new day when we awake we are promised God's mercy and faithfulness will be available to us. Scripture says, The steadfast love of the Lord never ceases; his mercies never come to an end; they are new every morning; great is your faithfulness.[10]

In sleep, God often equips and enables the obedient to help others. Isaiah said,

> The Sovereign Lord has given me a well-instructed
>   tongue,
> to know the word that sustains the weary.
> He wakens me morning by morning,
> wakens my ear to listen like one being instructed.
> The Sovereign Lord has opened my ears;
> I have not been rebellious,
> I have not turned away.[11]

Dreaming is now being called overnight therapy by some neuroscientists. Recent research discovered a major benefit of dreaming is in processing our daily emotional experiences so we can make sense of conflicting issues and move on with our lives.

Because we are daily faced with difficult issues, anxiety dreams are very common. They are usually triggered by internal stressors like angry emotions and impulses or external stressors like past trauma, a bad day at work, or an anxious response to whatever crisis the media is currently throwing at us. Typical anxiety dreams include,

- Teeth falling out
- Frequent nightmares
- Being back at school
- Losing your purse or wallet
- Tornadoes and storms
- Falling
- Flying
- Drowning
- Bathroom dreams
- Being chased
- Someone dying
- Earthquakes
- Spiders
- Tidal waves or flooding
- A deceased relative
- House issues
- Snakes
- Dogs
- Car issues
- Returning to a past relationship
- Naked in public
- Alligators
- Running late
- Unprepared for a test
- Forgetting something important

Research has discovered it's our time spent in REM dream sleep that helps to heal us from anxiety, stressful and traumatic experiences. This is because during REM sleep our brains are empty of the anxiety-triggering molecule noradrenaline and this absence allows us to process our distressing memories in a peaceful and secure setting.

Because anxiety dreams are so common secular, psychological,

New Age and Christian dream interpreters are all interested in them. It's just a matter of how they interpret them using their own opinions and worldviews.

I believe Christian books explaining possible meanings for these anxiety type of dreams can be useful. Yet we must always remember there are never any of these anxiety dreams in the Bible.

Joseph didn't lose his wallet. Pharaoh didn't go to the bathroom. Daniel wasn't chased by a snake. Nebuchadnezzar's teeth didn't fall out. Solomon wasn't naked in public and the Magi weren't flying in the sky, though Jacob was being chased in real life by his uncle Laban.

Bible dreams are very different dreams from anxiety dreams. They don't arise in the heart of man. They are from God to man and are all about the advancement of God's plans and purpose.

Our anxiety dreams are usually concerned with ourselves though they may occasionally be about getting us prepared and equipped to be involved in God's plans and purpose. These types of dreams can be a useful trigger for pastoral counselling and prayer ministry.

Modern research has also found non-REM sleep strengthens our individual memories but it is the REM sleep that helps us with creativity and problem solving. This means dreaming and not just sleep is important for our mental and physical health.

REM dreaming is also an activity that clearly differentiates our brains from computers. A computer retains facts and so may be said to have knowledge. Our brains also hold knowledge but they are able to exercise wisdom in understanding what that knowledge means and knowing how to apply it.

The latter wisdom-function is a major function of REM-sleep dreaming. This again reminds me of Isaiah's words,

> The Sovereign Lord has given me a well-instructed
>   tongue,
> to know the word that sustains the weary.

> He wakens me morning by morning,
> wakens my ear to listen like one being instructed.[12]

The benefits of a good night's sleep accompanied by REM dreaming is the most effective thing we can give to our brains and bodies each day.

They may also help us to better hear God's voice concerning His Eternal Plans and Purpose.

A SHORT HISTORY OF DREAMS

Dreams are a big deal!

People on planet earth receive at least thirty billion dreams every day.

Dreams are God's idea and a main way He communicates with people. The history of dreams is the history of humanity and the history of humanity has always been a war zone of confusion and deception from the gods of this world.

Yet from time immemorial people across cultures and nations have consistently come up with three very similar answers concerning dreams.

They've generally concluded dreams come from one of three sources; God, demons or the self. The Bible agrees with this position.

The following is a quick scan over the troubled and contested history of dreams in order to give us a sense of the difficulty and complexity of the subject. If you want more information you'll have to seek it outside the purview of this short chapter.

I believe it's really important to realise we are the inheritors of thousands of years of warfare concerning dreams. St Jerome's mistranslation is not the only successful attack from Satan who opposes all true sources of revelation from God.

Dreams have impacted all cultures from the simple indigenous peoples of America, Australia, Mexico and Ireland to the complex empires of Babylon and Egypt. Many of these people groups had a dream god or dream goddesses and some even had dreams books.

5,000 years before Christ, the Babylonians worshipped a dream goddess named Mamu, and used a special book for interpreting dreams.

Yet neither Mamu nor their book was of much use when God sent a disturbingly forgotten dream to the Babylonian King Nebuchadnezzar in 604 BC. Had it not been for the Hebrew prophet Daniel's relationship with the true God many of Mamu's faithful devotees would have been slaughtered.

In 3,000 BC the Egyptians also owned dream books and had a dream god called Serpis. Turned out Serpis wasn't much of a dream interpreter either for when Yahweh sent Pharaoh two dreams about a pending famine neither Serpis nor his devotees could interpret them.

In the end, only God's chosen dream interpreter, the Hebrew Joseph, was able to interpret Pharaoh's dreams.

Joseph who knew all revelation comes from God said, God will give Pharaoh the answer he desires.[1]

From around 2000 BC, some Egyptians slept on special dream beds in their sanctuaries and recorded their resultant dreams on papyrus. Over a thousand years before that the Sumerians of Mesopotamia had also slept on dream beds in their sanctuaries seeking dreams of divination.

Their poem, *The Epic of Gilgamesh* written in 2100 BC celebrates the prophetic power of dreams.

The Assyrian king Ashurnasirpal built a temple to Mamu at Imgur-Enlil, near Kalhu in the 800s BC and two hundred years later another Assyrian king called Ashurbanipal had a dream in which the goddess Ishtar turned a disastrous military predicament into victory.

The Assyrians and their Babylonian neighbours believed good dreams were from the gods and bad dreams were from demons.

The Greeks also had dream books and a dream god called Morpheus. They also slept in special shrines seeking prophetic dreams. Their first dream book was written in the 5th century BC by Antiphon.

The Greeks culled dream ideas from other nations. They also embraced a philosophical approach to dreams. Hippocrates[2] believed throughout the day the soul received images and during the night, it produced images.

Herodotus in *The Histories*, said, The visions that occur to us in dreams are, more often than not, the things we have been concerned about during the day.

The famous Greek philosopher Aristotle[3] rejected the supernatural and predictive power of dreams. Instead he believed dreams caused physiological activity and could be used to analyse illness and predict diseases.

Yet Aristotle's unbelief was a minority opinion. The vast majority of humanity continued to believe dreams were supernaturally sent by the gods and could contain valuable information and prophecy.

The Greeks also embraced the notion their souls left their bodies while asleep. The Chinese and the people of India had a similar understanding. The Chinese believed during sleep one part of their soul was able to journey in a dream realm, while the other part remained in the body.

The Indian text, *Upanishads*, written between 900 and 500 BC, made two statements concerning dreams. The first one said dreams are only an expression of inner desires while the second one claims the soul leaves the body and is guided until awakened.

In the *Mandukya Upanishad*, part of the Hindu Veda scriptures, a dream is said to be one of three states the soul experiences during its lifetime. The other two conditions being the waking state and the sleeping state.

This is similar to the Buddhist philosophers who say what we think of as the real world is probably just an illusion. Buddha Shakyamuni told his disciples to regard all phenomena as dreams. He claimed dreams merely represent one type of illusion.

The three great monotheistic religions of Judaism, Christianity and Islam generally agree on their approach to dreams.

The Hebrews believed their dreams were the voice of their one God called Yahweh. The Hebrews also differentiated between good dreams from Yahweh and bad dreams from evil spirits. Christians share the same belief.

Islam believes Allah speaks through prophetic dreams. In fact nowadays dream interpretation is the only way a Muslim can receive new revelations from Allah since the death of the prophet, Muhammad.

Islam classifies three types of dreams. Firstly, there is the true dream (al-ru'ya), then the false dream, which may come from the devil (shaytan), and finally, the meaningless everyday dream (hulm). This latter dream is thought to come from the dreamer's ego or base appetite issuing from their real world experiences.

Since the start of the church on Pentecost, the great deluge of dreams coming from God onto the earth has overwhelmed Satan's kingdom. Peter claimed this was the fulfilment of Joel's prophecy,

> In the last days, God says, I will pour out my Spirit on
> all people. Your sons and daughters will prophesy,
> your young men will see visions, your old men will
> dream dreams.[4]

Up until this time the Holy Spirit usually only rested on the prophet, priest and king. Then after His victory on the Cross and

His return to Heaven Jesus began to pour his Spirit, not just upon prophets, priests and kings, but upon all people.

No wonder Satan is overwhelmed. No wonder he has continually counterattacked dreams ever since, mainly through his usual methods of confusion, lies and deception.

The famous Byzantine work on dream interpretation, *The Oneirocriticon of Achmet* tells of how an Arab Christian called Achmet adapted Islamic Arabic material, which itself had been heavily influenced by Artemidorus of Daldis' *Oneirocriticon*, the earliest known classical Greek dream book.

Christians such as Tertullian, Augustine, and Synesius also adapted some of the pagan traditions of their contemporaries, as well as Hebrew traditions, in their attitudes to divination, prophecy and revelation, and dream classification.

We can see this in the history of the Christian Church's study of dreams and its resultant literature that has been a battlefield where all sorts of cross-pollination has occurred.

Christian dream literature basically falls into two major chronological and cultural groups. Firstly, there is the Western Christian (Latin and Greek) sources and secondly, the Eastern Christian (Arabic and Syrian) sources.

A study of early Christian sources shows Latin, Greek, and later Syriac and Arabic authors were strongly influenced in their study of dreams by how they sought to define and posture themselves against their traditional enemies, the Jews, the pagans, and the Muslims.

It wasn't just a simple study of dreams from the Bible. There were bigger issues of empire and authority at stake.

The question of how to discern divine from demonic dreams continued to trouble late-antique and medieval Christian writers.

The negative Greek monastic attitude to dreams influenced by Aristotle's anti supernatural stance persisted into the fifth and sixth centuries through texts such as the *Apophthegmata Patrum*, the sayings of the Egyptian desert fathers.

The study of dreams and their function in the world of medicine were also strongly influenced by philosophy, which was mostly divided into Platonist, Stoic, and Aristotelian schools.

And although Aristotelians such as Galen rejected the predictive power of dreams, Neo Platonists like the Greeks Evagrius and Athanasius of Alexandria and the Romans Ambrose, and Augustine were more positive about the possibility of the soul freeing itself from the shackles of the body in sleep.

The patristic tradition was also strongly influenced by philosophical and medical traditions on sleep and dreaming.

Canon law, and the acts of church councils also reflected ecclesiastical attitudes towards dreams rather than those of the lay or monastic people.

Those in authority as usual sought clerical control over dreams and communication from God.

Imagine the possible problems within the church hierarchy if God actually started speaking to His people in dreams!

Pope Gregory allegedly wrote *The Dialogues* a book typical of the Western adoption of the Greco-Roman oneirocritical heritage, in which dreams were accepted as an essential part of the Christian life, especially in monastic contexts.

Pope Gregory identified six ways in which dreams come to the soul,

1. A full stomach.
2. An empty stomach.
3. The illusions of the Devil, "the master of deceit."
4. Both through thought and illusion: (Dreams follow many cares).[5]
5. Divine revelation: e.g. Joseph's dreams.[6]
6. Both through thoughts in our mind and revelation, e.g. Nebuchadnezzar.[7]

Pope Gregory's classification of dream types has been simplified and is still used today in the Arabic-speaking world. They are dreams inspired by God; dreams inspired by the devil and disturbed dreams or nightmares inspired the nafs (ego or spirit) that dwell in each body.

This trichotomy neatly takes us right back to Tertullian in early Christian North Africa, and his identification of the three causes of dreams: those from God, those from a daemon, and those generated by the mind or soul.

Christian authors have often written about dreams. Some of the most important source works on dreams and prophecy include the *Ladder of Ascent* of John Climacus, the mystical writings of Isaac of Nineveh, and the letters of John of Dalyatha.

These three teachers who wrote during the sixth to eighth centuries were greatly influenced by the theologian Origen and the fourth century monk called Evagrius who reinforced the role of revelatory visions supported by ascetic virtue. Evagrius believed only the mature and holy received true dreams from God.

John Climacus, the seventh-century abbot of the Monastery of Mount Sinai also wrote negatively about the interpretation of dreams in *The Ladder Of Divine Assent.*

He shared Evagrius' suspicion of dreams particularly those of monastery novices. He believed dreams were associated with listlessness or despair. At the end of his discourse on dreams he said,

> The man who believes in dreams shows his inexperience, while the man who distrusts every dream is very sensible. Trust only the dreams that foretell torments and judgment for you, but even those dreams may also be from demons if they produce despair in you.

Abbot John wouldn't have been much use in the courts of Pharaoh[8] or Nebuchadnezzar.[9]

Interestingly nowadays while Christian dream interpretation has been largely sidelined for over a century by the psychoanalytical dream interpretations of Freud and Jung et al, Islam has never deviated for a moment from her belief in the supernatural power of dreams.

A billion Muslims believe Allah still speaks through the true dream.

GOD'S SOVEREIGN PURPOSE

God's sovereignty is rarely mentioned nowadays in Christian circles and never in secular society.

Yet we need some grasp of the reality of God's sovereignty in order to correctly understand God's dreams because every single Bible dream was sent to fulfil God's specific sovereign plans and purpose. Understanding God's purpose is a major key to unlocking God's dreams.

The Sovereignty of God is the biblical teaching that all things are under God's rule and control, and nothing happens without His direction or His permission.

This means God works not just some things but all things according to His will.[1] Throughout scripture Yahweh is revealed as the One True God who governs and directs all things for His Chosen People.

There's never a sense of God being a cosmic clockmaker who leaves human beings to their own devices. Instead He is shown actively intervening and interfering in human affairs through dreams in order to bring His kingdom plans and purpose to pass.

God really does cause everything to work together for the good of those who love Him and are called according to His purpose.[2] If God sends a dream there is a good purpose for that message.

Nothing takes God by surprise. He knew Jesus would save humanity long before Adam and Eve were created. He knew Abraham's descendants would be slaves in Egypt for four hundred years and afterwards come out with great wealth long before Abraham was born.

God's purposes are all encompassing and unstoppable.[3] The Sovereignty of God doesn't just mean God has the power and right to govern all things. It also means He continually does so. God is not only sovereign in principle. He is sovereign in practice.

God knows the future and takes an active part in influencing it. We see this in the way He uses dreams to warn King Abimelek not to hurt Abraham and Uncle Laban not to harm Jacob.

Dealing with God is like playing poker with someone who knows all the cards in your hand and the exact position of every card in the deck.

God's sovereignty means, God does what He wants, when He wants, the way He wants without asking our permission. Yet God's foreknowledge doesn't override our choices.

God gave Solomon a no brainer choice in a dream. He said if Solomon would serve God like his father David did then all his descendants and all of Israel would be greatly blessed but if he rejected God and served other gods then he and Israel would be cursed and put out of the Promised Land and their Temple destroyed.

Solomon disregarded God's warning and Israel still suffers today from Solomon's bad choice.

God's motivation is always love. Scripture says love must also be our goal,

> If I had the gift of prophecy, and if I understood all of
> God's secret plans and possessed all knowledge, and

if I had such faith that I could move mountains, but didn't love others, I would be nothing.[4]

God redeemed us from before the foundation of the world. He knows our ancestors and our descendants and how our choices will impact them.

God has good plans and purpose for His creation. He has good plans for our lives, our family's lives, our community's lives, our nation's lives and our world.

God desires daily fellowship with us based on intimacy and communication. He wants to give guidance and wisdom so we can be aligned with him. Ask of me and I will teach you unspeakable things you do not know![5]

The vast majority of biblical prophecy concerns Abraham's descendants and their homeland Israel. Other people and nations are mentioned only in as far as they interact with Israel. This also holds true for Bible dreams.

All Bible dreams concern God's Covenant with Abraham and God's promise to him of his descendant, the Messiah Jesus Christ, blessing all Nations.

Bible dreams show God's love for His people, as he constantly intervenes in their affairs for their benefit and the furtherance of His plans and purpose.

Bible dreams are specifically about God keeping the godly Messiah bloodline safe and on track for the cross on Calvary. It's all about the testimony of Jesus!

In order to fully grasp what God is doing today and how we can work in obedience with him we need to have some understanding of the history and future of Abraham's descendants, the Jewish people.

So far Jesus has fulfilled three hundred and fifty five biblical prophecies so it comes as no surprise to learn all the dreams in the Bible are in one way or another connected to God's covenant with Abraham and his descendant Jesus Christ.

Throughout Scripture God's purpose is to accomplish His prophecy made to Satan in Genesis 3 and His dream covenant made with Abraham in Genesis 15. The Messiah crushing Satan's head and blessing all nations and reigning with the Bride of Christ in heavenly places is the essence of God's vision for humanity.

We live in a wonderful day when the Gospel is being preached to all nations. After this task is finally completed Jesus will return and the next part of God's vision will kick in. Our role is never to formulate our own vision.

We play our part best when we understand God's plans and purpose are paramount, more important than anything else in our lives, more important than anything else in all creation.

Jesus understood this. He only did what He saw the Father doing.[6] When we align ourselves with God's purpose we become the happiest people on earth serving God without fear. This doesn't mean we won't suffer. It means our present and eternal needs are all taken care of by God. Jesus said,

> For the pagans run after all these things, and your heavenly Father knows that you need them. But seek first his kingdom and his righteousness, and all these things will be given to you as well. Therefore do not worry about tomorrow, for tomorrow will worry about itself. Each day has enough trouble of its own.[7]

God's covenant with Abraham changed his life and destiny, Israel's life and destiny and ultimately the whole world's life and destiny.

God's covenant with Abraham is still powerfully at work today as hundreds of thousands of people from all nations are daily born again into The Body of Christ.

GOD'S ETERNAL PLANS AND PURPOSE

God always functions out of His own eternal plans and purposes and everything He plans comes to pass. God always intended Jesus would destroy Satan's work and redeem humanity. For this purpose the Son of God was manifested, that He might destroy the works of the devil.[1]

Dreams have a specific purpose in implementing God's will as it's gradually revealed in the Bible. We see this occurring in all Bible dreams even though there are sometimes gaps of hundreds of years between dreams. Isaiah 55:10-11 says,

> As the rain and the snow
> come down from heaven,
> and do not return to it
> without watering the earth
> and making it bud and flourish,
> so that it yields seed for the sower and bread for the
> eater,
> so is my word that goes out from my mouth:
> It will not return to me empty,

but will accomplish what I desire
and achieve the purpose for which I sent it.

The Bible likens a dream from God as a word from God. Psalm 105, says,

> He sent a man before them, Joseph, who was sold as a slave. They afflicted his feet with fetters, He himself was laid in irons; Until the time that his word came to pass, The word of the Lord tested him.[2]

Here God is saying Joseph's two symbolic prophetic dreams were a word from Him and like any true word from God it would not return empty but would achieve the purpose for what it was sent.

God's dreams are actually words from God and they always accomplish their purpose. This happens in every recorded Bible dream.

In order to properly appreciate the big picture on the front of the jigsaw box of *God's Eternal Plans and Purpose* we need to start with Adam and Eve.

Contrary to popular belief Adam's creation wasn't the beginning of everything; it was the beginning of a plan and a purpose. Adam and Eve were created into history. There'd been others. There'd been a rebellion.

Although Genesis pulls a veil over the origins and nature of this rebellion we know sin existed before Adam and Eve. This is referred to in other scriptures.[3]

The Bible says, The morning stars sang together and all the sons of God shouted for joy when God laid the foundations of the earth.[4]

The leader of that choir was Lucifer/Satan, who before Adam's creation, rebelled taking a third of God's angels with him. Scripture also mentions principalities and powers and dominions in a realm far above all creation called heavenly places.

Before Adam and Eve the heavens and earth had been inhabited. But by the time they arrived Satan had lost his sphere of influence in the heavenly realms and the earth was empty.

At this point God gave our first parents the specific assignment of restocking the earth. He said, Be fruitful and increase in number; fill the earth and subdue it.[5]

Ten generations later Noah and his family were told the same thing after God had once again made the earth empty.[6]

But refilling the earth was God's secondary plan. There was a greater plan, a special plan unknown to prophets, priests, kings, angels and demons. A secret plan kept from Satan and the gods, a covert plan kept hidden in the heart of God, unknown and unknowable until thousands of years later when God revealed it to a Jewish prisoner chained to a soldier in the city of Rome.

This veiled plan revealed God's primary purpose, was to restock the heavenly realms left vacant by Satan and his angels and for this task He was going to use a special people. Paul, who received this revelation wrote,

> Although I am less than the least of all the Lord's
>   people, this grace was given me: to preach to the
>   Gentiles the boundless riches of Christ, and to
>   make plain to everyone the administration of this
>   mystery, which for ages past was kept hidden in
>   God, who created all things.[7]

In his letter to the Ephesians Paul further unwrapped this mystery. He said,

> God's hidden mystery was that through the church, the
>   manifold wisdom of God should be made known to
>   the rulers and authorities in the heavenly realms,

according to his eternal purpose that he accomplished in Christ Jesus our Lord.[8]

Paul is saying that from time immemorial God had predestined Jews and Gentiles who believed in Jesus Christ the Messiah to become the Church, the Body of Christ. This Bride of Christ would then take the place vacated by Satan and the fallen angels in the heavenly realms.

Paul underscores this when he says,

> God, raised Christ from the dead and seated him at his right hand in the heavenly realms, far above all rule and authority, power and dominion, and every name that is invoked, not only in the present age but also in the one to come. And God placed all things under his feet and appointed him to be head over everything for the church, which is his body, the fullness of him who fills everything in every way. And God raised us up with Christ and seated us with him in the heavenly realms in Christ Jesus, in order that in the coming ages he might show the incomparable riches of his grace, expressed in his kindness to us in Christ Jesus.[9]

God's eternal purpose was that we, the Bride of Christ, should occupy the heavenly realms vacated by Satan and the fallen angels.

No wonder Satan hates humanity for he can't make any more demons but all the time the earth's population is exploding and hundreds of thousands of people are daily pouring into God's kingdom.

This Great Mystery also called *The Secret of the Ages*[10] was prophetically hidden in the early pages of Genesis.

After Adam and Eve believed Satan's lies and fell from grace they took the world's first selfie! They lost God consciousness and became self-conscious.

Although the situation looked hopeless God wasn't fazed. He already had a plan in place, which He immediately released when He told Satan,

> And I will put enmity between you and the woman,
> And between your seed and her Seed; He shall
> bruise your head, And you shall bruise His heel.[11]

This new revelation was world history in a nutshell spoken in advance.

It lifted the veil and revealed God's eternal plans and purpose for a Messiah that would forever afterwards impact human history. We now know this Messiah to be Jesus Christ who in the final pages of Scripture is called The Lamb upon His Throne.[12]

This prophecy of a male child who'd destroy the works of the Devil is sometimes called the First Gospel. It clearly announced God's solution for humanity's dilemma and charted the ongoing theme for the rest of Scripture.

From the perspective of God's plans and purpose the outcome of this cosmic battle was never in doubt. But Satan was hell bent on preventing the woman's seed from ever being born. He instantly launched a manhunt that resulted in the ongoing constant conflict throughout Scripture.

Every battle, death, massacre, deception, fear, famine, idolatry, disease, betrayal, enslavement and evil was always Satan's attempt to thwart God's promised Messiah from coming to fulfilment.

Our next chapter looks more closely at Satan's frenzied attempts to do this.

SATAN'S HINDERING PURPOSE

In Scripture, Satan's primary focus was to thwart God's plans and purposes for humanity's redemption. His main mission was to destroy the promised royal seed of the woman.

To this end he tried his damnedest to wipe out the seed line that gave the Messiah and today he works to kill as many people as possible before they can come to the saving knowledge of Jesus Christ and take their rightful place in God's kingdom.

God often uses dreams to stop Satan succeeding.

After he lied and tempted Adam and Eve to sin God pronounced Satan's doom when he said,

> And I will put enmity between you and the woman,
> And between your seed and her Seed; He shall
> bruise your head, And you shall bruise His heel.[1]

Satan endeavoured to stop this prophecy from ever happening. He then started a manhunt in order to kill or corrupt all God-fearing male children that might possibly fulfil this prediction. His campaign kicked off with Cain killing Eve's first son Able.

Then as more and more sons of Adam and Eve were born Satan launched another plan. His new strategy was an attempt to corrupt the entire seed line of the woman and so prevent the birth of God's promised Messiah. Satan tried to achieve this by having fallen angels mate with human women, producing a corrupt hybrid race called the Nephilim.

Nephilim means fallen ones. The Genesis prophecy had mentioned Satan's seed. These Nephilim fulfilled that role. The Scripture says,

> When human beings began to increase in number on the earth and daughters were born to them, the sons of God saw that the daughters of humans were beautiful, and they married any of them they chose. Then the Lord said, My Spirit will not contend with humans forever, for they are mortal; their days will be a hundred and twenty years.
> The Nephilim were on the earth in those days—and also afterward—when the sons of God went to the daughters of humans and had children by them. They were the heroes of old, men of renown.
> The Lord saw how great the wickedness of the human race had become on the earth, and that every inclination of the thoughts of the human heart was only evil all the time. The Lord regretted that he had made human beings on the earth, and his heart was deeply troubled. So the Lord said, I will wipe from the face of the earth the human race I have created—and with them the animals, the birds and the creatures that move along the ground—for I regret that I have made them. But Noah found favour in the eyes of the Lord.[2]

Satan's strategy was working. Nephilim giants were effectively corrupting the seed of the woman and humanity was on the verge of extinction.

Things got so bad God regretted He'd created mankind at all for redemption would be impossible if every person was part fallen angel. So God judged the Earth with the flood. His purpose was threefold.

Firstly He wanted to destroy the Nephilim. Secondly He wanted to punish the fallen angels who'd had illicit sex with woman and make such an example of them so that no other angel would ever again try such a thing.

Jude said,

> And the angels who did not stay within their own
>   domain but abandoned their proper dwelling—
>   these He has kept in eternal chains under darkness,
>   bound for judgment on that great day.[3]

Peter said,

> God did not spare angels when they sinned, but sent
>   them to hell, putting them in chains of darkness to
>   be held for judgment.[4]

God's third purpose was to save humanity from certain annihilation. The flood was His way of preserving the human race and its bloodline. Had Satan managed to stop Jesus Christ from coming into the world there would be no hope for humanity. The Bible says,

> Noah was a just man and perfect in his generations,
>   and Noah walked with God.[5]

The Hebrew word for perfect in this verse is *tamiym*, which means complete or whole and concerns health and physical condition. It's the same word used to describe the state of acceptable animal sacrifices to the Lord.

So, *perfect in his generations means* Noah's genetic bloodline and ancestry was 100% human and untainted by the Nephilim hybrid corruption.

But the flood didn't stop Satan's attacks against the Messiah's seed line. Four hundred years later Noah's descendants were once again alienated from God and worshipping the sun, moon, stars and signs of the Zodiac in a tower built by giants in the land of Shinar.

After the flood, it seems the Nephilim were once more up to their old tricks. Certainly they were in the land of Canaan when the children of Israel entered it.

The Scripture says,

> And there we saw the Nephilim, the sons of Anak, who come of the Nephilim; and we were in our own sight as grasshoppers, and so we were in their sight.[6]

God then chose Abram, later renamed Abraham, for the purpose of launching His final plan for mankind's salvation. Abraham's descendants would defeat the giant races inhabiting The Promised Land and one of them, Jesus Christ of Nazareth, would be the Saviour of the whole world.

Before Abraham had been identified as the carrier of the Messiah seed line Satan had launched his general assault on mankind by causing the intermingling of Nephilim DNA with human DNA.

After Abraham was chosen Satan pinpointed his attacks against Abraham's descendants, the Jewish nation. Then after David's bloodline was chosen to birth the Messiah, Satan focused all his murderous efforts against David's seed line.

The following are some examples of Satan's vicious assaults

against the promised seed. They show something of the scope and intensity of his continual war against God's plans and purpose for the coming Messiah.

Most of God's Bible dreams were sent to destroy Satan's hindering plans against God's Messiah. Firstly, Abraham's wife Sarah was abducted by Pharaoh into his harem long before Isaac was born.[7]

Later Sarah was also snatched into King Abimelech's harem shortly before Isaac was born.[8]

Isaac's similar foolishness in Gerar of saying his wife was his sister also placed Abraham's family seed line in great danger.

Famines also threatened to wipe out Abraham's family line.

In Egypt, Satan launched a particularly cruel attack on Abraham's male line. The king of Egypt said to the Hebrew midwives,

> When you are helping the Hebrew women during childbirth on the delivery stool, if you see that the baby is a boy, kill him; but if it is a girl, let her live.[9]

Later when Abraham's descendants were finally fleeing Egypt, Satan again tried a last ditch attempt at their total destruction through Pharaoh's armies.[10]

Then Nathan prophesied to David the Messiah would come from his seed line - Your house and your kingdom will endure forever before me; your throne will be established forever.[11]

Afterwards Satan tried to wipe our David's line. His first major attack was in the marriage of David's descendant Jehoram and Ahab's evil daughter Athaliah. Satan caused Jehoram to murder all his brothers.[12]

Then the Arabs slew all David's male descendants except for Ahaziah.[13] Later Ahaziah was murdered by Jehu. When Athaliah the mother of Ahaziah realised her son was dead, she proceeded to destroy the whole royal family of the house of Judah.[14]

Only baby Joash was rescued and for six years he was kept hidden in the temple of the Lord before he became a king who reigned in Jerusalem forty years. At that point all God's covenant promises to Abraham, Isaac and Jacob rested on this one little baby boy.

We should never underestimate the value of a little child.

When David's descendant King Hezekiah was childless Satan again attempted to finally destroy the Abrahamic seed line through a double attack made by the King of Assyria and the King of Terrors but God kept His promises to Abraham, Isaac and Jacob.[15]

Later when Abraham's seed line were in captivity in Persia Satan used Haman in yet another infamous attempt to totally annihilate the children of Israel.[16]

In the New Testament Satan boldly tried to kill Jesus in Mary's womb. St Joseph was ready to divorce Mary when God sent a dream telling him not to be afraid of marrying Mary because she carried the promised seed.

Had Joseph exposed her pregnancy publicly Mary could well have been stoned to death and the Messiah seed line within her finally destroyed.[17]

Then shortly after Jesus was born Satan used King Herod in another attempt to murder the Messiah.[18]

Just before Jesus started his ministry Satan used a dream in order to try once again to kill the Messiah by tempting Jesus to jump from the top of the temple.[19]

Then when Jesus began his ministry at Nazareth Satan used the enraged synagogue congregation to again try to kill Jesus this time by throwing him off a cliff.[20]

Satan also tried to kill Jesus by the storm on the lake.[21] Later when Jesus told the Jews, Before Abraham was born, I am! they picked up stones to kill him.[22]

But all Satan's attempts to stop God's plans and purpose have failed and always will fail. As God says,

> Only I can tell you the future before it even happens.
> Everything I plan will come to pass, for I do whatever I wish.[23]

Genesis 3:15 was a remarkable prophecy given at the dawn of human history,

> And I will put enmity
> between you and the woman,
> and between your offspring and hers;
> he will crush your head,
> and you will strike his heel."

It is the first Messianic prophecy in the Bible. In it, God says a person born of the seed of woman (a virgin) will suffer a wound from Satan on his heel, but that person will then crush Satan's head.

The wound on the heel is symbolic of a non-lethal strike. This prophecy was fulfilled in the resurrection of Jesus from the dead. The wound on the head is symbolic of a lethal strike which will be finally fulfilled when Jesus returns and casts Satan into the lake of fire.

Two of the titles for Satan are often confusing and disturbing to Christians, *God of this world* and *Prince of this world.* They sometimes ask, If Satan is defeated how can he still have authority?

The answer is, Satan's ultimate defeat was sealed at The Cross, but hasn't yet been realised in history.

That's why many years after the Cross, the apostle John said the whole world lies in the power of the evil one".[24]

The writer of the book of Hebrews said although all things have been put in subjection to Christ, we do not yet see all things subjected to Him.[25]

The de-throning of Satan as the prince of this world was guaranteed by Jesus' victory over the Cross through the power of His resurrection. But Satan will not actually be removed from his throne until Jesus returns, at which time the God of peace will completely crush Satan.[26]

The total defeat of Satan is a delayed benefit of the Cross, just as is the receipt of our glorified bodies.

A key aspect of the conflict between God and Satan is all about dominion.

This earth was created for mankind. God granted dominion over the creation to Adam and Eve.[27] But when the two of them succumbed to Satan's temptation, that dominion was lost. Satan stole it, and he became the prince of this earth.

That's why Satan could legitimately tempt Jesus in a dream by offering Him all the kingdoms of the world if Jesus would only bow down and worship him. [28]

THE ANGEL OF THE LORD

Dreams are only one way God speaks to people. Apart from the Bible, there were other ways such as,

1. Throne Room Experience
2. Audible Voice of God
3. Visitation of God the Father
4. Visitation of the Lord Jesus
5. Manifestation of the Holy Spirit
6. Visitation from the Third Heaven
7. Heavenly Translation
8. Visitation of Angels
9. Visitations in a dream
10. Visitation in a vision
11. Open Visions
12. Dreams/Night visions
13. Inner visions
14. Trances
15. Experiences before waking and sleeping
16. Prophetic Word from a seasoned prophet

17. Discernment of Spirits
18. Word of Knowledge
19. Word of Wisdom
20. Scriptural Enlightenment
21. Nature
22. Déjà vu experiences
23. Urim & Thummim
24. Casting of Lots
25. Fleeces
26. Vague Pictures
27. Recognitions
28. Feelings that confirm revelation
29. Impressions that confirm revelation
30. Knowing through intuition and insight

God is not limited in the ways He interacts with His beloved creation or speaks to His people. Scripture records God appearing to Abraham ten times and to Jacob eight times.

The Bible says, The Lord appeared to Abram[1] and the Lord came to Abram in a vision[2]. It also says the Lord appeared to Abraham at the great trees of Mamre with two angels and ate food and had his feet washed by Abraham who worshiped him.[3]

Scripture also says Jacob physically wrestled with God and had his hip put out of joint. God appeared to many other people throughout Scripture, Abraham, Isaac, Rebecca, Jacob, Hagar, Gideon, Balaam, Moses, Joshua, Manoah, Isaiah, Elijah, Solomon and so on.

God said about Moses,

> When there is a prophet among you, I, the Lord, reveal myself to them in visions, I speak to them in dreams. But this is not true of my servant Moses; he is faithful in all my house. With him I speak face to

> face, clearly and not in riddles; he sees the form of the Lord.[4]

Then one day Moses asked God,

> Please show me Your glory. God answered, I will cause all My goodness to pass in front of you and I will proclaim My name, the Lord, before you. I will have mercy on whom I have mercy, and I will have compassion on whom I have compassion. And He added, You cannot see My face, for no one can see Me and live.[5]

What's happening here? On one hand the Bible says, The Lord would speak to Moses face to face, as one speaks to a friend[6]. Yet on the other hand God told Moses, You cannot see My face, for no one can see Me and live.[7]

So who is Moses speaking face to face with? Who exactly are all these people seeing when Scripture speaks of God appearing to them?

Jesus sheds light on this conundrum. He said, No one has ever seen God, but the one and only Son, who is himself God and is in closest relationship with the Father, has made him known.[8]

Later Jesus also said, No one has seen the Father except the one who is from God; only he has seen the Father.[9] If all these people saw God but they didn't see God the Father who then did they see?

Paul also told Timothy about God. He said,

> He alone is immortal and dwells in unapproachable light. No one has ever seen Him, nor can anyone see Him. To Him be honor and eternal dominion! Amen.[10]

There's a certain figure, a certain being, who keeps showing up throughout the law and the prophets. He's sometimes called the Angel of the Lord or One like the son of man. Sometimes He's called God and sometimes He has no name at all.

He's always worshipped and He speaks as God and He performs miraculous signs. People know He is God and expect to die after meeting Him face-to-face, but none of them actually do.

He speaks as God and He accepts worship as God but He can't be God the Father because Jesus said, No one has ever seen God, but the one and only Son, who is Himself God.

Here Jesus is simply saying no man has ever seen God the Father but the Bible plainly states people did see and talk with God. So, what's going on?

The short answer is these people are actually meeting with and talking to Jesus, a pre-incarnation appearance of Jesus Christ.

Hebrews says, The Son is the radiance of God's glory and the exact representation of his being.[11] In Matthew, Jesus describes Himself as God's mouthpiece on earth and God's revelation to mankind of what God is like.[12]

In John's Gospel, Phillip said, Lord, show us the Father and that will be enough for us. Jesus answered:

> Don't you know me, Philip, even after I have been among you such a long time? Anyone who has seen me has seen the Father. How can you say, Show us the Father? Don't you believe that I am in the Father, and that the Father is in me? The words I say to you I do not speak on my own authority. Rather, it is the Father, living in me, who is doing his work. Believe me when I say that I am in the Father and the Father is in me; or at least believe on the evidence of the works themselves.[13]

One of the many ways Jesus appeared throughout the Old Testament is as the Angel of the Lord. This Angel is very different from ordinary angels in that He is the only Angel in the Bible who accepts worship.

When He appeared to Moses[14] and Joshua[15] they were told to remove their sandals for they were standing on holy ground.

The Angel of the Lord is mentioned over fifty times in the Old Testament. In Exodus, He appeared to Moses in the burning bush and said, I am the God of your father, the God of Abraham, the God of Isaac, and the God of Jacob.[16]

Later God the Father told Moses and He would send an angel to guide and protect the Children of Israel in the wilderness. He called this angel, My angel and said, My name is in Him.[17]

The Angel of the Lord's main role was to carry messages to humanity from God. He gave orders to Balaam[18] and he instructed Gideon how to deliver Israel from the Midianite's.[19] He prophesied the birth of Samson[20] and he commanded David to build an altar in Jerusalem.[21]

He also led the Children of Israel in the wilderness as a pillar of cloud by day and fire by night[22] and he helped Elijah when he fled from Jezebel.[23]

He also appeared to Abraham, Isaac, Rebecca, Jacob, Hagar, Gideon, Balaam, Moses, Joshua, Manoah, Isaiah, Elijah and Solomon.

Jesus as the Angel of the Lord also functioned as God's avenger who executed judgment upon Israel's enemies. When the Nephilim Assyrian army threatened Jerusalem, it was the Angel of the Lord who killed 185,000 of them in one night.

In the Old Testament Jesus dealt with the Nephilim as the Angel of the Lord and in the New Testament He dealt with them in their spirit form of demons. They immediately recognised Him when He first appeared in His ministry at Capernaum. Scripture says,

> The people were amazed at his teaching, because he taught them as one who had authority, not as the teachers of the law. Just then a man in their synagogue who was possessed by an impure spirit cried out, What do you want with us, Jesus of Nazareth? Have you come to destroy us? I know who you are, the Holy One of God![24]

The demons instantly recognised Jesus because He is the one who'd killed them when they were Nephilim.

The Angel of the Lord as protector of Israel is mentioned in the Psalms, The angel of the Lord encamps around those who fear Him, and rescues them.[25] The Psalmist also says,

> Let those be ashamed and dishonoured who seek my life; Let those be turned back and humiliated who devise evil against me. Let them be like chaff before the wind, With the Angel of the Lord driving them on. Let their way be dark and slippery, With the Angel of the Lord pursuing them.[26]

The first couple of Biblical mentions of the Angel of the Lord concern Abraham's concubine, Hagar. After their initial encounter Hagar says, You are the God who sees me.[27]

At their second meeting the Angel of the Lord, speaks to Hagar about Ishmael and says, I will make him into a great nation.[28] This is something only God can do.

The Angel of the Lord also appears when Abraham is about to sacrifice Isaac on Mount Moriah and says, Do not lay a hand on the boy. Do not do anything to him. Now I know that you fear God, because you have not withheld from me your son, your only son.[29]

This is clearly God speaking. In this same incident Scripture says,

> The Angel of the Lord called to Abraham from heaven a second time and said, I swear by myself, declares the Lord, that because you have done this and have not withheld your son, your only son, I will surely bless you and make your descendants as numerous as the stars in the sky and as the sand on the seashore. Your descendants will take possession of the cities of their enemies, and through your offspring all nations on earth will be blessed, because you have obeyed me.[30]

This again is clearly God speaking and restating promises He already made to Abraham.

The fourth time we meet the Angel of the Lord is when Jacob wrestles with God and afterwards calls the wrestling place Peniel, saying he did so because I saw God face to face and yet my life was spared.[31] Hosea speaking of this incident with Jacob says,

> He struggled with the angel and overcame him; he wept and begged for his favour. He found him at Bethel and talked with him there— the Lord God Almighty, the Lord is his name[32]!

The fifth mention of the Angel of the Lord concerns Moses and the burning bush. Here the Angel of the Lord clearly identifies who He is by saying, I am the God of your father, the God of Abraham, the God of Isaac and the God of Jacob.[33]

The angel of the Lord also appears to Balaam[34] and Joshua[35] and four other times in the book of Judges. In Judges the Angel of the Lord told Israel,

> I brought you up out of Egypt and led you into the land I swore to give to your ancestors. I said, I will never

break my covenant with you, and you shall not make a covenant with the people of this land, but you shall break down their altars.[36]

Obviously this is God speaking. In Judges the Angel of the Lord also appears to Gideon.

After the angel consumed the meat and the bread by fire Gideon realised he'd been talking to God. He exclaimed Alas, Sovereign Lord! I have seen the Angel of the Lord face to face![37] Again, the Angel of the Lord is identified as none other than the Lord Himself.

Another interesting appearance of the Angel of the Lord in Judges concerns Samson's parents. When Samson's father Manoah was offering sacrifice the Angel of the Lord ascended in the flame and Manoah and his wife fell with their faces to the ground realising they had seen God. Manoah said, We are doomed to die! We have seen God![38]

My main point in this chapter is to remind us that Jesus appears throughout the Old Testament in many guises. There's a lot more than dreams and visions going on.

It's also interesting there are no instances of Jesus appearing as the Angel of the Lord in the New Testament. After Jesus became human the angel Gabriel was given the role of God's chief messenger. We see this in St. Joseph's four dreams.

Jesus as the Angel of The Lord is also very conspicuous concerning Jacob's dreams, Balaam's dreams, the dream concerning Gideon and some of Zechariah's dreams.

In fact Jesus as the Angel of the Lord actually interpreted *Jacob's 'Goats and Go Back Home' Dream.*

ANGELS IN BIBLE DREAMS

Twenty-two of the fifty-three dreams examined in this book include an angel or angels. Mainly, angels give instructions from God or interpret and explain God's revelation but they also have other functions.

In Jacob's Covenant Dream the angels are ascending and descending from Heaven, carrying out God's instructions.

In *Eliphaz's 'Demonic Nightmare' Dream* the spirit that frightens the dreamer is a fallen angel. We aren't told anything about *Job's Satanic Nightmares* but I suspect there were also fallen angels, especially Satan, involved.

In *Nebuchadnezzar's 'Large Tree' Dream* the angel called a watcher in some Bible versions, announces a decision made by the Heavenly Council and in *Daniel's 'Four Beasts' Dream* there's the same Heavenly Council and an angel interpreting and explaining things to Daniel.

In *Daniel's 'Ram, Goat and Little Horn' Dream* the angel Gabriel was sent to explain to Daniel the meaning of the dream but even with Gabriel's help Daniel lay exhausted for several days, appalled by the vision that was beyond his understanding.

In *Zechariah's Eight Night Vision Dreams* there were various angels and always an interpreting angel explaining things to Zechariah.

Three of St Joseph's four dreams mention an angel who gives instructions and it was probably the same angel who also gave instructions in the fourth dream.

In *Jesus Tempted By Satan Dream* we see the fallen angel Satan doing the tempting and afterwards God's angels came and ministered to Jesus.

GOD AND JESUS IN BIBLE DREAMS

Old Testament people who were reported as seeing God were really seeing Jesus in a pre-incarnate form because as John says, No one has seen God at any time.[1]

Paul confirms this when he says God the Father, alone can never die, and he lives in light so brilliant that no human can approach him. No human eye has ever seen him, nor ever will.[2]

John in the above verse goes on to say, The only begotten Son, who is in the bosom of the Father, He has declared Him.[3] Here John is saying the Old Testament people who were reported as seeing God were really seeing Jesus declaring God to them.

It's possible to hear God's voice but not possible to see Him. This is verified by a pronouncement God the Father made to Moses at Mt. Sinai, when he said, You cannot see My face, for no one may see Me and live.[4]

So when God appears as fire for example it can't be God the Father because no one can ever see God in any shape or form. The same thing holds true for God appearing as a smoking firepot with a blazing torch. No man has seen God!

Lets go through all the dreams of the Bible and look for God and Jesus.

In Abraham's Covenant Dream (Genesis 15:1-21) God talked to Abraham in a vision. Then He took Abraham outside and showed him the stars. The next day He continued the conversation and instructed Abraham to prepare the sacrificial animals in order to cut Covenant.

God then put Abraham into a deep sleep and continued to talk and prophesy to him in a dream. After it got dark God appeared as a smoking firepot with a blazing torch and passed between the sacrificial pieces.

This was Jesus who took Abraham outside and appeared as a smoking firepot with a blazing torch. It's the same Jesus who will take the punishment of death when the Covenant is broken.

In King Abimelek's Dream (Genesis 20:1-18) The Scripture says, God came to Abimelek in a dream one night and talked with him. This could have been either Jesus or God the Father because Abimelek only talked with God. There is no mention of Abimelek seeing anyone.

In Jacob's Covenant Dream (Genesis 28:10-22) Jacob saw Jesus as the Lord standing above the stairway. Interestingly Jesus also was the stairway.[5]

In Jacob's 'Goats and Go Back Home' Dream (Genesis 31:10-13) Jacob saw Jesus as the Angel of the Lord. Jesus also reminds Jacob they have met before at Bethel when he said, I am the God of Bethel, where you anointed a pillar and where you made a vow to me.

In Laban's 'Don't Harm Jacob' Dream - (Genesis 31:22-24) It could have been Jesus or God the Father who talked with Laban. As in King Abimelek's Dream there is no mention of anyone seeing God.

In Jacob Wrestles with God And Man Incident – (Genesis 32:24) Jacob was definitely wrestling with Jesus.

In Joseph's 'Sheaves of Grain' Dream (Genesis 37:1-11) There is no mention of God or Jesus. Though Joseph is a type of Jesus.

In Joseph's 'Sun, Moon & Stars' Dream (Genesis 37:1-11) There is no mention of God or Jesus. Though Joseph is a type of Jesus.

In Pharaoh's Cupbearer's Dream (Genesis 40:1-23) There is no explicit mention of God or Jesus. Though the vine is a type of Jesus (Jesus said, I am the vine) and the three branches could represent the three days Jesus was dead before he was resurrected and budded and blossomed so to speak..

In Pharaoh's Baker's Dreams (Genesis 40:1-23) There is no explicit mention of God or Jesus.

In Pharaoh's First Dream (Genesis 41:1-49) There is no explicit mention of God or Jesus.

In Pharaoh's Second Dream (Genesis 41:1-49) There is no explicit mention of God or Jesus.

In Jacob's 'Go Down To Egypt' Night Vision (Genesis 46:1-7) This is definitely Jesus speaking. He identifies himself as He did in Jacob's other dreams. He also promises to accompany Israel to and from Egypt.

In Balaam's 'Don't Curse Israel' Dream (Numbers 22:1-14) God spoke to Balaam in the dream. Jesus was in the seedline of the people Satan wanted Balaam to curse.

In Balaam's 'If They Call You' Dream (Numbers 22:15-38 (NKJV)) God spoke to Balaam in the dream. Afterwards Jesus appeared as the Angel of the Lord and reminded Balaam he was only to speak what God told him to speak concerning the Hebrews.

In The Midianite's Dream (Judges 7:9-18) There is no explicit mention of God or Jesus. But Gideon was specifically instructed by Jesus as the Angel of the Lord to go and hear the dream and its interpretation. The barley bread could be a symbol of Jesus and it was the Lord who caused the men throughout the camp to turn on each other with their swords.[6]

In Samuel's Night Vision Dream (1 Samuel 3:1-15) It could have been Jesus or God the Father who talked with Samuel. As in King Abimelek's Dream and Laban's Dream there is no mention of anyone being seen.

In Nathan's Dream For King David (2 Samuel 7:1-29) God spoke to Nathan in the dream. Jesus was symbolically referred to as the Son who would establish the kingdom forever.

In Solomon's 'Discerning Heart' Dream (I Kings 3:5-28) This was Jesus who appeared and talked with Solomon. God the Father, who no man can see, does not appear.

In Solomon's 'Warning' Dream (I Kings 9:1-9) This is Jesus who appeared to Solomon a second time, as He had appeared to him at Gibeon.

In Solomon 'Asks For Wisdom' Dream (2 Chronicles 1:7) This is Jesus who appeared to Solomon.

In The Brides Dream – (Song of Songs 3:15) This is Jesus she finds and holds close to her.

In Eliphaz's 'Demonic Nightmare' Dream (Job 4:12-21) The demon appears and tells lies about God.

In Job's – 'You Scare Me with Dreams' (Job 7:14) Job who is under attack from Satan mistakenly blames God for what Satan is doing.

In Jeremiah's 'Israel Will Return' Dream (Jeremiah 30:3 -31:26) This whole dream is a prophetic word from God.

In Nebuchadnezzar's 'Large Statue" Dream (Daniel 2:1-16) There is no explicit mention of God or Jesus. But the rock cut out not by human hands symbolised Jesus, and the huge mountain that filled the whole earth represented the Kingdom of God.

In Daniel's 'Mystery Revealed' Night Vision (Daniel 2:17-48) There is no explicit mention of God or Jesus but Daniel praised God for revealing the dream to him.

In Nebuchadnezzar's 'Large Tree Dream' (Daniel 4:4-37) I believe this holy angel is probably Jesus. "Behold, I send an angel before you, to **guard** you on the way and to bring you to the place which I have prepared" (Ex 23:20).

In Daniel's 'Four Beasts' Dream (Daniel 7:1-28) Daniel saw Jesus as the Ancient of Days.

In Daniel's Dream of the Ram and Goat (Daniel 8:1-27) There is no explicit mention of God or Jesus but the two holy ones speaking might have been God and Jesus. The angel Gabriel was sent to give the interpretation of this night vision.

In Zechariah's Eight Night Visions (Zechariah 1:7-6:15) Jesus is evident in all of the night visions.

In St. Joseph's 'Marry Mary' Dream (Matthew 1:20-25) Jesus appeared as the baby in Mary's womb and the angel said the baby's name was Jesus.

In The Magi's Dream (Matthew 2:1-12) There is no explicit mention of God or Jesus. We're not told much about the dream except they were directed to go home another way to protect the life of baby Jesus.

In St. Joseph's 'Escape To Egypt' Dream (Matthew 2:3-15) There is no explicit mention of God or Jesus though the dream is sent to protect the incarnate Jesus.

In St. Joseph's 'Back To Israel' Dream (Matthew 2:19-23) There is no explicit mention of God or Jesus though the dream is sent to protect the incarnate Jesus.

In St. Joseph's 'Go To Nazareth' Dream (Matthew 2:19-23) There is no explicit mention of God or Jesus though the dream is sent to protect the incarnate Jesus.

In Jesus' 'Tempted By Satan' Dream (Matthew 4:1-11) Jesus was lead by God's Holy Spirit into the wilderness to be tempted by Satan.

In Pilate's Wife's Dream (Matt 27:19) Jesus had appeared in her dream as an innocent man and she obviously recognised him.

In Peter interpreting Pentecost & quoting Joel (Acts 2:14-18) It is God who pours out His Spirit. It is Jesus who baptises us in the Holy Spirit.

In Saul's Vision on the Road to Damascus (Acts 9:1-9) It is Jesus who speaks with Saul later called Paul

In Ananias' Vision regards Paul. (Acts 9:10-19) It is Jesus who instructs Ananias.

In St Paul's Trance (Acts 22:2-21) Jesus identifies Himself as the One whom Paul is persecuting and God is seen as the One who chose Paul.

In Cornelius' 'Send For Peter' Vision (Acts 10:1-7) God is mentioned as hearing and responding to Peter's prayers.

In Peter's 'Kill and Eat' Trance (Acts 10:9-22) God, Jesus and the Holy Spirit are all evident in this vision.

In Peter's Revelation at Cornelius's House (Acts 10:44-48) It's Jesus who baptised the people at Cornelius's house in the Holy Spirit and then they are water baptised into Jesus Christs' name.

In Paul's 'Man Of Macedonia' Night Vision (Acts 16:6-11) There is no explicit mention of God or Jesus but God is directing Paul to preach in Macedonia.

In Paul's 'Fear Not' Night Vision (Acts 18:9-11) It is clearly Jesus who is speaking to Paul.

In Paul's 'Angelic' Night Vision Dream (Acts 27:20-25) The angel says God has graciously given Paul the lives of all who were sailing with him.

In Egypt's 'Dreadful Dreams (The Wisdom of Solomon 18:17-19) There is no explicit mention of God or Jesus though God has sent these dreams to explain why the first born are suffering.

In Esdras' Eagle and Lion' Dream (2 Esdras 11:1-48) (CEB) The Lion roused from the forest is Jesus.

In Esdras 'Man From The Sea' Dream (2 Esdras 13:1-57. (CEB) The man who rises from the sea is God's son Jesus Christ the Messiah.

In Mordecai's 'Two Great Dragons' Dream (Esther 10:4-13

(Addition F) (NRSVCE) God is seen answering Israel's prayers and working signs and wonders in order to deliver them from their enemies.

In Judas Maccabees' 'Golden Sword' Dream (2 Maccabees 15:6-16) God is mentioned as the One who gives the sword to Judas.

DREAM PURPOSE AND PROCESS

We must be constantly aware it is God and not us who interprets God's dreams. Joseph said, Do not interpretations belong to God?[1] The New Living Translation says it beautifully, Interpreting dreams is God's business.[2]

Daniel would agree. He knew God was the source of all true dream interpretation. He told King Nebuchadnezzar,

> No wise man, enchanter, magician or diviner can explain to the king the mystery he has asked about, but there is a God in heaven who reveals mysteries.[3]

Before we attempt to interpret any dream we should be in an attitude of prayer and total dependance upon God who is able to give us the proper interpretation. Just as Paul told us to pray for the power to interpret tongues[4] we should similarity ask God for the power to interpret dreams. A correct interpretation of a symbolic God given dream is a sovereign activity of God's Holy Spirit. All

God's symbolic Bible dreams are from the mind of God and as Paul reminds us,

> The Spirit searches all things, even the deep things of God. For who knows a person's thoughts except their own spirit within them? In the same way no one knows the thoughts of God except the Spirit of God.[5]

We should also be thankful God has allowed us the privilege of being involved in bringing His plans and purpose to pass.

The purpose is the reason why God sent the dream and the process is the method we use to try and discern the source of the dream and it's possible interpretation and purpose.

God's Bible dreams were sent so people could understand them and obey their message. God constantly used Bible dreams to reveal His kingdom purpose and to keep that purpose on track.

In Scripture God doesn't obscure or hide anything from the dreamer unless He has a reason for doing so. God wasn't just sending little riddles and puzzles to people to confuse them. After all most of his dreams were literal.

God's dreams were specifically sent from God to man in order to advance God's plans and purpose. If God decided to send a dream that required an interpretation then he also had a dream interpreter on hand.

In Scripture over 96% of the recorded dreams are God's dreams and God's dreams always have a purpose. So on one level Bible dreams are fairly easy to deal with because we know they are all God's dreams and not just random dreams from the Natural Man.

In our normal everyday life it's not always so easy. There, we have to discern the source of the dream first and then we have to interpret the dream usually using the *Symbol Replacement Method*.

More than half of all Bible dreams were literal but I don't think the same ratio holds true today. Certainly the vast majority of my own personal dreams are symbolic. The same goes for the many dreams I help others interpret.

Perhaps the reason for some of this is because people don't need me to interpret literal dreams. For example, if God tells someone in a dream to stop committing adultery or watching pornography then it's unlikely that person will need to share a dream like that with me.

Nowadays when presented with a dream we usually ask a series of questions some of which might be,

- What was the source of the dream?
- Was it a God dream, a soul dream or a satanic dream?
- Was the dream literal or symbolic?
- What was the subject matter?
- Who or what was the dream about?
- What was the context?
- How many dream scenes?
- What was the main point?
- Can we use the Symbol Replacement Method?
- Can the dreamer change the outcome?
- Is there a choice?
- Can the dreamer repent?
- Is it an impartation dream?
- Is it a repeated dream?
- Are there colours?
- Are their emotions?
- Is it a confirmation dream?
- Is it a sealed dream?
- What is the dreamer's metron?
- Is timing important?

But this was not the case with God's Bible dreams. God's Bible dreams were sent so people could understand them and obey their message. God didn't obscure or hide anything from the dreamer unless He had a reason for doing so. God wasn't just sending little riddles and puzzles to people to keep them amused or on edge.

After all most of His Bible dreams were literal. God's dreams were specifically sent from God to man in order to advance God's plans and purpose. If God decided to send a dream that required an interpretation then he always had a dream interpreter on hand.

My approach to dream interpretation is to put purpose first and process second. So my first response nowadays is not to run for the dream dictionary to see what this or that image means.

My first question is, Is this dream from God? And if it is from God then my second question is, For what purpose was it sent?

Obviously it's not a case of either/or. It's a case of both/and. Purpose and process are both important. But putting purpose first helps me focus firmly on God and His will. Knowing the dream was specifically sent to the dreamer's metron is also very helpful.

It's also never a case of, Please quickly explain this riddle so I can be blessed.

Consequently the checklist I use to interpret dreams is heavily weighted towards finding out God's purpose and knowing Him better.

GOD'S OVERALL PURPOSE FOR BIBLE DREAMS

Dreams and visions are the two main ways God speaks to people so they can obey and work with Him in accomplishing His intentions and advancing His Eternal Plans and Purpose.

Only believers receive visions while everyone can have a dream. God's dreams always carried an authority that demanded a response and all the dreamers were positively challenged to make crucial decisions because of them. God's dreams always changed the dreamer's view of God and His Chosen People. When the dreamers obeyed they were blessed, when they didn't they were cursed.

All Bible dreams were specifically targeted to the dreamer's personal life situation and metron. Most dreams were received in the midst of difficult life and death circumstances.

As well as having a personal meaning for the dreamer Bible dreams also held a significant importance for the dreamer's family, tribe and nation in the greater purpose of God.

Bible dreams were mainly sent to covenant people who were in a growing relationship with God. Abraham, Jacob, Joseph, Samuel, Nathan, Solomon, Jeremiah, Daniel, Zechariah, St Joseph, and Paul all had significant dreams that came as a result of their calling and their close and loving relationship with God.

These relationship dreams were also prophetic and encouraging. They contained warnings, instructions, directions and promises of future blessings. They also comforted the dreamers with a sense of the presence and care of God.

The four main functions of Bible dreams apart from love and relationship building was to be prophetic, to warn, to direct and to encourage. Sometimes, a single dream would accomplish two or three or all of these purposes.

For example, *Nebuchadnezzar's 'Large Tree' Dream* was prophetic and contained a warning while *Jacob's 'Goats and Go Back Home' Dream* was prophetic, encouraging and directional. *Abraham's Covenant Dream* was also prophetic and encouraging with the warning his descendants would be slaves for four hundred years in Egypt.

Solomon's 'Discerning Heart' Dream fulfilled all four of the main functions of Bible dreams. It was prophetic, encouraging, directional and warning. It was also the only dream in the Bible that actually imparted a spiritual gift to the dreamer.

As a general overview, forty one of the fifty three dreams examined in this book contained prophetic elements. Twenty five of them had warning elements, fourteen contained directional elements and thirty two had encouraging elements.

Overall, God's Bible dreams were a heavenly language and a potent means of divine revelation. They were sometimes audible and obvious and sometimes visual and symbolic requiring interpretation. When dreams were clearly understood and properly interpreted they usually changed people and their situations for the better. They also always destroyed the work of the devil.

Genesis contains over one third of all Bible dreams. The first six dreams are auditory message dreams in which God speaks in plain language easily understood by the dreamer. Although there is some symbolism there was no need for an interpretation in order that the dream be understood.

These dreams immediately impacted the dreamer and quickly achieved the required response. The next six dreams are symbolic dreams requiring differing degrees of interpretation and the final night vision dream is again an auditory message in plain language.

Afterwards all the dreams in the Old Testament require some level of interpretation. We're not told whether any New Testament dream requires an interpretation but I think it's unlikely.

In Joseph's first three dreams an angel speaks plainly to him and this probably also happened in his fourth dream. I suspect the Magi's and Pilates's wife's dreams were also auditory in plain speech.

In Paul's night vision in Acts the man from Macedonia spoke in plain speech.

Dreams like visions are one of God's main languages to his people. All dreams in Scripture whether they are conveyed in clear messages or in enigmatic symbols are a divine language that communicates a divine message to further God's divine plans and purpose.

GOD'S PURPOSE FOR EACH BIBLE DREAM

God used dreams in order to reveal His kingdom purpose and to keep that purpose on track. That kingdom purpose was always the revelation of Jesus Christ as the Messiah of all nations.

Sometimes God spoke of the dreamer's destiny and the destiny of their family lines like He did with Abraham, Jacob, Joseph and Solomon.

His purpose was often to give direction, encouragement, and reassurance. Sometimes He gave directions and instructions like He did with Abraham, Jacob, St. Joseph and the Magi.

Other times He encouraged and calmed the dreamer as He did with Abraham and Jacob when he spoke of their peaceful deaths at ripe old ages. Sometimes God revealed the future as He did with Abraham, Joseph, Pharaoh, Jeremiah, Nebuchadnezzar and Daniel.

Sometimes He encouraged them to trust Him by revealing Himself and His ways as he did with Abraham, Jacob, Samuel, Solomon and Nebuchadnezzar.

Sometimes God humbled them like He did with Nebuchadnezzar. Sometimes He warned them as he did with Abimelek, Laban, Pharaoh, the Midianite Soldier, Solomon, and Pilate's wife.

All the Jewish dreamers from Abraham's line were invited to join God in His work of bringing forth the Messiah. God spoke through dreams in order to create trust and motivation within the dreamer. He also sent dreams so the dreamer might know who God actually was as in the case of Nebuchadnezzar who gave one of the best descriptions of God in all of Scripture.

God used dreams to allow people to know Him better. He spoke to them in order to create faith and trust. So then faith comes by hearing, and hearing by the word of God.[1]

In **Abraham's Covenant Dream** God's main purpose was to cut covenant with Abraham and his seed line in order to bring the Messiah onto the earth. He also shared the future by telling Abraham what would happen to his descendants, Egypt and the Amorites over the next four hundred years. Finally He also blessed Abraham by telling him he would die in peace at a good old age.

In **King Abimelek's Dream** God's purpose was to keep His covenantal promises to Abraham concerning his descendants. He was also keeping the Messiah's mission on track. God also wanted to protect an innocent King and his nation from disaster so He had Abimelek return Sarah to Abraham under threat of death.

In **Jacob's Covenant Dream** God's purpose was to reveal himself to Jacob and explain to Jacob he was an inheritor of God's covenant with Abraham.

In **Jacob's 'Goats and Go Back Home' Dream** God's purpose was to get Jacob back to Canaan. Jesus appeared as the Angel of the Lord and showed Jacob how to prosper so he could obey God's instructions to bring his family back to the Promised Land.

In **Laban's 'Don't Harm Jacob' Dream** God's purpose was to keep the Abrahamic covenant on track. Consequently He warned Laban not to harm Jacob in any way.

In **Jacob Wrestles With God And Man** God's purpose was to test Jacob's faith and perseverance and convince Jacob that He was able to keep His covenant promises with Abraham, Isaac and Jacob no matter what.

In **Joseph's Two Dreams** God's purpose was to set the record straight and bring Joseph back to God's intended place for him as Jacob's inheritor after Laban's deceit had threatened God's plans. These dreams prepared Joseph for his calling as a saviour of Israel. God also gave Joseph's siblings a chance to repent of their bad attitude towards their brother.

In **Pharaoh's Cupbearer's Dream** God's purpose was to bring Joseph to a position of national prominence in Egypt in order to fulfil Joseph's previous two prophetic dreams and to bring about God's prophesy in Abraham's dream which said, Know for certain that for four hundred years your descendants will be strangers in a country not their own and that they will be enslaved and mistreated there.[2]

In **Pharaoh's Baker's Dream** God's purpose was to bring Joseph to a position of national prominence in Egypt in order to fulfil Joseph's previous two prophetic dreams and to bring about God's prophesy in Abraham's dream which said, Know for certain that for four hundred years your descendants will be strangers in a country not their own and that they will be enslaved and mistreated there.[3]

In **Pharaoh's Two Famine Dreams** God's purpose was to bring the children of Israel to the land of their enslavement. God was working His purpose out concerning the Messiah and keeping His Covenant prophetic promises to Abraham.

In **Jacob's 'Go Down To Egypt' Night Vision** God's purpose was to encourage Jacob to go down to Egypt so God could keep His covenantal promise to Abraham and descendants. God also comforted Jacob by telling him He would be with him, his family would become a great nation and Joseph would be with him when he died in bed.

In **Balaam's 'Don't Curse Israel' Dream** God's purpose was to stop the King of Moab from harming His Covenant People and their seedline.

In **Balaam's 'If They Call You' Dream** God's purpose was to stop the King of Moab from harming His Covenant People and their seedline. He also tested Balaam's heart with the stipulation, If the men come to call you.

In **The Midianite's Dream For Gideon** God's purpose was so Gideon and Purah could hear the dream and its interpretation in order that Gideon would be encouraged to believe God and go to war against vastly superior numbers.

In **Samuel's Night Vision** God's purpose was twofold. He wanted to call His new prophet into ministry and He also wanted to bring judgement on the old regime for not dealing with sin in its midst.

In **Nathan's Night Vision For King David** God's purpose was that Solomon should build the Temple because David was disqualified having killed so many people.

In **David's Bedtime Prayer** God's purpose was to show He could be trusted to protect his servant David.

In **Solomon's 'Discerning Heart' Dream** God's purpose was to equip and enable Solomon to rule God's Chosen People well. God also wanted to personally bless Solomon and enable him to live a long and fruitful life. God had been similarly concerned for the lives of Abraham and Jacob in their dreams. It's God's normal desire we be obedient so we can live long fruitful lives.

In **Solomon's 'The Bride's Dream'** - God's purpose was to reveal the sort of passionate lovers He desires. Another scripture similarly says, You will seek me and find me when you seek me with all your heart.[4]

In **Solomon's Warning Dream** God's purposes were to answer the powerful and beautiful prayers of Solomon and to instruct him about his role and his family's part in bringing them to pass. God was also renewing covenant with Solomon and explaining the responsibilities and penalties, the blessings and curses involved.

In **Solomon Asks For Wisdom Dream** God's purpose was to equip and enable Solomon to rule God's Chosen People well. God also wanted to personally bless Solomon and enable him to live a long and fruitful life. God's had been similarly concerned for the lives of Abraham and Jacob in their dreams. It's God's normal desire we be obedient so we can live long fruitful lives. (This is a retelling of Solomon's 'Discerning Heart' Dream)

In **Eliphaz's Demonic Nightmare Dream** Perhaps God's main purpose for leaving this dream in Scripture is to warn us to properly interpret and apply dreams otherwise we can innocently end up angering God just like Eliphaz.

In **Job's Satanic Nightmares** God's purpose was to reveal Satan as the accuser of the brethren and to highlight the righteous often suffer when under spiritual attack. We also learn God is Sovereign and has Satan on a leash.

In **Elihu's Dream Talk** God's purpose was to reveal that God speaks through dreams and visions to keep people alive even though they may not perceive this.

In **Jeremiah's 'Israel Will Return' Dream** God's purpose was to give Jeremiah profound insight into God's future plans and purpose and programs for Israel and the whole world. In the Abrahamic covenant God said all nations would be blessed through Abraham's posterity. One of the ways this was achieved was through God scattering Israel among the nations and gathering them home again. In Ezekiel 22:15 God said, I will disperse you among the nations and scatter you through the countries; and I will put an end to your uncleanness.

In **Nebuchadnezzar's Two Dreams** God's first purpose was to show proud King Nebuchadnezzar, then the most powerful man in the world, that God is the only One who controls the destiny of men and nations. His second purpose was to launch Daniel's long career as a political leader, trusted advisor, and well-known prophet in Babylon during Israel's dispersion.

In **Daniel's 'Mystery Revealed' Night Vision** God's purpose was to save Daniel's life and to elevate him into a position of favour, power and authority in Nebuchadnezzar's court, in the nation of Babylon and amongst Babylon's dream interpreters. God was also revealing His blue print concerning His people for the next six hundred years

In **Daniels' Four Beasts Dream** God's purpose was to share the future with His prophet. Amos 3:7 says, Surely the Sovereign Lord does nothing without revealing his plan to his servants the prophets. The overall theme of the Book of Daniel is God's sovereignty over history. It's so easy to be overwhelmed when God reveals a little of his knowledge. For example, after Daniel had a vision of the Messiah[5] he was told things the Jews must suffer at the hands of the Gentiles. Then in 35 verses of Daniel 10, we are treated to prophecies concerning 135 major events covering a period of 366 years. At that point we realise *God Knows Stuff* and although we can identify many of Daniel's fulfilled prophesies we are also aware there are many not yet understood and not yet fulfilled. Yahweh is the supreme God who reveals the future before it comes to pass. Almighty God sees the end from the beginning

In **Daniel's Ram, Goat and Little Horn Dream** God's purpose was to comfort Daniel and His Covenant People with the knowledge that He is the One in control and His plans and purpose are being patiently worked out.

In **Zechariah's Eight Dreams** God's overriding plan and purpose was to restore Israel and all nations into their right relationship with Him as Sovereign God and with one another. All eight night vision dreams further this purpose.

In **St Joseph's 'Marry Mary' Dream** God's purpose was to allay

Joseph's fears and encourage him to marry the Virgin Mary. God's purpose was to call Joseph as Jesus's foster father and protector in order that His promises to Abraham and Satan would come to pass.

In **The Magi's Dream** God's purpose was to keep the Messiah alive and well. There is also a prophecy from Jeremiah 31:15 being fulfilled around this incident. Herod will murder all the children around Bethlehem two years old and under; A voice is heard in Ramah, weeping and great mourning, Rachel weeping for her children and refusing to be comforted, because they are no more.

In **St. Joseph's 'Escape To Egypt' Dream** God's purpose was to instruct Joseph in order to protect the life of the Messiah. God, the eternal promise keeper, was also fulfilling His prophecy in Hosea 11:1 part of which says, out of Egypt I called my son.

In **St Joseph's 'Back To Israel' Dream** God's purpose was to bring the Messiah back to Israel now the threat of Herod had passed. God was also fulfilling His prophecy in Hosea 11:1 part of which says, out of Egypt I called my son.

In **St Joseph's 'Go To Nazareth' Dream** God's purpose was to allay Joseph's fears and bring the Messiah to a place of safety in Nazareth in Israel. God was also fulfilling his words spoken by the prophets, He shall be called a Nazarene. (This must have been an oral prophecy because there is no written text of these words in the Old Testament.)

In **Jesus Tempted By Satan Dream** God's purpose was that Jesus would overcome Satan with God's word.

In **Pilate's Wife's Dream** God's purpose was to let the proper authorities know Jesus was innocent. In fact everyone who would ever hear the story of Jesus' crucifixion would know God declared Jesus innocent by a dream given to Pilate's wife. There was also an opportunity for Pilate to listen to his wife and avert further suffering for her and him.

In **Peter Interpreting Pentecost** God's purpose is to keep His promise made to Abraham and Joel. He also is fulfilling Jesus' promise of power to His disciples for the work of His ministry of building His Church.

In **Saul's Vision On The Road To Damascus** God's purpose was to give Paul revelation of who Jesus really was and to launch Paul into his destiny and his life's work.

In **Ananias' Vision About Paul** God's purpose was to keep His visionary promise to Saul and heal him. He also wanted to release Saul into the next stage of his very special ministry.

In **St Paul's Trance** God's purpose was to save Paul's life and to move him into God's greater plans and purpose in the harvest fields of the Gentiles.

In **Cornelius' 'Send for Peter' Vision** God's purpose was to initiate a major worldview change for Jews and Gentiles. God was beginning to reveal more of what His promise to Abraham about blessing all nations would look like: salvation in the name of Jesus and baptism in the Holy Spirit.

In **Peter's 'Kill and Eat' Vision** God's purpose was to open Peter's eyes to the revelation that it was his duty to preach the Gospel to all people without prejudice because Jews, Samaritans and Gentiles all equally required cleansing from sin and all were coming into the kingdom of God.

In **Peter's Revelation at Cornelius's House** God's purpose was to show Peter and the church that God's promise to Abraham was coming to pass. The nations were being blessed with salvation through the Messiah Jesus Christ and the Holy Spirit was being poured out upon all flesh.

In **Paul's 'Man of Macedonia' Night Vision Dream** God's purpose was to clearly direct Paul to bring the Gospel to the Gentiles in Europe instead of Asia at that time.

In **Paul's 'Fear Not' Night Vision** God's purpose was encourage, protect and strengthen Paul in his ministry and to expand his vision of the harvest field.

In **Paul's 'Angelic' Night Vision Dream** God's purpose was to keep His servant Paul alive in order to bring the Gospel to Europe where Paul would write much of the New Testament.

In **Egypt's 'Dreadful Dreams** God's purpose was to reveal to the Egyptian firstborn sons exactly why they were suffering and dying.

In **Judas Maccabees' 'Golden Sword' Dream** God's purpose was to affirm and encourage Judas and his small army that God was with them and they were in God's will.

In **Mordecai's 'Two Great Dragons' Dream** God's purpose was to warn and instruct Mordecai in order to preserve the Jewish nation.

In **Esdras' Eagle and Lion' Dream** God's purpose was to bring peace to Ezra by answering his questions concerning why evil Babylon prospered while God's Chosen People languished.

In **Esdras 'Man From The Sea' Dream** God's purpose was to encourage and instruct Ezra and Abraham's descendants and calm their fears.

THE IMPORTANCE OF A DREAMER'S METRON

Understanding the biblical Greek term *metron* is really very helpful when it comes to making sense of dreams or any revelation.

The word metron refers to our God-given sphere of influence, our God-given responsibilities, concerning family, work, ministry, possessions, inheritance and so on.

All believers and non-believers have a specific metron for which they are responsible before God. Scripture says all authority comes from God and God will hold us responsible for how we exercise that authority.

A husband has responsibility for his wife and children. If he is a doctor his metron will also include his patients. If he is a cancer doctor his metron will include the cancer ward but will definitely not extend to the maternity unit.

A farmer's metron allows him to plant whatever seeds he wants in his own fields but gives him no permission to plant seeds in a neighbour's field. A pilot's metron covers only his own aeroplane.

When we understand our God-given sphere of influence, our metron, and stay within the orbit of our responsibilities we have little or no trouble. The problems start when we poke our noses into other people's metrons, other people's business.

Paul used the Greek term metron when explaining his God-given sphere of responsibility to the Church in Corinth. He said,

> We do not dare to classify or compare ourselves with some who commend themselves. When they measure themselves by themselves and compare themselves with themselves, they are not wise. We, however, will not boast beyond proper limits, (metron) but will confine our boasting to the sphere of service (metron) God himself has assigned to us, a sphere (metron) that also includes you.[1]

Paul is explaining God has given him influence and responsibility over the Corinthian Church. He has no metron or responsibility for the Jerusalem Church, which was under the metron of Peter, James and John.

Paul hoped the Corinthian church would grow and mature so his metron for spreading the Gospel amongst the gentiles would also expand. Paul was limited in his metron. Jesus on the other hand has an unlimited metron. He is the Alpha and the Omega. He has the Spirit without measure.

Like Paul we also have a limited metron relating to our present God-given responsibilities. The revelation we receive in dreams will always relate to our metron. Understanding this simple fact saves us untold trouble and helps us to stay focused and on track.

God just doesn't hand out revelation willy-nilly. All of our God given dreams concern our own metron. When we look carefully in Scripture we find all dreams are very specific to the dreamer's metron.

This is the only dream in the Bible in which God gives a prophetic message to the dreamer for another person. This was given to the prophet Nathan and a prophet is one who speaks God's messages to people. David was also within Nathan's metron because Nathan was a bold trusted member of David's royal court and one of his closest advisers.

Other examples are, Abraham's dream was about his family line , Abimelech's dream concerned his own and his household's safety and Jacob's dream of goats impacted his own financial future.

Laban's dream affected his own wellbeing. Joseph's dreams concerned his and his family's future. Pharaoh's cupbearer's and baker's dreams related to their own individual lives. Pharaoh's dream was about his responsibility concerning his nation.

The Midianite's dream was a warning for his own life although it also encouraged Gideon. Solomon's dream concerned his own increased metron as king. Likewise Nebuchadnezzar's dreams primarily concerned his own metron as King although they also had a wider worldwide prophetic significance.

In the New Testament St. Joseph's dreams all related to his metron as Jesus's foster father and guardian. The Magi's dream concerned what they should personally do and Pilate's wife's troubling dream related to her and her husband.

It's important to remember we have authority in both the natural and spiritual realms but it's a limited authority. If we are faithful with what God has given us we will be given more.[2]

We are like the children of Israel with the Promised Land. Even though the land was theirs by promise they were only ever able to possess it by hearing God's voice day by day and obeying Him. When they went off fighting their own battles they were always defeated.

There is also an important link between our natural and spiritual authority. Paul shows this when he writes to Timothy about appointing elders. He said an elder must manage his own family well and see that his children obey him, and he must do so in a manner worthy of full respect.

Here Paul stresses the connection between the natural and the spiritual when he says, If anyone does not know how to manage his own family, how can he take care of God's church?[3] Knowing the boundaries of one's metron, one's sphere of influence, one's measure of faith, one's area of responsibility, is vital.

So is an understanding of what we have been given responsibility for. As we look at all the dreams of the Bible we should always keep a close eye on the dreamer's metron. This helps us to understand exactly how much authority the dreamer carries and how God can use that authority.

For example Pharaoh's cupbearer was not in a place of authority to promote Joseph to a position of second in the land of Egypt but Pharaoh was. Yet the cupbearer's metron allowed him to introduce Joseph to Pharaoh.

If we are faithful and obedient in our metros we will all have a part to play in God's great plans and purpose.

GOD'S PURPOSE FOR EACH DREAMER'S METRON

All Bible dreams personally impact the dreamer. Although the dream's main goal is always to advance God's greater plans and purpose they all contain some personal element relating to the dreamer's metron and life situation.

The dreamer always has skin in the game, something to gain and something to lose.

Abraham's Dream concerned his land and children, which God had promised and which he was anxious about.

Abimelek's Dream concerned the safety and health of his life and that of his household and nation. He was completely unaware his life and metron were under attack; the women of his household were all struck barren and everyone was about to die

Jacob's First Dream was given when he was fleeing from his brother Esau. It concerned his safety and his future hopes because of the Covenant God had made with his grandfather.

Jacob's Second dream concerns his pending escape from Laban and about being reimbursed for all his hard work.

Jacob's Third dream calmed his fears and encouraged him to go down to Egypt with his family.

Laban's Dream concerned his own personal safety and that of his household.

Joseph's Two Dreams showed he'd be in a prominent position where he'd rule over the lives of the people of Israel and Egypt.

Pharaoh's Cupbearer's Dream concerned his imminent release from prison and his restoration to his position within Pharaoh's household.

Pharaoh's Baker's Dream concerned his imminent death for offending Pharaoh.

Pharaoh's Two Dreams concern his own safety, his household's safety and the safety of the land of Egypt.

The Midianite's Dream showed he and the Midianite army would be defeated by Gideon's army.

Balaam's First Dream meant he couldn't curse Israel and gain personal reward.

Balaam's Second Dream also hindered his desire for personal gain.

Samuel's Night Vision was also a personal call to be God's prophet.

Nathan's Night Vision Dream is the only dream in the Bible where the dreamer has a personal dream message for someone else. This dream was given to Nathan because of his metron of being King David's court prophet.

Solomon's First Dream was a personal offer from God to ask for whatever he wanted.

Solomon's Second Dream was a personal poetic love letter to God.

Solomon's Third Dream concerned a personal choice God gave him that would result in blessing or cursing for Solomon and his large metron.

Solomon 'Asks for Wisdom' Dream was a personal offer from God to give Solomon anything he wanted.

Eliphaz's 'Demonic Nightmare' Dream caused the dreamer great personal distress.

Job's Satanic Nightmares caused great personal fear and terror for the dreamer.

Jeremiah's Dream concerned his own personal return to Israel along with a remnant of the People of Israel.

Nebuchadnezzar's Two Dreams had personal messages with deep implications for him.

Daniel's Night Vision Dream concerned his own safety and that of his three friends as well as others and nations.

Daniels' Four Beasts Dream held deep personal pain for him. Daniel was deeply troubled by his thoughts, and his face turned pale.

Zechariah's Eight Dreams personally blessed the dreamer when he realised God was deeply interested in the lives of His people and not only the Temple building.

St Joseph's First Dream calmed his fears and encouraged him to marry Mary.

St Joseph's Second, Third and Fourth Dreams allowed Joseph to protect his own life and the lives of his wife and baby Jesus.

The Magi's Dream protected them personally from trouble with both Herod and God.

Jesus 'Tempted By Satan' Dream had incredible implications for Jesus' personal life.

Pilate's Wife's Dream caused her great personal distress.

Cornelius was personally informed by an angel, in a vision, that his prayers and gifts to the poor have come up as a memorial offering before God.

Peter's 'Kill and Eat' Vision enlightened his eyes and changed and enlarged his entire worldview.

Peter's Revelation at Cornelius's House shattered his ethnocentric theology and racial prejudice and opened him up to the whole church and the whole world.

Paul's "Man of Macedonia' Night Vision was a fresh start for his ministry. Paul's mission to Macedonia was one of the most important achievements in his missionary life.

Paul's 'Fear Not' Night Vision lifted him from a place of weakness and fear to a position where he was encouraged by the revelation God still had work for him and God would keep him safe and provide for him.

Paul's 'Angel of the Lord' Night Vision, strengthened Paul's faith when he learned God still had work for him to do and that neither him or the crew would die in the storm.

Egypt's 'Dreadful Dreams personally instructed each firstborn Egyptian why they were suffering and dying.

Judas Maccabees was personally affirmed and encouraged by his **'Golden Sword' Dream** that he and his small army were in God's will and God was with them.

Mordecai's 'Two Great Dragons' Dream enabled him to save his own life and that of the Jewish nation.

Esdras' 'Eagle and Lion' Dream brought peace and perspective to the dreamer.

Esdras 'Man From The Sea' Dream encouraged and instructed Ezra and calmed his fears.

GOD'S PURPOSES FOR BELIEVER'S METRONS

When I use the terms *Believers* and *Non-Believers* I'm really referring to Jews and Non-Jews; those who are in covenant with God and those who aren't. I'm sure all the dreamers in the Bible were believers in the unseen realm.

All the the *Believers* were Jewish dreamers from Abraham's family line. They were all inheritors and carriers of the Abrahamic Covenant. They were all strategic characters with major specific callings from God concerned with bringing about God's plans and purpose for his Messiah and his Kingdom.

All except Solomon were successful in their calling and metron. Solomon was incredibility blessed by God but he disregarded the warnings in his third dream and brought disaster upon himself and Israel by allowing the worship of other gods in Israel.

Moses said a king of Israel should not take many wives and not gather many horses and chariots, especially from Egypt. He also warned a king should not accumulate large amounts of silver and gold.[1]

Solomon blatantly disregarded all of these warnings. He married

700 wives and 300 concubines, many of them pagans. God cautioned marrying women outside of the covenant of Israel would lead to sensuality, idolatry and apostasy.

This is exactly what happened. Solomon's foreign wives lured him away from Yahweh into worship of their gods and idols.

God had a very special relationship with these believing dreamers. They were specially selected people from His Chosen People. They were very important to him; the apples of his eyes. He cared for them, and talked with them and gave them great success even though some of them endured much suffering and difficulty. He encouraged them and kept assuring them He would be with them and help them in their assignments.

Abraham's Metron: Abraham had a powerful metron that impacted all nations, all history and all time after him. God chose Abraham to be the Father of Faith for both Jews and Gentiles.

He was called to be the father of nations. His descendants would have their own country and be as numerous as the stars of heaven and one of them would be the Messiah. The prophetic word over Abraham was,

> I swear by myself, declares the Lord, that because you have done this and have not withheld your son, your only son, I will surely bless you and make your descendants as numerous as the stars in the sky and as the sand on the seashore. Your descendants will take possession of the cities of their enemies, and through your offspring all nations on earth will be blessed, because you have obeyed me.[2]

It was through Abraham's line the Promised One, who'd crush

Satan's head and destroy his works, would come: And I will put enmity between you and the woman, and between your offspring and hers; he will crush your head, and you will strike his heel.[3] God appeared to Abraham at least ten times!

Jacob's Metron: Jacob also had a powerful metron. He was Abraham's inheritor and the father of the leaders of the twelve tribes of Israel.

After Jacob wrestled with God his name was changed to Israel and this became both the name of the people and of the land. In a dream God told Jacob,

> I am the Lord, the God of your father Abraham and the
> God of Isaac. I will give you and your descendants
> the land on which you are lying. Your descendants
> will be like the dust of the earth, and you will
> spread out to the west and to the east, to the north
> and to the south. All peoples on earth will be
> blessed through you and your offspring. I am with
> you and will watch over you wherever you go, and I
> will bring you back to this land. I will not leave you
> until I have done what I have promised you.[4]

Jacob's metron included his special assignment to bring the children of Israel down to Egypt as promised to Abraham.

Joseph's Metron: Joseph's powerful metron was to prepare a place of safety and provision for the children of Israel in Egypt so the Messiah's seed line would be preserved.

God chose Joseph to be the heir of God's Covenant promises to

Abraham, Isaac and Jacob. 1 Chronicles 5:1-2 says, The rights of the firstborn belonged to Joseph.

Laban's trickery in marrying Leah off to Jacob meant God's plans for Joseph to be the firstborn were hindered. This is what caused such bad blood between Joseph's older brothers and him but God used Joseph's dreams to put things back on track.

Joseph correctly understood his dreams meant his family would one day be dependant on him and humbled before him.

This knowledge would have sustained him during the next thirteen years when he was bought and sold five times. Through Joseph, God was working His purpose out concerning the Messiah and keeping His Covenant dream promises to Abraham.

Samuel's Metron: Samuel's metron was to be an important prophet in Israel during a time when the word of the Lord was rare. The Lord was with Samuel as he grew up, and He let none of Samuel's words fall to the ground. All Israel from Dan to Beersheba recognised and accepted Samuel as God's prophet. The Lord continued to appear at Shiloh, and there He revealed himself to Samuel through his word.

Nathan's Metron: Nathan was a court prophet, a scribe and a trusted advisor during the reign of King David. He wrote histories of David and Solomon and was also responsible for the temple music. Nathan was a tough-love fearless prophet whom God used to speak to David during some dark and emotional times in David's personal life. God also employed Nathan to keep David on track as regards God's plans and purpose.

. . .

Solomon's Metron: Solomon was called to be Israel's King who would build a temple in Jerusalem for God to dwell in.

God's purpose was to equip and enable Solomon to rule God's Chosen People well. God also wanted to personally bless Solomon and empower him to live a long and fruitful life. God also anointed Solomon with incomparable heavenly wisdom, which Solomon foolishly squandered by disobeying God's commandments and ignoring God's warning dream.

Eliphaz's Metron: Eliphaz the Temanite came from the important Edom city of Teman. The Temanite's were famous for their wisdom. Eliphaz is Job's friend and believes in Job's God.

Job's Metron: Job had a major metron. He was a God fearing prophet with a large prosperous family. God trusted Job enough to allow Satan to test him. God was proud of Job. He called Job His servant and said, There is none like him on the earth, a blameless and upright man, who fears God and turns away from evil?[5] Ezekiel said Job was a righteousness man of the same calibre as Noah and Daniel.[6] James said Job was a blessed prophet, a shining example in the face of suffering. James also says Job's restoration was an example of God's compassion and mercy.[7]

Jeremiah's Metron: Jeremiah was a prophet to the nations, not only to Israel. He was told to write his revelation because it was intended to comfort and instruct many generations. Jeremiah the 'weeping prophet' had a major metron. He was one of God's major writing prophets.

With Baruch, his scribe, he penned the *Book of Jeremiah* the *Books of Kings* and the *Book of Lamentations*. Huldah the prophetess was his relative and a contemporary and Zephaniah and Isaiah were his mentors. The Book of Jeremiah with its revelation of a New Covenant has been foundational for Christianity.

Around forty direct quotations from the Book of Jeremiah are in the New Testament. Most occur in Revelation relating to Babylon's destruction.

Matthew showed how Jesus fulfilled Jeremiah's prophecies and Hebrews deals with the promised New Covenant by Jeremiah.

Daniel's Metron: Daniel was a major prophet with a worldwide and end time metron. He was gifted in dreams and visions[8] that prophesied world history, including that of Daniel's people Israel and all mankind in the latter days.[9] He also received revelation from the angel Gabriel.[10]

Daniel served in prominent positions in both Babylonian and Medo-Persian empires under Nebuchadnezzar, Belshazzar, Darius and Cyrus. In the first year of Darius's reign Daniel understood Jeremiah's prophecy which predicted a 70-year captivity of his people was soon coming to an end.[11]

Daniel prayed and fasted for his nation's sins and pleaded for God's mercy on himself, his fellow captives and all the inhabitants of Jerusalem.[12] He faithfully prayed three times a day even though this activity threatened his life.[13]

Ezekiel called him a righteous man alongside Noah and Job. Daniel's fame spread well beyond the borders of Israel.

When God granted Daniel the wisdom to interpret the king's dream, it launched Daniel's long career as a political leader, trusted advisor, major prophet and dream interpreter.

God's purpose for Daniel was to impact Babylon through revelation and dream interpretation in order to reveal God's sovereignty to the most powerful nation on earth.

Through Daniel's influence the God of Israel was revealed as the

Most High God who raises up and removes kings and establishes new world empires.

God was revealed as the Ancient of Days on the throne[14] and the God of heaven, whose kingdom will never end.[15] Daniel's dreams and visions showed God's faithfulness and care for His people Israel. God enabled Daniel to prophesy some of God's long-term plans for all nations including the Messiah, the temple, Jerusalem, and a coming kingdom of righteousness.

Zechariah's Metron: Zechariah was both a prophet and a priest born into a Levite family in Babylon. He returned to Jerusalem with the first batch of 50,000 Jews after their seventy-year exile.

He functioned at the same time as the prophet Haggai, the governor Zerubbabel and Joshua the high priest. While Haggai's preaching focused on Israel's sin and selfishness Zechariah's prophecy encouraged the harassed Israelites to rebuild the temple.

His metron was national and international. He prophetically saw the Messiah in both His first and His second comings. Zechariah has the largest number of messianic passages amongst all the Minor Prophets. The New Testament contains over forty of his references.

The Book of Revelation is greatly influenced by his imagery. Zechariah's main purpose was to assure Judah that although God disciplined them for seventy years in Babylon He was still their Covenant Keeping God who would bless them as He promised their fathers.

St Joseph's Metron: Saint Joseph had a unique metron. God chose him for the protection, education, and care of His only Son. Joseph is God's great hidden prophet; the patron saint of all prophets who daily go about their work in relative obscurity much like the seven thousand unknown to Elijah whom God had reserved for himself.[16]

There are no recorded words from Joseph in the Bible. He is only mentioned in a few sentences yet in his hiddenness and ordinariness he had the incredible privilege of spending more face to face time with Jesus than any other man.

God's purpose for Joseph was to be a covering and protection for Jesus and Mary. He was a man who heard clearly in his dreams and promptly obeyed.

Jesus' Metron: Scripture says, Jesus is the eternal Word made Flesh[17] and the Image of the Invisible God[18], He is the perfect manifestation of God; the very substance and embodiment of the Creator. He is also the only Mediator between God and man.[19] He is the Son of Man who gave Himself as a ransom for mankind. He is also Head over All Things.[20] His name of Christ refers to His position of highest dignity and honour at the Father's right hand. Scripture also says Jesus is,

- The Light of the World.[21]
- The Anointed One.[22]
- The Good Shepherd.[23]
- The Bread of Life.[24]
- Healer and Forgiver.[25]
- The Way, the Truth, the Life.[26]
- The Resurrection and Life.[27]
- He holds the keys of death.[28]
- Son of David.(Mark 10:47) [29]
- The Messiah-King.[30]
- Man of Sorrows.[31]
- Sinless and Holy.[32]
- Lamb of God.[33]
- Prince of Peace.[34]
- The Power and Wisdom of God.[35]

Peter's Metron: Peter was a colourful character, a wholehearted man of action totally committed to Jesus and constantly at the forefront of things.

He is always listed first among the Twelve Apostles. He was the first disciple called by Jesus. He was the first to confess Jesus as the Messiah. He was the first to walk upon water. He was the first to perform a miracle. He was the first to enter Jesus' empty tomb. He was the first to explain the baptism of the Holy Spirit.

Along with St Paul, God sovereignly chose Peter to take the Gospel to the whole world. Peter's opinion in the early Church's debate about Gentiles becoming converts was pivotal and crucial. Two New Testament epistles are attributed to Peter. Peter like Moses not only knew the Acts of God but he knew His Ways.[36]

Paul's Metron: Paul had a timeless worldwide metron. He was a leader of the first generation of Christians, and perhaps the most important person after Jesus in the history of Christianity. His surviving letters are the most influential writings after the Gospels. They've had an enormous influence on Christianity and secure Paul's place as one of the greatest religious leaders of all time.

His writings reveal a powerful mind grappling with the deep questions of Christianity such as how to articulate the relationship between Jesus the Christ and God the Father.

Peter affirming Paul's writings warned, Some parts of his letters are hard to understand, which ignorant and unstable people distort, as they do the rest of the Scriptures, to their own destruction.[37]

Esdras' Metron: Esdras functioned as a scribe and priest when the exiles returned after Nehemiah restored the Temple of Solomon and repaired Jerusalem. Esdras was a scholar of the Laws of Moses. Daily he reminded the Jews about their relationship and destiny with God and how important it was to worship God alone and live a holy life. He taught the people about the important plans and purposes God had for them as they returned to The Promised Land.

Mordecai's Metron: Mordecai was a Jew from the tribe of Benjamin living in exile in Persia. He was foster father to his cousin Esther. His faithfulness in this responsibility saved his own life and enabled him to help save the Jewish nation.

After Esther was made queen Mordecai was promoted to where he 'sat in the king's gate'. His faithfulness in this sphere of influence, this metron, enabled him to foil an assassination attempt on the king.

Later Mordecai refused to bow to the anti-Semite, Haman the Agagite, who'd been raised to the highest position at court. Haman responded by launching a plan of wholesale destruction of the Jewish exiles throughout the Persian Empire.

Mordecai and Esther thwarted Haman's plan and saved the Jewish nation. Haman was then executed on the gallows he'd erected for Mordecai's hanging. To this day, the Jews still celebrate the feast of Purim in memory of this great deliverance from their enemies.

Judas Maccabees' Metron; Judas Maccabeus was a Jewish priest and the son of a Jewish priest. He is best remembered as a guerrilla leader and a military genius who defended Israel from invasion by the Seleucid king Antiochus IV Epiphanies.

He defeated four Seleucid armies in quick succession and stopped the imposition of Hellenism upon Judea and preserved the Jewish religion.

His restoration of the Temple of Jerusalem is still yearly celebrated in Hanukkah the Jewish festival of lights.

Although the Seleucids offered the Jews freedom of worship, Judas continued the fight desiring political freedom as well as religious freedom. Although he was killed two years later, his younger brothers took over the fight, finally securing the independence of Judaea.

GOD'S PURPOSES FOR NON BELIEVER'S METRONS

All the dreamers in the Bible were believers in the unseen realm. So, when I use the terms *Believers* and *Non-Believers* I'm really referring to Jews and Non-Jews; those who knew God and who were in covenant with God and those who weren't.

God used Non-Jewish dreamers to prosper, bless and care for his Covenant People. God essentially used Abimelek, Laban, Pharaoh, Nebuchadnezzar, the Magi to keep His covenantal promises to Abraham on track.

Most of these Gentile dreamers held important and influential positions in life. Pharaoh was immensely rich and powerful and was considered a god by his people. Nebuchadnezzar was the richest and most powerful man in the world in his day.

Pharaoh's Cupbearer, Pharaoh's Baker and the Midianite soldier although bit players in the overall scheme of things still played important parts.

Pilate's wife, although not listened to by her husband, played the role of declaring Jesus innocent. She is the only recorded person in Scripture who publicly spoke out against the decision to kill Jesus.

When the dreamers were obedient they were generally blessed.

Abimelek's life was spared and his barren women were healed. Laban's life was spared and he made covenant with Jacob. Pharaoh's life and that of his household and nation were saved from famine.

Pharaoh's Baker's life was spared and he was restored to his former position. Nebuchadnezzar was restored to sanity and kingship and was also given a wonderful revelation of who God actually is.

The Magi got to see the Messiah and returned home safely. Pharaoh's Cupbearer on the other hand was beheaded for displeasing Pharaoh, the Midianite soldier and his friend were defeated in battle and history says Pilate and his wife suffered and died for not obeying her dream

Abimelek's Metron: Abimelek was the king of Gerar when Abraham travelled through the Philistine territory of Kadesh and Shur. God used Abimelek's influential metron and authority to keep His covenantal promises to Abraham on track.

Abimelek's metron included his family, household and the people of Gerar. All the women including his wife were afflicted with barrenness when he unknowingly got in the way of God's plans for Abraham.

God also used Abimelek to prosper Abraham by giving him a thousand shekels of silver, sheep and cattle and male and female slaves in order to cover his offence regarding Sarah.

He also gave Abraham a warm welcome and grazing rights for his animals. Abimelek said, My land is before you; live wherever you like. God used this incident concerning Sarah to give Abraham credibility and favour in Abimelek's eyes and before the community because it was Abraham's prayers that cured Abimelek's women of barrenness.

Later God used Abimelek to seal a covenant with Abraham.[1] This was a significant step concerning God's Promised Land pledge to

Abraham. During this covenant ceremony Abimelek received a tribute of seven female sheep from Abraham thereby acknowledging Abraham had dug the well and had a legal right to it. This was Abraham's first physical proof God was really giving His family the land of Canaan.

Laban's Metron: Laban was a natural family leader who first appeared as an adult spokesman for his father Bethuel's household.[2] He was impressed by the golden jewellery gifted to his sister Rebecca from Isaac, and had a key part in arranging their marriage.

His motives were all about gaining advantages for his family and this often set him at loggerheads with God's plans. Laban is symbolic of a man who seeks first his own kingdom.

In trying to work a good arrangement for his daughter Leah he unknowingly hampered God's plan of Joseph being Jacob's rightful heir. His concern over Jacob throwing away family safety in Aram for a risky prospect in the land of Canaan again put him in a position where he was opposing God's plans, this time for the Children of Israel to return to the Promised Land.

Nevertheless God used Laban's metron to provide safety, work and wives for Jacob. Although not mentioned in the Bible, Rabbinic sources identify Laban as the father of Bilhah and Zilpah, the concubines whom Jacob had children with.[3] If this is correct then Laban is the grandfather of all the Twelve Patriarchs of Israel.

Pharaoh's Cupbearer's Metron: The cupbearer's influential metron was that of a high ranking officer serving drinks in Pharaoh's court.

He had to be completely trustworthy because his role was to guard against Pharaoh being poisoned. To this end he was often required to swallow most of the drinks himself.

This proximity to Pharaoh placed the cupbearer in a position of great influence. When Pharaoh was still troubled by his dreams, after his magicians and wise men couldn't interpret them, God used the cupbearer to speak well of Joseph to Pharaoh.

This kickstarted Joseph's career and propelled him to a position of national prominence in Egypt. This helped fulfil Joseph's two prophetic dreams. It also helped bring about God's prophesy within *Abraham's Covenant Dream* which said, Know for certain that for four hundred years your descendants will be strangers in a country not their own and that they will be enslaved and mistreated there.[4]

Pharaoh's Baker's Metron: The Baker's influential metron was that of a high ranking officer baking bread and cakes for Pharaoh's court. He also had to be completely trustworthy because his role was to guard against Pharaoh being poisoned. Unfortunately his unmentioned offence was so great Pharaoh had him beheaded.

Perhaps the only personally redemptive thing for him concerning his dream interpretation was that he was able to put his house in order. Pharaoh's cupbearer was no doubt deeply impressed by the different fates between him and the baker. There dreams were matters of life and death.

Pharaoh's Metron: Pharaoh was worshipped as a god with absolute unchallenged authority in Egypt. He had the power of life and death as was evident in the incident concerning his cupbearer and baker. God used Pharaoh's metron to keep God's Covenant People alive and to bring them down to Egypt as prophesied to Abraham.

The Midianite's Metron: The Midianite and his friend were soldiers in the Midianite army. God's purpose was to use them and their dream interpretation to encourage and strengthen Gideon to finally believe God and go to war against vastly superior numbers.

Nebuchadnezzar's Metron: Nebuchadnezzar was the incredibility powerful King of Babylon. Jeremiah called him the destroyer of nations.[5] Similar to Joseph's situation, God used dream interpretation to propel Daniel into a position of great influence in Nebuchadnezzar's court as a political leader, trusted advisor and well-known prophet.

God used a dream to convince Nebuchadnezzar that the God of the Jews is the only sovereign God who controls the destiny of men and nations.

The Magi's Metron: The Magi were a group of prophetic non-Jews probably from the Persian priestly caste of Zoroastrianism who studied the stars.

The King James Version called them wise men; the same translation is applied to the wise men ruled over by Daniel in Babylon.[6] The Magi came from the East, where Balaam who prophesied about the Messiah came from. Balaam said,

> I see him, but not now; I behold him, but not near. A
>> star will come out of Jacob; a scepter will rise out of
>> Israel. He will crush the foreheads of Moab, the
>> skulls of all the people of Sheth.[7]

Both Darius and Cyrus were also thought to be Zoroastrians and possibly the influence of both the prophecies of Balaam and of Daniel may have been known by these Magi. God used these Gentiles to bring important prophetic presents to His only Son.

. . .

Pilate's Wife's Metron: Pilate's wife was a highborn, educated, wealthy Roman citizen married to the influential Roman governor of Judaea. Her closeness to Pilate, who had the power of life and death over people, gave her importance.

God's purpose through her dream was to let the proper authorities know Jesus was innocent. In fact everyone who would ever hear the story of Jesus's crucifixion would know God declared Jesus innocent by this dream to Pilate's wife.

Pilate's wife has the distinction of being the only person mentioned in the Bible who spoke out against the decision to kill Jesus.

DEFINITION OF A DREAM

On one level, it's really simple to tell the difference between a dream and a vision. A dream occurs when you are asleep and a vision occurs when you are wide-awake.

Jacob, Joseph, Pharaoh, Solomon and Nebuchadnezzar were all fast asleep when they had their dreams while Isaiah, Jeremiah, Ananias and Cornelius were wide awake when they received their visions.

Yet on another level it's not simple at all. Abraham was in the middle of a vision when God put him into a deep sleep and gave him a dream and Jeremiah seemed to be in the midst of a wide awake oracular vision when he suddenly said, At this I awoke and looked around. My sleep had been pleasant to me.[1]

Oops! So, all the foregoing prophetic revelation had really been received in a dream? And then did Jeremiah fall back to sleep and continue to dream?

I think so! That's why I included him in this study – *At this I awoke* – but I also wonder, how many other revelations considered as visions were really dreams. But that's an assignment for another day and perhaps another saint!

What about night visions? Were they visions given to people who went to bed and stayed awake or were they dreams given to people who went to bed and fell asleep.

Based on personal experience and on the fact Scripture never talks about day visions I have included them as dreams and call them night vision dreams.

The problem is, the Bible makes little or no distinction between dreams and visions. Sometimes we don't know whether the revelation has been a dream or a night vision.

Although there are over two hundred scriptural references to dreams and visions biblical writers are not particularly consistent or concerned with precise definitions. To the Hebraic mind the main point was the person had experienced a supernatural experience and revelation.

The book of Job says, In a dream in a vision of the night[2] while the book of Daniel uses phrases like, Your dream and the visions of your head[3], Visions of my dream, and a dream, a vision of the night. Isaiah also talks of a dream of a night vision.[4]

Webster's dictionary definition says a dream is a series of thoughts, images or emotions occurring during sleep and a vision is something seen otherwise than by natural sight - prophetic sight.

The main point for me is that in a dream the dreamer is asleep and not conscious. A good example would be Jacob's dream at Bethel. The Bible says, When Jacob awoke from his sleep, he thought, Surely the Lord is in this place, and I was not aware of it. [5]Jacob was asleep when he received his revelation.

The key point concerning a vision is that the visionary is conscious and not asleep. A good example would be *The Vision on the Mount of Transfiguration.*[6]

During that encounter the disciples were wide-awake and fully aware of their surroundings. Peter even spoke to Jesus during it. The Bible says,

> While he (Peter) was still speaking, a bright cloud covered them, and a voice from the cloud said, This is my Son, whom I love; with him I am well pleased. Listen to him! When the disciples heard this, they fell facedown to the ground, terrified. But Jesus came and touched them. Get up, he said. Don't be afraid. When they looked up, they saw no one except Jesus.[7]

In my understanding visions are basically the same as dreams, except dreams happen when a person is asleep and visions occur when a person is awake. Both can be literal and or symbolic.

In this study I've included Zechariah's eight night visions as dreams as I have with Samuel and Nathan's night visions. I've also judged Jeremiah's long piece of scripture from Jeremiah 30:3-31:40 to be a dream.

The more one studies Bible dreams the more one gets a sense and a feel for what a Bible dream really looks like. They are usually simple direct instructions or sometimes instructions given in a dialogue form. Occasionally when it suits God's purposes they are also symbolic messages requiring interpretation. Normally they are short, direct and very similar to a parable or a very short story.

In this sense, Zechariah's eight night visions have the typical feel of dreams. They are all like parables requiring interpretation.

Samuel's night vision is slightly different. We don't know if Samuel was asleep or awake but you'd think it'd be quite normal for a child of Samuel's age to go straight to sleep and sleep all night.

Anyway when Samuel hears God's voice he runs to Eli thinking he has been called. This happened three times until God speaks to him on the fourth occasion. And when God does speak He includes a bit more information than He usually does in a dream. His message goes to 90 words.

The same thing happens with Nathan's night vision dream in

which God gives a prophecy for King David that is 365 words long. This is far longer than any other Bible dream except of course, *Jeremiah's 'Israel Will Return' Dream* which runs to 1,227 words.

Yet although there are grey areas which other saints might someday shine better light on, my working definition for this book is that a dream occurs while the dreamer is asleep whereas, a vision happens while the visionary is awake. You see a dream while you are unconscious and you see a vision when you are fully conscious.

I receive much of my regular revelation through dreams. I also receive images and pictures, which I call inner visions, especially when I'm prophesying or interpreting tongues.

I've never to my knowledge received an open vision like Peter on the Mount of Transfiguration or Paul on the road to Damascus though I have received open visions in my dreams.

In this book I'm including a number of night visions because although there's no way of being 100% sure whether they are dreams or visions they certainly function like dreams and have an important message like dreams. They also all advance God's plans and purpose.

Still there are difficulties. In 1 Kings 3 we're told Solomon received his wisdom from God during a dream but when the same incident is reported in 2 Chronicles 1 there's no mention of this incident being a dream. We are only told, That night God appeared to Solomon.

Just how many other similar cases there are of this in Scripture we don't know. I pray some scribe may be called and anointed to unravel this area. I just wonder how many other incidents where it says, *God appeared* or *God spoke,* might well be dreams?

Also in *Jeremiah's They Will Return Dream*[8] the word dream is never mentioned yet we know this long revelation was a dream because it ends with the line, At this I awoke and looked around. My sleep had been pleasant to me.

It's obvious Jeremiah had been sleeping and dreaming but a Google search for Bible dreams wouldn't have shown this up.

FOUR KINDS OF BIBLE DREAMS

There are four kinds of dreams mentioned in Scripture.

- Firstly, there are *True Dreams* that are direct messages from God. These comprise 96% of all the recorded dreams in the Bible.
- Secondly, there are *Satanic Dreams*. There are only three mentions and two examples of such dreams.
- Thirdly there are *False Dreams* which are made-up delusions from the evil hearts and minds of men. We have no actual example of one of these dreams though God warns us about them.
- Fourthly there are *Natural Dreams* that arise from the dreamer's personal self. We have scriptures speaking about these dreams but no actual recorded examples.

God's True Dreams

This book focuses on and is full of the important ways God uses His true dreams to advance His plans and purpose. To this end we examine fifty three dreams and a few trances, visions and divine encounters.

Satanic Dreams

Concerning dreams from Satan we will examine how Eliphaz and Job were assailed by demonic dreams and nightmares. Although we know nothing about the actual content of Job's dreams we do know the spirit in Eliphaz's dream used half truths just like Satan did with Jesus, in *Jesus' Tempted By Satan Dream*. Unlike Jesus Eliphaz wasn't able to overcome the spirit by quoting God's word.

False Dreams

God through Jeremiah said these dreams are from deceitful prophets who have not stood in His presence and do not speak for Him. God calls them, lying prophets, who prophesy the delusions of their own minds?[1]

He tells His people not to listen to the made up dreams of these false prophets and mediums who try to fool God's people by prophesying lies in God's name.[2] The purpose of these false dreamers is to lead God's people into sin and away from God's plans and purpose.[3] Moses also warns about this,

> If a prophet, or one who foretells by dreams, appears among you and announces to you a sign or wonder, and if the sign or wonder spoken of takes place, and the prophet says, "Let us follow other gods" (gods you have not known) "and let us worship them," you must not listen to the words of that prophet or dreamer. The Lord your God is testing you to find out whether you love him with all your heart and with all your soul. It is the Lord your God you must follow, and him you must revere. Keep his commands and obey him; serve him and hold fast to him. That prophet or dreamer must be put to death for inciting rebellion against the Lord your God, who brought you out of Egypt and redeemed you from the land of slavery. That prophet or dreamer tried to turn you from the way the Lord your God commanded you to follow. You must purge the evil from among you.[4]

Joseph Smith who generated Mormonism and Muhammad who generated Islam all had dreams that led people away from a proper understanding and worship of Jesus as God.

Jeremiah also says God wants His true prophets to recount their dreams faithfully because their powerful dreams from Him will be like fire and a hammer that breaks a rock in pieces. The false prophets on the other hand steal words from one another and imagine fake dreams. Concerning these dreamers, God says,

> Indeed, I am against those who prophesy false dreams," declares the Lord. "They tell them and lead my people astray with their reckless lies, yet I did not send or appoint them. They do not benefit these people in the least," declares the Lord.[5]

In the New Testament, Jude also warns against false dreamers who defile their bodies, reject authority, and slander glorious beings.[6] Their evil dreams are not from God but from their own imaginations and sinful hearts.

Natural Dreams

God's purposes for sleep and dreams not only concern spiritual revelation. The vast majority of our dreams are from our natural selves. We have scriptures speaking about these dreams but no actual recorded examples. Nowadays we tend to identify these dreams with labels like *Processing Dreams* or *Soul Dreams.*

Soul Dreams seem to be processing dreams that have some sense of meaning to them. These dreams can often be interpreted. They tend to deal with suppressed emotions, attitudes, beliefs and issues we need to bring to the surface and bring to the Lord. They may refer to our past, present or even our concerns for the future.

Soul dreams often provide us with new insights into our inner world and occasionally they may even offer solutions for difficult personal problems. Soul dreams usually flag up issues that are best shared with pastors or other wise believers who can help us process these dreams and achieve a significant spiritual breakthrough in some relevant area.

As mentioned in chapter 17, God's General Purposes For Sleep and Dreams, these *Processing Dreams* are vital for good mental and emotional health. These God given REM dreams nightly recalibrate and fine-tune the emotional circuits of our brains. Proper sleep and dreaming resets and benefits our mental and physical health.

These dreams also show God's loving care because sleeping and dreaming are just as important for our lives as eating, drinking and breathing. The quality of our sleeping and dreaming is as vital to our well-being as the quality of our food, drink and air. The better the quality the better the life.

Dreaming is now being called 'overnight therapy' by some neuroscientists. Recent research discovered a major benefit of dreaming is in processing our daily emotional experiences so we can make sense of conflicting issues and move on with our lives.

Because we are daily faced with difficult issues, anxiety dreams are very common. They are usually triggered by internal stressors like angry emotions and impulses or external stressors like past trauma, a bad day at work, or an anxious response to whatever current crisis the media is throwing at us. These dreams can be about past events, repressed desires, and unfulfilled hopes. Wish fulfilment dreams about possible marriage partners fall into this category.

Isaiah likens such fleeting dreams to a hungry person who dreams of eating but wakens up still hungry and a thirsty person who dreams of drinking but wakens up faint and thirsty.[7]

Perhaps Solomon sums it up best when he says, Too much activity gives you restless dreams.[8]

WHERE DREAMS COME FROM

There are natural and supernatural dreams. For examples of natural dreams from the mind or the soul, please read the chapter called *God's General Purposes For Sleep And Dreams*.

All the recorded dreams in the Bible come from God apart from a couple from Satan. I believe Job's nightmares were attacks from Satan.[1] I also think Job's friend Eliphaz had a similar demonic attack.[2] I'm also considering the Temptation of Jesus[3] as a demonic dream attack.

Jeremiah also mentions false lying dreamers who prophesy the delusions of their own minds in an attempt to get God's people to worship Baal but we are never given a written example of any of these dreams.

Peter said no Bible prophecy ever came from the mind of the prophet. He said prophecy never had its origin in the human will but rather prophets spoke from God as they were carried along by the Holy Spirit.[4]

Peter is clearly saying the source of all Old Testament revelation including dreams was God and not man.

All Biblical prophecy came from a sovereign God who communicated directly through His prophets to His people. God's revelation came directly from God.

In the same way the recorded Bible dreams communicate God's thoughts and not man's thoughts. No recorded Bible dream ever originated from the mind of the dreamer.

This is where the water has been muddied. Bible dreams did not come from man's consciousness, man's unconsciousness or Carl Jung's idea of the collective unconsciousness.

All Biblical dreams came from a sovereign God who intervened into human history in order to further His own plans and purpose. All recorded Bible dreams came supernaturally from outside the dreamer.

The God of the Bible is unique. He created mankind in His own image and likeness and then revealed Himself to us. One important way was through dreams.

The main reason to study Bible dreams is to know what God's divine dreams and God's divine plans and purpose look like.

Dreams are important to God. Well over a third of the Bible concerns dreams and visions. Everybody dreams. Even babies in the womb.

From a Christian perspective the important thing is not who the dreamer is or what the dream is about. The vital question is whether the dream is from God or not.

Bible dreams were not sent primarily for the benefit of the dreamer, but so that Sovereign God's divine plans and purpose should come to pass. Dreams from God always advance God's redemptive work on the earth.

Are all dreams from God?

Definitely not!

Although there is no recorded description of any false dream in the Bible there are many references concerning false dreamers and false dreams.

Jeremiah explains false dreamers are people who have not stood in the council of the Lord to see or to hear his word. They have not heard from God and they lead people away from God.[5]

In Jeremiah 23, God also severely reprimands both God's prophets and Satan's prophets for telling lies and leading His people astray. Concerning Satan's prophets as represented by the prophets of Samaria, God said, I saw this repulsive thing: They prophesied by Baal and led my people Israel astray.[6]

As regards His own prophets, the prophets of Jerusalem, [7]God says, I have seen something horrible: They commit adultery and live a lie. They strengthen the hands of evildoers, so that not one of them turns from their wickedness.[8]

God also said, His Jewish prophets had become godless prophets who followed an evil course and used their power unjustly. God consequently warned His people not to listen to the made-up dreams and visions of these false prophets. He warned,

> Do not listen to what the prophets are prophesying to
> you; they fill you with false hopes. They speak
> visions from their own minds, not from the mouth
> of the Lord.[9]

The real problem was, none of these prophets had actually stood in the council of the Lord to see or to hear his word. They had merely imagined their dreams and visions and this resulted in them prophesying lies in God's name. God warned,

> They say, 'I had a dream! I had a dream!' How long will
> this continue in the hearts of these lying prophets,
> who prophesy the delusions of their own minds?
> They think the dreams they tell one another will
> make my people forget my name, just as their
> ancestors forgot my name through Baal worship.[10]

The purpose of these false dreams and false visions was to lead God's people away from the true worship of God. This has always been Satan's strategy.

In response God didn't tell His people to stop having dreams and visions. Instead He said,

> Let the prophet who has a dream recount the dream,
>   but let the one who has my word speak it faithfully.
>   For what has straw to do with grain?" declares the
>   Lord. "Is not my word like fire," declares the Lord,
>   "and like a hammer that breaks a rock in pieces?"[11]

God is not afraid of false prophets with their false dreams and visions. He uses His powerful dreams and visions to smash the false dreams and visions into smithereens.

Hebrews says,

> For the word of God is alive and active. Sharper than
>   any double-edged sword, it penetrates even to
>   dividing soul and spirit, joints and marrow; it
>   judges the thoughts and attitudes of the heart.
>   Nothing in all creation is hidden from God's sight.
>   Everything is uncovered and laid bare before the
>   eyes of him to whom we must give account.[12]

Jeremiah says the words of the false prophets are inedible straw easily blown away by the wind while God's word is a nourishing grain that satisfies.

God's word is a fire that quickly consumes their straw. His word is a hammer that cracks open stony hearts and smashes vain imaginations and false prophecy. Paul said,

> For the weapons of our warfare are not carnal, but

mighty through God to the pulling down of strong holds, Casting down imaginations, and every high thing that exalteth itself against the knowledge of God, and bringing into captivity every thought to the obedience of Christ[13]

God's true dreams and visions produce life and accomplish the purpose for which God sent them. We see this in every Bible dream. Isaiah 55:9-11 says,

> As the heavens are higher than the earth, so are my ways higher than your ways and my thoughts than your thoughts. As the rain and the snow come down from heaven, and do not return to it without watering the earth and making it bud and flourish, so that it yields seed for the sower and bread for the eater, so is my word that goes out from my mouth: It will not return to me empty, but will accomplish what I desire and achieve the purpose for which I sent it.

Jeremiah also spoke about God's purposes. Concerning the false prophets, he said,

> The anger of the Lord will not turn back until he fully accomplishes the purposes of his heart.[14]

Jeremiah said God was cross with the false prophets and dreamers because they didn't help the people to know and obey God. He wrote,

> God said, I am against those who prophesy false dreams. They tell them and lead my people astray

with their reckless lies, yet I did not send or appoint them. God also said He would punish them and their household for their foolish lies. Every imagined thing contrary to God's word is evil and despicable in God's eyes.[15]

God's plans and purpose will never be stopped. God says in Isaiah,

> Yea, since the day was I am he; and there is none that can deliver out of my hand: I will work, and who can hinder it?[16]

No human or demonic power can stop God's plans from coming to pass but that doesn't stop Satan from trying.

Satan's presence and work is always obvious in every dream of the Bible. He is always sniffing about looking for an opportunity to hinder God's work.

All the dreams of the Bible occur in the midst of a clash of kingdoms in the unseen realm.

DREAMS, NIGHT VISIONS AND EVENTS COVERED

In this book I explore all the fifty three dreams of the Bible. I also look at Jacob wrestling with God and man. I note Elihu's talk on dreams to Job.

I also examine the three important visionary events surrounding the gentiles coming into God's Kingdom at Cornelius's house and finish by inspecting five apocryphal dreams found in some Christian Bibles. The main focus is always on God's plans and purpose for His dreams, visions and events.

The dreams, visions and events are,

1. Abraham's Covenant Dream
2. King Abimelek's Dream
3. Jacob's Covenant Dream
4. Jacob's 'Goats and Go Back Home' Dream
5. Laban's 'Don't Harm Jacob' Dream
6. Jacob Wrestles With God And Man
7. Joseph's 'Sheaves of Grain' Dream
8. Joseph's 'Sun, Moon and Stars' Dream
9. Pharaoh's Cupbearer's Dream

10. Pharaoh's Baker's Dream
11. Pharaoh's Two Same 'Famine' Dreams (1)
12. Pharaoh's Two Same 'Famine' Dreams (2)
13. Jacob's 'Go Down To Egypt' Dream
14. Balaam's 'Don't Curse Israel' Dream
15. Balaam's 'If They Call You' Dream
16. The Midianite's Dream for Gideon
17. Samuel's Night Vision Dream
18. Nathan's Dream For King David
19. David's Bedtime Prayer
20. Solomon's 'Discerning Heart' Dream
21. Solomon's 'The Bride's Dream'
22. Solomon's Warning Dream
23. Solomon 'Asks For Wisdom' Dream
24. Eliphaz's 'Demonic Nightmare' Dream
25. Job's Satanic Nightmares
26. Jeremiah's 'Israel Will Return' Dream
27. Nebuchadnezzar's 'Large Statue' Dream
28. Daniel's 'Mystery Revealed' Night Vision
29. Nebuchadnezzar's 'Large Tree' Dream
30. Daniel's 'Four Beasts' Dream
31. Daniel's 'Ram, Goat and Little Horn' Dream
32. Zechariah's Dream of Horses
33. Zechariah's Dream of Horns and Craftsmen.
34. Zechariah's Dream of the Measuring Line
35. Zechariah's Dream/Vision of Joshua
36. Zechariah's Lampstand and Olive Trees
37. Zechariah's Dream/ Vision of the Flying Scroll
38. Zechariah's Dream of the Woman in a Basket
39. Zechariah's Dream of the Four Chariots
40. St Joseph's 'Marry Mary' Dream.
41. The Magi's Dream
42. St. Joseph's 'Escape To Egypt' Dream

43. St. Joseph's 'Back to Israel' Dream
44. St. Joseph's 'Go to Nazareth' Dream
45. Jesus 'Tempted By Satan' Dream
46. Pilate's Wife's Dream
47. Peter Interpreting Pentecost
48. Saul's Vision On The Road To Damascus
49. Ananias' Vision About Paul
50. St Paul's Trance
51. Cornelius' 'Send for Peter' Vision
52. Peter's 'Kill and Eat' Trance
53. Peter's Revelation at Cornelius's House
54. *Paul's 'Man Of Macedonia' Night Vision*
55. Paul's 'Fear Not' Night Vision
56. Paul's 'Angelic' Night Vision Dream
57. Egypt's 'Dreadful Dreams'
58. Esdras' Eagle and Lion' Dream
59. Esdras 'Man From The Sea' Dream
60. Mordecai's 'Two Great Dragons' Dream
61. Judas Maccabees' 'Golden Sword' Dream

THE BIBLE'S SYMBOLIC DREAMS

All of the following twenty five dreams require interpretation. Jesus' *Symbol Replacement Method of Interpretation* can be applied to them all. *Solomon's 'The Bride's Dream'* is unusual because it's a literary dream. Yet because it's a symbolic dream it's included in this section.

1. Joseph's 'Sheaves of Grain' Dream
2. Joseph's 'Sun, Moon and Stars' Dream
3. Pharaoh's Cupbearer's Dream
4. Pharaoh's Baker's Dream
5. Pharaoh's Two Same 'Famine' Dreams (1)
6. Pharaoh's Two Same 'Famine' Dreams (2)
7. The Midianite's Dream for Gideon
8. Nebuchadnezzar's 'Large Statue' Dream
9. Solomon's 'The Bride's Dream'
10. Daniel's 'Mystery Revealed' Night Dream
11. Nebuchadnezzar's 'Large Tree' Dream

12. Daniel's 'Four Beasts' Dream
13. Daniel's 'Ram, Goat and Little Horn' Dream
14. Zechariah's Dream of Horses
15. Zechariah's Dream of Horns and Craftsmen
16. Zechariah's Dream of the Measuring Line
17. Zechariah's Dream of Joshua
18. Zechariah's Lampstand and Olive Trees
19. Zechariah's Dream of the Flying Scroll
20. Zechariah's Dream of the Woman in a Basket
21. Zechariah's Dream of the Four Chariots
22. Judas Maccabees' 'Golden Sword' Dream
23. Mordecai's 'Two Great Dragons' Dream
24. Esdras' Eagle and Lion' Dream
25. Esdras 'Man From The Sea' Dream

THE BIBLE'S LITERAL DREAMS

*A*ll of the following twenty eight literal dreams were able to be understood and obeyed by the dreamer, even though there were sometimes symbolic and prophetic elements the dreamer may not have understood.

1. Abraham's Covenant Dream
2. King Abimelek's Dream
3. Jacob's Covenant Dream
4. Jacob's 'Goats and Go Back Home' Dream
5. Laban's 'Don't Harm Jacob' Dream
6. Jacob's 'Go Down To Egypt' Night Dream
7. Balaam's 'Don't Curse Israel' Dream
8. Balaam's 'If They Call You' Dream
9. Samuel's Night Vision Dream
10. Nathan's Night Vision Dream For King David
11. Solomon's 'Discerning Heart' Dream
12. Solomon's Warning Dream

13. Solomon 'Asks For Wisdom' Dream
14. Eliphaz's 'Demonic Nightmare' Dream
15. Job's Satanic Nightmares
16. Jeremiah's 'Israel Will Return' Dream
17. Daniel's 'Mystery Revealed' Night Dream
18. St Joseph's 'Marry Mary' Dream.
19. The Magi's Dream
20. St. Joseph's 'Escape To Egypt' Dream
21. St. Joseph's 'Back to Israel' Dream
22. St. Joseph's 'Go to Nazareth' Dream
23. Jesus Tempted By Satan Dream
24. Pilate's Wife's Dream
25. Paul's 'Man Of Macedonia' Night Dream
26. Paul's 'Fear Not' Night Vision Dream
27. Paul's 'Angelic' Night Vision Dream
28. Egypt's 'Dreadful Dreams'

THE TIMELINE OF BIBLE DREAMS

There are often hundreds of years between recorded dreams in the Bible. But throughout all those years God was still communicating with mankind in all sorts of ways; dreams, visions and personal appearances of Jesus and His angels. I suspect if all the dreams were written down it would be similar to what John said about the Lord,

> Jesus did many other things as well. If every one of them were written down, I suppose that even the whole world would not have room for the books that would be written.[1]

I have included this timeline of dreams because it helps us get a bird's eye view of where God used recorded dreams. I have also included references to Scriptural revelation concerning dreams.

The Garden of Eden and The Fall of Man occurred before 4000 BC. Job is said to be the oldest book in the Bible written sometime before 2100 BC.

2100 BC - Eliphaz's demonic Nightmare[2]
2100 BC - Job's Satanic Nightmares[3]
2100 BC - Elihu's Dream Talk[4]
71 years between dreams
2081 BC - Abraham's Covenant Dream. [5]
14 years between dreams
2067 BC - King Abimelek's Dream [6]
39 years between dreams
1928 BC - Jacob's Covenant Dream [7]
20 years between dreams
1908 BC - Jacob's 'Goats and Go Back Home' Dream [8]
1908 BC - Laban's 'Don't Harm Jacob' Dream [9]
2 years between dreams
1906 BC - Jacob Wrestles with God And Man[10]
100 years between dreams
1898 BC - Joseph's 'Sheaves of Grain' Dream[11]
1898 BC - Joseph's 'Sun, Moon & Stars' Dream[12]
11 years between dreams
1887 BC - Pharaoh's Cupbearer's Dream[13]
1887 BC - Pharaoh's Baker's Dreams[14]
2 years between dreams
1885 BC - Pharaoh's 'Seven Cows' Dream [15]
1885 BC - Pharaoh's Second Dream[16]
10 years between dreams
1875 BC – Jacob's 'Go Down To Egypt' Night Vision [17]
1445 BC - God's Declaration Concerning Dreams [18]
468 years between dreams
1407 BC - Balaam's 'Don't Curse Israel' Dream[19]
1407 BC - Balaam's 'If They Call You' Dream [20]
1406 BC - Laws Concerning Judging Dreams [21]

238 years between dreams
1169 BC - The Midianite's Dream [22]
99 years between dreams
1070 BC - Samuel's Night Vision Dream[23]
1010 BC -Saul Inquires of the Lord for Dreams[24]
17 years between dreams[25]
998 BC - Like those who Dream[26]
997 BC - Nathan's Night Vision For King David[27]
979 David's Bedtime Prayer[28]
30 Years between dreams
967 BC - Like a Fleeting Dream[29]
967 BC - Solomon's 'Discerning Heart' Dream[30]
967 BC - Solomon 'Asks For Wisdom' Dream[31]
17 years between dreams
950 BC - Solomon's Proverb Concerning Vision[32]
950 BC - The Brides Dream[33]
4 years between dreams
946 BC - Solomon's 'Warning' Dream[34]
946 BC - Solomon 'Asks For Wisdom' Dream[35]
835 BC - Joel's Promise of Future Dreams & Visions[36]
745 BC - God's Review of Old T History re Visions[37]
725 BC – God punished Israel by withholding dreams [38]
725 BC - Eyes and Ears Blessed Opened[39]
237 years between dreams
609 BC - Jeremiah's 'Israel Will Return' Dream[40]
609 BC- Jeremiah warns about False Dreamers [41]
609 BC - Jeremiah warns about False Dreamers [42]
5 years between dreams
604 BC - Daniel's Ability to Understand Dreams[43]
604 BC - Nebuchadnezzar's 'Large Statue" Dream[44]
604 BC – Daniel's 'Mystery Revealed' Night Vision[45]
22 years between dreams
582 BC - Nebuchadnezzar's 'Large Tree' Dream[46]

43 years between dreams
539 BC - Daniel Interprets Writing on the Wall[47]
539 BC - Daniel's 'Four Beasts' Dream[48]
539 BC -Daniel's Night Vision of the Ram and Goat[49]
539 BC -Daniel's Terrifying Vision of Jesus[50]
466 years between dreams
520 BC – Zechariah's Eight Dream/Visions[51]
520 BC -The Diviners' Lying Visions[52]
520 BC - Zechariah Prophesying Forth the Vision[53]
485 years between dreams
5 BC -St. Joseph's 'Marry Mary' Dream [54]
3 BC - The Magi's Dream[55]
3 BC - St. Joseph's 'Escape To Egypt' Dream[56]
1 BC - St. Joseph's 'Back To Israel' Dream[57]
1BC - St. Joseph's 'Go To Nazareth' Dream[58]
31 years between dreams
30 AD - Pilate's Wife's dream [59]
30 AD - Peter interpreting Pentecost, quoting Joel[60]
34 AD - Saul's Vision on the Road to Damascus[61]
34 AD - Ananias' Vision regards Paul[62]
37 AD - Cornelius' 'Send For Peter' Vision [63]
37 AD - Peter's 'Kill and Eat' Vision[64]
37 AD - Peter's Revelation at Cornelius's House[65]
12 years between dreams
49 AD - Paul's 'Man Of Macedonia' Night Vision[66]
51 AD - Paul's 'Fear Not' Night Vision [67]
10 years between dreams
61 AD - Paul's 'Angel of the Lord' Night Vision[68]
68 AD – False Dreamers - Jude 1:8
Ad 95 - The Visions of John (Book of Revelation)
Apocrypha Dreams
1446BC - Egypt's 'Dreadful Dreams'[69]
911 years between dreams

535 BC - Esdras' Eagle and Lion' Dream[70]
535BC - Esdras 'Man From The Sea' Dream[71]
52 years between dreams
483 BC - Mordecai's 'Two Great Dragons' Dream[72]
318 years between dreams
165 BC - Judas Maccabees' 'Golden Sword' Dream[73]

HOW JESUS INTERPRETS DREAMS

*Symbolic dreams are similar to parables.
A parable is a type of metaphorical analogy requiring a proper interpretation before it releases its message.

The simple Christian definition is, a parable is an earthly story with a heavenly meaning. This definition also recognises the need for interpretation.

Jesus told parables and explained to his disciples how to interpret all parables. This occurs in Mark in *The Parable of the Sower,* which is like a complex symbolic dream. We have to read the whole passage but it will be worth while. The Bible says,

> Again Jesus began to teach by the lake. The crowd that gathered around him was so large that he got into a boat and sat in it out on the lake, while all the people were along the shore at the water's edge. He taught them many things by parables, and in his teaching said: "Listen! A farmer went out to sow his seed. As he was scattering the seed, some fell along the path, and the birds came and ate it up. Some fell

on rocky places, where it did not have much soil. It sprang up quickly, because the soil was shallow. But when the sun came up, the plants were scorched, and they withered because they had no root. Other seed fell among thorns, which grew up and choked the plants, so that they did not bear grain. Still other seed fell on good soil. It came up, grew and produced a crop, some multiplying thirty, some sixty, some a hundred times."

Then Jesus said, "Whoever has ears to hear, let them hear."

When he was alone, the Twelve and the others around him asked him about the parables. He told them, "The secret of the kingdom of God has been given to you. But to those on the outside everything is said in parables so that,

"'they may be ever seeing but never perceiving,
and ever hearing but never understanding;
otherwise they might turn and be forgiven!'"

Then Jesus said to them, "**Don't you understand this parable? How then will you understand any parable?** The farmer sows the word. Some people are like seed along the path, where the word is sown. As soon as they hear it, Satan comes and takes away the word that was sown in them. Others, like seed sown on rocky places, hear the word and at once receive it with joy. But since they have no root, they last only a short time. When trouble or persecution comes because of the word, they quickly fall away. Still others, like seed sown among thorns, hear the word; but the worries of this life, the deceitfulness of wealth and the desires for other things come in and choke the word, making it unfruitful. Others, like seed sown on good soil, hear the word, accept it, and produce a crop—some thirty, some sixty, some a hundred times what was sown."[1]

The method Jesus uses to interpret this parable can be called *The Symbol Replacement Method.* The main eight images in this parable are,

- The farmer
- The seed
- The birds
- The sun
- The roots
- The path without soil
- The rocky place with little soil
- The good soil

In Mark, Jesus replaced these symbols with other images that helped to unlock the true meaning of the parable.

- The farmer obviously represented a preacher. (Though Jesus doesn't say this.)
- The seed represented the word of God.
- The birds represented Satan and his demons.
- The sun represented trouble or persecution because of God's word,
- The roots represented the ability to survive and flourish.
- The path without soil represents no capacity to receive or nurture God's word.
- The rocky place with little soil represents people with shallow faith.

- The good soil represents people of spiritual depth and faith who reproduce themselves.

So instead of the parable being a story about a farmer planting seed and facing difficulties it becomes a revelation of the process that occurs when a preacher or a prophet speaks the word of God. The world, the flesh and the devil all kick in and the hearer's hearts are tested.

Jesus said to his disciples, Don't you understand this parable? How then will you understand any parable? Here He was offering them a key.

What He really meant was, If you understand this parable then you will be able to understand all parables.

All the dream interpreters in the Bible including the interpreting angels use *The Symbol Replacement Method* of dream interpretation.

For example, Pharaoh dreamed two dreams in quick succession. His first dream contained seven skinny cows that ate up seven fat cows, and his second dream contained seven thin heads of grain that ate up seven full heads of grain.

Using *The Symbol Replacement Method* Joseph interpreted the seven fat cows and the seven full heads of grain as seven years of abundant food production. Using the same method he then interpreted the seven skinny cows and the seven thin heads of grain as seven years of famine.

Consequently Joseph's interpretation of Pharaoh's dream was, Seven years of great abundance are coming throughout the land of Egypt, but seven years of famine will follow them. For this Joseph was put in complete charge of the entire feeding program of the most powerful nation in the world. Not too difficult. Eh?

Another good example comes from Daniel in Babylon. Scripture says God gave Daniel knowledge and understanding of all kinds of literature and learning and in understanding visions and dreams of all kinds.[2]

Let's take a look at Daniel interpreting, *Nebuchadnezzar's 'Large Statue' Dream*. Now this process was a little more difficult because Nebuchadnezzar wouldn't or couldn't tell Daniel the dream and he was going to kill Daniel and others if they couldn't discover what his dream was and also interpret it. So Daniel had to get the dream from God and interpret it, which he did. Nebuchadnezzar's dream was,

> "Your Majesty looked, and there before you stood a large statue—an enormous, dazzling statue, awesome in appearance. The head of the statue was made of pure gold, its chest and arms of silver, its belly and thighs of bronze, its legs of iron, its feet partly of iron and partly of baked clay. While you were watching, a rock was cut out, but not by human hands. It struck the statue on its feet of iron and clay and smashed them. Then the iron, the clay, the bronze, the silver and the gold were all broken to pieces and became like chaff on a threshing floor in the summer. The wind swept them away without leaving a trace. But the rock that struck the statue became a huge mountain and filled the whole earth.[3]

The symbols in this dream are,

- The large statue
- The head of gold
- The chest and arms of silver
- The belly and thighs of bronze
- The legs of iron
- The feet, partly of iron and partly of baked clay
- The rock not cut by human hands

When Daniel used *The Symbol Replacement Method*, these symbols changed into what they represented.

- The large statue represented four kingdoms.
- The head of gold represented Nebuchadnezzar's' kingdom.
- The chest and arms of silver represented an inferior kingdom.
- The belly and thighs of bronze represented another inferior kingdom.
- The legs of iron also represented another inferior kingdom.
- The feet, partly of iron and partly of baked clay represented disunity.
- The rock not cut by human hands represented Jesus' eternal kingdom

When Daniel used *The Symbol Replacement Method*, to interpret this dream he basically replaced each dream symbol with what it represented in reality.

Because of this Daniel could explain Nebuchadnezzar was shown the successive kingdoms starting with his own kingdom that God would use to rule over Israel until their Messiah would come. With hindsight we now know, Nebuchadnezzar's dream spoke of four different empires - Babylon, Medo-Persia, Greece and Rome. Afterwards God would send His Messiah who'd establish His everlasting Kingdom.

The Scripture showing the *The Symbol Replacement Method*, in operation says,

> "This was the dream, and now we will interpret it to the king. Your Majesty, you are the king of kings. The God of heaven has given you dominion and

power and might and glory; in your hands he has placed all mankind and the beasts of the field and the birds in the sky. Wherever they live, he has made you ruler over them all. You are that head of gold.

"After you, another kingdom will arise, inferior to yours. Next, a third kingdom, one of bronze, will rule over the whole earth. Finally, there will be a fourth kingdom, strong as iron—for iron breaks and smashes everything—and as iron breaks things to pieces, so it will crush and break all the others. Just as you saw that the feet and toes were partly of baked clay and partly of iron, so this will be a divided kingdom; yet it will have some of the strength of iron in it, even as you saw iron mixed with clay. As the toes were partly iron and partly clay, so this kingdom will be partly strong and partly brittle. And just as you saw the iron mixed with baked clay, so the people will be a mixture and will not remain united, any more than iron mixes with clay.

"In the time of those kings, the God of heaven will set up a kingdom that will never be destroyed, nor will it be left to another people. It will crush all those kingdoms and bring them to an end, but it will itself endure forever. This is the meaning of the vision of the rock cut out of a mountain, but not by human hands—a rock that broke the iron, the bronze, the clay, the silver and the gold to pieces.

"The great God has shown the king what will take place in the future. The dream is true and its interpretation is trustworthy."[4]

It Is God Who Gives The Interpretation

~

Now all of that seems very simple, doesn't it? Well maybe not the bit about having to discover the contents of Nebuchadnezzar's dream otherwise you'll be killed.

So, before we begin to think it's as easy as painting by numbers I better mention something else. Both Joseph and Daniel understood this something else. Lets look at what they said about dream interpretation.

When Pharaoh's cupbearer and baker had dreams Joseph said, Do not interpretations belong to God? [5]

Later, Pharaoh said to Joseph, I had a dream, and no one can interpret it. But I have heard it said of you that when you hear a dream you can interpret it.

Joseph's truthful answer was, I cannot do it, but God will give Pharaoh the answer he desires.

Joseph was not being polite and self-effacing here. Although he intuitively understood *The Symbol Replacement Method* he also knew it was only God who could give the proper interpretation.

The same thing happened with Daniel. When Nebuchadnezzar asked him, Are you able to tell me what I saw in my dream and interpret it, Daniel honestly replied,

> No wise man, enchanter, magician or diviner can
> explain to the king the mystery he has asked about,
> but there is a God in heaven who reveals mysteries.
> He has shown King Nebuchadnezzar what will
> happen in days to come. [6]

Daniel also told Nebuchadnezzar,

> The revealer of mysteries showed you what is going to happen. As for me, this mystery has been revealed to me, not because I have greater wisdom than anyone else alive, but so that Your Majesty may know the interpretation and that you may understand what went through your mind.[7]

Daniel like Joseph was also not being polite and self-effacing. Although he also intuitively understood the *Symbol Replacement Method* he also knew it was only God who could give the proper dream interpretation.

But what about the pagan Midianite's dream you might say?

Good question! I'm glad you asked it because the soldier's friend also interpreted *The Midianite's Dream for Gideon* using the *Symbol Replacement Method.* The Bible says,

> Gideon arrived just as a man was telling a friend his dream. "I had a dream," he was saying. "A round loaf of barley bread came tumbling into the Midianite camp. It struck the tent with such force that the tent overturned and collapsed."
>
> His friend responded, "This can be nothing other than the sword of Gideon son of Joash, the Israelite. God has given the Midianites and the whole camp into his hands."[8]

The symbols in this dream are,

- A round loaf of barley bread
- The Midianite camp
- A tent

When the friend used *The Symbol Replacement Method,* these symbols changed into what they represented in reality.

- The round loaf of barley bread represented Gideon's sword of power and his small army.
- The Midianite camp represented the Midianite army
- The tent represented the protective covering and place of rest for the Midianite soldiers.

The soldier's friend understood these symbols and was able to declare God's truth that Gideon's small army would be victorious over the vastly superior Midianite army.

THE MCCAULEY DREAM CHECKLIST

This is a personal checklist I created based on Paul's prayer for the Ephesians,

> I keep asking that the God of our Lord Jesus Christ, the glorious Father, may give you the Spirit of wisdom and revelation, so that you may know him better. I pray that the eyes of your heart may be enlightened in order that you may know the hope to which he has called you, the riches of his glorious inheritance in his holy people, and his incomparably great power for us who believe.[1]

For me the checklist provides a consistency and an accountability to the interpretative process. It helps me stop cutting corners.

The McCauley Dream Checklist

The Dream Setting/Backstory

The Dream Scripture
The Problem
The Dreamer's Metron
The Message
God's Purpose
Satan's Purpose
Dreamer's Eyes Enlightened
Dreamer's Response and Application
Know God Better
The Dream Process.
The Usual Suspects
Takeaways

The Dream Setting/Backstory: Every dream typically arrives in the middle of a character's story and usually carries the answer to a problem. The Dream Setting/Backstory provides a context for the dream and allows us to get an idea of what's going on.

Understanding the Context of the dream helps us get a better sense of what's occurring in the bigger picture.

Context refers to the surrounding background circumstances and the specific environment or situation the dreamer finds himself in. This enables us to grasp an overview of the situation and its meaning and how the dream fits in.

The Dream Scripture: The dream scripture is our main focus. It also usually includes a sense of context. It always contains the dream, the dreamer and their response. Sometimes the dream is immediately understood and applied. Other times it requires interpretation. Sometimes it is a simple message about a simple situation, other times it can be very complex with a whole world impact

. . .

The Problem: God's dreams tend to answer and deal with problems that threaten to derail His greater plans and purpose. Often the dreamer knows nothing about the problem. Usually it's a case of God taking the initiative and intervening in the dreamer's life and circumstances in order to both care for the dreamer and to advance God's Own Kingdom Agenda.

In all the Bible dreams God is regularly shown as *The Great Trouble Shooter*. Psalm 46 says,

> God is our refuge and strength,
> an ever-present help in trouble.
> Therefore we will not fear, though the earth give way
> and the mountains fall into the heart of the sea.[2]

The Dreamer's Metron: The dreamer's metron also adds context to the dream. Metron refers to the dreamer's level of authority and sphere of influence. God always sends His dream to a credible person who is in a position to either share the dream or implement the dream's instruction.

For example Pharaoh's Cupbearer was totally unable to promote Joseph to a high position in Egypt but his metron allowed him to introduce Joseph to Pharaoh who did in fact have the metron to promote Joseph to the position God had intended for him.

The Message: The dream message is whatever communication God wants to give the dreamer in order to advance God's plans and purpose.

Many times it is clear and simple and can be taken literally. Other times it may be cryptic and symbolic and require interpretation, occasionally by an angel.

It's also possible the dreamer will not understand the dream. Sometimes they just have to get on with their lives. After *Daniel's 'Ram, Goat and Little Horn' Dream* the prophet said,

> I, Daniel, was worn out. I lay exhausted for several
> days. Then I got up and went about the king's
> business. I was appalled by the vision; it was beyond
> understanding.[3]

Other times the dream message can be implemented immediately like St Joseph instantly taking Mary and Jesus to a place of safety. With other dreams it can take years like Joseph with Pharaoh and sometimes like Daniel's dream it has to be sealed up for the distant future.[4]

God's Purpose: God who sustains all things by his powerful word, including billions of people, billions of planets and billions of galaxies, does nothing without purpose.[5]

Paul said God's mysterious purpose is that through the gospel the Gentiles are fellow heirs, fellow members of the body, and fellow partakers of the promise in Christ Jesus.[6]

He also spoke of God's ongoing purpose which is,

> Through the church, the manifold wisdom of God
> should be made known to the rulers and authorities
> in the heavenly realms, according to the eternal
> purpose that He accomplished in Christ Jesus our
> Lord.[7]

God's four main purposes for Bible dreams were,

1. To demonstrate His dominion over all the powers and principalities.
2. To encourage and guide His Covenant People with specific directions for their well-being and the safety of their seed line.
3. To prevent people and kings from harming His Covenant People and their seed line and to provide for His Covenant People and their seed line.
4. To encourage and help His New Testament Covenant People carry out the Great Commission of Jesus Christ.

Satan's Purpose: Jesus said, Satan comes only to steal and kill and destroy[8]. He also told Peter, Satan has asked to sift all of you as wheat[9] and Peter told us all to,

> Be alert and of sober mind. Your enemy the devil prowls around like a roaring lion looking for someone to devour.[10]

Satan's main mission is to thwart God's plans and purpose for humanity's redemption. As regards God's dreams Satan's primary focus was to destroy the Royal seed line of the woman so the Messiah could not come forth.

Today he still works to kill as many people as possible before they can come to the saving knowledge of Jesus Christ and take their rightful place in God's kingdom.

The proper interpretation and application of a dream from God always harms Satan's kingdom.

. . .

Dreamer's Eyes Enlightened: This focuses us to examine just how much the dreamer comprehends God's message and to what extent they understand what God required of them.

Dreamer's Response and Application: This allows us to see the dreamer's heart concerning their conformity to God's will and their obedience in doing God's will. The vast majority of dreamers are immediately obedient to God's will. One notable exception was Solomon whose longterm disobedience was tragic for Israel.

Know God Better: This section enables us to see God in action and to understand what's really important to Him. We also get to see His various attributes in action as He deals with His beloved Covenant people, the powers and principalities, humanity and His Only Beloved Son.

We were all born to know God. The purpose of all revelation is to know Him better.[11] Dreams are a main way God reveals His plans and purpose. Yet after a zillion years, when Satan has been defeated and the kingdom of this world has become the kingdom of our Lord and of his Messiah,[12] our primary goal will still be to know Him better.

The Dream Process: In the dream process we consider the nuts and bolts of the dream in order to seek for meaning and an interpretation. We ask who, what, where and when questions like, Who is it for? What does it concern? When will it happen? What weight does it carry? Is it of individual or national importance or does it have a spiritual impact through eons of time?

Is it literal or symbolic? Does it require interpretation? Does is contain, God, Jesus, Holy Spirit, angels etc. Does it contain a warning, an encouragement, directions or rebuke?

Usually we also consider the significance of various objects within the dream. For example in *Nebuchadnezzar's Large Statue Dream* we might try to figure out the importance and meaning of the head made of pure gold, the chest and arms of silver, the belly and thighs of bronze, the legs of iron and the feet partly of iron and partly of baked clay.

We'd certainly want to know what the rock not cut by human hands symbolised.

The Usual Suspects: This is a category I included for my own entertainment. God, Jesus, and Holy Spirit are all over the Bible often hidden in plain sight. Many of us are like the two disciples on the road to Emmaus.[13] We often can't join the dots up.

Satan is also all over the place trying to hinder God's plans. In this section I peek for evidence of God, Jesus, Holy Spirit and Satan in the dream.

Takeaways: Takaways are lessons, applications, key points revelations and so on that I especially feel are worth noting and remembering as regards the dream.

OLD TESTAMENT DREAMS

GOD'S PURPOSE FOR ABRAHAM

God's first Bible dream was a covenant dream given to Abraham. Thirty years earlier God had called Abraham and wasted no time in explaining His plans and purpose. He said,

> Go from your country, your people and your father's household to the land I will show you. I will make you into a great nation, and I will bless you; I will make your name great, and you will be a blessing. I will bless those who bless you, and whoever curses you I will curse; and all peoples on earth will be blessed through you.[1]

Jesus Christ was hidden in Abraham's call. With hindsight we know the One who will bless the nations is Jesus Christ, the same One spoken of in Genesis 3 that would someday crush Satan's head and bring redemption to mankind.

God's promise to Abraham is crucially important. Paul calls it the Gospel. He said,

> So also Abraham believed God, and it was credited to him as righteousness. Understand, then, that those who have faith are children of Abraham. Scripture foresaw that God would justify the Gentiles by faith, and announced the gospel in advance to Abraham: All nations will be blessed through you. So those who rely on faith are blessed along with Abraham, the man of faith.[2]

God's promise to Abraham and his descendants is the foundation of the Gospel message and any real understanding of God's plans and purpose through Jesus Christ depends upon an awareness of this.

When Paul was imprisoned for preaching the Gospel he said it was because of his hope in God's promises to the fathers of Israel, Abraham, Isaac and Jacob, that he was being condemned,

> And now I stand and am judged for the hope of the promise made of God unto our fathers.[3]

Scripture says people without Christ are strangers to the covenants of promise.[4] This means believers in Christ are connected to Abraham's Covenant. Paul says,

> Remember at that time you were separate from Christ, excluded from citizenship in Israel and foreigners to the covenants of the promise, without hope and without God in the world. But now in Christ Jesus you who once were far away have been brought near by the blood of Christ.[5]

One of the main reasons for Jesus Christ's work was to fulfil and confirm God's promise to Abraham. Paul writes,

> Now I say that Jesus Christ was a minister of the circumcision for the truth of God, to confirm the promises made unto the fathers.[6]

God's promises always produce faith when believed,

> By faith Abraham, when he was called to go out into a place, which he should after receive for an inheritance, obeyed; and he went out, not knowing whither he went.[7]

God motivated Abraham and imparted faith by revealing His plans and purpose. When God shares His intentions with us it creates faith and motivates us. This happens in Bible dreams to people like Abraham, Jacob, Joseph, Gideon, Solomon, Daniel and St Joseph.

God has work for us all but work without purpose is meaningless. Therefore God reveals His purpose so we'll be encouraged, motivated and full of faith. That's why we're told to desire spiritual gifts especially prophecy.[8]

God planned the Messiah Jesus Christ would come from Abraham's family line and bless all the people on earth. The nation of Israel would also come from Abraham's line and whoever blessed Israel would be blessed and whoever cursed Israel would be cursed.[9]

This theme of blessing and cursing runs throughout all Bible dreams. Those who obey are blessed and those who disobey are cursed. Even the great King Solomon was cursed when he disobeyed God's dream directives.[10]

God speaks to us to bring us into a loving relationship with Himself. This is God's highest goal and the main reason He communicates with us.

Today we have the advantage of 6,000 years of hindsight offered by the Bible.

Paul's writings in particular give us the bigger picture of God's plans and purpose across thousands of years of Jewish history.

We're now aware God always knew Jesus would crush Satan's head by dying on the cross long before Adam was ever created. We also know it was always part of God's plan that Jesus, the Lamb slain before the foundation of the world, would destroy Satan's authority.

We also know Jesus preached this Gospel to Adam and Eve and Satan in Genesis 3 and to Abraham in Genesis 7. This is the same Gospel being preached today to all nations in obedience to Jesus's last command.[11]

We know salvation has come to the Gentiles who are inheritors of Abraham's blessings by faith. We also know when the Gospel is finally preached to all nations the times of the Gentiles will be over and Jesus will return and all Israel will be saved.[12]

Satan will be thrown into the lake of fire[13] and then the Holy City, the new Jerusalem, will come down out of heaven from God, prepared as a bride beautifully dressed for her husband.[14] Then the real adventure will begin.

Abraham is a major character who today powerfully influences a third of all humanity through three major world religions. He is the founding father of the covenant between the Jewish people and God. In Christianity, he is the prototype of all believers, Jewish or Gentile and in Islam he is honoured in the chain of prophets beginning with Adam.

Abraham was no novice when it came to revelation. God appeared to him at least ten times, sometimes in a vision, sometimes physically in the figure of Jesus.

In Genesis, God gave him fourteen commands including, Get out of your country, Leave your father's house, Go to a land I will show you and Every male among you shall be circumcised.[15]

God also made forty-eight promises to Abraham. When he was childless God said he'd become a great nation that would inherit land.[16] God promised him everlasting possession of the Promised Land[17] and said he'd be the father of a numberless multitude.

Abram's name was changed to Abraham meaning father of many nations. God also said in Abraham's seed, meaning Jesus Christ, all the nations of the earth would be blessed.[18] Abraham's belief in God's promises was counted for righteousness.[19] God's promises confirmed by sacrifices became a covenant.[20]

Abraham also plays a very important role in the New Testament being mentioned seventy four times. He's called the friend of God,[21] and the father of all who believe[22] and the heir of the world.[23]

God viewed Abraham's faith in God's promises as righteousness.[24] We're told those who display Abraham's faith will also share Abraham's reward.[25]

The New Testament clarifies God's promises to Abraham in *Abraham's Covenant Dream* and says the unchangeableness of God's word was confirmed by His promise being combined with His oath.[26]

Hebrews 11 says, Abraham died in faith without receiving the promises but saw them afar off. Abraham really believed God was able to raise Isaac from the dead. Hebrews says those who died in faith without receiving the promises should not be made perfect apart from us.[27] Like Abraham we all must await Christ's return and the resurrection before we can fully receive all the promises.

Romans 4 says the reward of Abraham's promises are for all who share Abraham's faith. We're told Abraham's blessings extend to both Jews and Gentiles who believe in Christ[28] and those who are baptised into Christ become Abraham's seed and heirs of the promises.[29]

Abraham, Isaac and Jacob fiercely cherished their godly line and were totally against marriage with the Canaanites who'd intermarried with the fallen angel races and produced giants.

Abraham knew the Messiah would come from his family line. That's why thousands of years later Jesus could tell the Jews, Your father Abraham rejoiced at the thought of seeing my day; he saw it and was glad.[30]

Abraham had only one dream recorded in Genesis. His descendants Jacob and Joseph and the people they interacted with had the rest. Yet beyond these dreams there was a significant amount of communication with God taking place amongst the patriarchs and their families.

Rebekah, Isaac, Jacob, Hagar and Joseph all clearly heard from God. Paul said, those who have faith, meaning faith in Jesus, are children of Abraham and heirs to Abraham's blessings.[31]

God cut a covenant with Abraham. A covenant is the most sacred of all contracts between two people. The Hebrew word is b'rit, which carries the meaning of cutting the skin until blood flows.

In some cultures the parties involved cut into one another's arms and suck the blood. That's why it's called cutting a covenant. This mixing of blood makes them blood brothers of the covenant.

In God's covenant with Abraham the cutting by circumcision was the sign of the particular covenant. When Moses renewed the Abrahamic covenant on Mount Sinai half of the blood of the covenant sacrifice was sprinkled on the people and half upon the altar.

This symbolised God's mystical union with Israel. In the case of *Abraham's Covenant Dream* God put Abraham into a deep sleep and made a one-sided covenant with himself symbolising God was taking sole responsibility for the covenant.

Through the Abrahamic covenant and through God's dealings with Abraham and Israel God consistently revealed Himself as a promise maker and a promise keeper. This is a constant theme in all Bible dreams and God is still keeping His promises to Israel today.

God also told Abraham there was royalty in his linage, I will make you very fruitful; I will make nations of you, and kings will come from you.[32]

God's plan was to bless humanity through the Messiah who would come from Abraham's seed line. Paul wrote,

> Know then that it is those of faith who are the sons of Abraham. And the Scripture, foreseeing that God would justify the Gentiles by faith, preached the gospel beforehand to Abraham, saying, "In you shall all the nations be blessed." So then, those who are of faith are blessed along with Abraham, the man of faith.[33]

On this same theme Paul also said, Christ redeemed us from the curse of the law by becoming a curse for us, for it is written:

> Cursed is everyone who is hung on a pole. He redeemed us in order that the blessing given to Abraham might come to the Gentiles through Christ Jesus, so that by faith we might receive the promise of the Spirit.[34]

What all this means is before Adam and Eve ever sinned God had already made provision to redeem them and us. God doesn't want robots. He doesn't want to control our lives. We are free to choose His ways and free to align our lives with His great plans and purpose.

Paul also explains Jesus is the promised seed of Abraham and the Law of Moses is not applicable to us.

It was only given to the Jews until the Messiah would come. He also shows our blessings are linked back to Abraham's covenant and Abraham's type of faith and has nothing whatsoever to do with the Mosaic Law.

ABRAHAM'S COVENANT DREAM

Dream Setting/Backstory

Twenty generations after Adam and Eve things were in a really bad state. Fallen angels were breeding with the daughters of men and producing giants. God wasn't happy. He said,

> I will wipe from the face of the earth the human race I
> have created and with them the animals, the birds
> and the creatures that move along the ground for I
> regret that I have made them.[1]

God then judged the earth by a flood and began a new generation through his friend Noah. Four hundred years later Noah's descendants had once again abandoned God and were worshipping the sun, the moon, the stars and the signs of the Zodiac in a tower built by giants in the land of Shinar.[2]

They all spoke the same language but none spoke with God.

Again God wasn't happy. He destroyed the Tower of Babel, dispersed the people, confused their language and scattered their one world religion into a million pieces.

God then chose Abram, later renamed Abraham, for the purpose of launching His final plan for mankind's salvation. Abraham's descendants would later defeat the giant races inhabiting The Promised Land and one of them, Jesus Christ of Nazareth, would be the Saviour of the whole world.

God appeared to Abraham at least ten times. Initially He revealed Himself in a vision while Abraham was still in Mesopotamia. God said, Leave your country and your people, and go to the land I will show you.[3]

At Haran, God again encourages Abraham aged 75, to keep moving towards his destiny. He said,

> Go from your country, your people and your father's household to the land I will show you. I will make you into a great nation, and I will bless you; I will make your name great, and you will be a blessing. I will bless those who bless you, and whoever curses you I will curse; and all peoples on earth will be blessed through you.[4]

At their third meeting at Canaan after Abraham and Sarah had returned from Egypt because of famine and fear, God once again appeared to Abraham. He said,

> Look around from where you are, to the north and south, to the east and west. All the land that you see I will give to you and your offspring forever. At their fourth meeting after Lot had left, God said to Abraham, Look around from where you are, to the north and south, to the east and west. All the land

that you see I will give to you and your offspring forever. I will make your offspring like the dust of the earth, so that if anyone could count the dust, then your offspring could be counted. Go, walk through the length and breadth of the land, for I am giving it to you.[5]

Yet the clock was ticking and Abraham was still childless and landless. In Genesis 15, God intervened again to encourage Abraham and share new revelation. This time He used a vision and a dream. Initially they dialogued in the vision then God put Abraham to sleep and shared profound revelation through a dream.

The Dream Scripture
Genesis 15: 12-21

∼

After this, the word of the Lord came to Abram in a vision: "Do not be afraid, Abram. I am your shield, your very great reward. But Abram said, "Sovereign Lord, what can you give me since I remain childless and the one who will inherit my estate is Eliezer of Damascus?" And Abram said, "You have given me no children; so a servant in my household will be my heir." Then the word of the Lord came to him: "This man will not be your heir, but a son who is your own flesh and blood will be your heir." He took him outside and said, "Look up at the sky and count the stars, if indeed you can count them." Then he said to him, "So shall your offspring be."

Abram believed the Lord, and he credited it to him as righteousness.

He also said to him, "I am the Lord, who brought you out of Ur of the Chaldeans to give you this land to take possession of it." But

Abram said, "Sovereign Lord, how can I know that I will gain possession of it? So the Lord said to him, "Bring me a heifer, a goat and a ram, each three years old, along with a dove and a young pigeon." Abram brought all these to him, cut them in two and arranged the halves opposite each other; the birds, however, he did not cut in half. Then birds of prey came down on the carcasses, but Abram drove them away.

As the sun was setting, Abram fell into a deep sleep, and a thick and dreadful darkness came over him. Then the Lord said to him, "Know for certain that for four hundred years your descendants will be strangers in a country not their own and that they will be enslaved and mistreated there. But I will punish the nation they serve as slaves, and afterward they will come out with great possessions. You, however, will go to your ancestors in peace and be buried at a good old age. In the fourth generation your descendants will come back here, for the sin of the Amorites has not yet reached its full measure."

When the sun had set and darkness had fallen, a smoking firepot with a blazing torch appeared and passed between the pieces. On that day the Lord made a covenant with Abram and said, "To your descendants I give this land, from the Wadi of Egypt to the great river, the Euphrates— the land of the Kenites, Kenizzites, Kadmonites, Hittites, Perizzites, Rephaites, Amorites, Canaanites, Girgashites and Jebusites."

The Problem

~

Despite repeated promises from God about land and an heir Abraham was still childless, landless and anxious.

The Dreamer's Metron

∼

Abraham's enormous metron has impacted all nations for all time. God chose Abraham as the channel through which He released the knowledge of His plans and purpose for world salvation.

Abraham is the only person in Scripture called a friend of God[6] and God specifically chose His friend's seed line to bring forth Jesus Christ the Messiah.

Although far from perfect Abraham's great strength was to believe and obey his friend. Abraham was 100% convinced God always keeps His promises.

Consequently he was able to surrender himself to God's eternal plans and purpose and because of this Abraham is now called the father of faith and the faithful.[7]

Abraham essentially became the model for all believers by simply taking God at His word and trusting Him.

The Message

∼

God's communication concerned personal information for Abraham alongside future revelation concerning Israel, Egypt and Canaan.

The plain message spoken by God was, Know for certain that for four hundred years your descendants will be strangers in a country not their own and that they will be enslaved and mistreated there. (This was fulfilled when the nation of Israel was in Egypt for four hundred years)

But I will punish the nation they serve as slaves, and afterward they will come out with great possessions. (This happened before and during the Exodus from Egypt)

You, however, will go to your ancestors in peace and be buried at a good old age. (This was also fulfilled)

In the fourth generation your descendants will come back here, for the sin of the Amorites has not yet reached its full measure. (Although this part was partially fulfilled the complete fulfilment of this promise still hasn't happened. God promised land, from the Wadi of Egypt to the great river, the Euphrates— the land of the Kenites, Kenizzites, Kadmonites, Hittites, Perizzites, Rephaites, Amorites, Canaanites, Girgashites and Jebusites. Even though the Jews came back to their land in 1948 they're still not in possession of all of this land.)

There was no interpretation necessary in order for Abraham to understand this dream though there are some things he probably didn't fully understand. He wasn't told the name of the nation who'd enslave his people. Nor was he told explicitly that the fate of Jesus Christ the Messiah was sealed because of this dream.

God's Purpose

~

God's purpose was to reveal that Jesus Christ the Messiah would die for the sins of the whole world. He also wanted to encourage and strengthen Abraham and give him revelation about his descendants and the present occupiers of the Promised Land.

Earlier God had promised to rescue humanity from Satan's power through Eve's seed. We now know this rescue occurred when Jesus of Nazareth died on a cross 4,000 years later because of the unfaithfulness of Abraham's descendants.

Cutting animals in half and walking between them was a

common way of making covenant. The symbolism was if either of the parties didn't keep their end of the bargain then they'd suffer the same fate as the animals.

In Jeremiah, God says,

> Those who have violated my covenant and have not fulfilled the terms of the covenant they made before me, I will treat like the calf they cut in two and then walked between its pieces.[8]

Here God is saying anyone who violates the covenant will be killed like the sacrifices. Normally both parties walked between the slaughtered animals signifying they were jointly responsible to keep the covenant. In Abraham's dream only God in the form of a smoking pot and flaming torch passed between the animals. Through this symbolic act God was saying, I'll be the one to suffer death if this covenant is broken.

By making covenant with Abraham and taking sole responsibility for it God was condemning Jesus to death for there was no way in this world Abraham's descendants could ever keep the covenant. This meant God, through Jesus Christ, would suffer the death penalty.

Abraham's dream is perhaps the most important dream in all of Scripture. Later Abraham is asked to sacrifice his own son for God and he too is willing.

Satan's Purpose

Satan wanted to stop Abraham from believing God. His evil purpose was to hinder and prevent the Messiah from ever seeing the light of day. He would also be active in Egypt in enslaving and oppressing God's people. He was also polluting and populating the Promised Land with hybrid Nephilim giants.

Dreamer's Eyes Enlightened

∼

The prophet Abraham is clearly shown that God who cannot lie has unilaterally promised him children and land through an unbreakable covenant. Now nothing can stop this from happening, not even Abraham's sin.

Abraham also realises God knows the future and is acting according to His own higher sense of justice and purpose.

Abraham was also comforted to know he'd die in peace at a good old age and his descendants would finally possess the Promised Land after enduring a four hundred year struggle.

I wonder how much Abraham understood about Jesus Christ dying for the sins of humanity. We know when Paul said the Gospel was first preached to Abraham he is referring to God telling Abraham, All the nations shall be blessed in you.[9]

There's always a lot more happening in any encounter with God than we can fully understand and God isn't always ready or able to spill the beans. Jesus was with his disciples three and a half years before God told Peter that Jesus was the Messiah.[10]

Jesus also wasn't able to share all He wanted to with His disciples. Just before He left earth He told them,

> I still have much to tell you, but you cannot yet bear to hear it. However, when the Spirit of truth comes, He will guide you into all truth.[11]

Still it must have been hard for Abraham to learn his descendants would be slaves for four hundred years.

Dreamer's Response and Application

∽

Because Abraham's metron included all nations God spoke to him about Israel, Egypt and Canaan. Abraham didn't have to do anything apart from believing God. Scripture says, Abram believed the Lord, and He credited it to him as righteousness.[12]

Know God Better

∽

God is kind and compassionate with Abraham. He doesn't rebuke him for unbelief. Instead He reassures Abraham He hasn't forgotten His promises. He also comforts Abraham by letting him know his life will be long and end in peace.

God is also shown as a righteous judge who knows the future. In time He'll punish Egypt for her cruel treatment of the Jews. God always acts with a higher sense of purpose and justice. He knows just how long it will be before the sins of the Amorites cause them to lose Canaan.

The fruits of the Spirit, love, joy, peace, forbearance, kindness, goodness, faithfulness, gentleness and self-control are always evident with God. In this dream encounter we also see something of God's deeply hidden purpose. He is willing to die for the redemption of His creation in the form of His only Son Jesus.

The Dream Process

~

This dream encounter is mainly literal and can be understood as such by Abraham yet there are symbolic parts like the smoking pot and flaming torch, which symbolise God in the form of Jesus. All the Old Testament people who were reported as seeing God were really seeing Jesus in a pre-incarnate form because as John says, No one has seen God at any time.[13]

Paul confirms this when he says God the Father, alone can never die, and he lives in light so brilliant that no human can approach him. No human eye has ever seen him, nor ever will.[14]

We also see God as fire from other scriptures. God appeared to Moses as the fire burning in the bush. God also appeared as a pillar of fire when He brought Israel out of Egypt. Moses said, The Lord is a consuming fire. The glory of the Lord looked like a consuming fire on top of the mountain. God the Holy Spirit appeared like tongues of fire at Pentecost and Hebrews tells us our God is a consuming fire.

There is also the death sentence upon Jesus for those of us who can read between the lines. We don't know whether Abraham fully understood this or not. We do know Abraham wasn't told the name of the nation who's enslave his people.

While the dream is mainly literal it still requires a lot of reflection on the part of Abraham in order to comprehend the enormity of the message.

Although this short dream contains important revelation for Abraham personally it also includes revelation concerning Israel, Egypt and for the inhabitants of Canaan.

We are reminded of Amos 3:7,

> Surely the Sovereign Lord does nothing without
> revealing his plan to his servants the prophets.

I wonder if Abraham ever shared this dream with his wife and children? Did Jacob ever hear about it? Did Joseph?

The Usual Suspects

∽

The smoking firepot with a blazing torch reminds us of God in the form of Jesus who appeared as the pillar of cloud and fire, which led them out of Egypt. The ram also reminds us of Christ and the dove speaks of the Holy Spirit. The birds of prey and the land that will enslave Israel represent Satan and the gods.

Takaways

∽

The first recorded Bible dream was sent to Abraham in Genesis and the three last recorded Bible dreams were sent to Abraham's descendent Paul in *The Book of Acts* as he went about preaching the Gospel of Jesus Christ to both Jews and Gentiles. God's promise to Abraham of blessing the nations was coming to pass through his seed line.

God has been working out His plans and purpose from before creation. Here in *Abraham's Covenant Dream* we see His purpose for the Messiah moving forward.

God knows all things, He understands all things, He knows the end from the beginning. God is full of the fruit of the Spirit. He is kind and gentle and patient with Abraham. He is also a righteous judge.

Although He is merciful and full of grace, in the end no one or any nation gets away with anything. As Peter says,

> The Lord is not slow in keeping his promise, as some understand slowness. Instead he is patient with you, not wanting anyone to perish, but everyone to come to repentance.[15]

Reading between the lines there is also a sense of many future battles with the gods, the powers and principalities, before the Jewish nation will finally conquer all of the Promised Land.

We now know Israel had to defeat the gods of Egypt before they could escape their captivity. We also know the demonic giants and the gods within the Promised Land had to be defeated before Israel could take possession.

During Israel's captivity in Egypt the fallen angels were still mating with the daughters of men for some of these giants terrified the ten spies sent by Moses to spy out the land.

We're also aware, although the Jews have occupied a state in Israel since 1948, they still don't have complete possession of the land as promised to Abraham in this covenant dream.

The heavenly war continues.

KING ABIMELEK'S DREAM

Dream Setting/Backstory

King Abimelek's dream came fourteen years after *Abraham's Covenant Dream*. In the meantime Abraham made a couple of really big blunders. Firstly, instead of patiently waiting for God's promised heir he listened to Sarah and tried to help bring about God's promises by sleeping with Sarah's maid, Hagar.

This resulted, not in the promised child but in a problem child called Ishmael who became the spiritual father of all the Islamic nations still hell bent on destroying Israel.

Later, when Abraham was a hundred years old, God again appeared and affirmed His covenant. God emphasised it would be His plans and purpose that would come to pass and not Sarah's worldly scheme. God's sovereign intention was that His Messianic purpose would flow through Isaac's seed line and not Ishmael's seed line. God said,

> Your wife Sarah will bear you a son, and you will call him Isaac. I will establish my covenant with him as an everlasting covenant for his descendants after him.[1]

Abraham's second blunder also involved his beautiful wife Sarah. In Genesis 12 Abraham and Sarah were in Egypt due to a famine in Canaan. Abraham was afraid Pharaoh might kill him and steal his lovely wife. Eastern princes often exercised their right of collecting the beautiful women of their dominions into their harem.

In order to protect himself Abraham asked Sarah to say she was his sister (a half truth) and not his wife so Pharaoh might treat him favourably. This deception worked for a time.

Pharaoh gave Abraham a substantial amount of property, including sheep, oxen, assess, male and female slaves, she-asses, and camels. He also took Sarah into his harem and was very close to innocently committing adultery.

Then Pharaoh realised something was badly wrong when he and his household began to suffer various plagues. Afterwards when Pharaoh discovered Sarah was Abraham's wife he rebuked Abraham for his deception and expelled him and Sarah out of Egypt but he allowed them to keep their possessions.

There were three of these brother-sister subterfuges in Genesis. The one with Pharaoh, this one with Abimelek and a similar one involving Isaac and Rebecca in Genesis 26. Sins of the fathers?

Each time the powerful rulers rebuked the powerless nomads for telling lies but perhaps Abraham's and Isaac's fears are not without foundation because powerful royalty can be very treacherous. Queen Jezebel murdered Naboth in order to steal his vineyard and King David killed righteous Uriah in an effort to hide his sin and steal Bathsheba for himself.

Just before King Abimelek's dream Abraham and Sarah are up to their old tricks of telling half-truths and this has put a whole nation under God's judgement.

God had promised Isaac would be born within the year and now Sarah was in King Abimelek's harem awaiting adultery. Abraham's fear of telling the whole truth had put both Sarah and Abimelek in the dangerous position of derailing God's covenant plans.

The Dream Scripture
Genesis 20:1-18

∽

Now Abraham moved on from there into the region of the Negev and lived between Kadesh and Shur. For a while he stayed in Gerar, and there Abraham said of his wife Sarah, "She is my sister." Then Abimelek king of Gerar sent for Sarah and took her.

But God came to Abimelek in a dream one night and said to him, "You are as good as dead because of the woman you have taken; she is a married woman." Now Abimelek had not gone near her, so he said, "Lord, will you destroy an innocent nation? Did he not say to me, 'She is my sister,' and didn't she also say, 'He is my brother'? I have done this with a clear conscience and clean hands." Then God said to him in the dream, "Yes, I know you did this with a clear conscience, and so I have kept you from sinning against me. That is why I did not let you touch her. Now return the man's wife, for he is a prophet, and he will pray for you and you will live. But if you do not return her, you may be sure that you and all who belong to you will die."

Early the next morning Abimelek summoned all his officials, and when he told them all that had happened, they were very much afraid. Then Abimelek called Abraham in and said, "What have you done to us? How have I wronged you that you have brought such great guilt upon me and my kingdom? You have done things to me that should never be done." And Abimelek asked Abraham, "What was your reason for doing this?" Abraham replied, "I said to myself, 'There is surely no fear of God in this place, and they will kill me because of my wife.' Besides, she really is my sister, the daughter of my father though not of my mother; and she became my wife. And when God had me wander from my father's household, I said to her, 'This is how you can show your love to me: Everywhere we go, say of me, "He is my brother."'"

Then Abimelek brought sheep and cattle and male and female slaves and gave them to Abraham, and he returned Sarah his wife to him. And Abimelek said, "My land is before you; live wherever you like." To Sarah he said, "I am giving your brother a thousand shekels of silver. This is to cover the offense against you before all who are with you; you are completely vindicated."

Then Abraham prayed to God, and God healed Abimelek, his wife and his female slaves so they could have children again, for the Lord had kept all the women in Abimelek's household from conceiving because of Abraham's wife Sarah.

The Problem

God's plans and purpose for the seedline of the Messiah is under imminent threat. Abimelek is innocently sitting on a ticking time bomb totally unaware God is about to kill him and his entire household. So God mercifully makes all the women of Abimelek's household barren and sends a dream to get his attention.

The Dreamer's Metron

∼

Abimelek was the king of Gerar when Abraham travelled through the Philistine territory of Kadesh and Shur. He was in the powerful position of being able to bless or destroy Abraham and his household. God used Abimelek's influential metron to keep His covenantal promises to Abraham on track.

The Message

∼

The dream's plain message needs no interpretation. Basically God said, Abimelek, I know you did this with a clear conscience, and so I have kept you from sinning against me. That is why I did not let you touch her. Now return the man's wife, for he is a prophet, and he will pray for you and you will live. But if you do not return her, you may be sure that you and all who belong to you will die.

God's Purpose

∼

God's primary purpose was to advance His covenantal promises to Abraham concerning his descendants and the Messiah. It was God's intention Isaac should be born to Abraham and Sarah in order to inherit the Abrahamic Covenant.

God also used Abimelek to financially prosper Abraham just as He'd previously used Pharaoh. God was merciful to Abimelek. He was both firm but loving. Firm was, I'm going to kill you. Loving was, I know you didn't do it on purpose so repent and you'll live and everyone gets healed.

Satan's Purpose

Satan's purpose was to have Sarah commit adultery with Abimelek and thereby derail God's plans and promises.

Dreamer's Eyes Enlightened

Abimelek responded brilliantly! He immediately understood and received the dream's revelation and successfully interceded with God for his life and the lives of his people.

Abimelek showed himself to be an able and diplomatic leader. Even though he was not to blame he made amends and saved Sarah's reputation. His quick response saved numerous lives including the unborn. Had he not obeyed God's dream he and his people would have perished.

Dreamer's Response and Application

Abimelek believed God and wasted no time in appropriately responding. He successfully defended himself with God on the basis of the revelation and next morning put God's instructions into immediate effect.

He called his leaders together and contrary to Abraham's fearful assertion they really did fear God. Like a lot of modern Christians, Abraham made the classic mistake of wrongly judging non-followers of Yahweh as not being God fearing.

Abimelek rebuked Abraham but was also warm and generous to him and Sarah. He was very sensitive to Sarah's dilemma and graciously restored her honour before all the people. Abimelek's quick and decisive leadership turned a disastrous situation around and saved his nation. He was a worthy leader.

Know God Better

Sovereign God was decisive. He also kept His word to Abraham. The dream shows God has the power of life and death and will use it when He needs to. Yet He is gracious because He personally visited Abimelek in the dream instead of sending a man or an angel.

Through a dream God can prevent us from sinning against Him and incurring judgment upon our families. God in His mercy can stop pagan leaders from sinning and bringing a curse upon themselves and death to their people.

We see God knows all things and is just. There is judgment. There is mercy. He can bless, He can curse. He responds to repentance and brings reconciliation and healing. But He is always a promise keeper, always working His purpose for Jesus out.

God also showed He honours the delegated authority He gives to His ministers. He told Abimelek, Now return the man's wife, for he is a prophet, and he will pray for you and you will live. It was Abraham's anointed prayers that God used to heal Abimelek's household and to avert His wrath.

The Dream Process

∼

This is a literal dream in which God dialogues with the dreamer. It's a warning dream with corrective instructions. It's without symbolism and requires no interpretation but it does require a quick response. It was of personal, national and international importance.

Takeaways

∼

God's prophet's fear and half truths endangered God's plans and purpose and brought a whole nation under the judgement of God. A pagan leader's wise response and obedience to God brought blessing while a wrong response would have brought death.

Proper responses to God's dreams gain God's blessing. God speaks both to his followers and non-followers in dreams.

We can't use a modern Christian term non-believer to describe folk like Abimelek and other non-followers of Yahweh like Pharaoh and Nebuchadnezzar.

These leaders totally believed in the supernatural. They just didn't have the revelation of the true God before they had their dreams. Although only God's people experience God's visions, God speaks to all mankind through dreams.

That's what makes them such a great vehicle for revelation and instruction.

JACOB'S COVENANT DREAM

Dream Setting/Backstory

Jacob was an important Bible character. He was the father of the leaders of the Twelve Tribes of Israel. Apart from this dream God appeared to Jacob another seven times in Scripture. Jacob even wrestled with God in human form. This I believe was Jesus.

God sent *Jacob's Covenant Dream* thirty-nine years after *King Abimelek's Dream.* In the meantime God had appeared and prophesied to Isaac's wife Rebekah about the struggling twins in her womb. He revealed His purpose was that Jacob's line was to inherit the covenant blessing. God said,

> Two nations are in your womb, and two peoples from within you will be separated; one people will be stronger than the other, and the older will serve the younger.[1]

The twins were Esau the eldest and Jacob the youngest. The nations were Edom from Esau and Israel from Jacob. Normally Isaac's eldest son Esau was the one to inherit the spiritual covenant but he valued it so little he sold it to Jacob for a bowl of stew.

Esau continually chose the natural over the supernatural. His carelessness and impulsiveness finally disqualified him from leadership and the covenantal inheritance.

He also married two Hittite women in violation of God's will and Abraham's ruling not to take wives from among the Canaanites.[2] This rebellious act severed his children from the Abrahamic line.

Rebekah knew Jacob was God's chosen child[3] but instead of reminding Isaac of this prophecy she conspired with Jacob to deceive her husband. Like Sarah before her she tried to work out God's plans and purpose in her own way. This caused great pain for her and many others.

Just before this dream, seventy year old Jacob was fleeing for his life from Esau, whom Rebekah and Jacob had tricked out of his inheritance. Esau was now seething like Cain, who slew his brother Abel.

Again we see the work of Satan who constantly laboured to hinder God's plan of redemption by blocking the promised seed of the woman from being born through the prophesied lineage.

As Jacob sets off to flee five hundred miles away to Haran Isaac reminds him not to marry a Canaanite but to marry a woman from Laban's line in order to keep the Messiah Bloodline uncontaminated. Isaac also blessed Jacob with Abraham's blessing of descendants and land.

The Dream Scripture
Genesis 28:10-22

Jacob left Beersheba and set out for Harran. When he reached a certain place, he stopped for the night because the sun had set. Taking one of the stones there, he put it under his head and lay down to sleep.

He had a dream in which he saw a stairway resting on the earth, with its top reaching to heaven, and the angels of God were ascending and descending on it. There above it stood the Lord, and he said: "I am the Lord, the God of your father Abraham and the God of Isaac. I will give you and your descendants the land on which you are lying. Your descendants will be like the dust of the earth, and you will spread out to the west and to the east, to the north and to the south. All peoples on earth will be blessed through you and your offspring. I am with you and will watch over you wherever you go, and I will bring you back to this land. I will not leave you until I have done what I have promised you."

When Jacob awoke from his sleep, he thought, Surely the Lord is in this place, and I was not aware of it. He was afraid and said, How awesome is this place! This is none other than the house of God; this is the gate of heaven.

Early the next morning Jacob took the stone he had placed under his head and set it up as a pillar and poured oil on top of it. He called that place Bethel, though the city used to be called Luz.

Then Jacob made a vow, saying, If God will be with me and will watch over me on this journey I am taking and will give me food to eat and clothes to wear so that I return safely to my father's household, then the Lord will be my God and this stone that I have set up as a pillar will be God's house, and of all that you give me I will give you a tenth.

The Problem

Jacob's scheming had backfired and now he was fleeing for his life to a place five hundred miles away and facing an uncertain future. This lonely fugitive sleeping in the open field was being blessed because of the Abrahamic covenant. Jacob carried God's promises and the Messiah bloodline in his loins though he didn't realise this. All that was about to change.

The Dreamers Metron

Jacob had a powerful metron he had inherited from his grandfather Abraham. This was to bless all nations until the end of time. The dream also speaks of Jacob's offspring, which refers to Jacob's metron of being the father of twelve sons who would father the twelve tribes of Israel.

After Jacob wrestled with God his name was changed to Israel and this became both the name of the people and the land of God's Chosen People. God told Jacob,

> I am the Lord, the God of your father Abraham and the God of Isaac. I will give you and your descendants the land on which you are lying. Your descendants will be like the dust of the earth, and you will spread out to the west and to the east, to the north and to the south. All peoples on earth will be blessed through you and your offspring. I am with you and will watch over you wherever you go, and I will bring you back to this land. I will not leave you until I have done what I have promised you.[4]

Jacob's metron also included his call to bring the children of

Israel down to Egypt as promised to Abraham in his covenant dream.

The Message

God chose a significant time to affirm Jacob's call. Like Abraham and Isaac, God was going to multiply Jacob's descendants, give him land, protect him and bring him back to the Promised Land.

Prophetically this has also been the constant story of Israel until this very day. God's spoken message was clear and required no interpretation,

> I am the Lord, the God of your father Abraham and the God of Isaac. I will give you and your descendants the land on which you are lying. Your descendants will be like the dust of the earth, and you will spread out to the west and to the east, to the north and to the south. All peoples on earth will be blessed through you and your offspring. I am with you and will watch over you wherever you go, and I will bring you back to this land. I will not leave you until I have done what I have promised you.

God's Purpose

God's main purpose was to keep the Abrahamic Covenant on track. Here God is calling Jacob into play by activating his faith through prophecy. God's purpose was also to comfort and focus Jacob at this vulnerable time.

God didn't judge Jacob for his bad behaviour. Instead he revealed the treasures of his inheritance and prophesied about His world blessing future for Jacob and his offspring.

He also revealed more of Himself to Jacob. Before this Jacob knew Him only as the God of his father Isaac. In this dream Jacob was told the covenant promises made to Abraham and Isaac were now his as well. Jacob also received confirmation of all three major benefits of the covenant: dynasty, land and God's protection.

Satan's Purpose

Satan wanted to kill Jacob and nearly had Esau do it after he got angry when he realised the treachery of Rebekah and Jacob in stealing his birthright. When Jacob escaped, Satan then began working at making him fearful and discouraged.

Dreamer's Eyes Enlightened

Jacob got to see and hear God and was amazed and transformed by the dream. He said, Surely the Lord is in this place, and I was not aware of it. He was also afraid and said, How awesome is this place! This is none other than the house of God; this is the gate of heaven.

He didn't realise Jesus was the stairway to heaven and probably never knew it would be through Jesus Christ that all nations would be blessed.

Dreamer's Response and Application

Jacob is delighted with his dream. Yet unlike obedient and believing Abraham, Jacob was not fully convinced for he made a conditional vow saying if God would keep His word then he would tithe to God's work. Sounds a bit like doubting Thomas. There was still a long way to go before Jacob would totally trust God.

Know God Better

God is again seen as a loving covenant keeping God diligently caring for the Messiah's seed line. He's also shown as a God who wants a personal relationship with His people.

The Dream Process

The message is easily understood and doesn't require interpretation yet there was symbolism in the dream that Jacob couldn't understand but we with hindsight can clearly see.

This is a spectacular dream in which God in the form of Jesus appears with many angels who keep descending and ascending to heaven. Unlike the tower of Babel which was man's self effort to reach heaven these angels are carrying out God's work between heaven and earth in God's way.

Jesus is also hidden in plain sight for Jesus is the stairway to heaven and the offspring of Jacob who will bless all nations. He is the way the truth and the life. Jesus told Nathaniel,

> I tell you the truth, you will all see heaven open and the angels of God going up and down on the Son of Man, the one who is the stairway between heaven and earth.[5]

Yet this fuller interpretation was not necessary in order for Jacob to be encouraged and strengthened by the dream. The dream has personal, national and international importance. The dream covers thousands of years until Jesus finally comes back and saves all Israel.

The Usual Suspects

∼

God is there in the form of Jesus at the top of the stairs who reaffirms the Abrahamic covenant to Jacob. Jesus is also there as the stairway to heaven and the offspring of Jacob[6] who will bless all nations. Satan is seen as the cause of the fearful fleeing of Jacob.

Takeaways

∼

Bethel, which means house of God, was a significant place for Abraham and his descendants. They sought God there in times of trouble. When Abraham first entered Canaan his second encampment was between Bethel and Hai and when he returned from Egypt he went back to Bethel and called upon the name of the Lord.

When Jacob was fleeing Esau he met God in this dream at Bethel. When he later returned he again visited Bethel where God talked with him and he built an altar, calling the place El-beth-el.

Hosea said of Jacob, He found him at Bethel and talked with him there, the Lord God Almighty, the Lord is his name![7]

The Ark of the Covenant also spent time at Bethel. Samuel occasionally held court at Bethel and after Israel was divided Bethel became a seat of worship of the golden calf until Josiah dealt with Israel's idolatry. Israel's priests always remained at Bethel even after the king of Assyria destroyed the kingdom.

Jesus can be hidden in our dreams just like he was in Jacob's dream. Perhaps like Jacob and Abraham our dreams can be similar to the dreams of our ancestors for God has plans and purpose for family lines.

The dream covers thousands of years until Jesus returns. The trinity were in this dream. God was at the top of the stairway, Jesus was the stairway and the Holy Spirit gave the dream. Jacob is afraid and awestruck afterwards and there is the first ever mention of him setting up a memorial and worshipping God.

The Gospel is also mentioned again in this dream. Jacob was told, All peoples on earth will be blessed through you and your offspring.

JACOB'S 'GOATS AND GO BACK HOME' DREAM

The Dream Setting/Backstory

It's been twenty years since *Jacob's Covenant Dream*. In the meantime Jacob obeyed his father Isaac and took a wife from Laban's daughters. In fact due to Laban's scheming he ended up taking two wives and working for fourteen years to pay for them.

Family problems resulted from Laban's trickery. The emotional rivalry between Rachel and Leah was the daily battleground of Jacob's life. Yet God was working His purpose out and from this messy situation produced the founding fathers of the twelve tribes of Israel.

We're not told exactly when Jacob had this dream. Most likely it was before Joseph was born because after Joseph's birth Jacob asked Laban to allow him to return to Canaan with his family. Laban who'd learned through divination and experience that God was blessing him because of Jacob was reluctant to let this happen so they made a new business contract that appealed to cunning Laban.

In Jacob's day sheep were typically white and goats were typically black or brown. Streaked, speckled or spotted animals of either kind were rare. So when Jacob asked that his wages should only be the newborn streaked, speckled or spotted animals Laban knew by the laws of nature he was onto a good bet.

He also made sure the odds were even more stacked in his favour by deviously removing all the streaked, speckled or spotted animals from the flock.

The problem was Laban's selfish dishonesty had been getting in the way of God's plans and purpose. That's why God sent this dream. It was now God's timing for His covenant partner Jacob to return to Canaan so God decided to intervene and show Laban the truth of what Daniel discovered,

> Praise be to the name of God for ever and ever;
> wisdom and power are his. He changes times and
> seasons; he deposes kings and raises up others.[1]

Laban was about to learn God in His sovereignty also deposes goat and sheep breeders and raises up others when it suits his agenda.

∽

The Dream Scripture
Genesis 31:1-17

Jacob heard that Laban's sons were saying, "Jacob has taken everything our father owned and has gained all this wealth from what belonged to our father." And Jacob noticed that Laban's attitude toward him was not what it had been. Then the Lord said to Jacob, "Go back to the land of your fathers and to your relatives, and I will be with you." So Jacob sent word to Rachel and Leah to come out to the fields where his flocks were. He said to them, "I see that your father's attitude toward me is not what it was before, but the God of my father has been with me. You know that I've worked for your father with all my strength, yet your father has cheated me by changing my wages ten times. However, God has not allowed him to harm me. If he said, 'The speckled ones will be your wages,' then all the flocks gave birth to speckled young; and if he said, 'The streaked ones will be your wages,' then all the flocks bore streaked young. So God has taken away your father's livestock and has given them to me.

"In breeding season I once had a dream in which I looked up and saw that the male goats mating with the flock were streaked, speckled or spotted. The angel of God said to me in the dream, 'Jacob.' I answered, 'Here I am.' And he said, 'Look up and see that all the male goats mating with the flock are streaked, speckled or spotted, for I have seen all that Laban has been doing to you. I am the God of Bethel, where you anointed a pillar and where you made a vow to me. Now leave this land at once and go back to your native land.'"

Then Rachel and Leah replied, "Do we still have any share in the inheritance of our father's estate? Does he not regard us as foreigners? Not only has he sold us, but he has used up what was paid for us. Surely all the wealth that God took away from our father belongs to us and our children. So do whatever God has told you." Then Jacob put his children and his wives on camels, and he drove all his livestock ahead of him, along with all the goods he had accumulated in Paddan Aram, to go to his father Isaac in the land of Canaan.

The Problem

~

Laban was cheating Jacob out of his proper wages and this was hindering Jacob from obeying God's instructions to go back home.

The Dreamers Metron

∼

Jacob had a powerful metron. He had inherited Abraham's large metron to bless all nations until the end of time. Jacob's metron also included him being the father of twelve sons who'd birth the twelve tribes of Israel.

After Jacob wrestled with God his name was changed to Israel and this became both the name of the people and the land. God told Jacob,

> I am the Lord, the God of your father Abraham and the God of Isaac. I will give you and your descendants the land on which you are lying. Your descendants will be like the dust of the earth, and you will spread out to the west and to the east, to the north and to the south. All peoples on earth will be blessed through you and your offspring. I am with you and will watch over you wherever you go, and I will bring you back to this land. I will not leave you until I have done what I have promised you.[2]

Jacob's metron also included his call to bring the children of Israel down to Egypt as promised to Abraham. This is what is being worked on in this dream.

The Message

God's first message to Jacob was, Go back to the land of your fathers and to your relatives, and I will be with you. We aren't told whether this simple direction came through a dream, a vision or a personal appearance but its message is clear enough. It was God's time for Jacob to go home.

God then sent a dream in which Jesus, as the Angel of the Lord, identified Himself as the God of Bethel to whom Jacob made a vow. Jesus explained He has seen Laban's unjust dealings. He also showed Jacob how He was going to remedy it. He then repeated the message for Jacob to return to his native land.

God's Purpose

God's purpose was to safely bring Jacob back to Canaan. His prophecy to Abraham of four hundred years of slavery was still pending and Jacob needed to be in the right place at the right time for the next stage of things.

God had also promised to care for and bless Jacob. God accomplishes this by the wealth transfer from Laban to Jacob. God often freed His people from bad economic situations and used the oppressors to bless them.

God was also demonstrating His sovereignty to Laban by thwarting all his scheming and by giving Laban's livestock to Jacob.

Satan's Purpose

Satan's purpose was to use Laban's fear and greed to stop Jacob following God's instructions.

Dreamer's Eyes Enlightened

∼

Jacob now had proof God keeps His promises no matter what the circumstances. In *Jacob's Covenant Dream* God had said He would continuously protect Jacob and bring him safely back to Canaan.

Jacob also learned God sees all things and can easily bring justice to unfair situations. Now it was Jacob's time to keep his promise and tithe to God.

Initially Jacob tried to help God's promise by some kind of sympathetic magic but afterwards he admits it was God who was in charge,

> If Laban would say this, "the speckled will be your pay," then all the flock gave birth to speckled. And if he would say this, "the streaked will be your pay," then all the flock gave birth to streaked.[3]

Dreamer's Response and Application

∼

Jacob believed Jesus' dream interpretation and negotiated a new contract with Laban on the basis of it. He also added some notions of his own as to how it all might work out. He separated the animals and used stripped sticks as some sort of supernatural aid to help the speckled animals produce speckled offspring. Jesus had not told Jacob to do this.

Later when he retells the dream to Leah and Rachel, Jacob admits it was God who was in control of the situation and it was God who took away Laban's flocks and gave them to him. Jacob didn't claim it was the stripped magic sticks that prospered him.

Know God Better

～

God was still keeping His covenantal promises and caring for His chosen people. He was shown as a God who sees all things and can rectify economic injustice. He knows the future and can share revelation in order to place His servants in the right place at the right time.

He can use dreams to help us prosper and succeed in any life situation so that we can obey His greater plans and purpose.

God also used circumstances to lead Jacob. Grace and favour were being removed and Laban's sons were bad mouthing Jacob. God used these changes to make it very uncomfortable for him to remain in Haran.

The Dream Process

～

Jesus appeared as the Angel of the Lord and interpreted the image of the streaked, speckled and spotted male goats mating with the flock. His interpretation said He was going to bring economic redress to Jacob through the unlikely event of multiplying the rare streaked, speckled and spotted animals. Through this piece of prophetic insider information Jesus imparted faith and knowledge so that Jacob could negotiate his unusual new contract with Laban.

Jacob both hears and sees in this dream. He hears God call his name. He hears God instructing him to look. He sees which goats are mating. He hears God tell him He is aware of Laban's economic unfairness. He hears the angel of the Lord - Jesus – identify himself as the God who appeared to him of Bethel. He also hears God instructing him to leave and return to his native land.

This is a symbolic dream that requires interpretation. Without Jesus' interpretation Jacob would not have known what the image of the animals meant. By identifying Himself as the God of Bethel, Jesus also reminded Jacob of the whole issue of Covenant.

This is an enlightening, instructional and directional dream in which Jesus appears and interprets a dream. It's a dream of personal and national and international importance.

The Usual Suspects

Jesus manifests as the Angel of the Lord and intervenes in order to move God's plans forward. The Holy Spirit is seen in the anointed pillar and God is the Covenant God to whom the Bethel vow had been made. Satan is behind Laban's hindering plans. The gods will also appear in the household idols stolen by Rachel as they leave.

Takeaways

This is the only dream in Scripture that Jesus personally interpreted. At the time of telling this dream Jacob had fathered eleven of his twelve sons. It'd be around seventeen more years before God sent Joseph two dreams that resulted in him ending up in Egypt and over thirty more years before God sent Pharaoh two dreams beginning a process that resulted in Israel going down to Egypt for those four hundred years as promised to Abraham.

In our study of Bible dreams we regularly see the truth of the scripture which says,

> And he who searches our hearts knows the mind of the Spirit, because the Spirit intercedes for God's people in accordance with the will of God. And we know that in all things God works for the good of those who love him, who have been called according to his purpose.[4]

This means although God's chosen individuals make many mistakes the Holy Spirit prays for God's will to come to pass in their lives. God then works their problems out in such a way they turn out for good for those who are aligned with God in implementing His plans and purpose.

This principle functions in Jacob's life which is fortunate because Jacob had finally met his match in wheeler-dealer, small empire builder, Laban.

Even though Jacob put on a strange display as regards the stripped sticks God still gave him fairness and blessed him. So I suppose it's quite possible for prophets to do some strange unnecessary things yet God is a promise keeper who can overlook and clear up foolishness.

LABAN'S 'DON'T HARM JACOB' DREAM

The Dream Setting/Backstory

The dream setting began twenty years previously when Jacob agreed with Laban to work seven years for Rachel. At the end of these seven years Laban tricked Jacob into marrying his older daughter Leah justifying his deceit by citing local custom.

He then offered another seven-year deal for Rachel. Fourteen years later Jacob wanted to go home but Laban insisted he stay. Laban had discovered through divination that his prosperity was linked to God blessing Jacob.

Laban played a major part in God's plans for Abraham's family line. He had a key role in arranging Isaac's marriage to his sister Rebecca and Rabbinic sources say he was the father of the concubines, Bilhah and Zilpah, whom Jacob also had children with. If that is true then this would make Laban, like Isaac, a grandfather of the Twelve Tribes of Israel.

Laban's biggest problem was his self-interest, which caused

trouble for others especially Jacob and Joseph. Had Jacob married Rachel first then Joseph would have been the rightful heir and the other brothers would have had no reason to be so jealous. This dream was given in the midst of an emotionally charged life-threatening situation.

The Dream Scripture
Genesis 31:19-30

∼

When Laban had gone to shear his sheep, Rachel stole her father's household gods. Moreover, Jacob deceived Laban the Aramean by not telling him he was running away. So he fled with all he had, crossed the Euphrates River, and headed for the hill country of Gilead. On the third day Laban was told that Jacob had fled. Taking his relatives with him, he pursued Jacob for seven days and caught up with him in the hill country of Gilead.

Then God came to Laban the Aramean in a dream at night and said to him, "Be careful not to say anything to Jacob, either good or bad."

Jacob had pitched his tent in the hill country of Gilead when Laban overtook him, and Laban and his relatives camped there too. Then Laban said to Jacob, "What have you done? You've deceived me, and you've carried off my daughters like captives in war. Why did you run off secretly and deceive me? Why didn't you tell me, so I could send you away with joy and singing to the music of timbrels and harps? You didn't even let me kiss my grandchildren and my daughters goodbye. You have done a foolish thing.

I have the power to harm you; but last night the God of your father said to me, 'Be careful not to say anything to Jacob, either good or bad.'

Now you have gone off because you longed to return to your father's household. But why did you steal my gods?"

The Problem

∽

Jacob had deceitfully fled with Laban's daughters, their children and possessions. This was a huge dishonour and loss for Laban who then chased after them with a posse. Jacob's lack of integrity put God's covenant with Abraham and Isaac under threat. It also placed Laban and his men in a dangerous situation with God for in threatening God's direction for Jacob's life they were in the perilous position of thwarting God's plans for His Messiah.

The Dreamer's Metron

∽

Laban was a natural family leader who first appeared as a spokesman for his father, Bethuel's, household. He was impressed by the golden jewellery gifted to his sister Rebecca from Isaac. He also played a key part in arranging their marriage.

Laban's motives were always about gaining advantage for his family and this often set him at cross purposes with God's plans. Laban is symbolic of a man who seeks first his own kingdom.

In trying to work a good arrangement for his daughter Leah he unwittingly hampered God's plan of Joseph being Jacob's rightful heir.

His concern over Jacob throwing away family safety in Aram for a risky prospect in the land of Canaan also put him in a position where he was opposing God's plans, this time for the Children of Israel to return to the Promised Land.

Nevertheless God used Laban's metron to provide safety, work and wives for Jacob.

God also chose Laban to be a grandfather of all the Twelve Patriarchs of Israel.

The Message

The message was clear enough Do not harm Jacob.

It's similar to God's previous warnings to Pharaoh and Abimelech, which were also essentially, Don't harm those I'm in covenant with.

God's words to Laban weren't as harsh as those He spoke to Abimelek - You are as good as dead - but the implication was the same. There was a real sense of threat to Laban and his relatives if they disobeyed God's command.

God's Purpose

God was moving Jacob to the geographical area he needed to be in for the next stage of God's purpose. He has used Laban to prosper Jacob and his seed line and now He is protecting Jacob and Laban and their households from death and destruction.

God is essentially keeping His covenant with Abraham, Isaac and Jacob, as he moves forward his prophetic word from Genesis 3 about Jesus, the Messiah, the seed of the woman.

Satan's Purpose

Satan's purpose was to harm everyone. He wanted Laban to harm Jacob and his family and divert them from God's plans for them to be back in the Promised Land. Satan used greed, fear, anger, mistrust, offence, conflict, strife and deceit in an attempt to accomplish this.

Dreamer's Eyes Enlightened

Laban clearly understands God in his graciousness is warning him in order to save his own life and many other lives.

Dreamers Response and Application

Like Pharaoh and Abimelek before him Laban quickly changes his mind and obeys God's instructions and in so doing averts God's judgment on himself and his people.

Like Pharaoh and Abimelek, Laban also rebukes Jacob for his cowardly behaviour but there's a hallow ring to his questioning of Jacob. After all Laban, Pharaoh and Abimelek had all the power in these interactions and apart from God's intervention they would probably have used that power to harm God's chosen people.

Know God Better

God is once again shown as a wise and gracious promise keeper. He was also merciful to Laban. God knew angry Laban planned to harm Jacob and He warned him of the consequences of his intended actions. God kindly brought life and peace instead of strife and death.

The Dream Process

This is a simple literal dream with the instructions, Be careful not to say anything to Jacob, either good or bad. This is obviously an idiomatic expression basically meaning, Don't pick a fight with Jacob. It's a warning dream with corrective instructions requiring an immediate response. It has personal, family, national and international implications.

The Usual Suspects

God speaks in this dream. Jesus the seed of the woman is there as regards the Covenant bloodline under threat. Satan is evident in Laban's deception and anger and Jacob's fear and deceit. The god's appear in the guise of the household gods being stolen by Rachel.

Takeaways

∽

God is protecting the Messiah's bloodline and keeping covenant. He speaks clearly to Laban and takes the heat out of the situation. God can and will protect us from our bad decisions because of his covenant relationship with us. A God dream can bring peace to a very volatile life-threatening situation and can calm any storm.

The story of Jacob and Laban echoes and mirrors Abraham's dream in which God said,

> Your seed shall be a stranger in a land that is not theirs,
> and shall serve them and they shall afflict them,
> afterward they shall come out with great wealth.[1]

Similarly Abraham's grandson Jacob lived in the strange land of Paddam Aram as an indentured servant to Laban and was unjustly afflicted before leaving with great wealth on his return to the Promised Land.

So, symbolically Jacob's trouble with Laban foreshadowed Israel's future enslavement with Egypt.

This constant cycle of exile, persecution and return to the Promised Land is a recurrent motif impacting Israel until this very day.

JACOB WRESTLES WITH GOD AND MAN

This foolish plan of God is wiser than the wisest of human plans, and God's weakness is stronger than the greatest of human strength. (1 Cor 1:25 (NLT)

The Incident Setting/Backstory

Ninety years previously God had prophesied to Rebecca her younger twin Jacob would prevail over his brother Esau the rightful heir by birth order. Eventually this led to a family split during which Esau threatened to murder Jacob. When seventy year old Jacob fled for his life he'd an encounter with God in a dream at Bethel in which God identified himself as the God of Abraham and Isaac. God said He would give Jacob's offspring the land of Canaan.

God also prophetically spoke of Jacob's descendant, Jesus Christ, who'd bless all nations. God promised Jacob, I am with you and will watch over you wherever you go, and I will bring you back to this land. I will not leave you until I have done what I have promised you.[1]

It's now time for God to keep His promise to bring Jacob back to the Promised Land but this puts Jacob in big life threatening trouble with both his uncle Laban and his brother Esau.

The Incident Scripture
Genesis 32:1-32

Jacob also went on his way, and the angels of God met him. When Jacob saw them, he said, This is the camp of God. So he named that place Mahanaim. Jacob sent messengers ahead of him to his brother Esau in the land of Seir, the country of Edom. He instructed them: "This is what you are to say to my lord Esau: 'Your servant Jacob says, I have been staying with Laban and have remained there till now. I have cattle and donkeys, sheep and goats, male and female servants. Now I am sending this message to my lord, that I may find favour in your eyes.

When the messengers returned to Jacob, they said, We went to your brother Esau, and now he is coming to meet you, and four hundred men are with him.

In great fear and distress Jacob divided the people who were with him into two groups and the flocks and herds and camels as well. He thought, If Esau comes and attacks one group, the group that is left may escape.

Then Jacob prayed, "O God of my father Abraham, God of my father Isaac, Lord, you who said to me, 'Go back to your country and your relatives, and I will make you prosper,' I am unworthy of all the kindness and faithfulness you have shown your servant. I had only my staff when I crossed this Jordan, but now I have become two camps. Save me, I pray, from the hand of my brother Esau, for I am afraid he will come and attack me, and also the mothers with their children. But you have said, 'I will surely make you prosper and will make your descendants like the sand of the sea, which cannot be counted.'"

He spent the night there, and from what he had with him he selected a gift for his brother Esau: two hundred female goats and twenty male goats, two hundred ewes and twenty rams, thirty female camels with their young, forty cows and ten bulls, and twenty female donkeys and ten male donkeys. He put them in the care of his servants, each herd by itself, and said to his servants, "Go ahead of me, and keep some space between the herds."

He instructed the one in the lead: "When my brother Esau meets you and asks, 'Who do you belong to, and where are you going, and who owns all these animals in front of you?' then you are to say, 'They belong to your servant Jacob. They are a gift sent to my lord Esau, and he is coming behind us.'"

He also instructed the second, the third and all the others who followed the herds: "You are to say the same thing to Esau when you meet him. And be sure to say, 'Your servant Jacob is coming behind us.'" For he thought, "I will pacify him with these gifts I am sending on ahead; later, when I see him, perhaps he will receive me." So Jacob's gifts went on ahead of him, but he himself spent the night in the camp.

That night Jacob got up and took his two wives, his two female servants and his eleven sons and crossed the ford of the Jabbok. After he had sent them across the stream, he sent over all his possessions. So Jacob was left alone, and a man wrestled with him till daybreak. When the man saw that he could not overpower him, he touched the socket of Jacob's hip so that his hip was wrenched as he wrestled with the man. Then the man said, "Let me go, for it is daybreak."

But Jacob replied, "I will not let you go unless you bless me."

The man asked him, "What is your name?"

"Jacob," he answered.

Then the man said, "Your name will no longer be Jacob, but Israel, because you have struggled with God and with humans and have overcome."

Jacob said, "Please tell me your name."

But he replied, "Why do you ask my name?" Then he blessed him there.

So Jacob called the place Peniel, saying, "It is because I saw God face to face, and yet my life was spared."

The sun rose above him as he passed Peniel, and he was limping because of his hip. Therefore to this day the Israelites do not eat the tendon attached to the socket of the hip, because the socket of Jacob's hip was touched near the tendon.

The Problem

∼

Jacob just newly delivered from the threat of Laban and his armed men now learns his brother Esau is rushing towards him with four hundred armed men. This frightening news causes Jacob to intercede with the God of his fathers.

The Dreamer's Metron

∼

Jacob was Abraham's inheritor and the father of the leaders of the twelve tribes of Israel. After this incident of Jacob wrestling with

God his name was changed to Israel and this became both the name of the people and the land of God's chosen people.

> God told Jacob, I am the Lord, the God of your father Abraham and the God of Isaac. I will give you and your descendants the land on which you are lying. Your descendants will be like the dust of the earth, and you will spread out to the west and to the east, to the north and to the south. All peoples on earth will be blessed through you and your offspring. I am with you and will watch over you wherever you go, and I will bring you back to this land. I will not leave you until I have done what I have promised you.[2]

Jacob's metron also included his call to bring the children of Israel down to Egypt God as promised to Abraham.

The Message

The overall message of this incident is that God is keeping His promises to Jacob. When Jacob meets the company of angels he is reminded of the Bethel dream encounter and realises his camp is protected by God's camp, so he names the place Mahanaim, a Hebrew word meaning, two camps.

The main message is, God blesses you and your name will no longer be Jacob, but Israel, because you have struggled with God and with humans and have overcome.

God's Purpose

God was protecting Jacob and his seed line. God's purpose was also to convince Jacob He was able to keep His covenant promises. God was also testing Jacob's faith and perseverance in the midst of this incredibly pressurised situation.

As a reward for his tenacity Jacob receives a new name. Jesus who wrestles with him says he will no longer be called Jacob, meaning supplanter, but Israel, meaning, he struggles with God. Hosea later mentions this,

> In the womb he grasped his brother's heel; as a man he struggled with God. He struggled with the angel and overcame him; he wept and begged for his favour.[3]

A biblical name change is significant and signifies a new position with God and an increased level of faith. Abram was renamed Abraham meaning, father of nations. Sarai was renamed Sarah meaning princess. Simon was renamed Peter meaning rock and in Revelation one of the promises to the overcomer is a new name known only to the person who receives it.

After wrestling with God Jacob is a changed man, spiritually and physically. His famous limp is not so much a sign of God's discipline but a mark of faith and perseverance. His new name Israel was also inherited by his descendants who became know as the people of Israel and their Promised Land became Israel.

Satan's Purpose

Satan's plan was to hinder God's purpose by stirring up old wounds and animosities between Jacob and his brother Esau. He wanted to destroy the Messiah's bloodline. Satan's influence is also apparent in Jacob's fear and his gift giving and scheming.

Dreamer's Eyes Enlightened

Jacob is humbler and more committed than he was twenty years previously at Bethel. This life threatening incident has made him an intercessor. He finally realises all his wheeling and dealing and scheming is useless. He needs God's help.

He recognises his own unworthiness and reminds God of his obedience in returning to Canaan. Like a true intercessor he also reminds God of His promises,

> But you have said, I will surely make you prosper and
> will make your descendants like the sand of the sea,
> which cannot be counted.[4]

Dreamer's Response and Application

Jacob always sought and fought to be blessed. He persisted until he received his father's blessing unlike Esau who threw it away lightly for a bowl of stew. Revelation 3:15 says,

> I know your deeds, that you are neither cold nor hot. I
> wish you were either one or the other!

Jacob was always hot. He wrestled with Jesus all night and wouldn't let Him go until He blessed him. This tenacity in Jacob pleased God. Jeremiah said, You will seek me and find me when you seek me with all your heart.[5]

Jacob would have made a good Charismatic. Paul told the Corinthians, Covet earnestly the best gifts.[6] The word covet here has the meaning of lusting after something in a good way. Jacob always lusted after God's blessing.

He also finally understood God is able to do exceedingly abundantly above all that we ask or think. Jacob celebrated by calling the place Peniel, which means Face of God. He said, It is because I saw God face to face, and yet my life was spared.

Know God Better

We again see God as a Promise Keeping, Covenant Keeping God. An ever present help in times of trouble. A rewarder of those who diligently seek him.

The Incident Process

Jacob literally wrestles with Jesus and physically has his hip displaced. This incident is also symbolic of the nation of Israel, which is always wrestling with man and God. It has personal, national and international significance.

The Usual Suspects

∼

God is in the form of Jesus wrestling with Jacob and blessing him. Satan is there in the background opening up old wounds and animosities and causing fear in an attempt to kill the Messiah's bloodline.

Takeaways

∼

God will not test us beyond our endurance but will send us a way of escape. Yet God's testing can be fierce causing great distress and anxiety.

God knows the future and God keeps His promises. His words to Rebecca, Abraham, Isaac and Jacob were all fulfilled.

God is again seen as advancing His plans and purpose for the Messiah.

THE ERA OF THE DREAM INTERPRETER

When Jesus as the Angel of the Lord interpreted *Jacob's 'Goats and Go Back Home' Dream* He released what might be called, the era of the dream interpreter. Before this dream all dreamers understood their dreams at least to a level where they could quickly respond and apply the dream message.

God came to the non-Jews, Abimelek and Laban in simple literal dreams without any symbolism. We're not told whether these dreamers actually saw God or not. If they saw God then it would have been an appearance of Jesus.

The Jews on the other hand, all had dreams containing some degree of symbolism signalling deeper things. Abraham's covenant dream took place during a God induced deep sleep in the midst of thick and dreadful darkness when a smoking firepot with a blazing torch appeared and passed between pieces of dead birds and animals.

Jacob's covenant dream had God standing at the top of a heavenly stairway with angels ascending and descending. This was not fully understood or interpreted by Jacob who never knew the stairway was Jesus.

But Jacob's dream about goats required proper interpretation concerning the streaked, speckled and spotted goats mating.

Joseph's first two dreams required dream interpretation and although Jacob and his sons understood the gist of these dreams they also missed much of significance. Yet Jacob did correctly interpret Joseph's second dream. Pharaoh's dreams also required a dream interpreter and the intervention of God before their message was revealed.

Afterwards the vast majority of Old Testament dreams required some degree of interpretation in order to be understood.

With the arrival of Jesus as dream interpreter there was an immediate shift from open literal dreams to hidden symbolic dreams. It's as if Proverbs 25:2 kicked in,

> It is the glory of God to conceal a matter; to search out
> a matter is the glory of kings.

Now God's plans and purposes began to be concealed in parables, allegories, metaphors, similitudes, symbolism, typology, analogy and so on. This mainly continued throughout the rest of Scripture in dreams, visions and prophecy and especially in the parables of Jesus.

God's valuable hidden messages now required a seeking heart for an interpretation. The lukewarm and lazy remained ignorant. It's the same today.

We have no way of knowing if any New Testament dream required interpretation for we're never given any details of their content. We only know all New Testament dreamers always understood the meaning of their dreams.

In the New Testament it was the parables of Jesus that required interpretation. While Jesus walked the earth it was a parable interpreter and not a dream interpreter that was required.

JOSEPH'S 'SHEAVES OF GRAIN' DREAM

The Dream Setting/Backstory

Satan tried to mess up God's plans and purpose big time through Laban's self interest. Laban's daughter Rachel was God's divinely intended first wife for Jacob and Joseph was God's intended heir. Weak eyed Leah on the other hand was the result of Laban's greedy scheming.

Had Jacob not been tricked into marrying Leah he'd have married Rachel first and Joseph would've been his eldest son and rightful heir. Then no one would have objected to Joseph wearing his special long sleeved coat of many colours that identified him as Jacob's inheritor.

At the time of these dreams Jacob was 108 years old, Joseph was 17 and his brothers were all under 30. This was not exactly a very mature age for men at that time, considering Jacob was well over seventy before he married. In one sense the brothers' response to

Joseph's dreams was just the annoyance of immature teenagers. On the other hand their jealous hatred seemed demonically inspired.

The Dream Scripture
Genesis 37:1-17

∼

Jacob lived in the land where his father had stayed, the land of Canaan. This is the account of Jacob's family line. Joseph, a young man of seventeen, was tending the flocks with his brothers, the sons of Bilhah and the sons of Zilpah, his father's wives, and he brought their father a bad report about them. Now Israel loved Joseph more than any of his other sons, because he had been born to him in his old age; and he made an ornate robe for him. When his brothers saw that their father loved him more than any of them, they hated him and could not speak a kind word to him.

Joseph had a dream, and when he told it to his brothers, they hated him all the more. He said to them, "Listen to this dream I had: We were binding sheaves of grain out in the field when suddenly my sheaf rose and stood upright, while your sheaves gathered around mine and bowed down to it." His brothers said to him, "Do you intend to reign over us? Will you actually rule us?" And they hated him all the more because of his dream and what he had said.

The Problem

∼

God had sovereignly chosen Joseph to play a major part in implementing His plans for Abraham's descendants. This was resisted at every turn by Satan. Now God is revealing and advancing His plans through a dream and Satan and the brothers are not happy. The brothers hated Joseph because he was favoured by their father, Jacob. Problem was, Joseph was also favoured by God.

The Dreamer's Metron

Joseph was a prophet with a powerful metron concerning dreams and visions. His brothers mockingly called him a master of dreamers and that is what he actually was. When the magicians and wise men of Egypt couldn't interpret Pharaoh's dreams, Joseph with God's help was able to do so.

Afterwards God used Joseph to prepare a place of safety and provision for the children of Israel in Egypt so that the Messiah's royal seed line would be preserved.

God chose Joseph to be the heir of His covenant promises with Abraham, Isaac and Jacob. 1 Chronicles 5:1-2 says, The rights of the firstborn belonged to Joseph.

Laban's deceit in marrying Leah off to Jacob meant God's plans for Joseph to be the firstborn were threatened. This caused bad blood between Joseph and his older brothers but God used Joseph's dreams to put things back on track.

Joseph correctly understood his dreams meant his family would one day be dependant on him and humbled before him. This knowledge must have sustained him during the next thirteen years when he was bought and sold five times.

Through Joseph God was working His purpose out concerning the Messiah and keeping his covenant promises to Abraham.

The Message

The simple overall message of this dream is that God would restore Joseph to his proper place as inheritor and leader in the family. The symbolism of the grain foreshadows the time when the brothers will bow down before Joseph begging for grain. God would then place Joseph in a position where he would rule over the lives of his entire family and the entire people of Israel.

God's Purpose

In this dream God was encouraging and guiding His covenant people with specific direction for their well-being and the safety of their seed line but they didn't understand this. God's purpose was also to set the record straight and restore Joseph back to God's intended place for him as inheritor of the Covenant.

Joseph's dreams were never intended by God to be kept private. God had his own reason in compelling Joseph to speak. God was working out the next phase of His plans and purpose for the Messiah, His chosen people and the Promised Land. God was moving Joseph forward to his place of destiny and greatest ministry.

God was also exposing the hearts of Joseph's brothers.

Satan's Purpose

Satan was still trying to stop the Messiah's arrival. He did his damnedest to kill Joseph. He incensed Joseph's brothers to murder him so Joseph's dreams would never come to pass.

> Here comes that dreamer! they said to each other.
> Come now, let's kill him and throw him into one of these cisterns and say that a ferocious animal devoured him. Then we'll see what comes of his dreams.[1]

Satan's effort to remove Joseph was really an attempt to thwart God's plans and change the future. The brothers' reaction to Joseph's dreams is like the response of many Christians and non-Christians when they hear about God's sovereignty.

Many of us don't like it when we realise God is sovereign over our lives. He is sovereign to create us, sovereign to choose us, sovereign to save us and sovereign to condemn us.

The natural man hates that God has such power. Rebellious man wants to plan his own future. Nowadays he even wants to choose whether he should actually be a man or a woman. He scorns God's authority and challenges God's fairness and purpose.

Like Satan, he screams, I will have my own free will.

Dreamer's Eyes Enlightened

Joseph correctly understood the dream meant his family would one day be dependant on him and humbled before him in the future. This knowledge would have stayed with him during the next thirteen years when he was being bought and sold as a slave five times.

These dreams prepared and encouraged Joseph for the difficult days ahead.

Dreamer's Response and Application

∼

Unlike Mary who kept all things in her heart, Joseph shared his dreams with his father and brothers. Perhaps this family regularly shared their dreams with one another.

After all Joseph's father Jacob was a big dreamer who most likely would have shared the importance of his and Abraham's dreams with his family.

It's always been a common thing for my own large family to share and interpret our dreams around our meal table.

Joseph's response was to believe and share his dreams. This had a huge effect on his father and brothers. His father pondered them as future prophetic events that might impact his family.

The brothers were incensed. They mocked him. They said, Here comes the dreamer. The word used here is chalown which means master of dreams. They knew Joseph was a dreamer with a gift of dream interpretation.

Know God Better

∼

God is again seen as a promise keeper and a God of justice who can restore people and things to their proper place in His greater plans and purpose. Here once again God is working things out for the good of those who love him, who have been called according to his purpose.[2]

Sovereign God sees what's coming and often prepares us for it through dreams. Joseph is being shown no matter what happens in the future God is with him working His purposes out.

The Dream Process

On one level this is a simple symbolic dream, not particularly difficult to interpret. On another level it is an incredible prophetic dream that requires a good knowledge of Scripture in order to understand it better.

The brothers and Jacob both get the general gist of the dream. The brothers understand the dream but because hatred had darkened their minds they questioned Joseph's motives. They said, Do you intend to reign over us? Will you actually rule us?

The deeper spiritual truth was that God intended Joseph to rule over them in order to save their lives and the lives of their families and to bring His greater plans and purpose to come to pass for their nation and all nations. Their interpretation was clouded by jealousy and too narrow in scope.

This dream also foreshadowed Jesus who will be loved by His Father and rejected by His brothers whom He will finally save.

The Usual Suspects

God through this dream is working His Covenant plans and purpose out and is working all things together for good. Satan is enflaming the jealous brothers to kill Joseph and thereby change the future and prevent the Messiah from coming to crush his head.

Jesus, the bread of life, is prophetically in this dream. He is the sheaf of grain that will be bowed down before and worshipped by his brothers the Jewish people when they finally recognise and accept Him.

Takeaways

~

This dream kickstarts a series of incidents in which Joseph will be bought and sold five times. This process will bring Joseph to his preplanned place in God's plans and purpose prophesied to Abraham in his dream.

Through Joseph's two dreams God redressed Laban's manipulative actions that thwarted His plans for Joseph. The Bible records this setting of the record straight. It says,

> The sons of Reuben the firstborn of Israel (he was the firstborn, but when he defiled his father's marriage bed, his rights as firstborn were given to the sons of Joseph son of Israel; so he could not be listed in the genealogical record in accordance with his birthright, and though Judah was the strongest of his brothers and a ruler came from him, the rights of the firstborn belonged to Joseph).[3]

Joseph was the voice of God to his family and Israel through his dreams. His two simple dreams tested their hearts and motives. The brothers who already hated Joseph because their father treated him as his heir became even more jealous.

Jacob tried to keep the peace by rebuking Joseph but knew there was something of deeper significance in Joseph's dreams for his family's future.

God is not mentioned in either of these dreams but God is clearly working out His sovereign purpose through Joseph in the midst of great hostility and bitterness. When things were at their worse God was still in control. Even though Joseph would suffer thirteen years of exile and hardship there was nothing Satan or man could do to stop God's plans and purpose coming to pass. Psalm 105 says,

> He sent a man before them, even Joseph, who was sold for a servant: Whose feet they hurt with fetters: he was laid in irons: Until the time that his word came to pass, the word of the Lord tested him.[4]

In this verse the dreams from God are called the word of the Lord. It was the dreams, as the word of God, that tested Joseph.

The word of God is vitally important to a believer. Jesus told Satan, Man shall not live on bread alone, but on every word that comes from the mouth of God.[5]

Paul said, So then faith comes by hearing, and hearing by the word of God.[6]

A dream from God is a word from God.

It can sustain us, like Joseph, through many years.

A dream as the word of God also produces faith and faith leads to action. God often conveys His plans and purposes to us through dreams as His word.

When we receive and understand the message of God's word we receive faith to be God's representatives in bringing to pass His specific communicated plans and purpose.

JOSEPH'S 'SUN, MOON AND STARS' DREAM

The Dream Setting/Backstory

Satan tried to mess up God's plans and purpose big time through Laban's self interest. Laban's daughter Rachel was God's divinely intended first wife for Jacob and Joseph was God's intended heir. Weak eyed Leah on the other hand was the result of Laban's greedy scheming.

Had Jacob not been tricked into marrying Leah he'd have married Rachel first and Joseph would've been his eldest son and rightful heir. Then no one would have objected to Joseph wearing his special long sleeved coat of many colours that identified him as Jacob's inheritor.

At the time of these dreams Jacob was 108 years old, Joseph was 17 and his brothers were all under 30. This was not exactly a very mature age for men at that time, considering Jacob was well into his seventies before he married. In one sense the brothers' response to Joseph's dreams was just the annoyance of immature teenagers. On the other hand their hatred seemed demonically deep rooted. This dream came shortly after *Joseph's 'Sheaves of Grain' Dream*.

The Dream Scripture

∼

Then he had another dream, and he told it to his brothers. "Listen," he said, "I had another dream, and this time the sun and moon and eleven stars were bowing down to me." When he told his father as well as his brothers, his father rebuked him and said, "What is this dream you had? Will your mother and I and your brothers actually come and bow down to the ground before you?" His brothers were jealous of him, but his father kept the matter in mind.

The Problem

∼

God is setting the stage for the next part of his plans and purposes for Israel. These are the plans God shared with Abraham in *Abraham's Covenant Dream* but neither Joseph nor his father or brothers seem aware of this. In God's plans and purpose Abraham's descendants will spend four hundred years as slaves in Egypt. God sends these two dreams to kickstart the next phase of things.

The Dreamer's Metron

∼

Joseph was a prophet with a powerful metron concerning dreams and visions. His brothers mockingly called him a Master of Dreamers and that is what he actually was. When the magicians and wise men of Egypt couldn't interpret Pharaoh's dreams, Joseph with God's help was able to do so.

Afterwards God used Joseph to prepare a place of safety and provision for the children of Israel in Egypt so that the Messiah's royal seed line would be preserved.

God chose Joseph to be the heir of His Covenant promises with Abraham, Isaac and Jacob. 1 Chronicles 5:1-2 says, The rights of the firstborn belonged to Joseph.

Laban's deceit in marrying Leah off to Jacob meant God's plans for Joseph to be the firstborn were threatened. This caused bad blood between Joseph and his older brothers but God used Joseph's dreams to put things back on track.

Joseph correctly understood his dreams meant his family would one day be dependant on him and humbled before him. This knowledge must have sustained him during the next thirteen years when he was bought and sold five times.

Through Joseph's life God was working his purposes out concerning the Messiah and keeping his Covenant promises to Abraham.

The Message

The simple message of Joseph's two dreams is that God would restore Joseph to his proper place as inheritor and leader in the family. The symbolism of the grain in the first dream foreshadows the time when the brothers will bow down before Joseph begging for grain. God would then place Joseph in a position where he would rule over the lives of his family and the entire people of Israel.

In Joseph's second dream Jacob correctly interprets, (even though his wife was dead), that he was the sun, his wife was the moon, and his twelve children were the stars. Symbolically Abraham and Sarah are Israel's parents. Isaiah told Israel to,

> Look to the rock from which you were cut and to the quarry from which you were hewn; look to Abraham, your father, and to Sarah, who gave you birth.[1]

In *The Book of Revelation*, Israel is similarly symbolically shown as a woman clothed with the sun and moon and wearing a crown of stars.[2]

God's Purpose

In this dream God was encouraging and guiding His Covenant People with specific direction for their well-being and the safety of their seed line but they didn't understand it. God's purpose was also to set the record straight and bring Joseph back to God's intended place for him as inheritor of the Covenant.

Joseph's dreams were never intended by God to be kept private. God had his own reason in compelling Joseph to speak. God was working out the next phase of His plans and purposes for the Messiah, His chosen people and the Promised Land. God was moving Joseph forward to his place of destiny and greatest ministry.

Satan's Purpose

Satan was still trying to stop the Messiah's coming. He did his damnedest to kill Joseph. He incensed Joseph's brothers to murder him so Joseph's dreams would never come to pass.

> Here comes that dreamer! they said to each other.
> Come now, let's kill him and throw him into one of these cisterns and say that a ferocious animal devoured him. Then we'll see what comes of his dreams.[3]

Satan's effort to remove Joseph was really an attempt to thwart God's plans and change the future. The brothers' reaction to Joseph's dreams is like the response of most people when they hear about God's sovereignty.

Many of us don't like it when we realise God is sovereign over our lives. He is sovereign to create us, sovereign to choose us, sovereign to save us and sovereign to condemn us.

The natural man hates that God has such power. Rebellious man wants to plan his own future.

Nowadays he even wants to choose whether he should actually be a man or a woman. He scorns God's authority and challenges God's fairness and purposes. He screams, I will have my own free will.

Dreamer's Eyes Enlightened

Joseph correctly understood the dream meant his family would one day be dependant on him and humbled before him in the future.

This knowledge would have stayed with him during the next thirteen years when he was being bought and sold as a slave five times. These dreams prepared and encouraged Joseph for the difficult days ahead.

Dreamer's Response and Application

Unlike Mary who kept all things in her heart, Joseph perhaps unwisely shared these two dreams with his father and brothers. On the other hand, maybe this family regularly shared their dreams with one another. It's always been normal for my own family to share and interpret our dreams around our meal table.

After all Joseph's father Jacob was a big dreamer who most likely would've shared the importance of his and Abraham's dreams with his family.

Joseph's response was to believe and share his dreams. This had a huge effect on his father and brothers. His father wisely pondered them as possible future prophetic events that might impact his family.

The brothers were incensed. They mocked him. They said, Here comes the dreamer. The word used here is chalown which means master of dreams. They knew Joseph was a dreamer with a gift of dream interpretation and they didn't like it.

Know God Better

God is again seen as a Promise Keeper and a God of justice who can restore people and things to their proper place in His greater plans and purpose. Here once again God is working for the good of those who love him, who have been called according to his purpose.[4]

Sovereign God sees the future and often prepares us for it through dreams. Joseph is being shown no matter what happens in the future God is with him working His purposes out.

The Dream Process

On one level both of Josephs dreams are the same dream. They are simple symbolic dreams, not particularly difficult to interpret. On another level they are incredible prophetic dreams that require a good knowledge of scripture in order to understand.

The brothers understood Joseph's dreams on a very superficial level and wrongly and partially interpreted them through their dark cloud of hatred. This made them question Joseph's motives. They said, Do you intend to reign over us? Will you actually rule us?

The deeper spiritual truth was that God intended Joseph to rule over them in order to save their lives and the lives of their families and to bring God's greater plans and purposes to come to pass for their nation.

This second dream about the sun and moon and eleven stars bowing down to Joseph, (the twelfth star) was again generally understood by the brothers and Jacob. The brothers responded by adding jealously to their hatred while Jacob, who well understood that a dream can change one's fortune, pondered the matter.

Jacob better interprets the dream. He realises it's a prophetic dream about him and his family being dependant on Joseph and humbled before him.

Though I don't think he saw the full significance of the sun, the moon and the stars as being the foundation of Israel that was as glorious at the heavenly bodies that brought light and time onto the earth. Similarly Israel would bring the light of the Gospel of Jesus Christ to the whole world.

There is also possibly another level of meaning to the sun, moon and stars imagery. It can mean the gods of other nations. Moses warned Israel,

> And when you look up to the sky and see the sun, the moon and the stars—all the heavenly array—do not be enticed into bowing down to them and worshiping things the Lord your God has apportioned to all the nations under heaven.[5]

On this level, the sun, moon and stars imagery could also represent Egypt's gods who will bow down before Joseph because he is able to interpret Pharaoh's dreams and they are not. All of Egypt would also bow down to Joseph in order to receive food during their time of famine. On another level Joseph is a type of Jesus Christ. Prophetically the dream also speaks about all creation bowing down before Jesus.

The Usual Suspects

∼

God through His dreams to Joseph is working His Covenant plans and purpose out and is working all things together for good. Satan is enflaming the jealous brothers to kill Joseph and thereby change the future and prevent the Messiah from coming to crush his head. Jesus is prophetically in the dreams. He is the sheaf of grain that will be worshipped by His brothers the Jewish people when they finally recognise Him. He is also the One to whom all creation and all gods will eventually bow down to as represented by the sun, moon and stars.

Takeaways

~

In Deuteronomy Moses warns Israel against idolatry. He says,

> And when you look up to the sky and see the sun, the moon and the stars—all the heavenly array—do not be enticed into bowing down to them and worshiping things the Lord your God has apportioned to all the nations under heaven. But as for you, the Lord took you and brought you out of the iron-smelting furnace, out of Egypt, to be the people of his inheritance, as you now are.[6]

In the above scripture Israel is warned never to worship other gods, not because other gods don't exist, but because God Almighty has decided to take complete personal responsibility for ruling Israel Himself.

The other gods would rule the rest of the world's nations.

Joseph's two dreams have a major prophetic significance for the Messiah of whom Joseph is a type. In this sense Joseph's dreams symbolise the day when the crucified Messiah Jesus Christ, the man of sorrows who was despised and rejected of men[7] and who was rejected by his brothers in the nation of Israel will be recognised and received by those who once destained him.

The heart-breaking event in Genesis 45 when Joseph was

revealed and reconciled to his brothers who had hated and rejected him will be played out once again between Jesus and the saved remnant of Israel on the day when God, will pour out on the house of David and the inhabitants of Jerusalem a spirit of grace and supplication. Scripture says,

> They will look on me, the one they have pierced, and they will mourn for him as one mourns for an only child, and grieve bitterly for him as one grieves for a firstborn son.[8]

> The Lord God shall give Him the throne of His father David, and He shall reign over the house of Jacob forever, and of His kingdom there shall be no end.[9]

PHARAOH'S CUPBEARER'S DREAM

The Dream Setting/Backstory

Pharaoh's cupbearer and baker were in the same prison as Joseph awaiting judgement for offending and angering their powerful master. Joseph was serving them. One night they both had a dream concerning their respective metrons.

The Dream Scripture
Genesis 40:1-13

Some time later, the cupbearer and the baker of the king of Egypt offended their master, the king of Egypt. Pharaoh was angry with his two officials, the chief cupbearer and the chief baker, and put them in custody in the house of the captain of the guard, in the same prison where Joseph was confined. The captain of the guard assigned them to Joseph, and he attended them.

After they had been in custody for some time, each of the two men—the cupbearer and the baker of the king of Egypt, who were being held in prison—had a dream the same night, and each dream had a meaning of its own. When Joseph came to them the next morning, he saw that they were dejected. So he asked Pharaoh's officials who were in custody with him in his master's house, "Why do you look so sad today?" "We both had dreams," they answered, "but there is no one to interpret them." Then Joseph said to them, "Do not interpretations belong to God? Tell me your dreams."

So the chief cupbearer told Joseph his dream. He said to him, "In my dream I saw a vine in front of me, and on the vine were three branches. As soon as it budded, it blossomed, and its clusters ripened into grapes. Pharaoh's cup was in my hand, and I took the grapes, squeezed them into Pharaoh's cup and put the cup in his hand."

"This is what it means," Joseph said to him. "The three branches are three days. Within three days Pharaoh will lift up your head and restore you to your position, and you will put Pharaoh's cup in his hand, just as you used to do when you were his cupbearer. But when all goes well with you, remember me and show me kindness; mention me to Pharaoh and get me out of this prison.

The Problem

∼

God was moving His agenda for Joseph forward. He used the cupbearer's life and death dream to kickstart this process. Like the rest of Egypt the cupbearer and the baker believed Pharaoh was a god, the reincarnation of the Egyptian god Horus. To have angered such a god man who wielded absolute power over his subjects was no small thing.

The Dreamer's Metron

∽

The cupbearer's influential metron was that of a high-ranking officer serving drinks in Pharaoh's court. He had to be completely trustworthy because his most important role was to guard against Pharaoh being poisoned.

To this end he was often required to swallow some of the drinks before serving them. This intimate relationship and proximity to Pharaoh placed the cupbearer in a position of great influence.

When Pharaoh was troubled by his dreams, after his magicians and wise men couldn't interpret them, God used the cupbearer to speak well of Joseph to Pharaoh and thereby give him access to Pharaoh

The Message

∽

Joseph's clear interpretation was that Pharaoh would forgive and reinstate the cupbearer to his former position within three days.

God's Purpose

∽

God's purpose was to raise Joseph to a position of influence within Egypt so Joseph could advance God's plans and purpose. Consequently God gave an unforgettable experience to the cupbearer. His testimony was told to Pharaoh when God's timing was right.

God was still firmly focused on keeping His promises to Abraham and bringing forth the Messiah. This is the first in a series of dreams God uses to bring Joseph to a position of national prominence in Egypt in order to fulfil Joseph's previous two prophetic dreams and to bring about God's prophesy in Abraham's dream which said,

> Know for certain that for four hundred years your descendants will be strangers in a country not their own and that they will be enslaved and mistreated there. But I will punish the nation they serve as slaves, and afterward they will come out with great possessions.[1]

Satan's Purpose

Joseph had always been a target for Satan who wanted him dead. He'd tried to rob Joseph's birthright by making Jacob marry Leah first. He caused Joseph's brothers to be jealous enough to nearly kill Joseph and ultimately sell him into slavery.

Satan also filled Potiphar's wife with lust and lies that landed Joseph in prison. Satan was also probably trying to kill the cupbearer and the baker just because he was a murderer from the beginning. God worked all these bad situations for good and used them to further His plans to bring Jacob and his family down to Egypt.

Dreamer's Eyes Enlightened

∽

Within three days the relieved cupbearer realised Joseph's God had given him a correct interpretation to his dream.

Dreamer's Response and Application

∽

The dreamer didn't have any part whatsoever in bringing the dream to pass. This dream as the word of God was like the seed that fell on rocky ground. The cupbearer received it with joy but having no root soon forgot all about his promise to Joseph. Like the nine lepers healed by Jesus he never thought to be thankful. He forgot all about it and quickly returned to his old way of life.

Know God Better

∽

God is again seen as a dependable promise keeper who can work all things together for good for those who are called according to his purposes.[2] He used this dream incident with the cupbearer to further His own plans and purpose and to bless His faithful servant Joseph.

The Dream Process

Joseph acknowledged God as the Divine Dream Interpreter and immediately gave a succinct correct interpretation to this complex symbolic dream referring specifically to the dreamer's metron.

Using the *The Symbol Replacement Method* he revealed the three branches are three days and interprets the squeezing of grapes into Pharaoh's cup as the cupbearer's former work situation being restored. There's a bustling sense of new life bursting forth throughout this dream.

With hindsight the dream also seems to contain symbolic reference to the coming Messiah. We now know Jesus referred to himself as the true vine. We also know Jesus arose from the dead after three days and we know his blood has been poured out as a sin offering, a drink offering for all nations.

So, on a symbolic level the cupbearer's dream could represent Christ's sacrificial offering that freed sinners from Satan's power and the prison of their transgressions. The vine then represents the true vine, Jesus Christ. The cupbearer squeezed the fruit of the vine into the royal cup, and brought it to his lord for acceptance. This prophetically speaks of the shed blood of Jesus before the Father.

The cupbearer's goblet of crushed grapes reminds us of Jesus who before the crucifixion fell with his face to the ground and prayed, My Father, if it is possible, may this cup be taken from me. Yet not as I will, but as you will.[3]

Unlike the cupbearer Jesus had to die but in three days like the three vine branches He rose again. Jesus had also refered back to Abraham when He says, This cup which is poured out for you is the new covenant in My blood.[4]

Today, this new covenant in Jesus blood continually bursts forth with new life all over the world resulting in 200,000 new believers daily.

The Usual Suspects

∽

Joseph says God is the One who interprets dreams. It was Satan that caused Potiphar's wife to lust after Joseph and tell lies that landed him in prison. Jesus is seen in the image of the vine, the three days of resurrection and the cup of blessing.

Takeaways

∽

This is the first time in Scripture God uses dream interpretation as a means of placing His servants into positions of power in a world government.

God will again use this same strategy with Daniel in Babylon over twelve hundred years later.

Jesus is the same yesterday, today and forever so no doubt some Christian master dream interpreters will find themselves in similar circumstances in future.

That God can work all things together for good is again apparent. We are also beginning to see how dreams can impact and save nations.

PHARAOH'S BAKER'S DREAM

The Dream Setting/Backstory

*P*haraoh's cupbearer and baker were in prison awaiting judgement for offending and their powerful master. One night they both had a dream concerning their respective metrons. Joseph who was serving them has just given an encouraging interpretation to the cupbearer.

The Dream Scripture
(Genesis 40:16-23)

When the chief baker saw that Joseph had given a favourable interpretation, he said to Joseph,

"I too had a dream: On my head were three baskets of bread. In the top basket were all kinds of baked goods for Pharaoh, but the birds were eating them out of the basket on my head."

"This is what it means," Joseph said. "The three baskets are three days. Within three days Pharaoh will lift off your head and impale your body on a pole. And the birds will eat away your flesh."

Now the third day was Pharaoh's birthday, and he gave a feast for all his officials. He lifted up the heads of the chief cupbearer and the chief baker in the presence of his officials: He restored the chief cupbearer to his position, so that he once again put the cup into Pharaoh's hand—but he impaled the chief baker, just as Joseph had said to them in his interpretation. The chief cupbearer, however, did not remember Joseph; he forgot him.

The Problem

God was advancing His agenda for Joseph forward. He used the baker's life and death dream to underline this process. Like the rest of Egypt the cupbearer and the baker believed Pharaoh was a god, the reincarnation of the Egyptian god Horus. To have angered such a god man who wielded absolute power over the life and death of his subjects was a really big problem.

The Dreamer's Metron

The Bakers metron was that of a high-ranking officer making bread and cakes for Pharaoh's court. He was well known by Pharaoh. He had to be completely trustworthy because his role was to guard against Pharaoh being poisoned. His offence was so great Pharaoh had him beheaded. Perhaps the only personally redemptive thing for him concerning this dream interpretation was that he was able to put his house in order. Pharaoh's cupbearer was no doubt deeply impressed by the contrasting and different fates between him and the baker. It was a matter of life and death.

The Message

Joseph's interpretation was that Pharaoh would kill the baker within three days and impale his body on a pole.

God's Purpose

God's purpose was to use this difficult situation to highlight Joseph's credibility as a dream interpreter in the eyes of the cupbearer and later Pharaoh. God was advancing His Messianic purpose, still focused on keeping His promises to Abraham. This is the second in a series of dreams God uses to bring Joseph to a position of national prominence in Egypt in order to fulfil Joseph's previous two prophetic dreams and to bring about his prophesy in Abraham's dream which said,

> Know for certain that for four hundred years your descendants will be strangers in a country not their own and that they will be enslaved and mistreated there. But I will punish the nation they serve as

slaves, and afterward they will come out with great possessions.[1]

Satan's Purpose

∽

Joseph had always been a target for Satan who wanted him dead. He'd tried to rob Joseph's birthright by making Jacob marry Leah first. He caused Joseph's brothers to be jealous enough to nearly kill Joseph and ultimately sell him into slavery.

Satan also filled Potiphar's wife with the lust and lies that landed Joseph in prison. Satan was also probably trying to kill the cupbearer and baker just because he was a murderer from the beginning.

God worked all these bad situations for good and used them to further His plans to bring Jacob down to Egypt.

Dreamer's Eyes Enlightened

∽

The baker's eyes were opened to the awful fact he would soon be dead and his body would impaled on a pole for all to see. I'm sure he hoped Joseph's interpretation was wrong.

Dreamer's Response and Application

∽

We are not told. Hopefully he was able to set his house in order before Pharaoh killed him.

Know God Better

∽

God is again seen as a dependable Promise Keeper who can work all things together for good for those who are called according to his purpose.[2] He was able to use this incident concerning the baker to further His own plans and purpose and to bless His faithful servant Joseph. God was able to warn the baker of his impending demise and perhaps allow him time to put his house in order.

The Dream Process

∽

Joseph has no problem interpreting this complex symbolic dream concerning the baker's metron. Again he immediately gave a succinct correct interpretation.

Using the *The Symbol Replacement Method* he revealed the three baskets were three days. He interpreted the birds eating Pharaoh's goods off the top basket on the baker's head as the baker suffering loss of life just as there is a loss of bread. Bread is often called the staff of life. It's interesting there is no covering or protection over the bread. Perhaps the baker had been careless with his work or words.

Unlike the cupbearer's dream that was bustling with life there is a strong sense of loss in the baker's dream. The cupbearer had fresh new grape juice to serve to Pharaoh while the birds stole the baker's produce.

With hindsight the cupbearer's and baker's dreams can be seen to contain some symbolic references to the future Messiah. On this level the cupbearer's dream could represent Christ's sacrificial offering that freed sinners from Satan's power and the prison of their transgressions.

The vine could represent the true vine, Jesus Christ. The cupbearer squeezed the fruit of the vine into the royal cup, and brought it to his lord for acceptance. This prophetically speaks of the shed blood of Jesus before the God the Father.

On the other hand, the baker brought the fruit of his own works and found it defiled by birds representing demons and unacceptable to his lord. We are reminded of Paul who said,

> Now to the one who works, wages are not credited as a gift but as an obligation. However, to the one who does not work but trusts God who justifies the ungodly, their faith is credited as righteousness.[3]

The bakers goods ended up as food for the birds symbolising demons and brought no redemption while the cupbearer's cup of crushed grapes reminds us of Jesus who before the crucifixion fell with his face to the ground and prayed, My Father, if it is possible, may this cup be taken from me. Yet not as I will, but as you will.[4]

> Isaiah said, He was wounded for our transgression; He was bruised for our iniquities; the chastisement of our peace was upon Him, and with His stripes we are healed.[5]

The three branches could symbolise Jesus lying in the tomb for three days and three nights while his disciples waited for his resurrection. The grapes pressed into the cup could also speak of the blood of Jesus Christ that flowed from his wounded side and the cup symbolises the cup of endless blessing Jesus presented to God the Father.

The cursed baker whose body was impaled on a pole could be construed as an echo of Christ who was also impaled on a tree.[6]

The Usual Suspects

∼

God gives the interpretation and Satan is seen in the birds of the air who destroy the bread. Jesus is seen in the bread and the three days and the body impaled on the pole.

Takeaways

∼

This is the first time in Scripture we see God using dream interpretation as a means of placing his servants into positions of power in a world government.

God will again use this same strategy with Daniel in Babylon over twelve hundred years later.

Jesus is the same yesterday, today and forever so no doubt some Christian Master Dream interpreters will find themselves in similar circumstances in future.

That God can work all things together for good is again apparent. We are also beginning to see how dreams can impact and save nations.

PHARAOH'S TWO SAME 'FAMINE' DREAMS

The Dream Setting/Backstory

*T*hese couple of dreams occur two years after *The Cupbearer's Dream* and *The Baker's Dream*. God who perfectly understands times and seasons is patiently working His purpose out. Joseph was still in prison. The Cupbearer forgot to mention him to Pharaoh.

The Psalmist said,

> He sent a man before them, even Joseph, who was sold for a servant: Whose feet they hurt with fetters: he was laid in irons: Until the time that his word came to pass, the word of the Lord tested him.[1]

It's now time for the next phase of God's plans and purpose for Israel. So God sends two dreams, one immediately after another and troubles the most powerful man in the world.

The Dream Scripture
Genesis 41:1-46

∼

When two full years had passed, Pharaoh had a dream: He was standing by the Nile, when out of the river there came up seven cows, sleek and fat, and they grazed among the reeds. After them, seven other cows, ugly and gaunt, came up out of the Nile and stood beside those on the riverbank. And the cows that were ugly and gaunt ate up the seven sleek, fat cows.

Then Pharaoh woke up. He fell asleep again and had a second dream:

Seven heads of grain, healthy and good, were growing on a single stalk. After them, seven other heads of grain sprouted—thin and scorched by the east wind. The thin heads of grain swallowed up the seven healthy, full heads.

Then Pharaoh woke up; it had been a dream. In the morning his mind was troubled, so he sent for all the magicians and wise men of Egypt. Pharaoh told them his dreams, but no one could interpret them for him. Then the chief cupbearer said to Pharaoh, "Today I am reminded of my shortcomings. Pharaoh was once angry with his servants, and he imprisoned me and the chief baker in the house of the captain of the guard. Each of us had a dream the same night, and each dream had a meaning of its own. Now a young Hebrew was there with us, a servant of the captain of the guard. We told him our dreams, and he interpreted them for us, giving each man the interpretation of his dream. And things turned out exactly as he interpreted them to us: I was restored to my position, and the other man was impaled."

So Pharaoh sent for Joseph, and he was quickly brought from the dungeon. When he had shaved and changed his clothes, he came before Pharaoh. Pharaoh said to Joseph, "I had a dream, and no one can interpret it. But I have heard it said of you that when you hear a dream you can interpret it."

"I cannot do it," Joseph replied to Pharaoh, "but God will give Pharaoh the answer he desires." Then Pharaoh said to Joseph,

"In my dream I was standing on the bank of the Nile, when out of the river there came up seven cows, fat and sleek, and they grazed among the reeds. After them, seven other cows came up—scrawny and very ugly and lean. I had never seen such ugly cows in all the land of Egypt. The lean, ugly cows ate up the seven fat cows that came up first. But even after they ate them, no one could tell that they had done so; they looked just as ugly as before.

Then I woke up.

"In my dream I saw seven heads of grain, full and good, growing on a single stalk. After them, seven other heads sprouted—withered and thin and scorched by the east wind. The thin heads of grain swallowed up the seven good heads.

I told this to the magicians, but none of them could explain it to me." Then Joseph said to Pharaoh, "The dreams of Pharaoh are one and the same. God has revealed to Pharaoh what he is about to do. The seven good cows are seven years, and the seven good heads of grain are seven years; it is one and the same dream. The seven lean, ugly cows that came up afterward are seven years, and so are the seven worthless heads of grain scorched by the east wind: They are seven years of famine.

"It is just as I said to Pharaoh: God has shown Pharaoh what he is about to do. Seven years of great abundance are coming throughout the land of Egypt, but seven years of famine will follow them. Then all the abundance in Egypt will be forgotten, and the famine will ravage the land. The abundance in the land will not be remembered, because the famine that follows it will be so severe. The reason the dream was given to Pharaoh in two forms is that the matter has been firmly decided by God, and God will do it soon.

"And now let Pharaoh look for a discerning and wise man and put him in charge of the land of Egypt. Let Pharaoh appoint commissioners over the land to take a fifth of the harvest of Egypt during the seven years of abundance. They should collect all the food of these good years that are coming and store up the grain under the authority of Pharaoh, to be kept in the cities for food. This food should be held in reserve for the country, to be used during the seven years of famine that will come upon Egypt, so that the country may not be ruined by the famine."

The plan seemed good to Pharaoh and to all his officials. So Pharaoh asked them, "Can we find anyone like this man, one in whom is the spirit of God?" Then Pharaoh said to Joseph, "Since God has made all this known to you, there is no one so discerning and wise as you. You shall be in charge of my palace, and all my people are to submit to your orders. Only with respect to the throne will I be greater than you."

So Pharaoh said to Joseph, "I hereby put you in charge of the whole land of Egypt." Then Pharaoh took his signet ring from his finger and put it on Joseph's finger. He dressed him in robes of fine linen and put a gold chain around his neck. He had him ride in a chariot as his second-in-command, and people shouted before him, "Make way!" Thus he put him in charge of the whole land of Egypt.

Then Pharaoh said to Joseph, "I am Pharaoh, but without your word no one will lift hand or foot in all Egypt." Pharaoh gave Joseph the name Zaphenath-Paneah and gave him Asenath daughter of Potiphera, priest of On, to be his wife. And Joseph went throughout the land of Egypt.

Joseph was thirty years old when he entered the service of Pharaoh king of Egypt.

The Problem

∼

The most powerful man in the most powerful empire on Earth is troubled by two God given dreams and his magicians and wise men can't interpret them.

The Dreamer's Metron

∼

All-powerful Pharaoh was both the political and religious leader of Egypt. He held the titles of Lord of the Two Lands and High Priest of Every Temple. He was the supreme ruler and was worshipped as a god on earth, the intermediary between the gods and the people.

As the High Priest of Every Temple, it was his duty to build great temples and monuments celebrating his own achievements and paying homage to the gods of the land. He officiated at religious ceremonies and choose the sites of temples.

As Lord of the Two Lands he made laws, owned all the land and collected taxes, and made war or defended Egypt against aggression. The people believed he was the reincarnation of the Egyptian god Horus. His word was law.

The Message

∼

Joseph's interpretation and application were clear and simple. Soon, there was coming seven years of great abundance followed by seven years of famine. A fifth of each abundant year's harvest must be stored up in order for Egypt to survive the famine years.

God's Purpose

∼

God is working his purpose out concerning His Messiah and also keeping His covenant dream promises to Abraham. He is setting the stage for the children of Israel to come to the land of their enslavement. *Abraham's Covenant Dream* had warned,

> Know for certain that for four hundred years your descendants will be strangers in a country not their own and that they will be enslaved and mistreated there. But I will punish the nation they serve as slaves, and afterward they will come out with great possessions.[2]

God interprets Pharaoh's dreams and by this shows He is greater than all the gods of Egypt. Four hundred years later He will begin to punish and destroy the whole Egyptian Empire. But here God is merciful in sending Pharaoh a dream and enabling Joseph to interpret it. God is also bringing forth Joseph's children Manasseh and Ephraim who each will receive an inheritance in the Promised Land.

Satan's Purpose

∼

Satan's purpose was to destroy God's chosen people during the famine.

Dreamer's Eyes Enlightened

∼

Pharaoh immediately witnessed to Joseph's interpretation and application of his dream.

Dreamer's Response and Application

∼

This dream's interpretation caused Pharaoh to exhibit the gift of discerning of spirits. He immediately recognised Joseph has the spirit of God. He also realised Joseph has a discerning and wise spirit.

Pharaoh wholeheartedly believed and received Joseph's dream interpretation and application and immediately took whatever steps were necessary in order to apply its truths. He promoted Joseph to being second in command of all Egypt in order to save the nation from famine.

Pharaoh also changed Joseph's name to Zaphenath-Paneah and gave him a wife; Asenath daughter of Potiphera, priest of On.

Having your name changed, being promoted from prison to second in command to a god-man in the most powerful nation on earth and being given a high ranking priest's daughter as your wife is quite a career upgrade merely for interpreting a couple of dreams.

Know God Better

Once again we see God as a trustworthy, sovereign, all knowing promise keeper. We know from *Abraham's Covenant Dream* that the sins of the Amorites had not yet reached the point to where God could justify removing them from the land.

We also realise God can send dreams that instantly trouble the most powerful rulers on earth.

The Dream Process

Both dreams are simple symbolic God crafted dreams requiring interpretation. The dreams were powerful enough to trouble powerful Pharaoh's mind yet enigmatic enough to keep their meaning hidden from his magicians and wise men.

Proverbs 25:2 says, It is the glory of God to conceal a matter. Yet after we are shown the interpretation or a dream or a riddle then it all seems so simple. That's why we can be lured into thinking Pharaoh's dreams were not really very difficult dreams to interpret. The same thing can happen when we read of Solomon's wisdom concerning the two mothers and the live baby.[3]

But the truth is if God conceals something then it is impossible for man or demon to unseal it. We can see this *sealed revelation* truth in action when Daniel is unable to understand the angel's explanation of Daniel's vision. The angel says,

> Daniel, go about your business, because the meaning of

this message will remain secret until the end of time.[4]

But with Pharaoh God made Joseph look good. After the interpretation things seemed to fit together. Using *The Symbol Replacement Method* we realise the River Nile appearing in the dream represented the issue of food for Egypt was totally dependent on the Nile for good crops. Joseph then interpreted both sets of seven as seven years; seven years of plenty and seven years of famine.

Both dreams are mirror images of one another containing the same message. The seven fat and sleek cows and the seven full and good heads of grain represent seven year of abundant provision from the River Nile.

The seven ugly and gaunt cows and the seven thin and scorched heads of grain represent seven year of famine from the River Nile. The seven famine years will totally consume all provision and produce from the abundant years.

During the first seven years the cows feed from the abundant reeds by the Nile and the grain is nourished from the stalk but afterwards the cows and the heads of grain both only feed from what has gone before. There was now nothing new and growing for them to consume.

The East wind represented severe conditions sent from God. In Egypt the dry East wind hardens the earth and shrivels the grain. In Exodus, Moses summoned the east wind to carry the locusts that plagued Egypt and to part the Red Sea so that the Children of Israel could escape Pharaoh's armies who were being punished by God.[5]

Several other Biblical references connect the east wind with destruction, particularly the destruction of the wicked by God. In this dream God's hand was behind the East wind that would cause the famine. Joseph said the matter of the famine been firmly decided by God, and God will do it soon.

In Hosea God had similarly used an east wind to punish Israel represented by Ephraim. God said,

> Even though he thrives among his brothers.
> An east wind from the Lord will come,
>   blowing in from the desert;
> his spring will fail
>   and his well dry up.
> His storehouse will be plundered
>   of all its treasures.[6]

Joseph also says a couple of things that are not immediately evident within the dreams. He mentions the reason the dream was given to Pharaoh in two forms was because the matter had been firmly decided by God, and God was about to do it soon. I think this was probably a word of knowledge in operation as opposed to a universal dream truth.

I don't think every dream that is repeated is about to happen soon. Like Joseph we must always hear from God and not just apply some principles like Pharaoh's magicians.

Similarly, Josephs plan to appoint commissioners who would take a fifth of the harvest during the seven years of abundance and store it in cities was not evident from anything within the dream. This also was a word of wisdom God gave to Joseph in order to impress and convince Pharaoh of Joseph's ability to deal with the pending famine.

The Usual Suspects

The gods and their disciples are powerless to interpret Pharaoh's two dreams and helpless against the famine. The fat and sleek cows represent God's blessing and the ugly and lean cows represent God's cursing. Pharaoh's revelation concerning Joseph was evidence of the Holy Spirit moving upon him. Jesus is hidden in the seed line of the Chosen People who are about to be saved from famine because of theses dreams from God.

Takeaways

Dreams got Joseph into trouble and dreams got Joseph out of trouble. Here dream interpretation propels Joseph into a position of prominence in a powerful foreign kingdom.

God will again use this same dream tactic with Daniel before Nebuchadnezzar in Babylon over twelve hundred later. God will similarly prepare the stage for Daniel to calm a troubled ruler and gain credibility before another bunch of magicians and wise men who can't fathom God's dreams.

These are the only two situations in scripture where a ruler has a dream that requires an interpretation. In both cases the local dream interpreters are unable to decipher God's dreams.

Nevertheless there must have been incredible pressure on Joseph as he interpreted dreams for a god man who wielded the power of life and death as Joseph well knew from the incident with the Baker.

God gives dreams according to the dreamer's metron. Pharaoh, Nebuchadnezzar and King Abimelek were all given dreams relevant for their metron, their lives and their nations. They also had the authority and clout to implement the application of their dreams.

JACOB'S 'GO DOWN TO EGYPT' NIGHT VISION DREAM

The Dream Setting/Backstory

This dream occurs nine years after Joseph interpreted Pharaoh's two dreams. Jacob's household are now in their second year of the crippling famine Pharaoh's dream had predicted and Jacob sends ten of his sons to Egypt to buy grain. He keeps Benjamin at home.

In Egypt, Joseph recognised his brothers and initiated a series of ploys that resulted in Benjamin being brought to Egypt and Joseph revealing himself to his brothers.

Then the literal part of Joseph's first dream was fulfilled when his eleven brothers bowed down, prostrating themselves before him.

By now Joseph had gained a deeper understanding of God's greater plans and purpose for his life and his nation. He said,

> I am your brother Joseph, the one you sold into Egypt!
> And now, do not be distressed and do not be angry

with yourselves for selling me here, because it was to save lives that God sent me ahead of you. For two years now there has been famine in the land, and for the next five years there will be no ploughing and reaping. But God sent me ahead of you to preserve for you a remnant on earth and to save your lives by a great deliverance.[1]

God had now placed Joseph into a position where he could provide refuge and food for Jacob's household in Goshen in Egypt. Jacob's sons returned to Hebron with twenty additional donkeys laden with supplies and various transport wagons to carry Jacob's household down to Egypt.

The Dream Scripture
Genesis 46:1-7

∽

So Israel set out with all that was his, and when he reached Beersheba, he offered sacrifices to the God of his father Isaac.

And God spoke to Israel in a vision at night and said, "Jacob! Jacob!"

"Here I am," he replied.

"I am God, the God of your father," he said. "Do not be afraid to go down to Egypt, for I will make you into a great nation there. I will go down to Egypt with you, and I will surely bring you back again. And Joseph's own hand will close your eyes."

Then Jacob left Beersheba, and Israel's sons took their father Jacob and their children and their wives in the carts that Pharaoh had sent to transport him. So Jacob and all his offspring went to Egypt, taking with them their livestock and the possessions they had acquired in Canaan. Jacob brought with him to Egypt his sons and grandsons and his daughters and granddaughters—all his offspring.

The Problem

∼

Jacob had struggled to believe Joseph was alive and was the governor of all Egypt. How could he trust the words of his conniving sons who'd deceived him so badly? But as he listened to their story and saw the provisions and the carts Joseph had sent to carry them to Egypt he said, I'm convinced! My son Joseph is still alive. I will go and see him before I die. Afterwards Jacob travelled twenty-five miles to Beersheba and offered sacrifices to God in an effort to seek confirmation and guidance.

The Dreamers Metron

∼

Jacob has inherited Abraham's enormous metron to bless all nations until the end of time. Jacob was also the father of twelve sons who'd lead the twelve tribes of Israel. After Jacob wrestled with God his name was changed to Israel and this became both the name of the people and the land of God's Chosen People.

God told Jacob,

> I am the Lord, the God of your father Abraham and the
> God of Isaac. I will give you and your descendants
> the land on which you are lying. Your descendants
> will be like the dust of the earth, and you will

spread out to the west and to the east, to the north and to the south. All peoples on earth will be blessed through you and your offspring. I am with you and will watch over you wherever you go, and I will bring you back to this land. I will not leave you until I have done what I have promised you.²

Jacob's metron also included his call to bring the children of Israel down to Egypt as promised to Abraham. This is what is being worked on in this dream.

The Message

~

The message is plain enough. God identifies himself as the God of Jacob's father Isaac. God then calms Jacob's concerns. He said, Do not be afraid to go down to Egypt, for I will make you into a great nation there. I will go down to Egypt with you, and I will surely bring you back again. And Joseph's own hand will close your eyes.

This reads very much like a précised version of the message God already gave Jacob in *Jacob's Covenant Dream* at Bethel. God again assures Jacob He will go with him and will bring him back again to the Promised Land. He also comforts Jacob by revealing Joseph, whom Jacob thought dead, would be with him at his own death.

God's Purpose

~

God is moving His plans and purposes for the Messiah forward. To this end he reassures Jacob he's doing the right thing in going to Egypt. He also comforts Jacob with the revelation Joseph's own hand will close his eyes.

He further comforts Jacob by promising to be with him in Egypt and also to bring his body back to the Promised Land.

Satan's Purpose

Satan who had been behind all the scheming and jealousy of Joseph's brothers is still trying to stop Jacob from moving in God's will through fear and unbelief.

Dreamer's Eyes Enlightened

This was the eight interaction of God with Jacob in Scripture. Jacob recognised God's voice and his eyes were opened to realise it was God's will for him to go down to Egypt.

Dreamer's Response and Application

Jacob continued on his way to Egypt with the comfort of knowing he had God's approval and blessing on his journey and God would accompany him.

Know God Better

God is again seen working all things together for good. He is a promise keeper who can sympathise with our weaknesses and help us overcome all circumstances through His sufficient grace.[3] He can weave all our sin and weakness into a beautiful tapestry bringing beauty from ashes.[4]

The Dream Process

We're not told whether Jacob saw God or not. If he did see Him then it would have been Jesus. But I suspect it's just a case of Jacob hearing God's voice.

This dream came after Jacob responded positively to Joseph's invitation. On his way he offered sacrifice to God who then encouraged Jacob in his choice. God spoke directly to the issue on Jacob's heart and created faith for the journey.

This is a literal dream similar to the earlier Genesis dreams in which God gives instructions to the dreamer. There is no interpretation required, only obedience. The dream is of personal, national and international importance. It's primary objective was to move God's chosen people to the next stage of their journey as foretold in *Abraham's Covenant Dream*.

The Usual Suspects

∽

God is speaking in this dream calming Jacob's fears and giving him direction and comforting words. Satan is the one who caused Jacob's fears. God's promise of being with Jacob reminds us of Jesus' words to his disciples, And surely I am with you always, to the very end of the age.[5] Jesus was also in the chosen people's seed line.

Takeaways

∽

In the first Genesis dream God spoke to childless Abraham about his descendants going down to a land where they would be slaves for four hundred years.

In this last Genesis dream God specifically directed Abraham's descendants through Jacob to go to that land.

I wonder did Jacob have any inkling Egypt would be the land of those four hundred years of captivity? I wonder did Jacob ever learn of *Abraham's Covenant Dream*. I also wonder did Jacob ever share his dreams and Abraham's dream with Joseph?

Surely there's a warning here that we should share our dreams and revelation with our children so they might better know who they are and for what purpose they were placed upon this earth.

Then they might gain some understanding of how God is working out His plans and purposes within our family lines for His greater Glory.

BALAAM'S 'DON'T CURSE ISRAEL' DREAM

The Dream Setting/Backstory

This dream was sent nearly five hundred years after the last Genesis dream. God had finally released His chosen people from Egypt and had given them various victories over their enemies on their way to the Promised Land. When they arrived at the plains of Moab, King Balak who'd heard of their recent triumph over the Amorites was frightened. He decided to hire a soothsayer named Balaam to curse them and weaken them.

The Dream Scripture
Numbers 22:1-14

Then the Israelites travelled to the plains of Moab and camped along the Jordan across from Jericho. Now Balak son of Zippor saw all that Israel had done to the Amorites, and Moab was terrified because there were so many people. Indeed, Moab was filled with dread because of the Israelites. The Moabites said to the elders of Midian, "This horde is going to lick up everything around us, as an ox licks up the grass of the field." So Balak son of Zippor, who was king of Moab at that time, sent messengers to summon Balaam son of Beor, who was at Pethor, near the Euphrates River, in his native land. Balak said:

"A people has come out of Egypt; they cover the face of the land and have settled next to me. Now come and put a curse on these people, because they are too powerful for me. Perhaps then I will be able to defeat them and drive them out of the land. For I know that whoever you bless is blessed, and whoever you curse is cursed."

The elders of Moab and Midian left, taking with them the fee for divination. When they came to Balaam, they told him what Balak had said.

"Spend the night here," Balaam said to them, "and I will report back to you with the answer the Lord gives me." So the Moabite officials stayed with him.

God came to Balaam and asked, "Who are these men with you?"

Balaam said to God, "Balak son of Zippor, king of Moab, sent me this message: 'A people that has come out of Egypt covers the face of the land. Now come and put a curse on them for me. Perhaps then I will be able to fight them and drive them away.'"

But God said to Balaam, "Do not go with them. You must not put a curse on those people, because they are blessed."

The next morning Balaam got up and said to Balak's officials, "Go back to your own country, for the Lord has refused to let me go with you."

So the Moabite officials returned to Balak and said, "Balaam refused to come with us."

The Problem

∼

King Balak of Moab wanted Balaam to curse God's Chosen People.

The Dreamer's Metron

∼

Balaam was a Gentile prophet who heard clearly from God and gave some beautiful prophecies. Balaam was not a false prophet. He had the gift but not the character. Scripture calls him a wicked prophet because in his heart he served money and as Jesus said,

> "No one can serve two masters. Either you will hate the one and love the other, or you will be devoted to the one and despise the other. You cannot serve both God and money.[1]

∼

The Message

∼

God's clear message to Balaam concerning Moab and Israel was was, "Do not go with the people of Moab. You must not put a curse on the people of Israel, because they are blessed."

God's Purpose

～

God's purpose was to stop the King of Moab from harming His Covenant People and their seed line.

Satan's Purpose

～

Satan's purpose was that Balaam should curse curse Israel and prevent their progress towards the Promised Land.

Dreamer's Eyes Enlightened

～

Balaam clearly heard God's will and was in no doubt as to what he should do.

Dreamer's Response and Application

～

Balaam was obedient to God's instructions and immediately upon rising from his bed told Balak's officials he couldn't return with them to curse Israel because God had refused to allow him to do so.

Know God Better

Israel's covenant keeping God is once again protecting His chosen people and their seedline from kings and others who would harm them.

The Dream Process.

We're not told whether Balaam saw God or not. If he did see Him then it would have been Jesus. But I suspect it's a similar dream to *Jacob's 'Go Down To Egypt' Dream* in which Jacob just heard God's voice.

This is a simple literal dream in which God dialogues with the dreamer. God asks Balaam about the Moabites who are staying with him. Balaam explains they are representatives of King Balak who wants him to curse Israel.

God then clearly tells Balaam not to side with Balak and curse His chosen people because He has blessed them.

The Usual Suspects

God spoke to Balaam in the dream. Jesus was in the seedline of the people Satan wanted Balaam to curse.

Takeaways

Although Balaam was more than happy to curse Israel for money he had enough spiritual sense to realise he needed God's permission to do so. He had some understanding of what Proverbs teaches about curses,

> Like a fluttering sparrow or a darting swallow, an
> undeserved curse does not come to rest.[2]

Balak and Balaam were also on very dangerous ground concerning the issue of cursing Israel because God had already promised Abraham,

> Blessed is everyone who blesses you, And cursed
> is everyone who curses you.[3]

The reality was Balak and Balaam were in great danger of being personally cursed by God. Balaam must have understood something of this when he told Balak,

> How can I curse
> those whom God has not cursed?
> How can I denounce
> those whom the Lord has not denounced?[4]

Through this whole encounter God never allowed Balaam to curse Israel. In fact in Balaam's last prophecy concerning Israel, God has Balaam pronounce the great truth,

> Blessed is everyone who blesses you, And cursed
> is everyone who curses you.[5]

BALAAM'S 'IF THEY CALL YOU' DREAM

The Dream Setting/Backstory

*I*n his first dream God told Balaam to have nothing to do with Balak's offer of reward and his intentions to curse Israel. Balaam obeyed God's instructions. Now Balak ups the ante and appeals to Balaam's materialistic ego by sending more distinguished officials to restate his generous offer of money.

The Dream Scripture
Numbers 22:15-38 (NKJV)

Then Balak again sent princes, more numerous and more honorable than they. And they came to Balaam and said to him, "Thus says

Balak the son of Zippor: 'Please let nothing hinder you from coming to me; for I will certainly honour you greatly, and I will do whatever you say to me. Therefore please come, curse this people for me.' "

Then Balaam answered and said to the servants of Balak, "Though Balak were to give me his house full of silver and gold, I could not go beyond the word of the Lord my God, to do less or more. Now therefore, please, you also stay here tonight, that I may know what more the Lord will say to me."

And God came to Balaam at night and said to him, "If the men come to call you, rise and go with them; but only the word which I speak to you—that you shall do." So Balaam rose in the morning, saddled his donkey, and went with the princes of Moab.

Then God's anger was aroused because he went, and the Angel of the Lord took His stand in the way as an adversary against him. And he was riding on his donkey, and his two servants were with him. Now the donkey saw the Angel of the Lord standing in the way with His drawn sword in His hand, and the donkey turned aside out of the way and went into the field. So Balaam struck the donkey to turn her back onto the road. Then the Angel of the Lord stood in a narrow path between the vineyards, with a wall on this side and a wall on that side. And when the donkey saw the Angel of the Lord, she pushed herself against the wall and crushed Balaam's foot against the wall; so he struck her again. Then the Angel of the Lord went further, and stood in a narrow place where there *was* no way to turn either to the right hand or to the left. And when the donkey saw the Angel of the Lord, she lay down under Balaam; so Balaam's anger was aroused, and he struck the donkey with his staff.

Then the Lord opened the mouth of the donkey, and she said to Balaam, "What have I done to you, that you have struck me these three times?"

And Balaam said to the donkey, "Because you have abused me. I wish there were a sword in my hand, for now I would kill you!"

So the donkey said to Balaam, "Am I not your donkey on which you have ridden, ever since I became yours, to this day? Was I ever disposed to do this to you?"

And he said, "No."

Then the Lord opened Balaam's eyes, and he saw the Angel of the Lord standing in the way with His drawn sword in His hand; and he bowed his head and fell flat on his face. And the Angel of the Lord said to him, "Why have you struck your donkey these three times? Behold, I have come out to stand against you, because *your* way is perverse before Me. The donkey saw Me and turned aside from Me these three times. If she had not turned aside from Me, surely I would also have killed you by now, and let her live."

And Balaam said to the Angel of the Lord, "I have sinned, for I did not know You stood in the way against me. Now therefore, if it displeases You, I will turn back."

Then the Angel of the Lord said to Balaam, "Go with the men, but only the word that I speak to you, that you shall speak." So Balaam went with the princes of Balak.

Now when Balak heard that Balaam was coming, he went out to meet him at the city of Moab, which is on the border at the Arnon, the boundary of the territory. Then Balak said to Balaam, "Did I not earnestly send to you, calling for you? Why did you not come to me? Am I not able to honour you?"

And Balaam said to Balak, "Look, I have come to you! Now, have I any power at all to say anything? The word that God puts in my mouth, that I must speak." So Balaam went with Balak, and they came to Kirjath Huzoth. Then Balak offered oxen and sheep, and he sent some to Balaam and to the princes who were with him.

The Problem

King Balak won't take no for an answer and Balaam still loves money.

The Dreamer's Metron

Balaam was a Gentile prophet who heard clearly from God and gave some beautiful prophecies over Israel. Balaam was not a false prophet. He had the gift but not the character. Scripture calls him a wicked prophet because in his heart he served money and as Jesus said,

> "No one can serve two masters. Either you will hate the one and love the other, or you will be devoted to the one and despise the other. You cannot serve both God and money.[1]

The Message

God's plain message was, *If* the men come to call you, rise and go with them; but only the word which I speak to you—that you shall do.

God's Purpose

God's purpose was to stop the King of Moab from harming His Covenant People and their seed line. He also tested Balaam's heart with the stipulation, *If* the men come to call you.

Satan's Purpose

Satan's purpose was that Balaam should curse Israel and prevent their progress towards the Promised Land.

Dreamer's Eyes Enlightened

Balaam knew the exact details what he was allowed to do.

Dreamer's Response and Application

Balaam didn't wait for the men to come to call him. Instead he rose early in the morning, quickly prepared and rushed out to meet Balak's entourage. Jude said Balaam's sin was that he ran greedily into an error for reward.[2]

Know God Better

God, although likely annoyed by Balaam's childish repeating of the same answered question, was willing to work with him. To this end God applied a stipulation that would test Balaam's heart.

The Dream Process.

This is a simple literal dream in which God clearly instructs the dreamer. God said, *If* the men come to call you, rise and go with them. God also told Balaam to only speak the words God told him to say.

The Usual Suspects

God spoke to Balaam in the dream. Jesus appeared as the Angel of the Lord and reminded Balaam he was only to speak what God told him to speak concerning the Hebrews. Satan was using the Moabites to tempt Balaam to curse Israel.

Takeaways

Balaam clearly heard from God. He also understood his metron. He said, How can I curse those whom God has not cursed? How can I denounce those whom the Lord has not denounced?[3]

He also gave seven beautiful prophecies over Israel, one of which foretold the Messiah,

> A star will come out of Jacob; a sceptre will rise out of Israel. He will crush the foreheads of Moab, the skulls of all the people of Sheth.[4]

Despite all this Balaam loved money rather than God and was more concerned about his own self-centred desires than about God's plans and purpose.

God wanted His Chosen People protected and although Balaam couldn't curse Israel directly he came up with a plan of how they could be tempted to bring a curse upon themselves.

He told Balak how to lure them with prostitutes and idolatry. As a result Israel ended up worshiping Baal of Peor and committing fornication with Midianite women. Because of these sins God plagued Israel, and 24,000 of their men died.[5]

Scripture condemns Balaam as a prophet for hire[6] and reports his execution[7] as punishment for his part in the Baal Peor incident[8], where he is blamed for inciting Moabite women to entice Israelite men to sin.

Peter said Balaam loved the wages of wickedness[9] and Jude associates Balaam with the selling of one's soul for money.[10] Jesus also depicted Balaam as an evil prophet when He warned the church in Pergamum,

> There are some among you who hold to the teaching of Balaam, who taught Balak to entice the Israelites to sin so that they ate food sacrificed to idols and committed sexual immorality.[11]

Satan hates God's people and his strategies are always the same. If he can't curse them directly he'll always fall back on his usual temptations of sexual immorality and idolatry, the girls, the guys, the gold and the glory.

Same old, same old!

THE MIDIANITE'S DREAM FOR GIDEON

The Dream Setting/Backstory

God sent this dream to an unnamed Midianite soldier over 700 years after the last of the Genesis dreams and over two hundred years after Balaam's two dreams. In those days dreams were scarce.

God's prophecy in Abraha*m's Covenant Dream* had come to pass. The sins of the Amorites eventually reached their full measure and Israel had been resident in the Promised Land for nearly four hundred years. Moses had warned,

> When you enter the land the Lord your God is giving
> you, do not learn to imitate the detestable ways of
> the nations there. Let no one be found among you
> who sacrifices their son or daughter in the fire, who
> practices divination or sorcery, interprets omens,
> engages in witchcraft, or casts spells, or who is a

medium or spiritist or who consults the dead.
Anyone who does these things is detestable to
the Lord; because of these same detestable practices
the Lord your God will drive out those nations
before you. You must be blameless before
the Lord your God.[1]

The main problem was whenever Israel prospered and had peace for any amount of time they foolishly turned their backs on God and began to imitate the detestable ways of their enemies. This was such a time.

Deborah's victory over Israel's foes resulted in forty years of peace and prosperity but when God's Chosen People again turned to idols God delivered them into the hands of the Midianites for seven years.

Israel soon became impoverished, reduced to hiding in caves and mountains and eating coarse barley bread, a food usually fed to animals. Eventually they turned to God. The Scripture says,

> When the people of Israel cried out to the Lord on
> account of the Midianites, the Lord sent a prophet
> to the people of Israel. And he said to them, "Thus
> says the Lord, the God of Israel: I led you up from
> Egypt and brought you out of the house of slavery.
> And I delivered you from the hand of the Egyptians
> and from the hand of all who oppressed you,
> and drove them out before you and gave you their
> land. And I said to you, 'I am the Lord your
> God; you shall not fear the gods of the Amorites in
> whose land you dwell.' But you have not obeyed my
> voice.[2]"

God reminded His chosen people how He'd kept the covenantal

promises but how they'd broken them. The Angel of the Lord then appeared to a young man, Gideon from the tribe of Manasseh, and called him to deliver the people and condemn their idolatry. The Angel of the Lord was Jesus.

There were seven interactions between God and Gideon. In Gideon's first conversation with The Angel of the Lord, Jesus tells Gideon he is called to save Israel from the oppression of Midian.

Gideon wasn't convinced. He wanted a sign so Jesus caused supernatural fire to shoot up out of a rock and consume an offering. Then He vanished.

The second conversation occurred later that night in an incident reminiscent of a dream in which Gideon was given specific instructions to destroy Baal's alter and grove and build an altar to the Lord and sacrifice on it.

The third and forth conversations occurred around two supernatural signs Gideon wanted concerning a fleece over two consecutive nights. The fifth and sixth conversations between Gideon and God resulted in the Israeli army being reduced from 32,000 soldiers to 10,000 soldiers to 300 soldiers.

God only wanted a small group of soldiers in order to show Israel it was Him and not man who delivered them.

The seventh conversation occurred during the night and has great similarities to early Genesis dreams. During this incident God instructs Gideon to either immediately begin the battle or if he is still fearful to take his servant Purah and go down to the enemy's camp and listen to what they are saying so he could be encouraged.

God is willing to work with Gideon's further need for confirmation and more faith. After all, Gideon is about to embark on what looks like an impossible mission. He is going to war against a vast and powerful well trained army with only his three hundred men.

The Dream Scripture

Judges 7:9-15

The Lord said to Gideon, "With the three hundred men that lapped I will save you and give the Midianites into your hands. Let all the others go home." So Gideon sent the rest of the Israelites home but kept the three hundred, who took over the provisions and trumpets of the others. Now the camp of Midian lay below him in the valley. During that night the Lord said to Gideon, "Get up, go down against the camp, because I am going to give it into your hands. If you are afraid to attack, go down to the camp with your servant Purah and listen to what they are saying. Afterward, you will be encouraged to attack the camp." So he and Purah his servant went down to the outposts of the camp. The Midianites, the Amalekites and all the other eastern peoples had settled in the valley, thick as locusts. Their camels could no more be counted than the sand on the seashore.

Gideon arrived just as a man was telling a friend his dream. "I had a dream," he was saying. "A round loaf of barley bread came tumbling into the Midianite camp. It struck the tent with such force that the tent overturned and collapsed."

His friend responded, "This can be nothing other than the sword of Gideon son of Joash, the Israelite. God has given the Midianites and the whole camp into his hands."

When Gideon heard the dream and its interpretation, he bowed down and worshiped. He returned to the camp of Israel and called out, "Get up! The Lord has given the Midianite camp into your hands."

The Problem

Despite all his interactions with Jesus as the Angel of the Lord, Gideon still didn't have the required level of faith to commence the battle. So God allowed him to hear a relevant dream being interpreted in order to increase his faith. Remember, faith comes by hearing, and hearing by the word of God.[3] A dream from God is a word from God.

The Dreamer's Metron

Gideon's metron increased rapidly from that of an idol maker's son to a mighty warrior who'd deliver Israel from all her enemies. Although Gideon's call was to save all Israel, God had him first work with his metron closer to home. He was told,

> Tear down your father's altar to Baal and cut down the Asherah pole beside it. Then build a proper kind of altar to the Lord your God on the top of this height.[4]

Our metrons concerning our family and neighbours are often the hardest and most intimidating assignments to accomplish. The stakes are usually highest in the home mission field.

After his obedience and success in the local area Gideon's metron quickly expanded into a national one. He was anointed when the Spirit of the Lord came on him. Afterwards he blew a trumpet, summoning the Abiezrites to follow him. He also sent messengers throughout Manasseh, Asher, Zebulun and Naphtali, calling them to join with him.

The importance of ministering to those closest to us within our metron is stressed throughout Scripture. When God called Abraham, He said,

> For I have chosen him so that he will command his
> children and his house after him to keep the way of
> the Lord by doing what is right and just. This is
> how the Lord will fulfil to Abraham what He
> promised him.[5]

It's always much easier to preach to people we might never set eyes on again than it is to minister to our own spouse, children, friends, and loved ones. All authentic ministry starts from the home place.

The Message

The message is clear enough; Gideon will win this battle because God is with him.

God's Purpose

God was still keeping his covenantal promises to Abraham. When Israel again turned to Him and asked for help from their enemies God immediately responded by raising up Gideon as a deliverer.

God also sent this dream to the Midianite soldier so Gideon could hear its interpretation and have his faith strengthened enough to believe God and obey him. God also arranged the timing of this divine appointment so Gideon would be in the right place at the right time.

Satan's Purpose

∽

Satan's purpose was to wipe out God's chosen people by a vastly superior army including lots of Nephilim soldiers and thereby stop the Messiah from coming to crush his head.

Dreamer's Eyes Enlightened

∽

The dreamer's eyes are enlightened. The Midianite soldier now knows he is on the losing side of this battle because Israel's God has given the whole camp into Gideon's hands. Hopefully the Midianite used this dream interpretation to save himself and his friend.

This dream interpretation was really meant for Gideon. The significant thing as regards God's plans and purpose is that Gideon's eyes are enlightened and his faith is strengthened.

Dreamer's Response and Application

∽

We're not told what the dreamers response was but we know Gideon was finally encouraged enough to believe and obey God and to go to war against overwhelming odds.

Know God Better

God patiently worked with Gideon until Gideon's faith level was strong enough for him to believe God and take decisive action. God also wanted Israel to know it was His power and not the strength of man that brought victory. God was still keeping His thousand-year-old covenantal promises to Abraham, Isaac and Jacob and Joseph. He was still moving his agenda for the Messiah forward.

Through this dream and its implementation God also displayed His total superiority over the gods of the Midianites, the Amalekites and all the other eastern peoples. God is the One who can protect His Son's seedline.

The Dream Process

This is a simple symbolic dream easily interpreted by the Midianite soldier's friend. Using *The Symbol Replacement Method* the round loaf of barley bread represents Gideon and his rough army who are reduced to eating coarse barley bread. Perhaps *Barleybread* was a Midianite nickname for Gideon.

This loaf that overturned and collapsed the Midianite tent symbolised Gideon's army supported by a God powerful enough to destroy the vast Midianite camp of soldiers.

This is the only place in the Bible where a dreamer's dream is for someone else and the dreamer didn't realise this fact. The dream has national importance and international importance.

The Usual Suspects

∼

God is patiently waiting in the wings for his beleaguered people to ask him for help. Satan and the gods on the other hand are seducing and harassing the people. God has removed His hand of protection because His people are ignoring His words through Moses and are worshiping the gods of the Amorites in whose land they now live. Jesus is everywhere as the Angel of the Lord and the Holy Spirit came upon Gideon and anointed him for battle.

Takeaways

∼

Through this dream and it's implementation God demonstrates His total dominion over the powers and principalities attacking His covenant people and their seed line. He also shows His complete ability to protect his chosen ones.

Although Gideon talked with Jesus and was anointed by the Holy Spirit his life didn't end too well. Moses had warned Israel before they entered the Promised Land, that their king must not take many wives or his heart would be led astray. He also must not accumulate large amounts of silver and gold.[6]

Like Solomon after him Gideon violated both of these warnings. Fame went to his head. He had seventy sons from his many wives. Gideon then went on to make an ephod[7] out of the gold won in battle, which eventually caused all of Israel to turn away from God yet again.

There was peace in Israel for forty years during the life of Gideon but as soon as Gideon died of old age, the Israelites again turned to worship the false god Baal-Berith and ignored the family of Gideon.

Gideon had failed to instruct his children after him. Like Solomon, a dreamer who started off well and ended up badly, Gideon didn't leave a good legacy.

Dreams and supernatural encounters are wonderful things but we still need to pay careful attention and obedience to the word of God.

We still need to look after our families.

SAMUEL'S NIGHT VISION DREAM

The Dream Setting/Backstory

This night vision came nearly one hundred years after *The Midianite's Dream for Gideon*. Eli the high priest ministered before The Ark of the Covenant and judged Israel for forty years. Young Samuel was given into Eli's care to fulfil a vow made to God by Samuel's mother Hannah.

Eli's sons Hophni and Phinehas who ministered with their father were wicked men with no regard for the Lord or the custom of the priests with the people.

They were sleeping with the holy women who served at the temple entrance. They also took prime cuts of meat, sometimes by force, from the sacrifices instead of honouring the random method God had ordained for this process.[1]

Eli rebuked them too lightly and they continued in their sin. Scripture says, Eli's sons were scoundrels; they had no regard for the Lord.[2]

Even though revelation was scarce in those days God still sent an unnamed prophet to tell Eli he had honoured his sons above the Lord because he did not rebuke them and remove them from office.

Because of Eli's toleration of his son's sin, forever afterwards, all of Eli's male descendants would die before reaching old age.

The King James Version says it poetically, They shall die in the flower of their age.[3]

The unknown prophet said the sign of his prophecy coming to pass would occur when Hophni and Phinehas would die on the same day.

The Dream Scripture
1 Samuel 3:1-15

∽

The boy Samuel ministered before the Lord under Eli. In those days the word of the Lord was rare; there were not many visions.

One night Eli, whose eyes were becoming so weak that he could barely see, was lying down in his usual place. The lamp of God had not yet gone out, and Samuel was lying down in the house of the Lord, where the ark of God was. Then the Lord called Samuel.

Samuel answered, "Here I am." And he ran to Eli and said, "Here I am; you called me."

But Eli said, "I did not call; go back and lie down." So he went and lay down.

Again the Lord called, "Samuel!" And Samuel got up and went to Eli and said, "Here I am; you called me."

"My son," Eli said, "I did not call; go back and lie down."

Now Samuel did not yet know the Lord: The word of the Lord had not yet been revealed to him.

A third time the Lord called, "Samuel!" And Samuel got up and went to Eli and said, "Here I am; you called me."

Then Eli realised that the Lord was calling the boy. So Eli told Samuel, "Go and lie down, and if he calls you, say, 'Speak, Lord, for your servant is listening.'" So Samuel went and lay down in his place.

The Lord came and stood there, calling as at the other times, "Samuel! Samuel!"

Then Samuel said, "Speak, for your servant is listening."

And the Lord said to Samuel: "See, I am about to do something in Israel that will make the ears of everyone who hears about it tingle. At that time I will carry out against Eli everything I spoke against his family—from beginning to end. For I told him that I would judge his family forever because of the sin he knew about; his sons blasphemed God, and he failed to restrain them. Therefore I swore to the house of Eli, 'The guilt of Eli's house will never be atoned for by sacrifice or offering.'"

Samuel lay down until morning and then opened the doors of the house of the Lord. He was afraid to tell Eli the vision, but Eli called him and said, "Samuel, my son."

Samuel answered, "Here I am."

"What was it he said to you?" Eli asked. "Do not hide it from me. May God deal with you, be it ever so severely, if you hide from me anything he told you." So Samuel told him everything, hiding nothing from him. Then Eli said, "He is the Lord; let him do what is good in his eyes."

The Problem

∼

God's spiritual leaders were wicked men with little regard for the Lord or His instructions. God was about to change the guard.

It was like when Isaiah said, These people draw near to Me with their mouths and honour Me with their lips, but their hearts are far from Me.⁴

The priests and people were not seeking the Lord and God was not pleased. Isaiah said dreams and visions being rare was a sign of God's punishment. He wrote,

> Be stunned and amazed,
> > blind yourselves and be sightless;
> be drunk, but not from wine,
> > stagger, but not from beer.
> The Lord has brought over you a deep sleep:
> > He has sealed your eyes (the prophets);
> > he has covered your heads (the seers).
> For you this whole vision is nothing but words sealed in a scroll. And if you give the scroll to someone who can read, and say, "Read this, please," they will answer, "I can't; it is sealed." Or if you give the scroll to someone who cannot read, and say, "Read this, please," they will answer, "I don't know how to read.⁵"

When God refuses to give dreams and visions and interpretation we are all in trouble. King Saul who continually disobeyed God cried out,

> I am in great distress. The Philistines are fighting against me, and God has departed from me. He no longer answers me, either by prophets or by dreams.⁶

Micah also spoke about a time when Israel disobeyed God. He said,

> Therefore night will come over you, without visions, and darkness, without divination. The sun will set for the prophets, and the day will go dark for them. The seers will be ashamed and the diviners disgraced. They will all cover their faces because there is no answer from God. But as for me, I am filled with power, with the Spirit of the Lord, and with justice and might, to declare to Jacob his transgression, to Israel his sin. Hear this, you leaders of Jacob, you rulers of Israel, who despise justice and distort all that is right.[7]

The Dreamer's Metron

Samuel had a deep and wide metron in a range of leadership roles. He was a seer, priest, nazarite, judge, prophet, and military leader. God used Samuel to set up Israel's monarchy. Initially he resisted Israel's desire for a king but conceded after God said it was okay.

He then anointed Saul as king and later David. Afterwards he prophesied Saul's rejection as king three times. The third rejection occurred after the Witch of Endor conjured up Samuel's spirit at King Saul's insistence.

Samuel has the distinction of being only one of two ghosts, apart from the Holy Ghost, who appears in Scripture. The other is Moses on the Mount of Transfiguration. Remember Elijah never died.

Samuel arrived on the scene at a pivotal time in Israel's history. After Joshua's death Israel entered the days of the judges, a time without a centralised government. During this era, God in response to the peoples' prayer would raise up certain individuals like Gideon to deliver Israel from her enemies for a time.

The Book of Judges records twelve judges and First Samuel

presents Eli and Samuel. Samuel was the last judge. After Samuel's time Israel was led by kings.

Samuel was born when words from the Lord were rare and scarce. God used Samuel to usher in the era of the prophets, a time when Israel was awash with prophets and revelation that still blesses the whole world today.

The Message

As often happens in a new move of God, judgement began at the house of the Lord.[8] Eli knew his sons were sinning but he failed to properly deal with them. Now God's clear message said He was about to swiftly judge them in a manner that will shock all of Israel.

God's Purpose

God was keeping His Covenantal Promises to Abraham concerning caring for Israel. God's purpose was twofold. He planned to bring judgement on the old regime for not dealing with sin in its midst and He wanted to start speaking again to the nation through his new prophet Samuel.

Satan's Purpose

Satan's purpose as usual was to resist God's plans and purpose and to lead men astray from the true worship of God. Hophni and Phinehas like Satan were full of pride, lust, greed and rebellion. Like Satan they were no longer fit for purpose.

Dreamer's Eyes Enlightened

God bursts on the scene and starts speaking to Samuel. Overnight Samuel receives divine revelation concerning the nation and begins to function as a prophet.

Dreamer's Response and Application

Young Samuel was afraid to tell Eli of his revelation and didn't know what to do until Eli encouraged him to reveal it under the threat of God dealing severely with him if he withheld anything from Eli.

So Samuel shared everything he received with his spiritual mentor. Samuel's dream revelation was a confirmation of what the prophet had said earlier. Eli's response was lethargic. As a priest he should have interceded with God for his sons. Instead he just let things take their course.

Know God Better

God is still the Promise Keeper yet He is also a God of justice able and willing to judge His people. In this incident God raises up a new innocent next-generation of prophetic people who will press in to know Him better.

The Dream Process

∼

This is a literal dream. Although Samuel doesn't need an interpretation he did need instruction on how to properly respond to God. It was all new to Samuel. He assumed God's voice was the High Priest's Eli's voice, so he kept going to Eli until Eli realised God was talking to Samuel.

Perhaps God had similarly spoken to Eli in the past. When Samuel eventually recognised God as the source of the voice he says, Speak, for your servant is listening. At that point God delivered his plain message.

The Usual Suspects

∼

The lamp and the Ark of God was there. The Lord who came and stood there, calling as at the other times was probably Jesus. Satan was evident in the actions of Hophni and Phinehas.

Takeaways

∼

Like Gideon before him and David and Solomon after him, Eli didn't properly discipline his sons. The children's hearts were not turned to their father and the land was cursed.[9]

Samuel didn't do much better. The Bible says,

> When Samuel grew old, he appointed his sons as Israel's leaders. The name of his firstborn was Joel and the name of his second was Abijah, and they served at Beersheba. But his sons did not follow his ways. They turned aside after dishonest gain and accepted bribes and perverted justice. So all the elders of Israel gathered together and came to Samuel at Ramah. They said to him, "You are old, and your sons do not follow your ways; now appoint a king to lead us, such as all the other nations have.[10]"

Lack of integrity and no fear of God within the next generation opened a door for Israel to reject God as King and instead choose a man to rule over them. Samuel was displeased at this but the Lord told him:

> Listen to all that the people are saying to you; it is not you they have rejected, but they have rejected me as their king.[11]

The people were able to reject God as king because of the neglected character flaws within Samuel's sons.

NATHAN'S DREAM FOR KING DAVID

The Dream Setting/Backstory

This dream arrives nearly one hundred years after *Samuel's Night Vision Dream*. At this time God had given King David rest from all his enemies and grateful David wanted to build a temple to house the ark of God.

The Dream Scripture
2 Samuel 7:1-29

After the king was settled in his palace and the Lord had given him rest from all his enemies around him, he said to Nathan the prophet, "Here I am, living in a house of cedar, while the ark of God remains in a tent."

Nathan replied to the king, "Whatever you have in mind, go ahead and do it, for the Lord is with you."

But that night the word of the Lord came to Nathan, saying:

"Go and tell my servant David, 'This is what the Lord says: Are you the one to build me a house to dwell in? I have not dwelt in a house from the day I brought the Israelites up out of Egypt to this day. I have been moving from place to place with a tent as my dwelling. Wherever I have moved with all the Israelites, did I ever say to any of their rulers whom I commanded to shepherd my people Israel, "Why have you not built me a house of cedar?"'

"Now then, tell my servant David, 'This is what the Lord Almighty says: I took you from the pasture, from tending the flock, and appointed you ruler over my people Israel. I have been with you wherever you have gone, and I have cut off all your enemies from before you. Now I will make your name great, like the names of the greatest men on earth. And I will provide a place for my people Israel and will plant them so that they can have a home of their own and no longer be disturbed. Wicked people will not oppress them anymore, as they did at the beginning and have done ever since the time I appointed leaders over my people Israel. I will also give you rest from all your enemies.

"'The Lord declares to you that the Lord himself will establish a house for you: When your days are over and you rest with your ancestors, I will raise up your offspring to succeed you, your own flesh and blood, and I will establish his kingdom. He is the one who will build a house for my Name, and I will establish the throne of his kingdom forever. I will be his father, and he will be my son. When he does wrong, I will punish him with a rod wielded by men, with floggings inflicted by human hands. But my love will never be taken away from him, as I took it away from Saul, whom I removed from before you. Your house and your kingdom will endure forever before me; your throne will be established forever.'"

Nathan reported to David all the words of this entire revelation.

Then King David went in and sat before the Lord, and he said:

"Who am I, Sovereign Lord, and what is my family, that you have brought me this far? And as if this were not enough in your sight, Sovereign Lord, you have also spoken about the future of the house of your servant—and this decree, Sovereign Lord, is for a mere human!

"What more can David say to you? For you know your servant, Sovereign Lord. For the sake of your word and according to your will, you have done this great thing and made it known to your servant.

"How great you are, Sovereign Lord! There is no one like you, and there is no God but you, as we have heard with our own ears. And who is like your people Israel—the one nation on earth that God went out to redeem as a people for himself, and to make a name for himself, and to perform great and awesome wonders by driving out nations and their gods from before your people, whom you redeemed from Egypt? You have established your people Israel as your very own forever, and you, Lord, have become their God.

"And now, Lord God, keep forever the promise you have made concerning your servant and his house. Do as you promised, so that your name will be great forever. Then people will say, 'The Lord Almighty is God over Israel!' And the house of your servant David will be established in your sight.

"Lord Almighty, God of Israel, you have revealed this to your servant, saying, 'I will build a house for you.' So your servant has found courage to pray this prayer to you. Sovereign Lord, you are God! Your covenant is trustworthy, and you have promised these good things to your servant. Now be pleased to bless the house of your servant, that it may continue forever in your sight; for you, Sovereign Lord, have spoken, and with your blessing the house of your servant will be blessed forever."

The Problem

∼

David had the wonderful idea of building a temple to house the Ark of God but this was not part of God's plans and purpose.

The Dreamer's Metron

∼

Nathan was a court prophet, a scribe and a trusted advisor during the reign of King David. He wrote histories of David[1] and Solomon[2] and was also responsible for the temple music.[3]

Nathan was a tough-love fearless prophet. God used him to speak to David during some dark and emotional times in David's personal life.

It was Nathan who informed David he was not the one to build the Temple in Jerusalem. Instead, in a passage known as *Nathan's Oracle*, he prophesied God would build a dynasty for David.

Later, he boldly reprimanded David for committing adultery with Bathsheba and for murdering her faithful husband Uriah the Hittite.[4]

After the death of David and Bathsheba's love child Bathsheba became pregnant again. At this point, God sent Nathan to tell them He loved their new child. They called the baby, Solomon 'Jedidiah,' a name meaning, beloved of the Lord.[5]

Later David and Bathsheba called one of their sons Nathan, probably to honour Nathan's long faithful service and friendship.[6]

Nathan also bravely warned the dying David about Adonijah's plot to become king. This resulted in God's choice of Solomon becoming king instead.[7]

The Message

God pointed out, He has not asked David to build him a house. In fact, it is God who will build a house for David. God also promised to make David's name great and to give peace and space to His chosen people. God also told David He had chosen one of David's sons to build a house for His Name.

God's Purpose

God's purpose was that Solomon should build the Temple. 1 Chronicles says David was disqualified because he'd killed so many people,

> David said to Solomon: "My son, I had it in my heart to build a house for the Name of the Lord my God. But this word of the Lord came to me: 'You have shed much blood and have fought many wars. You are not to build a house for my Name, because you have shed much blood on the earth in my sight. But you will have a son who will be a man of peace and rest, and I will give him rest from all his enemies on every side. His name will be Solomon, and I will grant Israel peace and quiet during his reign. He is the one who will build a house for my Name. He will be my son, and I will be his father. And I will establish the throne of his kingdom over Israel forever.'[8]

Satan's Purpose

∼

Satan's purpose was to have David proceed with his own good intentioned plans without consulting God.

Dreamer's Eyes Enlightened

∼

Nathan clearly heard from God the message he should give to David.

Dreamer's Response and Application

∼

Nathan reported to David all the words of this entire revelation.

Know God Better

∼

God's plans and purpose must always be accomplished in God's way.

The Dream Process

∼

This is the only dream in the Bible where the dreamer receives a dream for another person. (Daniel was shown Nebuchadnezzar's dream but it was still Nebuchadnezzar's dream.) This is a literal dream in which God plainly told Nathan what to say to David on a number of important issues concerning David's metron. There is also some prophetic symbolism hidden in the dream with a possible reference to Jesus,

> He is the one who will build a house for my Name, and I will establish the throne of his kingdom forever. I will be his father, and he will be my son.[9]

The Usual Suspects

∽

God spoke to Nathan in the dream. Jesus was symbolically referred to as the Son who would establish the kingdom forever and Satan wanted David to do his own good intentioned thing without consulting God first.

Takeaways

∽

This is the only dream in the Bible in which God gives a prophetic message to the dreamer for another person. Interestingly it was given to a prophet and a prophet is one who speaks God's messages to people. David was also within Nathan's metron because Nathan was a bold trusted member of David's royal court and one of his closest advisers.

DAVID'S BEDTIME PRAYER

The Dream Setting/Backstory

David is about to lie down for the night. Outside his men are surrounded by a powerful army who have tracked him down. This was probably jealous King Saul.[1]

The Pre-Dream Scripture
Psalm 17:1-15

Hear, O LORD, my righteous plea;
listen to my cry.
Give ear to my prayer—
it comes from lips free of deceit.
May my vindication come from Your presence;

may Your eyes see what is right.
You have tried my heart;
You have visited me in the night.
You have tested me and found no evil;
I have resolved not to sin with my mouth.
As for the deeds of men—
by the word of Your lips
I have avoided the ways of the violent.
My steps have held to Your paths;
my feet have not slipped.
I call on You, O God,
for You will answer me.
Incline Your ear to me;
hear my words.
Show the wonders of Your loving devotion,
You who save by Your right hand
those who seek refuge from their foes.
Keep me as the apple of Your eye;
hide me in the shadow of Your wings
from the wicked who assail me,
from my mortal enemies who surround me.
They have closed their callous hearts;
their mouths speak with arrogance.
They have tracked us down, and now surround us;
their eyes are set to cast us to the ground,
like a lion greedy for prey,
like a young lion lurking in ambush.
Arise, O LORD, confront them!
Bring them to their knees;
deliver me from the wicked by Your sword,
from such men, O LORD, by Your hand—
from men of the world
whose portion is in this life.

> May You fill the bellies of Your treasured ones and
> satisfy their sons,
> so they leave their abundance to their children.
> As for me, I will behold Your face in righteousness;
> when I awake, I will be satisfied in Your presence.

∼

The Problem

∼

David and his army are surrounded by a superior enemy army.

The Dreamer's Metron

∼

King David was a shepherd boy who became Israel's third greatest king after Hezekiah[2] and Josiah[3] though he was far more famous. David has more mentions in the Old Testament than anyone else and only Jesus has more references in the New Testament.

David, God's 'anointed one'[4] was from the tribe of Judah[5] and Bethlehem which Luke refers to as 'the town of David.[6]

Despite his many obvious flaws, David is called a man after God's own heart.[7] Paul says, this was because of his obedience to God.[8]

David was also an anointed musician whose songs chased demons away.[9]. He wrote half of the Book of Psalms.[10]

He was also giant slayer, world famous for killing the Philistine Nephilim giant Goliath.[11] David was a brave warrior and leader of men.[12]

The Message/Prayer

∼

David knows he is in good standing with God with no unresolved issues. So he asks God to protect him and deal with his enemies. As he heads off to sleep he tells God he will see His face in righteousness, perhaps in a dream? He also looks forward to when he awakes. He knows he will not die or be killed in his sleep.

God's Purpose

∼

God's purpose was to care for and protect His friend and the leader of His Covenant People.

Satan's Purpose

∼

Satan's purpose was that David would be anxious and fearful and would lose a good night's sleep.

Prayer's Eyes Enlightened

∼

David knew God would answer his prayers and keep him as the apple of God's eye.

Dreamer's Response and Application

∼

David prayed to God in the midst of his predicament and then drifted off to sleep confident God would prevent David's enemies from harming His Covenant People and their seed line.

Know God Better

∼

David knew God was completely dependable. So he confidently prayed beautiful words,

> Show the wonders of Your loving devotion,
> You who save by Your right hand
> those who seek refuge from their foes.
> Keep me as the apple of Your eye;
> hide me in the shadow of Your wings

The Prayer Process

∼

David's prayer begins with a plea for deliverance from his life threatening enemies and ends with the confident assertion of having been heard and consequently being able to sleep in peace under God's loving protection.

David knows his enemies are unjustly accusing him. Typical of Satan. So, he asks his friend God for help and pleads his innocence citing his intimate relationship with God as justification.

After all God knows all about him for God has tried his heart and has also often visited him in the night, most likely in dialoguing dreams.

On this basis David asks God for vindication. David then asks God to be his refuge. He wants to be kept safe like the apple of God's eye and protected like a little bird under its mother's wing.

David describes his pitiless enemies who wish to tear him apart like a bunch of wolves and lions. He then affirms his belief in the resurrection by saying while their hope is only for this life, his hope is in the righteousness of God. Then he heads off to sleep knowing God will still be there in the morning.

There are both literal and symbolic levels to David's prayer. On the physical level David and his army actually are surrounded by a fierce life threatening army and David is happy to go off to sleep under God's protection. He knows Sovereign God is the one in control.

On the symbolic level David is also prophesying about the final sleep of death. In this picture even though Satan and his demons are surrounding and accusing us, we who have placed our faith in the saving power of Jesus's sacrifice will awake to the presence of God in eternity.

Like David our eyes are not focused on temporal treasures, but on the eternal and satisfying riches of the Lord Jesus Christ.

There are also prophetic lines that look forward to Jesus on the cross,

> My steps have held to Your paths;
> my feet have not slipped.
> I call on You, O God,

for You will answer me.
Incline Your ear to me;
hear my words.[13]

Keep me as the apple of Your eye;
hide me in the shadow of Your wings
from the wicked who assail me,
from my mortal enemies who surround me.[14]

The Usual Suspects

∽

David prays to God. Jesus the Messiah will come from David's seed line and Satan is seen in the actions of the surrounding army crouched like a lion greedy for prey.

Takeaways

∽

David is very familiar with God visiting him in the night. I'm sure many of those visits were in dreams.

SOLOMON'S 'DISCERNING HEART' DREAM

The Dream Setting/Backstory

This dream was sent a hundred years after Samuel's night vision. Dreams were still rare in these days. God usually spoke to kings through prophets but in this case He appeared in a dream and asked Solomon what he wanted. Solomon was being tested. His response would reveal his heart.

The Dream Scripture
Kings 3:5-28

At Gibeon the Lord appeared to Solomon during the night in a dream, and God said, "Ask for whatever you want me to give you." Solomon answered, "You have shown great kindness to your servant, my father David, because he was faithful to you and righteous and upright in heart. You have continued this great kindness to him and have given him a son to sit on his throne this very day. "Now, Lord my God, you have made your servant king in place of my father David. But I am only a little child and do not know how to carry out my duties. Your servant is here among the people you have chosen, a great people, too numerous to count or number. So give your servant a discerning heart to govern your people and to distinguish between right and wrong. For who is able to govern this great people of yours?"

The Lord was pleased that Solomon had asked for this. So God said to him, "Since you have asked for this and not for long life or wealth for yourself, nor have asked for the death of your enemies but for discernment in administering justice, I will do what you have asked. I will give you a wise and discerning heart, so that there will never have been anyone like you, nor will there ever be. Moreover, I will give you what you have not asked for—both wealth and honour—so that in your lifetime you will have no equal among kings. And if you walk in obedience to me and keep my decrees and commands as David your father did, I will give you a long life."

Then Solomon awoke—and he realised it had been a dream.

The Problem

Solomon, the youngest of his brothers, had been made king and was now at the helm of the vehicle God was using to bring forth the Messiah. Solomon was just twenty-three when he had this dream. The main problem was he had never been equipped for kingship.

The Dreamer's Metron

∽

King Solomon was incredibly blessed by God and is still known worldwide. God made him the wisest man who ever lived. He was a prolific writer, poet, and scientist. He wrote Proverbs, the Song of Solomon, Ecclesiastes, and two psalms as well as 3,000 proverbs and 1,005 songs.

He organised and ruled Israel with fairness and built the first temple in Jerusalem alongside a majestic palace, gardens, roads, and government buildings. Solomon's skills in architecture and management turned Israel into the showplace of the Middle East. He made treaties and alliances that brought great peace to his kingdom. He traded with other nations and made Israel wealthy.

The Message

∽

Solomon desired a discerning heart in order to govern Israel well. God's clear message was He would indeed give Solomon a wise and discerning heart.

In fact, God was so pleased with Solomon's request He said He'd give Solomon what he had not asked for, both wealth and honour, so that in Solomon's lifetime there would be no king like him.

God then made Solomon a final conditional promise. He said, If you walk in obedience to me and keep my decrees and commands as David your father did, I will give you a long life.

God's Purpose

God was still keeping His Covenant Promises to Abraham about the coming Messiah. God's main purpose was to equip Solomon to rule Israel well. God also wanted Solomon to live a long and fruitful life. God was similarly concerned for the lives of Abraham and Jacob in their dreams.

Seems it's God's desire we be obedient and live long fruitful lives. God gifted Solomon with incomparable heavenly wisdom, which Solomon foolishly squandered by disobeying God's commandments.

Satan's Purpose

Satan's purpose was that Solomon should be disobedient to God's decrees and commands. Solomon's downfall began when he disobeyed the word of God spoken through Moses who said,

> The king, moreover, must not acquire great numbers
> of horses for himself or make the people return to
> Egypt to get more of them, for the Lord has told
> you, "You are not to go back that way again." He
> must not take many wives, or his heart will be led
> astray. He must not accumulate large amounts of
> silver and gold.
> When he takes the throne of his kingdom, he is to
> write for himself on a scroll a copy of this law,
> taken from that of the Levitical priests. It is to be
> with him, and he is to read it all the days of his
> life so that he may learn to revere the Lord his God
> and follow carefully all the words of this law and

these decrees and not consider himself better than his fellow Israelites and turn from the law to the right or to the left. Then he and his descendants will reign a long time over his kingdom in Israel.[1]

Solomon ignored God's decrees not to multiply horses, wives and gold. He also didn't read his Bible each day.

After his political marriage to Pharaoh's daughter lust became a problem. Many of Solomon's 700 wives and 300 concubines were foreign women who worshipped other gods. Eventually they lured Solomon's heart away from Yahweh into the worship of their false gods and idols.

Satan gained a great victory through Solomon's disobedience. Even today Freemasons boldly promote Solomon as an affluent wise spiritual leader of men who happily embraced and worshipped many Gods.

Dreamer's Eyes Enlightened

∼

Solomon clearly knew God answered his request for a wise and discerning heart. He knew this would bring him fame. He also knew God would bless him with such great wealth and honour that in his lifetime he would have no equal among kings. He understood if he walked in obedience and kept God's decrees and commands as his father David had then God would give him a long life

Dreamer's Response and Application

∼

On one hand Solomon believed God and received the wonderful wisdom. On the other hand he didn't obey God like his father David and he didn't receive a long life. God's first two promised gifts concerning wisdom and wealth were unconditional. The third promise of a long life was conditional on Solomon's obedience.

This last promise never came to pass because Solomon weakened into sin and rebellion and died aged sixty. He broke all of Moses' instructions for a godly king.

Know God Better

God is pleased when we humbly desire to be responsible and succeed in our metron. He is also willing to give us more than we can ask or think. Paul said,

> Now to him who is able to do immeasurably more than
> all we ask or imagine, according to his power that is
> at work within us, to him be glory in the church
> and in Christ Jesus throughout all generations, for
> ever and ever! Amen.[2]

We also realise there are consequences for disobedience. We can die young and leave no legacy to our descendants. Nehemiah said,

> Was it not because of marriages like these that
> Solomon king of Israel sinned? Among the many
> nations there was no king like him. He was loved by
> his God, and God made him king over all Israel, but
> even he was led into sin by foreign women.[3]

The Dream Process

～

This is a literal dream in which God appears. This appearance of God would have been Jesus because no man has ever seen God. The dream doesn't require an interpretation. It is clear and simple.

It concerns Solomon's life and the Israeli nation. It's a calling dream with impartation and a conditional promise. It's also an interactive dream in which the dreamer dialogues with God very similar to *King Abimelek's Dream*. It is of personal, nation and international importance.

The Usual Suspects

～

Jesus is in the dream dialoguing with Solomon. God is there in His life giving word and decrees. Satan and the gods are waiting in the wings for Solomon's disobedience to open a door for them to destroy God's people and hinder God's plans.

Takeaways

～

Initially, Solomon's focus was firmly on God's plans and purpose. He desired wisdom so he could rule God's people well. God was pleased with this attitude and gave him what Jesus promised,

> But seek first his kingdom and his righteousness, and
> all these things will be given to you as well.[4]

Solomon is a good example of gift versus character.

Despite God's mighty anointing and gifting, Solomon didn't fully pay attention to God's written word. This brought about an early death for Solomon and great disaster for Israel. The Three G's took him out in the end. The Girls, the Gold and the Glory.

SOLOMON'S 'THE BRIDE'S' DREAM

The Dream Setting/Backstory

This is a literary dream created by a man instead of the usual spiritual dreams sent by God. Solomon penned this love poem dream seventeen years after his first recorded dream.

Because God is nowhere mentioned there was much debate before the *Song of Solomon* was accepted into the Jewish scriptures. It was finally included only because of its possible allegorical interpretation as a love relationship between God and His covenant people.

The Song of Solomon, also called the *Song of Songs* is an ancient love poem/song created to be performed before a live audience accompanied by music. There are differing interpretations of this simple yet complex poem. Some theologians suggest it refers to Solomon while others believe it's a song about a shepherd and a shepherdess.

Both interpretations find textual support. Essentially it's a celebration of erotic yearning between a man and a woman.

The main point for the dream interpreter is this dream was authored by man and not by God. So, unlike all other Bible dreams it doesn't contain clear crisp specific instructions from God. Nevertheless God has allowed it to become part of Scripture so I'll treat it as I've done all other Bible dreams.

The Dream Scripture
Song of Songs 3:1-5:16

∽

All night long on my bed
   I looked for the one my heart loves;
   I looked for him but did not find him.
I will get up now and go about the city,
   through its streets and squares;
I will search for the one my heart loves.
   So I looked for him but did not find him.
The watchmen found me
   as they made their rounds in the city.
   "Have you seen the one my heart loves?"
Scarcely had I passed them
   when I found the one my heart loves.
I held him and would not let him go
   till I had brought him to my mother's house,
   to the room of the one who conceived me.
Daughters of Jerusalem, I charge you
   by the gazelles and by the does of the field:
Do not arouse or awaken love
   until it so desires.
   Who is this coming up from the wilderness

    like a column of smoke,
perfumed with myrrh and incense
    made from all the spices of the merchant?
 Look! It is Solomon's carriage,
    escorted by sixty warriors,
    the noblest of Israel,
all of them wearing the sword,
    all experienced in battle,
each with his sword at his side,
    prepared for the terrors of the night.
 King Solomon made for himself the carriage;
    he made it of wood from Lebanon.
 Its posts he made of silver,
    its base of gold.
Its seat was upholstered with purple,
    its interior inlaid with love.
Daughters of Jerusalem, come out,
    and look, you daughters of Zion.
Look on King Solomon wearing a crown,
    the crown with which his mother crowned him
on the day of his wedding,
    the day his heart rejoiced.

He

How beautiful you are, my darling!
    Oh, how beautiful!
    Your eyes behind your veil are doves.
Your hair is like a flock of goats
    descending from the hills of Gilead.
 Your teeth are like a flock of sheep just shorn,
    coming up from the washing.
Each has its twin;
    not one of them is alone.

Your lips are like a scarlet ribbon;
    your mouth is lovely.
Your temples behind your veil
    are like the halves of a pomegranate.
Your neck is like the tower of David,
    built with courses of stone;
on it hang a thousand shields,
    all of them shields of warriors.
Your breasts are like two fawns,
    like twin fawns of a gazelle
    that browse among the lilies.
Until the day breaks
    and the shadows flee,
I will go to the mountain of myrrh
    and to the hill of incense.
You are altogether beautiful, my darling;
    there is no flaw in you.
Come with me from Lebanon, my bride,
    come with me from Lebanon.
Descend from the crest of Amana,
    from the top of Senir, the summit of Hermon,
from the lions' dens
    and the mountain haunts of leopards.
You have stolen my heart, my sister, my bride;
    you have stolen my heart
with one glance of your eyes,
    with one jewel of your necklace.
How delightful is your love, my sister, my bride!
    How much more pleasing is your love than wine,
and the fragrance of your perfume
    more than any spice!
Your lips drop sweetness as the honeycomb, my bride;

milk and honey are under your tongue.
The fragrance of your garments
   is like the fragrance of Lebanon.
You are a garden locked up, my sister, my bride;
   you are a spring enclosed, a sealed fountain.
Your plants are an orchard of pomegranates
   with choice fruits,
   with henna and nard,
    nard and saffron,
   calamus and cinnamon,
   with every kind of incense tree,
   with myrrh and aloes
   and all the finest spices.
You are a garden fountain,
   a well of flowing water
   streaming down from Lebanon.

She

Awake, north wind,
   and come, south wind!
Blow on my garden,
   that its fragrance may spread everywhere.
Let my beloved come into his garden
   and taste its choice fruits.

He

I have come into my garden, my sister, my bride;
   I have gathered my myrrh with my spice.
I have eaten my honeycomb and my honey;
   I have drunk my wine and my milk.

Friends

Eat, friends, and drink;
   drink your fill of love.

She

I slept but my heart was awake.
   Listen! My beloved is knocking:
"Open to me, my sister, my darling,
   my dove, my flawless one.
My head is drenched with dew,
   my hair with the dampness of the night."
I have taken off my robe—
   must I put it on again?
I have washed my feet—
   must I soil them again?
My beloved thrust his hand through the latch-
   opening;
   my heart began to pound for him.
I arose to open for my beloved,
   and my hands dripped with myrrh,
my fingers with flowing myrrh,
   on the handles of the bolt.
I opened for my beloved,
   but my beloved had left; he was gone.
   My heart sank at his departure.
I looked for him but did not find him.
   I called him but he did not answer.
The watchmen found me
   as they made their rounds in the city.
They beat me, they bruised me;
   they took away my cloak,
   those watchmen of the walls!
Daughters of Jerusalem, I charge you—
   if you find my beloved,
what will you tell him?
   Tell him I am faint with love.

Friends

How is your beloved better than others,

most beautiful of women?
How is your beloved better than others,
   that you so charge us?

She

My beloved is radiant and ruddy,
   outstanding among ten thousand.
His head is purest gold;
   his hair is wavy
   and black as a raven.
His eyes are like doves
   by the water streams,
washed in milk,
   mounted like jewels.
His cheeks are like beds of spice
   yielding perfume.
His lips are like lilies
   dripping with myrrh.
His arms are rods of gold
   set with topaz.
His body is like polished ivory
   decorated with lapis lazuli.
His legs are pillars of marble
   set on bases of pure gold.
His appearance is like Lebanon,
   choice as its cedars.
His mouth is sweetness itself;
   he is altogether lovely.
This is my beloved, this is my friend,
   daughters of Jerusalem.

The Problem

This young love-struck virgin who yearns to be wed and enjoying the marriage bed, dreams of seeking and finding her lover. Then the dream repeats itself with the different outcome of her been beaten by night watchmen and not finding her lover.

Dreamer's Metron

This beautiful virgin is around sixteen years old. Her metron comes from her intense love for her future husband. This love empowers her. Her friends call her blessed. Sounds a lot like the young Virgin Mary.

The Message

The allegorical dream message is clear, Those who selflessly seek God will find him despite all the difficulties.

God's Purpose

God's purpose for this dream is to reveal the sort of lover He desires. Lovers willing to overcome all obstacles in their pursuit of Him. Other scriptures say similar,

> You will seek me and find me when you seek me with all your heart.[1]

> But if from there you seek the Lord your God, you will find him if you seek him with all your heart and with all your soul.[2]

> My soul yearns for you in the night; in the morning my spirit longs for you. You, God, are my God, earnestly I seek you; I thirst for you, my whole being longs for you, in a dry and parched land where there is no water.[3]

> As the deer pants for streams of water, so my soul pants for you, my God.[4]

Satan's Purpose

Satan's purpose is seen in the actions of the watchmen who hinder the girl in her search. They beat her and bruise her and steal her cloak representing her anointing.

Dreamer's Eyes Enlightened

The virgin realised there is great pain and difficulty in true love yet she could not be stopped in her quest. This is perhaps best said in chapter eight, Many waters cannot quench love; rivers cannot sweep it away.

Dreamer's Response and Application

～

The dreamers' response is to overcome adversity and keep seeking. She longs for the wedding bed in her mother's house. This is not some secret liaison. She openly tells the daughters of Jerusalem how painful true love can be yet she always keeps the prize in her sight and forever praises her wonderful lover.

Know God Better

～

God has a consuming love for us. He wants the same in return. We were created for intimacy. Satan tried to mess this up. But God sent His son born of a woman to destroy the works of Satan.

Jesus' death opened the doorway to intimacy once again. The curtain of separation has been torn. We can now boldly enter the Most Holy Place by the blood of Jesus by a new and living way opened for us through the curtain, that is, his body.[5] God who is love wants love!

The Dream Process

～

The first part of this repeated dream depicts God's plans and purpose for the girl in that she finds the desire of her heart. The second part shows Satan's hindering actions to thwart God's plans and purpose for the girl and her lover. This represents Jesus and His Bride.

This dream requires interpretation. For the Jew the dream conjures up images of the chosen covenant people longing for the presence of their God,

> I have posted watchmen on your walls, Jerusalem;
>   they will never be silent day or night.
> You who call on the Lord,
>   give yourselves no rest,
> and give him no rest till he establishes Jerusalem
>   and makes her the praise of the earth.[6]

For the Christian the image is of a lovelorn people yearning for the final return of their lover Jesus. Like the Shulamite we see Christ by faith through a glass, darkly. But at His second coming we shall see him face to face. Then our marriage will take place and the bliss begin. Then the words of Jesus will come to pass,

> Father, I want those you have given me to be with me
>   where I am, and to see my glory, the glory you have
>   given me because you loved me before the creation
>   of the world.[7]

The Usual Suspects

∼

God who is love is everywhere in the Song of Solomon. He is the air they breathe. Jesus is also everywhere apparent in the form of the desired lover. He is the Lily of the Valley, the bright morning star.

He is especially obvious in the picture of the beloved outside the virgin's door;

> Behold, I stand at the door and knock. If anyone hears My voice and opens the door, I will come in to him and dine with him, and he with Me.[8]

Satan is also obvious in the hindering persecution of the watchers on the wall who steal the virgin's cloak.

Takeaways

∾

Love is the lifeblood in our relationship with God. Jesus said the most important of all God's commands was to Love the Lord your God with all your heart.[9]

We were all created with a love yearning that can only be satisfied by knowing God. Our route to intimacy is like the Shulamite's who passionately pursued her lover. Before He returned to heaven Jesus said,

> Anyone who loves me will obey my teaching. My Father will love them, and we will come to them and make our home with them. Anyone who does not love me will not obey my teaching. These words you hear are not my own; they belong to the Father who sent me. All this I have spoken while still with you. But the Advocate, the Holy Spirit, whom the Father will send in my name, will teach you all things and will remind you of everything I have said to you. Peace I leave with you; my peace I give you.

I do not give to you as the world gives. Do not let your hearts be troubled and do not be afraid. You heard me say, 'I am going away and I am coming back to you.*10*

SOLOMON'S WARNING DREAM

The Dream Setting/Backstory

Twenty years after Solomon's 'Discerning Heart' Dream, God again appeared to Solomon after he'd moved the Ark of the Covenant into the House of the Lord at Gibeon.

While Solomon was praying the Glory Cloud so powerfully filled the Temple that the priests couldn't stand. Solomon prayed beautiful prayers reminding God of his covenant with Israel. He said,

> I have provided a place there for the ark, in which is
> the covenant of the Lord that he made with our
> ancestors when he brought them out of Egypt.[1]

Solomon also reminded God of his covenant with David. He said,

> Now Lord, the God of Israel, keep for your servant
> David my father the promises you made to him

when you said, You shall never fail to have a successor to sit before me on the throne of Israel, if only your descendants are careful in all they do to walk before me faithfully as you have done.[2]

Afterwards God sent this dream.

The Dream Scripture
I Kings 9:1-6

∽

When Solomon had finished building the temple of the Lord and the royal palace, and had achieved all he had desired to do, the Lord appeared to him a second time, as he had appeared to him at Gibeon. The Lord said to him:

"I have heard the prayer and plea you have made before me; I have consecrated this temple, which you have built, by putting my Name there forever. My eyes and my heart will always be there.

"As for you, if you walk before me faithfully with integrity of heart and uprightness, as David your father did, and do all I command and observe my decrees and laws, I will establish your royal throne over Israel forever, as I promised David your father when I said, 'You shall never fail to have a successor on the throne of Israel.'

"But if you or your descendants turn away from me and do not observe the commands and decrees I have given you and go off to serve other gods and worship them, then I will cut off Israel from the land I have given them and will reject this temple I have consecrated for my Name. Israel will then become a byword and an object of ridicule among all peoples. This temple will become a heap of rubble. All who pass by will be appalled and will scoff and say, 'Why has the Lord done such a thing to this land and to this temple?' People will answer, 'Because they have forsaken the Lord their God, who brought their ancestors out of Egypt, and have embraced other gods, worshiping and serving them—that is why the Lord brought all this disaster on them.'"

The Problem

∼

Solomon's continuing blessing and success were conditional on his obedience to God.

The Dreamer's Metron

∼

King Solomon was profoundly blessed by God. God made him the wisest man who ever lived. He was a prolific writer, poet, and scientist. He wrote Proverbs, the Song of Solomon, Ecclesiastes, and two psalms.

I Kings says he wrote 3,000 proverbs and 1,005 songs. He organized and ruled Israel with fairness and built the first temple in Jerusalem alongside a majestic palace, gardens, roads, and government buildings.

Solomon's skills in architecture and management turned Israel into the showplace of the Middle East. He made treaties and alliances that brought great peace to his kingdom. He traded with other nations and made Israel incredibly wealthy.

The Message

God assured Solomon He had heard and accepted his prayers and had consecrated the building. He also promised His eyes and heart would be on Jerusalem continually just as Solomon asked.

God then renewed the Davidic covenant with Solomon in much the same way as He'd previously renewed and affirmed the Abrahamic covenant with Isaac and Jacob.

God then made a conditional promise to Solomon concerning his destiny, the destiny of his descendants and the destiny of all Israel. God said if Solomon would walk faithfully before him like his father David had then there would always be one of his family line on the Throne of Israel.

On the other hand if Solomon or his descendants left following God and went off to serve and worship other gods then terrible things would happen not only for Solomon's line but also for the whole nation of Israel.

God's Purpose

God's purpose was to tell Solomon that his prayers had been accepted and would be answered. His purpose was also to remind Solomon how to be successful in his life and calling.

Solomon knew what to do. He had prayed,

> Now Lord, the God of Israel, keep for your servant
> David my father the promises you made to him
> when you said, You shall never fail to have a

successor to sit before me on the throne of Israel, if only your descendants are careful in all they do to walk before me faithfully as you have done.[3]

In this dream God was again affirming his covenant with Solomon and underlining the responsibilities and penalties, the blessings and curses involved.

Satan's Purpose

As usual Satan's purpose was to hinder God's plans and purpose. God clearly explained Satan's plans and purposes to Solomon. God knew Satan would tempt Solomon and Israel to disregard God's commands and decrees and to serve other gods and worship them. Satan was very successful in his schemes concerning Solomon.

Dreamer's Eyes Enlightened

Solomon had clearly and powerfully heard God's plans and purpose for him, his family and for Israel. He knew what was required of him.

Dreamer's Response and Application

Solomon's response and application were awful, the worst in all Scripture. The pagan Kings, Abimelek and Pharaoh were obedient to God's voice in their dreams and they and their people were blessed because of this.

Solomon instead was totally disobedient to God's conditional promise and he and his people were cursed. Before the children of Israel entered Canaan, Moses warned that a king of Israel should not take many wives and not to gather many horses and chariots, especially from Egypt. He also warned a king should not accumulate large amounts of silver and gold.[4]

Solomon blatantly disregarded all of these warnings. God knew marrying women outside of the covenant of Israel would lead to sensuality, idolatry and apostasy. This is what happened with Solomon. Scripture says,

> King Solomon, however, loved many foreign women besides Pharaoh's daughter—Moabites, Ammonites, Edomites, Sidonians and Hittites. They were from nations about which the Lord had told the Israelites, "You must not intermarry with them, because they will surely turn your hearts after their gods." Nevertheless, Solomon held fast to them in love. He had seven hundred wives of royal birth and three hundred concubines, and his wives led him astray. As Solomon grew old, his wives turned his heart after other gods, and his heart was not fully devoted to the Lord his God, as the heart of David his father had been. He followed Ashtoreth the goddess of the Sidonians, and Molek the detestable god of the Ammonites. So Solomon did evil in the eyes of the Lord; he did not follow the Lord completely, as David his father had done.

> On a hill east of Jerusalem, Solomon built a high place
> for Chemosh the detestable god of Moab, and for
> Molek the detestable god of the Ammonites. He did
> the same for all his foreign wives, who burned
> incense and offered sacrifices to their gods.
> The Lord became angry with Solomon because his
> heart had turned away from the Lord, the God of
> Israel, who had appeared to him twice.[5]

God was outraged with Solomon's idolatry and punished him by removing ten of the twelve tribes from Israel. Yet in His mercy He delayed His judgement until after Solomon's early death and because of His promise to David He gave one tribe to Solomon's son.

Know God Better

∾

God is a trustworthy covenant keeper who honours His word. He is ready to instruct and guide us in the good way we should go. He is more than willing to explain the blessings and curses inherent in any situation. If we obey Him we will be blessed. If we continually disobey Him we will be cursed.

The Dream Process

∾

The dream process is very similar to Solomon's first dream only this time God does all the talking. As no man has ever seen God this is Jesus who is appearing and talking to Solomon.

And just like in Solomon's first dream at Gibeon Jesus warns him about the dangers of disobedience and the blessings of obedience. This is a literal dream that doesn't require an interpretation but it does require strict obedience on the part of Solomon and his dependants.

It's scope impacts Solomon's life, his family line and the Israeli nation to this very day. It's a dream that answered questions asked in prayer. It also contained a wonderful conditional promise for Solomon and his family line and six dreadful warnings about not keeping covenant and worshiping other gods.

The Usual Suspects

∼

Jesus appears in the dream dialoguing with Solomon. God is there in Solomon's life giving words and decrees. Earlier Solomon had experienced the Holy Spirit in the Glory Cloud. Satan and the gods are still waiting in the wings for Solomon's disobedience to open a door for them to destroy the people of God and hinder God's plans. They patiently wait to exploit Solomon's weaknesses.

Takeaways

∼

Solomon's downfall began when he married Pharaoh's daughter for political advancement. Then lust became a problem. Among Solomon's 700 wives and 300 concubines were foreign women who worshipped foreign gods. Eventually they seduced Solomon away from the worship of Yahweh.

Solomon's sins speak loudly to our materialistic culture. When we too value fame and fortune above God we're also headed for a fall. Solomon started off well and finished badly.

Despite his stunning gifts of wisdom and prosperity and his anointing Solomon still fell into idolatry. Despite experiencing the Lord's Glory Cloud Solomon ended up publicly worshipping the detestable gods Chemosh and Molech.

As he sacrificed innocent children to Molech on the Mount of Olives, Solomon was also sacrificing his own children's future. Unlike faithful Abraham, Solomon did not teach his children after him the ways of the Lord.

God had said,

> For I have chosen him, so that he will direct his children and his household after him to keep the way of the Lord by doing what is right and just, so that the Lord will bring about for Abraham what he has promised him.[6]

Solomon didn't continue to follow and obey God, nor did he teach his children to follow the God of his father David. This was Solomon's greatest failure. He gained the whole world and lost his family.

He got caught up in the trappings of fame and power and failed in being responsible in the main area of his metron, his descendants and the nation of Israel.

The same thing also happened to Gideon. He too left a poor legacy to his children. He too got caught up in the girls, the gold and the glory.

SOLOMON 'ASKS FOR WISDOM' DREAM

The Dream Setting/Backstory

This is a 2 Chronicles retelling of *Solomon's 'Discerning Heart' Dream* from 1 Kings 3.

The interesting thing is there is no mention of the word dream in this incident. We are only told, That night God appeared to Solomon, though from reading about this incident in 1 Kings 3 we know it definitely was a dream.

This begs the question about just how many other situations were really dreams when we read words like *God appeared* or *God spoke*. The rest of my comments on this dream are similar to what was said concerning the same incident in *Solomon's 'Discerning Heart' Dream*.

This dream occurs over one hundred years after *Samuel's Night Vision Dream*. Dreams were still rare in those days. God usually spoke to kings through prophets but in this case God took the initiative, appeared in a dream, and asked Solomon what he wanted from

God. There was also a degree of testing in this offer for Solomon's response would reveal much about his heart.

The Dream Scripture
2 Chronicles 1:1-17

∼

Solomon son of David established himself firmly over his kingdom, for the Lord his God was with him and made him exceedingly great. Then Solomon spoke to all Israel—to the commanders of thousands and commanders of hundreds, to the judges and to all the leaders in Israel, the heads of families— and Solomon and the whole assembly went to the high place at Gibeon, for God's tent of meeting was there, which Moses the Lord's servant had made in the wilderness. Now David had brought up the ark of God from Kiriath Jearim to the place he had prepared for it, because he had pitched a tent for it in Jerusalem. But the bronze altar that Bezalel son of Uri, the son of Hur, had made was in Gibeon in front of the tabernacle of the Lord; so Solomon and the assembly inquired of him there. Solomon went up to the bronze altar before the Lord in the tent of meeting and offered a thousand burnt offerings on it.

That night God appeared to Solomon and said to him, "Ask for whatever you want me to give you."

Solomon answered God, "You have shown great kindness to David my father and have made me king in his place. Now, Lord God, let your promise to my father David be confirmed, for you have made me king over a people who are as numerous as the dust of the earth. Give me wisdom and knowledge, that I may lead this people, for who is able to govern this great people of yours?"

God said to Solomon, "Since this is your heart's desire and you have not asked for wealth, possessions or honour, nor for the death of your enemies, and since you have not asked for a long life but for wisdom and knowledge to govern my people over whom I have made you king, therefore wisdom and knowledge will be given you. And I will also give you wealth, possessions and honour, such as no king who was before you ever had and none after you will have."

Then Solomon went to Jerusalem from the high place at Gibeon, from before the tent of meeting. And he reigned over Israel.

Solomon accumulated chariots and horses; he had fourteen hundred chariots and twelve thousand horses, which he kept in the chariot cities and also with him in Jerusalem. The king made silver and gold as common in Jerusalem as stones, and cedar as plentiful as sycamore-fig trees in the foothills. Solomon's horses were imported from Egypt and from Kue—the royal merchants purchased them from Kue at the current price. They imported a chariot from Egypt for six hundred shekels of silver, and a horse for a hundred and fifty. They also exported them to all the kings of the Hittites and of the Arameans

The Problem

∽

Solomon although the youngest of his brothers had been made king over God's people Israel. He is now at the helm steering the vehicle God was using to bring forth the Messiah. Solomon was around twenty-three when he had this dream. Solomon's main problem then was he'd never been trained for leadership.

The Dreamer's Metron

∽

Solomon was super abundantly blessed by God. God made him the wisest man who ever lived. He was a prolific writer, poet, and scientist. He wrote Proverbs, the Song of Solomon, Ecclesiastes, and two psalms.

I Kings says he wrote 3,000 proverbs and 1,005 songs. He organised and ruled Israel with fairness and built the first temple in Jerusalem alongside a majestic palace, gardens, roads, and government buildings.

Solomon's skills in architecture and management turned Israel into the showplace of the Middle East. He made treaties and alliances that brought great peace to his kingdom. He traded with other nations and made Israel incredibly wealthy.

The Message

Solomon desired a discerning heart in order to govern Israel well. God's clear message was He was more than happy to give Solomon a wise and understanding heart. This is really the Holy Spirit, the spirit of wisdom and revelation that St Paul mentions in Ephesian 1:17.

God was so pleased with Solomon's answer He also freely gives him unequalled wealth and honour.

In this version of the dream there is no record of God's conditional promise concerning a long life mentioned in Solomon's 'Discerning Heart' Dream,

> And if you walk in obedience to me and keep my decrees and commands as David your father did, I will give you a long life.[1]

God's Purpose

God's purpose was to equip and enable Solomon to rule God's Chosen People well. God also wanted to bless Solomon and enable him to live a long and fruitful life. God was similarly concerned for the lives of Abraham and Jacob in their dreams. Seems it's God's normal desire that we be obedient to him so we can live long fruitful lives.

Satan's Purpose

Satan as usual was waiting in the wings to tempt Solomon and hinder God's plans. He would use the women, the horses and the gold. He would succeed by getting Solomon to be disobedient to God's word.

Dreamer's Eyes Enlightened

Solomon clearly knew God answered his request for a wise and discerning heart. He knew this would bring him fame. He also knew God would bless him with such great wealth and honour that in his lifetime he would have no equal among kings. He also knew if he walked in obedience to God and kept God's decrees and commands as his father David had then God would give him a long life

Dreamer's Response and Application

∼

The first two promised gifts of wisdom and wealth and honour were unconditional. They kicked in without any effort on Solomon's part. The third promised gift of a long life was conditional on Solomon's obedience and never came to pass because Solomon deteriorated into sin and rebellion and died aged sixty. This passage from 2 Chronicles doesn't specifically mention obedience but in this same incident in 1 Kings 3 we're told Solomon's long life would depend on his obedience.

Also Moses had warned Israel,

> The king, moreover, must not acquire great numbers of horses for himself or make the people return to Egypt to get more of them, for the Lord has told you, "You are not to go back that way again." He must not take many wives, or his heart will be led astray. He must not accumulate large amounts of silver and gold. When he takes the throne of his kingdom, he is to write for himself on a scroll a copy of this law, taken from that of the Levitical priests. It is to be with him, and he is to read it all the days of his life so that he may learn to revere the Lord his God and follow carefully all the words of this law and these decrees and not consider himself better than his fellow Israelites and turn from the law to the right or to the left. Then he and

his descendants will reign a long time over his kingdom in Israel.[2]

Solomon disregarded all these commandments. He didn't read from a copy of the law all the days of his life. He sent people to Egypt and acquired many horses. He married Pharaoh's daughter. He multiplied wives and he accumulated vast amounts of gold. Consequently he didn't live a long life and the consequences were even worse for his metron; his descendants and the people of Israel.

Know God Better

God is still keeping covenant with Abraham and his descendants. He is pleased when we're humble and desire to be responsible and succeed in our metron. He is also able and willing to give us more than we can ask or think. Ephesians 3:20-21 says,

> Now to him who is able to do immeasurably more than
> all we ask or imagine, according to his power that is
> at work within us, to him be glory in the church
> and in Christ Jesus throughout all generations, for
> ever and ever! Amen.

The Dream Process

This is a literal dream in which God appears. This is Jesus because no man apart from Jesus has ever seen God. The dream doesn't require an interpretation. It concerns Solomon's life and the Israeli nation.

It's a calling dream with a supernatural impartation of wisdom. It's also an interactive dream in which the dreamer dialogues with God very similar to other Genesis dreams. It has personal, national and international significance.

The Usual Suspects

Jesus appeared and dialogued with Solomon. Satan was waiting in the wings. The Holy Spirit was anointing Solomon for his calling. God was keeping His promises to Abraham, Isaac and Jacob.

Takeaways

God's gifts are excellent. They are blessings with no trouble added.[3] Solomon is a good example of the thorny issue of gift versus character.

Although he was mightily anointed and gifted yet he didn't obey God's warnings or pay daily attention to God's word. This brought about an early death and ultimately great disaster for Israel.

ELIPHAZ'S 'DEMONIC NIGHTMARE' DREAM

The Dream Setting/Backstory

*E*liphaz's dream is unique in Scripture. Apart from Solomon's literary dream it's one of only two recorded Bible dreams not from God. In this study I'm also treating Jesus' temptation by Satan as a dream.

Eliphaz's dream is also the only recorded nightmare in the Bible apart from *Egypt's Dreadful Dreams* from *The Wisdom of Solomon* in the Apocrypha which were probably all nightmares.

In *The Book of Job*, God initiated intense spiritual warfare by allowing Satan to test Job. Satan kicked off by destroying all Job's prosperity and killing his ten children.

Throughout Job's entire story none of the characters ever really understand what's going on. The three friends Eliphaz the Temanite, Bildad the Shuhite and Zophar the Naamathite came alongside Job and tried to comfort him with their worldly advice but it never helped.

Their natural wisdom wasn't divine revelation and the understanding they had was flawed. You can't cast out the flesh or discipline a demon. Eliphaz the dreamer is the oldest and kindest of Job's friends. He came from the important Edom city of Teman. The Temanite's were famous for their wisdom. Eliphaz was the first of Job's three visitors and was always the first to speak in all their discussions.

The Dream Scripture
Job 4:12-21

∼

A word was secretly brought to me, my ears caught a whisper of it. Amid disquieting dreams in the night, when deep sleep falls on people, fear and trembling seized me and made all my bones shake. A spirit glided past my face, and the hair on my body stood on end. It stopped, but I could not tell what it was. A form stood before my eyes, and I heard a hushed voice: 'Can a mortal be more righteous than God? Can even a strong man be more pure than his Maker? If God places no trust in his servants, if he charges his angels with error, how much more those who live in houses of clay, whose foundations are in the dust, who are crushed more readily than a moth! Between dawn and dusk they are broken to pieces; unnoticed, they perish forever. Are not the cords of their tent pulled up, so that they die without wisdom?

The Problem

∼

Job is in deep trouble and Eliphaz who doesn't have God's revelation offers his own advice as wisdom. Eliphaz received this dream experience from a demonic source and quoted it as if it was the revealed word of God. He also made the classic mistake of applying a personal dream to another's situation. He was using a possible rhema word as logos. This is always very dangerous but especially dangerous when the source of the word is Satan. Remember the book of Job is all about unseen and unrecognised intense spiritual warfare.

Dreamer's Metron

Eliphaz the Temanite came from the important Edom city of Teman. The Temanite's were famous for their wisdom. Eliphaz is Job's friend and believes in Job's God.

The Message

Everything about this dream situation is wrong. It reads like the script from a bad horror b-movie. The dream experience is terrifying and the message condemns rather than gives clear direction. In the midst of distressing dreams there is whispering and a hushed voice and fear and trembling and hair standing on end. Doesn't sound much like the Holy Spirit.

The message is also condemning. It misrepresents God's character and God's attitude to man as seen in other Bible dreams. There is no sense whatsoever of a Covenant Keeping God who loves His creation. Instead God is represented as lofty and distant and distrustful of man who He might destroy without mercy at any moment. This is a demonic dream.

God's Purpose

~

Perhaps God's main purpose for leaving this dream in Scripture is to warn us to properly interpret and apply dreams otherwise we can innocently end up angering God just like Eliphaz.

Satan's Purpose

~

God said Job was blameless and upright, a man who fears God and shuns evil. Satan violently attacked God's assessment of Job through this demonic dream. His purpose as usual was to misrepresent the character of God and cause a rift in our relationship with our Heavenly Father. He did this with Adam and Eve. He lied in order to make mankind believe God is cruel and unloving just like himself.

Satan's strategy in this dream was to give Eliphaz a cocktail of truth and lies. The truth part was no man could be more righteous and pure than God.

The lies part was God places no trust in His servants or His angels. God always trusted His servants the prophets and His righteous angels. He trusted the Virgin Mary and Joseph with Jesus and He trusted Job to pass this test.

Satan also depicted God as cruel and uncaring while the exact opposite is true. Jesus said,

> Are not two sparrows sold for a penny? Yet not one of them will fall to the ground outside your Father's care.[1]

Dreamer's Eyes Enlightened

∼

Eliphaz was deceived when he believed this dream was from God. His eyes were darkened as opposed to enlightened. This reminds us of Jesus' words, If then the light within you is darkness, how great is that darkness![2]

Eliphaz wrongly preached this dream message as if it was God's word and he influenced others like Bildad into believing and repeating it. At the end of Job God rebuked Eliphaz and said, I am angry with you and your two friends, because you have not spoken the truth about me, as my servant Job has.

Eliphaz's dream experience was not from God and didn't speak the truth about God. God then tells Eliphaz,

> So now take seven bulls and seven rams and go to my servant Job and sacrifice a burnt offering for yourselves. My servant Job will pray for you, and I will accept his prayer and not deal with you according to your folly.[3]

God recognized Eliphaz was foolish as opposed to being malicious and He forgave him his sin. This is the direct opposite of Eliphaz's dream message that depicts God as an angry deity ever ready to crush His distrusted creation for the slightest thing.

Having Job pray for Eliphaz reminds us of God having Abraham pray for Abimelek who was also in error but innocent in intent.

Dreamer's Response and Application

∾

Eliphaz made the novice's mistake of using a rhema word as a logos word. He used a personal revelation as if it was God's word to all mankind and wrongly applied it to Job. Eliphaz's dream brought no relief nor produced no faith in Job. Instead it just condemned and confused him even more.

Know God Better

∾

God places trust in His servants who are made in His image and likeness and is willing to let them undergo testing by the rebel Satan. Job was everything Satan wasn't. The Lord had told Satan,

> "Have you considered my servant Job? There is no one on earth like him; he is blameless and upright, a man who fears God and shuns evil.*4*"

The Dream Process

∾

This dream process is not entirely clear. From the dream scripture it's not totally apparent whether the spirit is within the dream or outside the dream. The dream experience itself produces great fear and physical manifestations. The whispering and hushed voice of the indistinct spirit reminds us of Isaiah's warning,

> When someone tells you to consult mediums and
> spiritists, who whisper and mutter, should not a
> people inquire of their God? Why consult the dead
> on behalf of the living? Consult God's
> instruction and the testimony of warning. If anyone
> does not speak according to this word, they have no
> light of dawn.[5]

The dream message itself is plain and literal and required no interpretation but it did need discernment. This half truth message claimed God was greater and purer than distrusted mankind who He was willing to crush at any time. This was a lie. There was also perhaps a little sting in the tail for the dreamer. The dream spirit said, Men die without wisdom.

Eliphaz came from Teman a place famous for wisdom.

The Usual Suspects

∼

It is God who initiates and oversees this interaction with Satan. In Job 42:5 when the Lord speaks to Job out of the storm Job says, My ears had heard of you but now my eyes have seen you. This would have been Jesus that Job saw.

Takeaways

∼

Satan loves the battleground of debate and theology but he is no match for God. In 1 Corinthians the apostle Paul quoted the words of Eliphaz about God catching those who are wise in their own eyes.

The quote is, He catches the wise in their craftiness, and the schemes of the wily are swept away. ⁶ Paul says, For the wisdom of this world is foolishness in God's sight. As it is written: 'He catches the wise in their craftiness.'

In the Book of Job, God caught Satan in his craftiness and once again worked all things together for good for His called servant.

JOB'S SATANIC NIGHTMARES

The Dream Setting/Backstory

Job, who is under intense personal spiritual attack from Satan, is totally unaware of the real source of his problems. He wrongly assumes it is God who is tormenting him in his dreams and visions.

The Dream Scripture
Job 7:11-16

Therefore I will not keep silent;
I will speak out in the anguish of my spirit,
 I will complain in the bitterness of my soul.
Am I the sea, or the monster of the deep,

>   that you put me under guard?
>   When I think my bed will comfort me
>   and my couch will ease my complaint,
>   even then you frighten me with dreams
>   and terrify me with visions,
>   so that I prefer strangling and death,
>   rather than this body of mine.
>   I despise my life; I would not live forever.
>   Let me alone; my days have no meaning.

The Problem

~

God has lifted His hand of protection from Job and has allowed Satan limited permission to test him. This includes the area of Job's dream life.

Dreamer's Metron

~

Job had a major metron. He was a God fearing prophet with a large prosperous family. God trusted Job enough to allow Satan to test him. God was proud of Job. He called Job His servant and said, There is none like him on the earth, a blameless and upright man, who fears God and turns away from evil?[1]

Ezekiel said Job was a righteous man of the same calibre as Noah and Daniel.[2]

James said Job was a blessed prophet, a shining example in the face of suffering. James also says Job's restoration was an example of God's compassion and mercy.[3]

The Message

∽

This is no specific recorded dream with a specific message. This dream scripture refers to many frightening dreams and visions from Satan.

Perhaps the real message here is Satan frightens and terrifies people with dreams and tries to shift the blame onto God.

Dreamer's Eyes Enlightened

∽

Job's eyes were not enlightened by these horrifying dreams. Instead he was confused and wrongly interpreted Satan's attack as God's punishment.

Job had no idea why all this awfulness was happening to him yet without any specific revelation of what was really happening in the unseen spiritual realm he remained faithful to God.

Dreamer's Response and Application

∽

Job wrongly blamed God for these satanic dreams. He had the wrong interpretation, wrong response and wrong application. In the end Job never ever found out the full truth of his situation though he finally understood his affliction was within God's will even though he despaired at not knowing why.

The Dream Process

∼

We know nothing about the dreams and visions except the dreams frightened Job and the visions terrified him.

God's Purpose

∼

As mentioned in the previous dream God has many purposes in the Book of Job. He revealed Satan as the accuser of the brethren and showed the continual spiritual warfare going on.

We learn the righteous often suffer when under spiritual attack and sometimes God's plans and purpose involve testing, pain and suffering. They certainly did for Jesus.

We also learn God is Sovereign and has Satan on a leash. God also shows us our self-righteousness is not enough. We all need a redeemer. God's overall purpose was to prove to Satan that Job was a righteous man who loved and served him even when times were awful and he didn't understand why he was suffering.

Know God Better

∼

We see God is willing to let His choice servants go through times of incredible testing in order to teach Satan and the gods a lesson.

The evil spirit in *Eliphaz's Demonic Nightmare Dream* said God places no trust in his servants. This was a blatant lie for God was more than willing to trust His servant Job.

God only allowed Satan to afflict Job because God knew faithful Job would never turn away from Him. We also see Sovereign God isn't obliged to explain Himself to His creation. When God finally speaks He neither justified the reason for Job's suffering nor defended His justice.

The Usual Suspects

It is God who initiates and oversees this interaction with Satan. In Job 42:5 when the Lord speaks to Job out of the storm Job says, My ears had heard of you but now my eyes have seen you. This would have been Jesus that Job saw and not God the Father.

Satan is very evident in these dreams and visions by the effect they have upon Job. Satan's relentless attacks caused Job anguish of spirit and bitterness of soul. Satan frightened and terrified Job so much he even despaired of his life, which he felt was meaningless.

Takeaways

The big lesson for the Christian dream interpreter is that it's entirely possible to give a wrong interpretation and like Eliphaz and Job blame God for what is really the work of Satan.

I've read some Christian dream interpreters who claimed these dream and visions of Job were nightmares from God. How foolish is that? Why would God, who was so proud of Job, send him terrifying dreams? God is not a capricious sadist who sends terrifying dreams to righteousness believers. That's Satan's role.

Christian dream interpreter's really do need to know God better. To this end we should say Paul's prayer often;

> I keep asking that the God of our Lord Jesus Christ, the
> glorious Father, may give you the Spirit of
> wisdom and revelation, so that you may know him
> better. I pray that the eyes of your heart may be
> enlightened in order that you may know the hope
> to which he has called you, the riches of his glorious
> inheritance in his holy people, and his
> incomparably great power for us who believe.[4]

Job's beautiful declaration, I know that my redeemer lives, and that in the end he will stand on the earth[5], is a lovely prophetic reference to Christ as our Redeemer. It has become the wellspring of several Christian hymns as well as being the famous opening lines of Part III of Handel's Messiah.

ELIHU'S DREAM TALK

The Dream Setting/Backstory

Job experienced a series of frightening dreams and visions as mentioned in *Job's Satanic Nightmares*. Job's main grievance was God didn't answer him in his distress.

Elihu countered Job's complaint with this revelation about how God often uses dreams and visions to answer our prayers though we may not recognise this. Elihu said God uses warning dreams in order to stop us from sinning and to guide us in the way we should go.

The Dream Scripture
Job 33:12-18

> But I tell you, in this you are not right,
>> for God is greater than any mortal.
> Why do you complain to him
>> that he responds to no one's words?
> For God does speak—now one way, now another—
>> though no one perceives it.
> In a dream, in a vision of the night,
>> when deep sleep falls on people
>> as they slumber in their beds,
> he may speak in their ears
>> and terrify them with warnings,
> to turn them from wrongdoing
>> and keep them from pride,
> to preserve them from the pit,
>> their lives from perishing by the sword.

∼

The Problem

∼

Job feels God disregards his prayers and difficulties and Elihu is trying to advise him.

Dreamer's Metron

∼

Elihu's metron is that of a truth teller who brings perspective. He plays a cameo role in the Book of Job. His entrance scene is,

But Elihu son of Barakel the Buzite, of the family of Ram, became very angry with Job for justifying himself rather than God.[1]

Elihu then speaks four times and disappears.

Elihu reaches the same conclusion as Eliphaz, Bildad, and Zophar but while they say Job is suffering because he sinned, Elihu said Job sinned verbally because of his suffering.

God's overall verdict was Job was a faultfinder who spoke without knowledge and put God in the wrong. Elihu says the same three things. In the end God clears Job and condemns Eliphaz, Bildad, and Zophar but says nothing regarding Elihu. The main points of Elihu's four speeches to Job are;

- God is not silent; he spoke through your pain.
- God is not unjust. He'll sort out the wicked.
- You may be trivial compared to God but righteous living is not purposeless.
- You're wrong to criticise God. Better to fear him.

The Message

∼

Elihu's message is clear enough. God speaks to us in ways we often miss. Sometimes He speaks in warning dreams and visions that frighten us.

God's Purpose

God's purpose for warning dreams and visions is to keep us from sinning against Him and suffering the consequences. God's dreams can save us from pride, which can cause us to fall. These dreams can also keep us alive and well and save us from hell.

Satan's Purpose

Satan's purpose is to keep us confused and disorientated so we begin to blame God for our problems.

Dreamer's Eyes Enlightened

What Elihu says about dreams can be generally true but was not really applicable in Job's case. His interpretation left Job none the wiser because Job's dreams were from Satan and not from God.

Nevertheless God's dreams can indeed frighten and warn people. We see this in Abimelek who repented and saved many lives. God also warned Laban who obeyed and saved lives. Pharaoh's Baker was probably terrified when he realised he was going to die at the hand of Pharaoh.

The Midianite's Dream about Gideon defeating their army probably also frightened him and his friend.

Samuel's night vision dream sternly warned Eli about his erring children. Solomon was also warned in a dream. Nebuchadnezzar was troubled, terrified and warned by his two dreams.

The interesting thing is apart from Abimelek and Laban none of the others were able or willing to act upon the warnings from God.

Dreamer's Response and Application

∽

There is always an opportunity for the dreamer to obey God and apply the warning and change their future for the better. In many dreams God encourages and guides His covenant people with specific direction for their well being and the safety of their seed line.

Sometimes a dream from God can be physically and emotionally hard to bear. For example, after *Daniel's 'Ram, Goat and Little Horn' Dream* the dreamer was overwhelmed. He said,

> I, Daniel, was worn out. I lay exhausted for several days. Then I got up and went about the king's business. I was appalled by the vision; it was beyond understanding.[2]

Know God Better

∽

God is a good Father. He loves us. God's intentions are always good towards His creation. He wants to save people. That's why God sends warning dreams. Peter says,

> With the Lord a day is like a thousand years, and a thousand years are like a day. The Lord is not slow in keeping his promise, as some understand

slowness. Instead he is patient with you, not wanting anyone to perish, but everyone to come to repentance.[3]

The Dream Process

Elihu doesn't mention any particular dream process. But he does say God does speak, now one way, now another though no one perceives it. He also said God may speak in their ears and terrify them with warnings. He says God does this to turn them from wrongdoing and going to hell. In context he was applying this logic to Job's dreams and in this case he was wrong.

The Usual Suspects

God the Father is there caring for his people and warning them about the results of their sinful actions. Satan is there telling lies, confusing people and maligning God. Jesus is hidden as the Redeemer who preserves them from the pit.

Takeaways

There's a teaching about 'sealed dreams' from Elihu's above dream talk that has gained popularity amongst some Christian dream interpreters. The King James Version of Job 33:16, says, Then He opens the ears of men, And seals their instruction. It's this phrase, *And seals their instruction,* that we're looking at.

This *'sealed dream teaching'* takes the position that sometimes God sends us *'sealed dreams'* we don't remember because God wants to bring about some radical change or course direction in our lives that we're not currently ready for.

So God sends a dream that 'seals His instruction' in our spirit and then 'pop' just at the right moment God releases the seal and the dream kicks in and we have a déjà vu moment. We then live out the dream moment without any decision or obedience on our part. Sounds great!

The only problem is there is not one dream in all of the Bible that fits this profile. Some folk have also taught these 'Sealed Dreams' or 'Concealed Dreams' are actually the best dreams to have. I don't think so.

In Daniel 2, Nebuchadnezzar couldn't remember his *'Large Statue' Dream.* He became angry and furious because none of the wise men of Babylon could tell him his dream and interpret it.

Imagine what would have happened if Daniel had waltzed in and said, Hi Nebuchadnezzar, don't you know that's a 'sealed dream', one of the best dreams you can have?

Instead Daniel sought the Lord and God revealed the dream to him and in so doing preserved Daniel's life, that of his friends and the lives of all the wise men of Babylon.

It was Daniel's faith and anointing to hear from God that propelled him into prominence in Nebuchadnezzar's court and not some lame teaching about 'sealed dreams'.

Also imagine what would have happened if Joseph had said to Mary, I had a dream last night that I can't remember?

Would Mary have replied, Oh, that's a 'sealed dream' Joseph. Well get a big surprise when the answer arrives!

The only Biblical dream that mentions a sealed dream interpretation is from Daniel 8. Here the dream is seen and written down but Daniel can't understand the angel's interpretation. The Scripture says,

> "The vision of the evenings and mornings that has been given you is true, but seal up the vision, for it concerns the distant future."
> I, Daniel, was worn out. I lay exhausted for several days. Then I got up and went about the king's business. I was appalled by the vision; it was beyond understanding.

This is a far cry from a 'sealed dream' that just pops out in a déjà vu moment.

The New International Version of Job 33: 16 uses the phrase, *He may speak in their ears and terrify them with warnings*. So in the NIV, *seals their instructions*, becomes *terrify them with warnings*.

The sense is God is speaking warnings to people in order to save then from trouble. As we've mentioned above, God did this to Abimelek, Laban and Nebuchadnezzar amongst others. Even Daniel was greatly troubled and turned pale after seeing *Daniel's 'Four Beasts' Dream*.

Throughout Scripture God used dreams for various reasons. He mainly spoke through Bible dreams in order to reveal His kingdom purpose and to keep that purpose on track. His main kingdom purpose was the revelation of Jesus Christ the Messiah.

Sometimes God spoke of the dreamer's destiny and the destiny of their family lines like He did with Abraham, Jacob, Joseph and Solomon.

Sometimes He gave directions and instructions like He did with Abraham, Jacob, St. Joseph and the Magi.

Sometimes He encouraged and settled people as He did with

Abraham and Jacob when he spoke of their peaceful deaths at ripe old ages.

Sometimes God revealed the future as He did with Abraham, Joseph, Pharaoh, Jeremiah, Nebuchadnezzar and Daniel.

Sometimes He encouraged them to trust Him by revealing Himself and His ways as He did with Abraham, Jacob, Samuel, Solomon and Nebuchadnezzar.

Sometimes God humbled them like He did with Nebuchadnezzar. Sometimes He warned them as he did with Abimelek, Laban, Pharaoh, The Midianite Soldier, Solomon, and Pilate's wife.

The dreamers from Abraham's line were all invited to join God in His work of bringing forth the Messiah. God spoke through dreams in order to create trust and motivation within the dreamer.

He also sent dreams in order that the dreamer should know who God actually was, as in the case of Nebuchadnezzar who gave one of the most wonderful descriptions of God in all of Scripture.

God used dreams to allow people to know Him better. God spoke to us in order to create faith and trust. So then faith comes by hearing, and hearing by the word of God.

But nowhere in the Bible is there one example of a *'Sealed Dream'*.

The is nothing like, One day Solomon was helping The Queen of Sheba off her elephant when 'pop' he had a déjà vu moment.

In fact God usually spoke quite plainly and openly We have no example of any Biblical 'sealed dream' and déjà vu moment.

ISAIAH'S ORACLE ON DREAMS

I've considered examining some of Isaiah's material as possible dreams. Isaiah 2:1 tells us Isaiah received his revelation when he saw a word. The Scripture says,

> The word that Isaiah the son of Amoz saw concerning Judah and Jerusalem.[1]

Similarly Psalm 105:17-19 says,

> He sent a man before them, even Joseph, who was sold for a servant: Whose feet they hurt with fetters: he was laid in irons: Until the time that his word came to pass, the word of the Lord tested him.

In the above verse Joseph's dreams from God are called the word of the Lord. It was these dreams as the word of God that tested Joseph. So Isaiah seeing a word could possibly mean Isaiah saw a dream.

Isaiah begins with the words, *The vision of Isaiah*. Finis Jennings Dake in his Bible says the Hebrew word *chazon is translated* vision here. Dake says *chazon* has the meaning of to see mentally; dream; see a vision; have revelation, receive an oracle.

But the more I studied the many visions of Isaiah I realised none of them really looked and felt like dreams. All of the other dreams in this book apart from *Jeremiah's 'Israel Will Return' Dream* are either simple plain literal messages requiring no interpretation or parable like messages requiring some interpretation.

None of them apart from Jeremiah's dream are lengthy oracles and declarations like Isaiah's. So I have stuck with tradition and not considered any of Isaiah's visions as dreams. Perhaps someone else might do further research on this.

Jeremiah's 'Israel Will Return' Dream is considered a dream because in Jeremiah 31:26 the prophet says, At this I awoke and looked around. My sleep had been pleasant to me.

So, the foregoing had been a dream. Then Jeremiah went back to sleep and continued in the same vein. As far as I can see *Jeremiah's 'Israel Will Return' Dream* is the only dream in the Scripture that is given in oracle form.

The Oracle Setting/Backstory

∾

God's Covenant People are walking in darkness and faking their religion. They no longer love and worship their creator. So God decides to punish them by withholding revelation. He has also decided to punish their enemies who are trying to destroy his people and their seed line.

The Dream Scripture
Isaiah 29:1-16

Woe to you, Ariel, Ariel,
>   the city where David settled!
Add year to year
>   and let your cycle of festivals go on.
Yet I will besiege Ariel;
>   she will mourn and lament,
>   she will be to me like an altar hearth.
I will encamp against you on all sides;
>   I will encircle you with towers
>   and set up my siege works against you.
Brought low, you will speak from the ground;
>   your speech will mumble out of the dust.
Your voice will come ghostlike from the earth;
>   out of the dust your speech will whisper.
But your many enemies will become like fine dust,
>   the ruthless hordes like blown chaff.
Suddenly, in an instant,
>   the Lord Almighty will come
with thunder and earthquake and great noise,
>   with windstorm and tempest and flames of a devouring fire.
Then the hordes of all the nations that fight against Ariel,
>   that attack her and her fortress and besiege her,
will be as it is with a dream,
>   with a vision in the night—
as when a hungry person dreams of eating,
>   but awakens hungry still;
as when a thirsty person dreams of drinking,

but awakens faint and thirsty still.
So will it be with the hordes of all the nations
   that fight against Mount Zion.
Be stunned and amazed,
   blind yourselves and be sightless;
be drunk, but not from wine,
   stagger, but not from beer.
The Lord has brought over you a deep sleep:
   He has sealed your eyes (the prophets);
   he has covered your heads (the seers).

For you this whole vision is nothing but words sealed in a scroll. And if you give the scroll to someone who can read, and say, "Read this, please," they will answer, "I can't; it is sealed." Or if you give the scroll to someone who cannot read, and say, "Read this, please," they will answer, "I don't know how to read."

The Lord says:
"These people come near to me with their mouth
and honour me with their lips,
but their hearts are far from me.
Their worship of me
is based on merely human rules they have been taught.
Therefore once more I will astound these people
with wonder upon wonder;
the wisdom of the wise will perish,
the intelligence of the intelligent will vanish."
Woe to those who go to great depths
to hide their plans from the Lord,
who do their work in darkness and think,
"Who sees us? Who will know?"
You turn things upside down,
as if the potter were thought to be like the clay!
Shall what is formed say to the one who formed it,

"You did not make me"?
Can the pot say to the potter,
"You know nothing"?

The Problem

∽

God's Covenant People no longer genuinely love and worship their creator. They are also surrounded by their enemies who want to destroy them and their seed line.

The Dreamer's Metron

∽

Isaiah was a major Hebrew prophet who lived 700 years before Jesus. His writings are beautiful and his vision is stunning. Isaiah spoke of the greatness, grace, and glory of God, the virgin birth, dual nature, earthly life, sufferings, and the resurrection of the Messiah.

He also prophesied the coming tribulation and the wonders of the millennium. Although primarily a prophet to Judah his metron included all Israel.

To this end, he condemned the nation's sin and pronounced future judgment upon them but mercifully he also prophesied their restoration

Isaiah proclaimed the Holiness of God[2] and explained the reason for Satan's Fall.[3] He pronounced God's Judgement on Israel.[4] yet he also testified about God's great Mercy and Grace towards them.[5]

He also exposed Israel's blindness yet predicted a time when their eyes would be opened.[6] Isaiah also called God's Chosen People to repentance[7] and like Jeremiah predicted their restoration to their promised homeland.[8]

Because of his emphasis on the Messiah, Isaiah has been called the 'Evangelical Prophet' and his book has been entitled 'The Fifth Gospel'. Isaiah 53 perfectly depicts Jesus on the Cross the only hope for fallen humanity.[9]

Isaiah also rejoiced when he saw Israel and the world restored when he prophesied about a new heaven and a new earth.[10]

The Message

The message for God's people was God was going to punish them by withholding revelation and interpretation from their prophets and seers.

The message for his enemies was that their plans for victory over Israel would evaporate like a soulish dream.

God's Purpose

God's purpose was to warn and punish His people by withholding revelation from them. He also wanted them to know He was still protecting them and still keeping Covenant.

Satan's Purpose

Satan's purpose was to steal Israel's heart from their God. He also wanted their enemies to wipe them out.

Dreamer's Eyes Enlightened

Isaiah clearly knew God's intentions for His people and their enemies.

Dreamer's Response and Application

Isaiah wrote down the vision and declared it to the people.

Know God Better

One main way God shows His displeasure with His people is to stop speaking to them through His prophets and seers. Consequently they can't interpret and understand God's dreams and visions any longer. Then they just stumble through life like drunken blind people and get on with their lifeless religion based on human rules they have been taught by men.

The Vision Process

The message is clearly spoken as a declarative oracle. It requires no interpretation.

The Usual Suspects

God is warning both his people and their enemies. Satan is seducing the people away from God and also trying to kill them by an enemy army. Jesus is in the seed line of Israel.

Takeaways

Paul said Israel was 'blind in part' and had experienced a hardening in part until the full number of the Gentiles has come in.[11] Today Israel is not able to fully understand her own scriptures. But a time will come when their eyes will be opened[12] and God will lift their veil of blindness.

God will also open the eyes of the Gentiles as well. The mystery mentioned in Ephesians concerning the Gentiles being fellow heirs with Israel, and partakers of the promise in Christ Jesus through the gospel[13] will be finally revealed and God's sheepfold will be full of Old and New Testament saints who follow one Shepherd.[14]

Cessationism is a belief that claims the miraculous gifts of the Holy Spirit, ceased being practiced early in the Christian Church history. So for Christian Cessationists there are no more wonderful gifts of the word of knowledge, increased faith, the gifts of healing, the gift of miracles, prophecy, the discernment of spirits, diverse kinds of tongues and the interpretation of tongues.

Isn't it sad when Christians are happy to remove prophets and seers and the revelatory gifts of the Holy Spirit from the body of Christ. Isaiah knew being in such a blind and deaf state was evidence of being punished by God.

JEREMIAH'S 'ISRAEL WILL RETURN' DREAM

The Dream Setting/Backstory

We know this portion of Scripture is a dream because in Jeremiah 31:26 the prophet says, At this I awoke and looked around. My sleep had been pleasant to me. All the foregoing had been a dream. Then Jeremiah went back to sleep and continued in the same vein.

This dream comes over three hundred years after Solomon's dreams. Solomon disobeyed God's *Warning Dream* at Gibeon and brought national disaster upon Abraham's descendants. Instead of bestowing blessing upon his family line and Israel he was seduced by money, sex and power into serving and worshiping other gods.

God then kept His promise of punishment and national captivity: I will cut off Israel from the land I have given them and will reject this temple I have consecrated for my Name.[1]

After Solomon's death Israel broke into two kingdoms. The ten northern tribes kept the name Israel and headquartered at Samaria, while the southern tribes of Judah, Benjamin and some of Levi became known as Judah.

Both kingdoms turned away from their covenant with God and their descendants suffered the consequences.

Jeremiah's dream came over two hundred years after Solomon's dream. By then the fruit of Solomon's disobedience had advanced to the point where the ten northern tribes were deported as captives to what is now modern Iran. Afterwards they were scattered to the ends of the earth and became the Ten Lost Tribes.

The southern Kingdom of Judah were just as bad. They too continually ignored God's prophets. For forty years Jeremiah had condemned their false worship and social injustice. He'd pleaded with them to abandon their idols but they wouldn't listen.

Now God is about to keep His promise and discipline them. Nebuchadnezzar's powerful armies are outside attacking the gates, inside famine is raging and the Beloved City is about to be destroyed. Jeremiah is in prison awaiting trail for treason. He'd told God's people to willingly go into captivity in Babylon.

The Dream Scripture
Jeremiah 30:3-31:40

∽

This is the word that came to Jeremiah from the Lord: "This is what the Lord, the God of Israel, says: 'Write in a book all the words I have spoken to you. The days are coming,' declares the Lord, 'when I will bring my people Israel and Judah back from captivity and restore them to the land I gave their ancestors to possess,' says the Lord."

"At that time," declares the Lord, "I will be the God of all the families of Israel, and they will be my people."

This is what the Lord says:
"The people who survive the sword
will find favour in the wilderness;
I will come to give rest to Israel."
The Lord appeared to us in the past, saying:
"I have loved you with an everlasting love;
I have drawn you with unfailing kindness.
I will build you up again,
and you, Virgin Israel, will be rebuilt.
Again you will take up your timbrels
and go out to dance with the joyful.
Again you will plant vineyards
on the hills of Samaria;
the farmers will plant them
and enjoy their fruit.
There will be a day when watchmen cry out
on the hills of Ephraim,
'Come, let us go up to Zion,
to the Lord our God.'"
This is what the Lord says:
"Sing with joy for Jacob;
shout for the foremost of the nations.
Make your praises heard, and say,
'Lord, save your people,
the remnant of Israel.'
See, I will bring them from the land of the north
and gather them from the ends of the earth.
Among them will be the blind and the lame,
expectant mothers and women in labour;
a great throng will return.
They will come with weeping;
they will pray as I bring them back.
I will lead them beside streams of water

on a level path where they will not stumble,
because I am Israel's father,
and Ephraim is my firstborn son.
"Hear the word of the Lord, you nations;
proclaim it in distant coastlands:
'He who scattered Israel will gather them
and will watch over his flock like a shepherd.'
For the Lord will deliver Jacob
and redeem them from the hand of those stronger than they.
They will come and shout for joy on the heights of Zion;
they will rejoice in the bounty of the Lord—
the grain, the new wine and the olive oil,
the young of the flocks and herds.
They will be like a well-watered garden,
and they will sorrow no more.
Then young women will dance and be glad,
young men and old as well.
I will turn their mourning into gladness;
I will give them comfort and joy instead of sorrow.
I will satisfy the priests with abundance,
and my people will be filled with my bounty,"
declares the Lord.
This is what the Lord says:
"A voice is heard in Ramah,
mourning and great weeping,
Rachel weeping for her children
and refusing to be comforted,
because they are no more."
This is what the Lord says:
"Restrain your voice from weeping
and your eyes from tears,
for your work will be rewarded,"
declares the Lord.

"They will return from the land of the enemy.
So there is hope for your descendants,"
declares the Lord.
"Your children will return to their own land.
"I have surely heard Ephraim's moaning:
'You disciplined me like an unruly calf,
and I have been disciplined.
Restore me, and I will return,
because you are the Lord my God.
After I strayed,
I repented;
after I came to understand,
I beat my breast.
I was ashamed and humiliated
because I bore the disgrace of my youth.'
Is not Ephraim my dear son,
the child in whom I delight?
Though I often speak against him,
I still remember him.
Therefore my heart yearns for him;
I have great compassion for him,"
declares the Lord.
"Set up road signs;
put up guideposts.
Take note of the highway,
the road that you take.
Return, Virgin Israel,
return to your towns.
How long will you wander,
unfaithful Daughter Israel?
The Lord will create a new thing on earth—
the woman will return to the man."
This is what the Lord Almighty, the God of Israel, says: "When I

bring them back from captivity, the people in the land of Judah and in its towns will once again use these words: 'The Lord bless you, you prosperous city, you sacred mountain.'

People will live together in Judah and all its towns—farmers and those who move about with their flocks.

I will refresh the weary and satisfy the faint."

At this I awoke and looked around. My sleep had been pleasant to me.

"The days are coming," declares the Lord, "when I will plant the kingdoms of Israel and Judah with the offspring of people and of animals. Just as I watched over them to uproot and tear down, and to overthrow, destroy and bring disaster, so I will watch over them to build and to plant," declares the Lord. "In those days people will no longer say,

'The parents have eaten sour grapes,
   and the children's teeth are set on edge.'

Instead, everyone will die for their own sin; whoever eats sour grapes—their own teeth will be set on edge.

"The days are coming," declares the Lord,
   "when I will make a new covenant
with the people of Israel
   and with the people of Judah.
It will not be like the covenant
   I made with their ancestors
when I took them by the hand
   to lead them out of Egypt,
because they broke my covenant,
   though I was a husband to them,"
declares the Lord.
"This is the covenant I will make with the people of Israel
   after that time," declares the Lord.
"I will put my law in their minds
   and write it on their hearts.

I will be their God,
    and they will be my people.
No longer will they teach their neighbour,
    or say to one another, 'Know the Lord,'
because they will all know me,
    from the least of them to the greatest,"
declares the Lord.
"For I will forgive their wickedness
    and will remember their sins no more."
This is what the Lord says,
he who appoints the sun
    to shine by day,
who decrees the moon and stars
    to shine by night,
who stirs up the sea
    so that its waves roar—
    the Lord Almighty is his name:
"Only if these decrees vanish from my sight,"
    declares the Lord,
"will Israel ever cease
    being a nation before me."
This is what the Lord says:
"Only if the heavens above can be measured
    and the foundations of the earth below be searched out
will I reject all the descendants of Israel
    because of all they have done,"
declares the Lord.

"The days are coming," declares the Lord, "when this city will be rebuilt for me from the Tower of Hananel to the Corner Gate. The measuring line will stretch from there straight to the hill of Gareb and then turn to Goah. The whole valley where dead bodies and ashes are thrown, and all the terraces out to the Kidron Valley on the east as far as the corner of the Horse Gate, will be holy to the Lord. The city will never again be uprooted or demolished."

The Problem

∼

Israel had gone too far. God's assessment was,

> Your wound is incurable, your injury beyond healing. There is no one to plead your cause, no remedy for your sore, no healing for you. All your allies have forgotten you; they care nothing for you. I have struck you as an enemy would and punished you as would the cruel, because your guilt is so great and your sins so many.[2]

Now God is about to send His beloved people to Babylon for seventy years. Like the children of Israel in the desert most of them will die there. Afterwards God will continue His covenantal promises and plans and purpose with a new generation:

> I will restore the fortunes of Jacob's tents and have compassion on his dwellings; the city will be rebuilt on her ruins, and the palace will stand in its proper place.[3]

Jeremiah's dream offers hope to that generation and also speaks thousands of years into the future.

The Dreamer's Metron

Jeremiah was a prophet to the Nations, not only to Israel. He was told to write his revelation because it was intended to comfort and instruct many generations. Jeremiah the 'weeping prophet' had a major metron. He was one of God's major writing prophets.

With Baruch, his scribe, he penned the *Book of Jeremiah* the *Books of Kings* and the *Book of Lamentations*. Huldah the prophetess was his relative and a contemporary and Zephaniah and Isaiah were his mentors. The Book of Jeremiah with its revelation of a New Covenant has been foundational for Christianity.

Around forty direct quotations from the Book of Jeremiah are in the New Testament. Most occur in Revelation relating to Babylon's destruction.

Matthew showed how Jesus fulfilled Jeremiah's prophecies and The Letter to the Hebrews deals with the promised New Covenant prophesied by Jeremiah.

The Message

This dream reaffirms what God had already said about His Covenant with Israel. It was never God's intention to destroy Israel but always to bring her to repentance and obedience.

Here God is sending the nation into captivity for seventy years for their sins but afterwards there will be a joyful restoration to their land. Then Jerusalem will be rebuilt, their numbers will increase and their government will be established once more. Then God's Covenant with them will be renewed and all their enemies will be eliminated.

God's Purpose

Once again God is seen as a long-suffering covenant keeper and promise keeper. On the one hand He is keeping His word and punishing Israel for her idolatry. On the other hand like a good Father He is telling His children He loves them and is speaking of His good plans and purpose for their future restoration.

Satan's Purpose

Satan's purpose was to seduce God's people into sin and idolatry so God would have to punish them.

Dreamer's Eyes Enlightened

Jeremiah is given profound insight into God's marvellous future plans and purpose for Israel and the whole world.

Dreamer's Response and Application

Jeremiah was obedient. He wrote down the words of the dream in a book as instructed.

The Dream Process

∼

This is a long complex symbolic prophetic dream with some literal parts. It comes in the form of prophetic declarations from God. It requires lots of interpretation and much of it is still hidden today.

It's an incredibly uplifting dream for all of God's people. It's been a great source of encouragement and comfort to Abraham's descendants who've been scattered worldwide for thousands of years.

Know God Better

∼

Once again God is shown to be a trustworthy Promise Keeper who takes an active part in bringing His promises to pass. God does what he says. He isn't some sort of heavenly Santa Claus who just keeps blessing his children year after year.

Through Moses, God warned the people of Israel. He said, I will bless you and your children if you are obedient and I will curse you and your children if you disobey.[4]

There are consequences for sin. When God is judging and punishing His people for their idolatry He is still being a faithful Promise Keeper. In the same way God deals with Israel He also deals with us today. Paul warns us,

> Do not be deceived: God cannot be mocked. A man reaps what he sows. Whoever sows to please their flesh, from the flesh will reap destruction; whoever

sows to please the Spirit, from the Spirit will reap eternal life.[5]

Time after time God warned Israel they'd be scattered if they persisted in their idolatry;

> Then the Lord will scatter you among all nations, from one end of the earth to the other. There you will worship other gods—gods of wood and stone, which neither you nor your ancestors have known. Among those nations you will find no repose, no resting place for the sole of your foot. There the Lord will give you an anxious mind, eyes weary with longing, and a despairing heart. You will live in constant suspense, filled with dread both night and day, never sure of your life.[6]

Takeaways

∼

Many times, God had good reason to wipe out Israel but He always chose to be merciful to her because of His covenant with Abraham, Isaac and Jacob.

Jeremiah's most important prophecy occurred in this dream as God spoke of a time when He would make a covenant with Israel that would replace the old Mosaic Covenant.

In those days God would write His law upon the hearts of men, rather than on tables of stone, and all would know God personally and receive his forgiveness.[7]

This New Covenant prophecy is quoted in Hebrews 8 and fills Jesus' words at the Last Supper: This cup is the new covenant in my blood.

Jeremiah's dream has a scope far beyond Israel's initial return from Babylon. It reaches across thousands of years to our present day and stretches forth to a time when God will restore the full fortunes of all Israel.

Today the State of Israel is largely made up of only Judah's descendants. God's prophecies concerning the Second Exodus clearly speak of both Judah and Israel.

Jeremiah's dream was partially fulfilled when hundreds of thousands of Jews returned to their historical land and founded the modern State of Israel in 1948.

Today God's chosen people don't have all of the land promised to Abraham, Isaac and Jacob. They still have a lot of hardship and tribulation to endure before they finally inherit the complete fulfilment of God's promise.

NEBUCHADNEZZAR'S 'LARGE STATUE' DREAM

The Dream Setting/Backstory

Nebuchadnezzar's dream arrived five years after *Jeremiah's 'Israel Will Return' Dream.* Jeremiah's exile prophecy had kicked in and Daniel was already one year in Babylon.

The Jewish exile occurred in three stages over a twenty-year period. The royal family, nobility and court officials went first. Then the upper classes, politicians and craftsmen including the prophet Ezekiel and lastly the everyday people when the temple and city were finally destroyed.

Daniel and his three friends Hananiah, Mishael and Azariah were in the first group and were chosen to be trained for senior positions in Nebuchadnezzar's court. God had already chosen them before the foundation of the world to be His witnesses in Babylon before its powers and principalities.

The Dream Scripture
Daniel 2:1-49

～

In the second year of his reign, Nebuchadnezzar had dreams; his mind was troubled and he could not sleep. So the king summoned the magicians, enchanters, sorcerers and astrologers to tell him what he had dreamed. When they came in and stood before the king, he said to them, "I have had a dream that troubles me and I want to know what it means." Then the astrologers answered the king, "May the king live forever! Tell your servants the dream, and we will interpret it."

The king replied to the astrologers, "This is what I have firmly decided: If you do not tell me what my dream was and interpret it, I will have you cut into pieces and your houses turned into piles of rubble. But if you tell me the dream and explain it, you will receive from me gifts and rewards and great honour. So tell me the dream and interpret it for me." Once more they replied, "Let the king tell his servants the dream, and we will interpret it."

Then the king answered, "I am certain that you are trying to gain time, because you realise that this is what I have firmly decided: If you do not tell me the dream, there is only one penalty for you. You have conspired to tell me misleading and wicked things, hoping the situation will change. So then, tell me the dream, and I will know that you can interpret it for me."

The astrologers answered the king, "There is no one on earth who can do what the king asks! No king, however great and mighty, has ever asked such a thing of any magician or enchanter or astrologer. What the king asks is too difficult. No one can reveal it to the king except the gods, and they do not live among humans."

This made the king so angry and furious that he ordered the execution of all the wise men of Babylon. So the decree was issued to put the wise men to death, and men were sent to look for Daniel and his friends to put them to death. When Arioch, the commander of the king's guard, had gone out to put to death the wise men of Babylon, Daniel spoke to him with wisdom and tact. He asked the king's officer, "Why did the king issue such a harsh decree?" Arioch then explained the matter to Daniel. At this, Daniel went in to the king and asked for time, so that he might interpret the dream for him.

Then Daniel returned to his house and explained the matter to his friends Hananiah, Mishael and Azariah. He urged them to plead for mercy from the God of heaven concerning this mystery, so that he and his friends might not be executed with the rest of the wise men of Babylon. During the night the mystery was revealed to Daniel in a vision. Then Daniel praised the God of heaven and said:

"Praise be to the name of God for ever and ever; wisdom and power are his. He changes times and seasons; he deposes kings and raises up others.

He gives wisdom to the wise and knowledge to the discerning. He reveals deep and hidden things;

he knows what lies in darkness,

and light dwells with him. I thank and praise you, God of my ancestors: You have given me wisdom and power,

you have made known to me what we asked of you, you have made known to us the dream of the king."

Then Daniel went to Arioch, whom the king had appointed to execute the wise men of Babylon, and said to him, "Do not execute the wise men of Babylon. Take me to the king, and I will interpret his dream for him."

Arioch took Daniel to the king at once and said, "I have found a man among the exiles from Judah who can tell the king what his dream means."

The king asked Daniel (also called Belteshazzar), "Are you able to tell me what I saw in my dream and interpret it?"

Daniel replied, "No wise man, enchanter, magician or diviner can explain to the king the mystery he has asked about, but there is a God in heaven who reveals mysteries. He has shown King Nebuchadnezzar what will happen in days to come. Your dream and the visions that passed through your mind as you were lying in bed are these:

"As Your Majesty was lying there, your mind turned to things to come, and the revealer of mysteries showed you what is going to happen. As for me, this mystery has been revealed to me, not because I have greater wisdom than anyone else alive, but so that Your Majesty may know the interpretation and that you may understand what went through your mind.

"Your Majesty looked, and there before you stood a large statue—an enormous, dazzling statue, awesome in appearance. The head of the statue was made of pure gold, its chest and arms of silver, its belly and thighs of bronze, its legs of iron, its feet partly of iron and partly of baked clay. While you were watching, a rock was cut out, but not by human hands. It struck the statue on its feet of iron and clay and smashed them. Then the iron, the clay, the bronze, the silver and the gold were all broken to pieces and became like chaff on a threshing floor in the summer. The wind swept them away without leaving a trace. But the rock that struck the statue became a huge mountain and filled the whole earth.

"This was the dream, and now we will interpret it to the king. Your Majesty, you are the king of kings. The God of heaven has given you dominion and power and might and glory; in your hands he has placed all mankind and the beasts of the field and the birds in the sky. Wherever they live, he has made you ruler over them all. You are that head of gold.

"After you, another kingdom will arise, inferior to yours. Next, a third kingdom, one of bronze, will rule over the whole earth. Finally, there will be a fourth kingdom, strong as iron—for iron breaks and smashes everything—and as iron breaks things to pieces, so it will crush and break all the others. Just as you saw that the feet and toes were partly of baked clay and partly of iron, so this will be a divided kingdom; yet it will have some of the strength of iron in it, even as you saw iron mixed with clay. As the toes were partly iron and partly clay, so this kingdom will be partly strong and partly brittle. And just as you saw the iron mixed with baked clay, so the people will be a mixture and will not remain united, any more than iron mixes with clay.

"In the time of those kings, the God of heaven will set up a kingdom that will never be destroyed, nor will it be left to another people. It will crush all those kingdoms and bring them to an end, but it will itself endure forever. This is the meaning of the vision of the rock cut out of a mountain, but not by human hands—a rock that broke the iron, the bronze, the clay, the silver and the gold to pieces.

"The great God has shown the king what will take place in the future. The dream is true and its interpretation is trustworthy."

Then King Nebuchadnezzar fell prostrate before Daniel and paid him honour and ordered that an offering and incense be presented to him. The king said to Daniel, "Surely your God is the God of gods and the Lord of kings and a revealer of mysteries, for you were able to reveal this mystery."

Then the king placed Daniel in a high position and lavished many gifts on him. He made him ruler over the entire province of Babylon and placed him in charge of all its wise men. Moreover, at Daniel's request the king appointed Shadrach, Meshach and Abednego administrators over the province of Babylon, while Daniel himself remained at the royal court.

The Problem

∽

Nebuchadnezzar had defeated the Jewish nation and believed his god Marduk was more powerful than the Jewish God. Yahweh decided to fix Nebuchadnezzar's worldview. So He sent him a troubling dream.

The Dreamer's Metron

Nebuchadnezzar was the longest-reigning and most powerful monarch of the Neo-Babylonian Empire. Scripture depicts him as the demolisher of Solomon's Temple and the architect of the Babylonian captivity. Jeremiah called him the destroyer of nations.[1]

God used Nebuchadnezzar both to punish Israel and to witness to Babylon and the whole world about the greatness of God.

Nebuchadnezzar had a prophetic dream of international importance about the rise and fall of world powers beginning with his own kingdom. He saw thousands of years into the future.

The Message

Nebuchadnezzar's dream spoke of four different empires - Babylon, Medo-Persia, Greece and Rome - that would rule over God's chosen people. Afterwards God would send His Messiah who'd establish His everlasting Kingdom.

In Scripture, nations and kings only got a mention if they impacted upon Israel. The basic message of Nebuchadnezzar's dream is that Daniel's God is the sovereign God who knows and shapes the future.

The Book of Daniel concerns end time revelation and spiritual warfare but its main purpose is to reveal God as King of Kings and Lord of Lords and not just some defeated Jewish deity.

Nebuchadnezzar's dream revealed one day the Kingdom of God in the form of Jesus Christ the Messiah would rule over all other kingdoms, earthly and heavenly. This resonates with Revelation, which says,

> The kingdom of the world has become the kingdom of our Lord and of his Messiah, and he will reign for ever and ever.[2]

Nebuchadnezzar was also shown the successive kingdoms starting with his own kingdom that God would use to rule over and enforce his discipline upon Israel until their Messiah would arrive for the first time.

God's Purpose

God's purpose was to humble Nebuchadnezzar by showing him that He and He alone controls the destiny of men and nations. Through his interaction with Daniel and his friends Nebuchadnezzar is brought to a place where he believes in Daniel's God.

The interplay between God and Nebuchadnezzar also symbolises God's general dealings with all gentile nations and their idolatrous failure to recognise His sovereignty. They all need to know the Most High is sovereign over all earthly kingdoms and gives them to whosoever He wishes.

Satan's Purpose

~

Satan tried to use this dream to have Daniel and his three friends killed and so hinder God's plans and purpose for Israel and their Messiah.

Dreamer's Eyes Enlightened

~

After this dream Nebuchadnezzar realised it is God who rules supreme in heaven and on earth and that he was merely a tool in God's hand to punish rebellious Israel.

He also realised Yahweh is not just a defeated Jewish deity but is in fact the God of all nations. He also understood his gods and his magicians, enchanters, sorcerers and astrologers were very limited in their ability to understand spiritual reality. They were also theologically wrong when they said, What the king asks is too difficult. No one can reveal it to the king except the gods, and they do not live among men.

Dreamer's Response and Application

~

Nebuchadnezzar was so disturbed by his dreams his first response was to change his dream interpreters' job descriptions and working terms and conditions.

Instead of him telling them his dream and rewarding them for their interpretation he now wanted his wise men to both tell him his dream and correctly interpret it otherwise they and their families would be destroyed.

The wise men's dream jobs had quickly turned into a collective nightmare.

Nebuchadnezzar's second response after Daniel's correct interpretation was to humble himself and immediately accept the interpretation and reward the interpreter.

He honoured Daniel and acknowledged his God Yahweh as the Supreme God. Then he gave Daniel gifts and made him the ruler over Babylon.

He then put him in charge over the whole menagerie of wise men, magicians, enchanters, sorcerers and astrologers. He also gave Daniel's three friends positions of power at Daniel's request.

Know God Better

No matter how bad things seem God is still in control. In *The Book Of Daniel*, the God of Israel is shown as the God of wisdom and power who understands times and seasons and is patiently working His purpose out. He's also presented as a personal God who cares for and speaks encouragingly to his servants.

Nebuchadnezzar's dream also reveals it is God and not man who is the real kingmaker; He sets them up and removes them. He also gives wisdom to the wise and knowledge to people of understanding. He reveals deep things and secret things. He dwells in light yet knows what is in darkness. He answers prayer and gives power and wisdom to his servants. He is still keeping His covenant with Abraham and still bringing forth the Messiah.

The Dream Process

∼

This extremely difficult dream process required the interpreter not only to interpret the dream but to also actually receive the dream from God before he interpreted it.

All this occurred under a strict time pressure and threat of death. There is no other dream process like it in Scripture.

This dream interpretation required earnest intercession from Daniel and his three friends. In response God revealed Nebuchadnezzar's dream and its interpretation to Daniel in a night vision dream.

This is a complex, prophetic and symbolic dream requiring interpretation with incredible significance for all mankind. The dream was symbolic and the images used were gold, silver, a mountain, a rock, clay, chaff, wind, as well as the man-made substances of bronze and iron.

Daniel used *The Symbol Replacement Method* in interpreting this dream. His interpretation was that Nebuchadnezzar's dream spoke of four different empires. The gold symbolised Babylon, the silver symbolised Medo-Persia, the bronze represented Greece and the iron represented Rome. These are the empires God would use to care for and discipline His chosen people. Afterwards God would send His rock the Messiah who'd establish His everlasting Kingdom.

And just as each material was of lesser value so would each empire be of lesser importance. The fourth kingdom, the Roman Empire was represented as a mixture of iron and baked clay. This was interpreted as a weak mixture that would lack coherent unity.

When the king heard this dream and its interpretation it witnessed to his spirit so much that he fell down before Daniel.

As with Joseph, Daniel was also honoured and placed into a high position because of dream interpretation.

The Usual Suspects

Jesus is the rock cut out not by human hands that takes over the whole world. The one who cuts Him out is God. Satan is seen in his disgraced servants, the magicians, enchanters and astrologers who cannot discover or interpret Nebuchadnezzar's dream. Satan was willing to sacrifice his servants in order to kill Daniel. Satan is also seen in the inability of servants to come up with Nebuchadnezzar's dream and its interpretation.

Takeaways

Initially Nebuchadnezzar assumed his god Marduk had defeated the Jewish Yahweh but he eventually realised God ruled supreme and he and Marduk were merely tools in God's hand to punish rebellious Israel. Yahweh is revealed as the God of All Nations.

The Book of Daniel lifts the veil and allows us a glimpse of the greater cosmic conflict in the heavenly realms scheduled to continue until Jesus Christ the Messiah returns and fully establishes his kingdom.

Christian dream interpreters need not fear the new age or other occultist groups. Perhaps in the future Christian dream interpreters who know God will save the lives of many soothsayers. Satan's kingdom is seen as very limited in its capacity to reveal hidden things and the future. They were totally defeated by Nebuchadnezzar's request.

Satan also couldn't lift a finger to protect any of his servants in the Kings court. God on the other hand was totally able to equip Daniel to do that what was impossible amongst men.

The same thing occurred during *The Writing on the Wall* incident when Nebuchadnezzar's son Belshazzar was king in Daniel 5. Satan's servants couldn't interpret that either.

Proud Nebuchadnezzar was spiritually deceived. God was merciful by sending him a dream, the sort mentioned by Elihu in Job 33;

> For God does speak—now one way, now another—
> though no one perceives it. In a dream, in a vision
> of the night, when deep sleep falls on people as they
> slumber in their beds, he may speak in their ears
> and terrify them with warnings, to turn them from
> wrongdoing and keep them from pride, to preserve
> them from the pit, their lives from perishing by the
> sword.[3]

Nebuchadnezzar's dream fits Elihu's description perfectly. God terrified Nebuchadnezzar in order to deal with his pride issue though it will take another dream and seven years of madness until the king fully bows the knee.

DANIEL'S 'MYSTERY REVEALED' NIGHT VISION DREAM

The Dream Setting/Backstory

This dream came five years after *Jeremiah's 'Israel Will Return' Dream*. It revealed to Daniel the contents and the interpretation of *Nebuchadnezzar's Large Statue Dream*.

The Dream Scripture
Daniel 2:14-20

When Arioch, the commander of the king's guard, had gone out to put to death the wise men of Babylon, Daniel spoke to him with wisdom and tact. He asked the king's officer, Why did the king issue such a harsh decree? Arioch then explained the matter to Daniel. At this, Daniel went in to the king and asked for time, so that he might interpret the dream for him.

Then Daniel returned to his house and explained the matter to his friends Hananiah, Mishael and Azariah. He urged them to plead for mercy from the God of heaven concerning this mystery, so that he and his friends might not be executed with the rest of the wise men of Babylon. During the night the mystery was revealed to Daniel in a vision. Then Daniel praised the God of heaven and said: Praise be to the name of God for ever and ever; wisdom and power are his. He changes times and seasons; he deposes kings and raises up others. He gives wisdom to the wise and knowledge to the discerning. He reveals deep and hidden things; he knows what lies in darkness, and light dwells with him. I thank and praise you, God of my ancestors. You have given me wisdom and power, you have made known to me what we asked of you, you have made known to us the dream of the king."

The Problem

∽

Daniel and his three friends, Hananiah, Mishael and Azariah, are about to be executed with the rest of the wise men of Babylon unless Daniel comes up with the content and interpretation of Nebuchadnezzar's dream. This required a miracle.

The Dreamer's Metron

∽

Daniel was a major prophet with a worldwide and end time metron. He was gifted in dreams and visions that prophesied world history, including Daniel's people, Israel and all mankind in the latter days. He also received revelation from the angel Gabriel.

Daniel served in prominent positions in both Babylonian and Medo-Persian empires under Nebuchadnezzar, Belshazzar, Darius and Cyrus. In the first year of Darius's reign Daniel understood the prophecy of Jeremiah that predicted a 70-year captivity of his people was soon coming to an end.

Daniel often prayed and fasted for his nation's sins and pleaded for God's mercy on himself, his fellow captives and all the inhabitants of Jerusalem. He faithfully prayed three times a day even when this activity threatened his life.

Ezekiel called him a righteous man alongside Noah and Job. Daniel's fame spread well beyond the borders of Israel. When God granted Daniel the wisdom to interpret the king's dream, it launched Daniel's long career as a political leader, trusted advisor, major prophet and dream interpreter.

God's purpose for Daniel was to impact Babylon through revelation and dream interpretation in order to reveal God's sovereignty to the then most powerful nation on earth. Through Daniel's influence Israel's God was revealed as the Most High God who raises and removes kings and establishes new world empires. He is the Ancient of Days on the throne and the God of heaven, whose kingdom will never end.

Daniel's dreams and visions showed God's faithfulness and care for His people Israel. God enabled Daniel to prophesy some of God's long-term plans for all nations including the Messiah, the temple, Jerusalem, and a coming kingdom of righteousness.

The Message

God revealed Nebuchadnezzar's withheld dream and its interpretation to Daniel in answer to prayer. Nebuchadnezzar's dream disclosed four different empires - Babylon, Medo-Persia, Greece and Rome - that would affect God's Chosen People. Afterwards God would send His Messiah who'd establish His everlasting Kingdom.

The basic message is that Daniel's God is the sovereign God who knows and shapes the future. Although the Book of Daniel concerns end time revelation and spiritual warfare its main purpose is to present God as King of Kings and Lord of Lords as opposed to just some defeated Jewish deity.

Nebuchadnezzar's dream revealed that one day the Kingdom of God in the form of Jesus Christ the Messiah would rule over all other kingdoms, earthly and heavenly.

This resonates with Revelation 11;15,

> The kingdom of the world has become the kingdom of our Lord and of his Messiah, and he will reign for ever and ever.

God's Purpose

God had a number of purposes for this dream. He saved Daniel's life and revealed to Daniel and his friends just how powerful and dependable He actually was. God also elevated Daniel into a position of favour and authority in Nebuchadnezzar's court and amongst Babylon's dream interpreters. From this position of authority Daniel could help God's Chosen People.

Daniel would still be there when Nebuchadnezzar's dynasty ended and Cyrus would return the Jews to Israel as revealed to

Daniel through Jeremiah's writings. God also disclosed His blueprint concerning His people for the next six hundred years. Daniel's roles in Babylon and Persia left an eternal testimony for all nations, for all time.

God also wanted to show Nebuchadnezzar He was not just a minor Jewish deity defeated by the Babylonian god Marduk. When God revealed the contents of the king's dream to Daniel this enabled him to witness to the astonished Nebuchadnezzar by declaring,

> No wise man, enchanter, magician or diviner can
> explain to the king the mystery he has asked about,
> but there is a God in heaven who reveals
> mysteries.[1]

Satan's Purpose

Satan tried to use this dream to have Daniel and his three friends killed and so hinder God's plans and purpose for Israel and the Messiah from coming to pass.

Dreamer's Eyes Enlightened

Daniel fully understood the dream and its interpretation. He knew what to do to save his life. Through this interpretation Daniel realised everything happening to himself, Israel, Babylon and King Nebuchadnezzar was under God's sovereign control.

This fundamental understanding of a sovereign God who knows and controls all things is central to all Biblical prophecy. Prophecy after all is essentially the announcement of God's future plans and purpose in advance. The magicians and wise men in the most powerful nation on earth had no idea about the future yet God enabled His servant Daniel to see 2,500 years into the future.

Dreamer's Response and Application

~

Daniel's immediate response was to thank God for saving his life. He then started praising God using some of his recent revelation from the night vision;

> I thank thee, and praise thee, O thou God of my
> fathers, who hast given me wisdom and might, and
> hast made known unto me now what we desired of
> thee: for thou hast now made known unto us the
> king's matter.[2]

He then spoke to Nebuchadnezzar and gave God the glory for revealing and interpreting the dream. He said,

> No wise man, enchanter, magician or diviner can
> explain to the king the mystery he has asked about,
> but there is a God in heaven who reveals
> mysteries.[3]

Daniel then gave the dream and its interpretation to Nebuchadnezzar.

Know God Better

∼

God is clearly seen as sovereign with all wisdom and power. He is the one who changes times and seasons; He deposes kings and raises up others. He gives wisdom to the wise and knowledge to the discerning.

He intervenes in the life of His people in order to advance His own plans and purpose and also to care for them. It was God who was taking a proactive part in moving His plans and purpose forward. He left nothing to chance. He both sent the dream and the dream interpreter.

The Dream Process

∼

This revelation of national and international importance was given in a night vision but we're not told whether Daniel was awake or asleep. We do know Daniel had open visions. We also know it was a comprehensive and accurate rerun of Nebuchadnezzar's withheld dream, the only place in scripture where God uses a dream to reveal the contents of another dream.

The statue in Nebuchadnezzar's dream foretold the sequence of successive world empires that would impact Israel. Although there are minor disagreements amongst theologians, the basic consensus is the golden head symbolised Nebuchadnezzar's Babylonian Empire. Isaiah called Babylon the golden city and Jeremiah said Babylon was a gold cup in the Lord's hand.

The chest and arms of silver were symbolic of the inferior Medo-Persian powers that conquered Babylon. Jeremiah said the Medes would make Babylon a desolation and Daniel confirmed this when he said, Darius the Mede took over the kingdom, at the age of sixty two.

The brass thighs symbolised the Greek empire of Alexander the Great and the iron legs with the iron and clay feet symbolised the Roman Empire.

These are the empires that have successively dominated the Eurasian Mideast region for 2500 years and have impacted the 'diaspora' - the dispersed Jews the most. Bible prophecy never mentions nations or world events not connected with Israel.

The rock cut out not by human hands represented the Messiah, Jesus Christ. All other kingdoms will be blown away like chaff but His Kingdom shall grow and fill the whole earth.

Every day 200,000 new believers are pouring into His Kingdom. Jesus referred to himself as being a rock in Matthew;

> Have you never read in the Scriptures: The stone the builders rejected has become the cornerstone; the Lord has done this, and it is marvellous in our eyes? Therefore I tell you that the kingdom of God will be taken away from you and given to a people who will produce its fruit. Anyone who falls on this stone will be broken to pieces; anyone on whom it falls will be crushed.[4]

The Roman Empire that crucified the Messiah was finally crushed in 300 AD while the Messiah's Kingdom continues to flourish.

The Usual Suspects

God is presented as the all powerful revealer of mysteries and the One who sends His Messiah that will destroy all other kingdoms. Jesus is the rock not cut out by human hands whose Kingdom will fill the whole earth.

Satan is seen in Nebuchadnezzar's murderous threats to the dream interpreters. Satan was willing to sacrifice his servants in order to kill Daniel and his three friends. Satan is also seen in the inability of servants to come up with Nebuchadnezzar's dream and its interpretation.

Takeaways

Both Joseph and Daniel were raised into positions of national influence because of their gifting in dream interpretation. Not only did God send the dreams no one could interpret, He also sent His own dream interpreters.

In both cases it was God's will to place one of Abraham's descendants into a strategic position of authority where they'd serve God's purpose for Israel and their coming Messiah.

Joseph and Daniel influenced the pagan superpowers of their day. They demonstrated the God of Abraham, Isaac and Jacob to be the supreme ruler of nations and kings. Pharaoh and Nebuchadnezzar both ended up acknowledging and worshipping Yahweh.

Often it's the most difficult and dangerous circumstances that propel God's people into their destiny. Daniel's life and the life of his three friends were under urgent threat.

Like us all, Daniel had to have faith God would answer his prayers. Afterwards he was delighted when he realised his sovereign God had everything under control.

NEBUCHADNEZZAR'S 'LARGE TREE' DREAM

The Dream Setting/Backstory

This powerful prophetic dream occurs twenty-two years after *Nebuchadnezzar's Large Statue Dream,* the correct interpretation of which propelled Daniel into a position of prominence and put egg on the face of Babylon's magicians, enchanters, astrologers and diviners.

Nothing much has changed. Nebuchadnezzar is still proud and his wise men still can't interpret God's dreams.

Nebuchadnezzar who'd finished all his wars was wealthy beyond measure and the proud ruler of the world's first great empire. Babylon was an international centre of trade and industry with its wonderful hanging gardens, one of the seven wonders of the world. God in His mercy spoke to Nebuchadnezzar in a dream

The Dream Scripture
Daniel 4:4-37

∼

I, Nebuchadnezzar, was at home in my palace, contented and prosperous. I had a dream that made me afraid. As I was lying in bed, the images and visions that passed through my mind terrified me. So I commanded that all the wise men of Babylon be brought before me to interpret the dream for me. When the magicians, enchanters, astrologers and diviners came, I told them the dream, but they could not interpret it for me. Finally, Daniel came into my presence and I told him the dream. (He is called Belteshazzar, after the name of my god, and the spirit of the holy gods is in him.)

I said, "Belteshazzar, chief of the magicians, I know that the spirit of the holy gods is in you, and no mystery is too difficult for you. Here is my dream; interpret it for me. These are the visions I saw while lying in bed: I looked, and there before me stood a tree in the middle of the land. Its height was enormous. The tree grew large and strong and its top touched the sky; it was visible to the ends of the earth. Its leaves were beautiful, its fruit abundant, and on it was food for all. Under it the wild animals found shelter, and the birds lived in its branches; from it every creature was fed.

"In the visions I saw while lying in bed, I looked, and there before me was a holy one, a messenger, coming down from heaven. He called in a loud voice: 'Cut down the tree and trim off its branches; strip off its leaves and scatter its fruit. Let the animals flee from under it and the birds from its branches. But let the stump and its roots, bound with iron and bronze, remain in the ground, in the grass of the field.

"'Let him be drenched with the dew of heaven, and let him live with the animals among the plants of the earth. Let his mind be changed from that of a man and let him be given the mind of an animal, till seven times pass by for him.

"'The decision is announced by messengers, the holy ones declare the verdict, so that the living may know that the Most High is sovereign over all kingdoms on earth and gives them to anyone he wishes and sets over them the lowliest of people.'

"This is the dream that I, King Nebuchadnezzar, had. Now, Belteshazzar, tell me what it means, for none of the wise men in my kingdom can interpret it for me. But you can, because the spirit of the holy gods is in you." Then Daniel (also called Belteshazzar) was greatly perplexed for a time, and his thoughts terrified him.

So the king said, "Belteshazzar, do not let the dream or its meaning alarm you."

Belteshazzar answered, "My lord, if only the dream applied to your enemies and its meaning to your adversaries! The tree you saw, which grew large and strong, with its top touching the sky, visible to the whole earth, with beautiful leaves and abundant fruit, providing food for all, giving shelter to the wild animals, and having nesting places in its branches for the birds—Your Majesty, you are that tree! You have become great and strong; your greatness has grown until it reaches the sky, and your dominion extends to distant parts of the earth.

"Your Majesty saw a holy one, a messenger, coming down from heaven and saying, 'Cut down the tree and destroy it, but leave the stump, bound with iron and bronze, in the grass of the field, while its roots remain in the ground. Let him be drenched with the dew of heaven; let him live with the wild animals, until seven times pass by for him.'

"This is the interpretation, Your Majesty, and this is the decree the Most High has issued against my lord the king: You will be driven away from people and will live with the wild animals; you will eat grass like the ox and be drenched with the dew of heaven. Seven times will pass by for you until you acknowledge that the Most High is sovereign over all kingdoms on earth and gives them to anyone he wishes. The command to leave the stump of the tree with its roots means that your kingdom will be restored to you when you acknowledge that Heaven rules. Therefore, Your Majesty, be pleased to accept my advice: Renounce your sins by doing what is right, and your wickedness by being kind to the oppressed. It may be that then your prosperity will continue."

All this happened to King Nebuchadnezzar. Twelve months later, as the king was walking on the roof of the royal palace of Babylon, he said, "Is not this the great Babylon I have built as the royal residence, by my mighty power and for the glory of my majesty?"

Even as the words were on his lips, a voice came from heaven, "This is what is decreed for you, King Nebuchadnezzar: Your royal authority has been taken from you. You will be driven away from people and will live with the wild animals; you will eat grass like the ox. Seven times will pass by for you until you acknowledge that the Most High is sovereign over all kingdoms on earth and gives them to anyone he wishes."

Immediately what had been said about Nebuchadnezzar was fulfilled. He was driven away from people and ate grass like the ox. His body was drenched with the dew of heaven until his hair grew like the feathers of an eagle and his nails like the claws of a bird.

At the end of that time, I, Nebuchadnezzar, raised my eyes toward heaven, and my sanity was restored. Then I praised the Most High; I honoured and glorified him who lives forever. His dominion is an eternal dominion; his kingdom endures from generation to generation. All the peoples of the earth are regarded as nothing.

He does as he pleases with the powers of heaven
and the peoples of the earth.
No one can hold back his hand
or say to him: "What have you done?"

At the same time that my sanity was restored, my honour and splendour were returned to me for the glory of my kingdom. My advisers and nobles sought me out, and I was restored to my throne and became even greater than before. Now I, Nebuchadnezzar, praise and exalt and glorify the King of heaven, because everything he does is right and all his ways are just. And those who walk in pride he is able to humble.

The Problem

∼

Twenty-two years earlier God had humbled Nebuchadnezzar by sending *Nebuchadnezzar's 'Large Statue' Dream*. Its main purpose was to show him that God alone controlled the destiny of men and nations. Nebuchadnezzar responded by telling Daniel,

> Surely your God is the God of gods and the Lord of
> kings and a revealer of mysteries, for you were able
> to reveal this mystery.[1]

Yet twenty-two tears later in the midst of all his worldly success Nebuchadnezzar was as proud and deceived as ever. So God sent him a dream!

The Dreamer's Metron

∼

Nebuchadnezzar was the longest reigning and most powerful monarch of the Neo-Babylonian Empire. Scripture depicts him as the demolisher of Solomon's Temple and the architect of the Babylonian captivity. Jeremiah called him the destroyer of nations.[2] God used Nebuchadnezzar both to punish Israel and to witness to Babylon and the whole world about the greatness of God. Nebuchadnezzar had a prophetic dream of international importance about the rise and fall of world powers beginning with his own kingdom. He saw thousands of years into the future.

The Message

The message is plain enough. It was repeated three times; the Most High is sovereign over all kingdoms on earth and gives them to anyone he wishes.

Nebuchadnezzar had grown strong; his greatness had grown until it reached the sky, and his dominion extended to distant parts of the earth. But self-centred Nebuchadnezzar had forgotten God was the power behind his throne. He was living a settled life of exploitative power with no thought or care for the poor and needy in his kingdom.

Because of this God issued a decree that Nebuchadnezzar was to live like a wild animal for seven years. Then he would acknowledge the sovereignty of God and God would restore him.

Daniel who had a spirit of wisdom and revelation and who knew the ways of God offered a way out. He told Nebuchadnezzar, Renounce your sins by doing what is right, and your wickedness by being kind to the oppressed. It may be that then your prosperity will continue.

Essentially Daniel was saying, Repent and care for the poor and needy.

God's Purpose

God's purpose was that Nebuchadnezzar should know Him better. God desired Nebuchadnezzar should realise the Most High is sovereign over all kingdoms on earth and gives them to anyone he wishes and sets over them the lowliest of people. God was demonstrating His dominion over all powers and principalities especially Babylon where His exiled people were living.

Nebuchadnezzar believed his success was due to himself. He also believed he could wield his enormous power without being answerable to anyone.

God decided to show Nebuchadnezzar there is only one King who is sovereign and His name is Yahweh. God also wanted Nebuchadnezzar to know he had a responsibility before God to treat ordinary people with respect and justice.

Nebuchadnezzar was about to learn what true kingship entailed;

> May all kings bow down to him and all nations serve him. For he will deliver the needy who cry out, the afflicted who have no one to help. He will take pity on the weak and the needy and save the needy from death. He will rescue them from oppression and violence, for precious is their blood in his sight.[3]

Satan's Purpose

Satan's purpose was to blind the eyes of Nebuchadnezzar and hinder all of God's plans. Through powerful Nebuchadnezzar, Satan tried to kill as many people as possible. He had attempted to kill Daniel and his friends and all the magicians, enchanters, sorcerers and astrologers at the time of Nebuchadnezzar's first dream.

Dreamer's Eyes Enlightened

∽

It seems Nebuchadnezzar was none the wiser after this dream. It was going to take another eight years before he'd finally become fully enlightened. A year after the dream he was still boasting about how great he was when God's decree kicked in and he ended up living like an animal for seven years.

Dreamer's Response and Application

∽

We're not told about Nebuchadnezzar's initial reaction to the dream. He certainly didn't respond properly to God's warning. Nor did he heed appropriately to Daniels advice to repent and care for the poor and needy.

It was really only after his punishment that Nebuchadnezzar becomes enlightened and transformed. Only then was he able to apply the dream's message. Only then was he able to comprehend and fully declare the greatness and sovereignty of God. Nebuchadnezzar was now a believer who told the whole world,

> Now I, Nebuchadnezzar, praise and exalt and glorify the King of heaven, because everything he does is right and all his ways are just. And those who walk in pride he is able to humble.[4]

Know God Better

∼

God showed great mercy to Nebuchadnezzar by sending this dream. It's the sort of dream mentioned by Elihu in Job 33;

> For God does speak—now one way, now another—
> though no one perceives it. In a dream, in a vision
> of the night, when deep sleep falls on people as they
> slumber in their beds, he may speak in their ears
> and terrify them with warnings, to turn them from
> wrongdoing and keep them from pride, to preserve
> them from the pit, their lives from perishing by the
> sword.

Nebuchadnezzar's dream fits Elihu's description perfectly. Although Nebuchadnezzar didn't respond appropriately to the dream and offset the angel's decree God was still merciful.

The seven years of lycanthropy suffered by Nebuchadnezzar brought transformation and salvation. Peter speaks of this aspect of God when he says;

> The Lord is not slow in keeping his promise, as some
> understand slowness. Instead he is patient with you,
> not wanting anyone to perish, but everyone to
> come to repentance.[5]

God is also revealed as a kind and loving God who cares for justice for the poor and needy, the widow and orphan. The Psalmist says,

> Who is like you, Lord? You rescue the poor from those
> too strong for them, the poor and needy from those
> who rob them.[6]

The Psalmist also says concerning the covenant keeping God of Abraham, Isaac and Jacob;

> Blessed are those whose help is the God of Jacob, whose hope is in the Lord their God. He is the Maker of heaven and earth, the sea, and everything in them – he remains faithful for ever. He upholds the cause of the oppressed and gives food to the hungry. The Lord sets prisoners free, the Lord gives sight to the blind, the Lord lifts up those who are bowed down, the Lord loves the righteous. The Lord watches over the foreigner and sustains the fatherless and the widow, but he frustrates the ways of the wicked.[7]

The Dream Process

This is a complex symbolic personal warning dream requiring interpretation. There is also an angel making decrees.

Daniel again uses *The Symbol Replacement Method*. The great tree represented Nebuchadnezzar. The bound stump symbolised the possibility of restoration. The brass and iron that bound the stump reminds us of Greece and Rome from Nebuchadnezzar's earlier dream. Till seven times pass by was interpreted as seven years.

Daniel also adds a word of wisdom to his dream interpretation to the effect that caring for the poor and needy is a big deal for God. Heeding this advice would have given Nebuchadnezzar a *Get Out of Jail Free Card*.

The Usual Suspects

∼

God is represented by the angel making decrees. The Holy Spirit is evident in Nebuchadnezzar's declaration of the spirit of the holy gods being in Daniel. Jesus is glimpsed in Nebuchadnezzar's salvation. The stump left in the ground also reminds me of Jesus as the root of Jesse from Isaiah 11.

Takeaways

∼

In this dream we see the Divine Council from Psalm 82 in operation. They send a messenger who enforces their judgement and who declares the purpose of that judgement,

> The decision is announced by messengers, the holy ones declare the verdict, so that the living may know that the Most High is sovereign over all kingdoms on earth and gives them to anyone he wishes and sets over them the lowliest of people.'[8]

There's more recorded in Scripture about Nebuchadnezzar than any other Gentile ruler. Nebuchadnezzar's first dream was prophetic and international in scope while the second dream dealt with personal issues involving the King's own lifestyle.

It was about Nebuchadnezzar's fall from power followed by his restoration. God resists the proud but still desires to bring them to Himself. The dream typifies God's dealing with rebellious men who forget God and in their arrogance strive to build their own empires. Like the Tower of Babel their house of cards will always fall.

God is known as the God of widows and orphans and the poor and needy.[9] Yet he is no respecter of persons. There is an interesting scripture in Ezekiel that speaks of Nebuchadnezzar working for God. Ezekiel says,

> On April 26, the first day of the new year, during the twenty-seventh year of King Jehoiachin's captivity, this message came to me from the Lord: "Son of man, the army of King Nebuchadnezzar of Babylon fought so hard against Tyre that the warriors' heads were rubbed bare and their shoulders were raw and blistered. Yet Nebuchadnezzar and his army won no plunder to compensate them for all their work. Therefore, this is what the Sovereign Lord says: I will give the land of Egypt to Nebuchadnezzar, king of Babylon. He will carry off its wealth, plundering everything it has so he can pay his army. Yes, I have given him the land of Egypt as a reward for his work, says the Sovereign Lord, because he was working for me when he destroyed Tyre.[10]

God was also very patient with Nebuchadnezzar. Peter says,

> But do not forget this one thing, dear friends: With the Lord a day is like a thousand years, and a thousand years are like a day. The Lord is not slow in keeping his promise, as some understand slowness. Instead he is patient with you, not wanting anyone to perish, but everyone to come to repentance.[11]

After his first dream Nebuchadnezzar realised God was the God of gods and a revealer of mysteries. Then after the fiery furnace incident he declared there was no other God who could rescue His people like Yahweh.

Then following his seven years of madness Nebuchadnezzar was finally transformed and able to proclaim,

> All the peoples of the earth are regarded as nothing. He does as he pleases with the powers of heaven and the peoples of the earth. No one can hold back his hand or say to him: "What have you done?" ... Now I, Nebuchadnezzar, praise and exalt and glorify the King of heaven, because everything he does is right and all his ways are just. And those who walk in pride he is able to humble.[12]

Two years later Nebuchadnezzar died.

DANIEL'S 'FOUR BEASTS' DREAM

The Dream Setting/Backstory

Daniel received two night vision dreams thirty years after Nebuchadnezzar's *Big Tree Dream*. A generation had come and gone and Nebuchadnezzar's son Belshazzar was now reigning.

The overall theme of these revelations - *Daniel's 'Four Beasts' Dream* and *Daniel's 'Ram, Goat and Little Horn'* Dream once again concern God's sovereignty over history and nations.

Before we look at *Daniel's 'Four Beasts' Dream* it's important to realise we have no certain way of knowing the exact names of the kings and empires depicted in this dream. In *Nebuchadnezzar's 'Large Statue' Dream* we know Nebuchadnezzar was the head of gold so historically we can easily fit in the empires that followed him into some sort of schema. In fact Daniel was so sure of his proper interpretation of *Nebuchadnezzar's 'Large Statue' Dream* that he risked his life on it.

This is not the case with *Daniel's 'Four Beasts' Dream*. After this dream Daniel was so traumatised and troubled that he kept the matter to myself.

God had blessed Daniel in knowledge and understanding of all kinds of literature and learning. Daniel was also anointed in understanding visions and dreams of all kinds.

So if Daniel with the help of the interpreting angel couldn't fully interpret this dream then you can bet your bottom dollar I'm not going to exhaust myself trying.

The Dream Scripture
Daniel 7:1-28

∼

In the first year of Belshazzar king of Babylon, Daniel had a dream, and visions passed through his mind as he was lying in bed. He wrote down the substance of his dream.

Daniel said: "In my vision at night I looked, and there before me were the four winds of heaven churning up the great sea. Four great beasts, each different from the others, came up out of the sea.

"The first was like a lion, and it had the wings of an eagle. I watched until its wings were torn off and it was lifted from the ground so that it stood on two feet like a human being, and the mind of a human was given to it.

"And there before me was a second beast, which looked like a bear. It was raised up on one of its sides, and it had three ribs in its mouth between its teeth. It was told, 'Get up and eat your fill of flesh!'

"After that, I looked, and there before me was another beast, one that looked like a leopard. And on its back it had four wings like those of a bird. This beast had four heads, and it was given authority to rule.

"After that, in my vision at night I looked, and there before me was a fourth beast—terrifying and frightening and very powerful. It had large iron teeth; it crushed and devoured its victims and trampled underfoot whatever was left. It was different from all the former beasts, and it had ten horns.

"While I was thinking about the horns, there before me was another horn, a little one, which came up among them; and three of the first horns were uprooted before it. This horn had eyes like the eyes of a human being and a mouth that spoke boastfully.

"As I looked,
"thrones were set in place,
 and the Ancient of Days took his seat.
His clothing was as white as snow;
the hair of his head was white like wool.
His throne was flaming with fire,
and its wheels were all ablaze.
A river of fire was flowing,
coming out from before him.
Thousands upon thousands attended him;
ten thousand times ten thousand stood before him.
The court was seated,
and the books were opened.

"Then I continued to watch because of the boastful words the horn was speaking. I kept looking until the beast was slain and its body destroyed and thrown into the blazing fire. (The other beasts had been stripped of their authority, but were allowed to live for a period of time.)

"In my vision at night I looked, and there before me was one like a son of man, coming with the clouds of heaven. He approached the Ancient of Days and was led into his presence. He was given authority, glory and sovereign power; all nations and peoples of every language worshiped him. His dominion is an everlasting dominion that will not pass away, and his kingdom is one that will never be destroyed.

The Interpretation of the Dream

"I, Daniel, was troubled in spirit, and the visions that passed through my mind disturbed me. I approached one of those standing there and asked him the meaning of all this.

"So he told me and gave me the interpretation of these things: 'The four great beasts are four kings that will rise from the earth. But the holy people of the Most High will receive the kingdom and will possess it forever—yes, for ever and ever.'

"Then I wanted to know the meaning of the fourth beast, which was different from all the others and most terrifying, with its iron teeth and bronze claws—the beast that crushed and devoured its victims and trampled underfoot whatever was left. I also wanted to know about the ten horns on its head and about the other horn that came up, before which three of them fell—the horn that looked more imposing than the others and that had eyes and a mouth that spoke boastfully.

As I watched, this horn was waging war against the holy people and defeating them, until the Ancient of Days came and pronounced judgment in favour of the holy people of the Most High, and the time came when they possessed the kingdom.

"He gave me this explanation: 'The fourth beast is a fourth kingdom that will appear on earth. It will be different from all the other kingdoms and will devour the whole earth, trampling it down and crushing it. The ten horns are ten kings who will come from this kingdom. After them another king will arise, different from the earlier ones; he will subdue three kings. He will speak against the Most High and oppress his holy people and try to change the set times and the laws. The holy people will be delivered into his hands for a time, times and half a time.

"'But the court will sit, and his power will be taken away and completely destroyed forever. Then the sovereignty, power and greatness of all the kingdoms under heaven will be handed over to the holy people of the Most High. His kingdom will be an everlasting kingdom, and all rulers will worship and obey him.'

"This is the end of the matter. I, Daniel, was deeply troubled by my thoughts, and my face turned pale, but I kept the matter to myself."

The Problem

~

Troubled times are coming for God's people. Daniel was shown vast quantities of revelation about coming kingdoms over an extensive period of time. He was also shown the coming Messiah and something of what will happen to Abraham's seed at the conclusion of time.

The Dreamer's Metron

~

Daniel was a major prophet with a worldwide and end time metron. He was gifted in dreams and visions that prophesied world history, including Daniel's people, Israel and all mankind in the latter days. He also received revelation from the angel Gabriel.

Daniel served in prominent positions in both Babylonian and Medo-Persian empires under Nebuchadnezzar, Belshazzar, Darius and Cyrus. In the first year of Darius's reign Daniel understood the prophecy of Jeremiah that predicted a 70-year captivity of his people was soon coming to an end.

Daniel often prayed and fasted for his nation's sins and pleaded for God's mercy on himself, his fellow captives and all the inhabitants of Jerusalem. He faithfully prayed three times a day even thought this activity threatened his life.

Ezekiel called him a righteous man alongside Noah and Job. Daniel's fame spread well beyond the borders of Israel. When God granted Daniel the wisdom to interpret the king's dream, it launched Daniel's long career as a political leader, trusted advisor, major prophet and dream interpreter.

God's purpose for Daniel was to impact Babylon through revelation and dream interpretation in order to reveal God's sovereignty to the then most powerful nation on earth. Through Daniel's influence Israel's God was revealed as the Most High God who raises and removes kings and establishes new world empires. He is the Ancient of Days on the throne and the God of heaven, whose kingdom will never end.

Daniel's dreams and visions showed God's faithfulness and care for His people Israel. God enabled Daniel to prophesy some of God's long-term plans for all nations including the Messiah, the temple, Jerusalem, and a coming kingdom of righteousness.

The Message

∽

The message of this apocalyptic dream is simple enough. It's another case of, The Most High is sovereign over all earthly kingdoms and gives them to anyone he wishes and sets over them the lowliest of people.[1]

Daniel is also shown that despite all the coming cruel kingdoms and despite all the great suffering they'll inflict on Abraham's descendants, in the end the Messiah will appear and set up His everlasting Kingdom.

Then the sovereignty, power and greatness of all the kingdoms under heaven will be handed over to the holy people of the Most High. His kingdom will be an everlasting kingdom, and all rulers will worship and obey him.

God's Purpose

∾

God's purpose was to comfort Daniel and His covenant people with the knowledge He is in control. Despite how awful things might appear at any particular time we must always remember it is God's plans and purpose that will ultimately prevail. God's Messiah will arrive and His Kingdom will come. It's also a case of Amos 3:7, Surely the Sovereign Lord does nothing without revealing his plan to his servants the prophets.

Satan's Purpose

∾

Satan, as the ruler of this world, continues to war against God's holy people using ungodly and despotic world leaders but ultimately he is no match for the Ancient of Days who judged him at The Cross and will finally judge him and cast him into the lake of burning sulphur with the beast and the false prophet.[2]

The title Ancient of Days is only mentioned three times in the Bible and they all occur in the above verses, Daniel 7:9, 13, and 22. I believe they all refer to Jesus as God and man.

Dreamer's Eyes Enlightened

∽

Daniel's eyes were once again enlightened to God's amazing sovereignty. God and the interpreting angel, possibly Gabriel, give Daniel a thumbnail sketch of thousands of years of world history from his era until the Messiah returns and rules on Earth. Daniel was not given specific names of the kings and their empires but this has not stopped generations of enthusiastic Christians from trying to fill in the blanks. After all, It is the glory of God to conceal a matter, But the glory of kings is to search out a matter.[3]

Dreamer's Response and Application

∽

During this apocalyptic dream Daniel's initial response was to be greatly troubled in spirit and mind. Then upon waking his immediate response was to write down the substance of the dream.

Although Daniel was perplexed over many of the dream's mysteries he generally understood the central theme, which concerned the victory of the saints and the establishment of God's Kingdom on earth.

Overall, Daniel was traumatised by this apocalyptic revelation. His mind was deeply troubled, the blood left his face and he withdrew into himself.

Know God Better

Once again God's sovereignty is showcased for the whole world. Isaiah speaking for God said,

> I make known the end from the beginning, from
> ancient times, what is still to come. I say, 'My
> purpose will stand, and I will do all that I please.[4]'

Daniel experiences something of this great truth in this dream. This dream also shows how easily one can become overwhelmed when God shares even a little of his vast knowledge. Yet God in His kindness only shares what we can bear.

In The Gospel of John, Jesus spoke to his disciples who had been with him for three and a half years. He said,

> I have much more to say to you, more than you can
> now bear. But when he, the Spirit of truth, comes,
> he will guide you into all the truth. He will not
> speak on his own; he will speak only what he hears,
> and he will tell you what is yet to come.[5]

God knows just how much revelation a human being can take at any one time. Sometimes prophetic revelation can be very heavy to carry. For example, after Daniel's vision of the Messiah he was told things the Jews must suffer at the hands of the Gentiles. Then in just thirty-five verses God gives Daniel revelation concerning one hundred and thirty five major events covering a period of three hundred and sixty six years.

At that point we realise God knows stuff and although we can identify many of Daniel's fulfilled prophesies there are many more not yet understood and fulfilled. Yahweh is the supreme sovereign God who reveals the future before it comes to pass.

Isaiah wrote,

> I am God and always will be. No one can escape from
> my power; no one can change what I do.[6]

The Dream Process

~

Daniel was able to reflect within the dream on what exactly he was seeing. This was a highly symbolic dream full of difficult imagery, in which Daniel dialogued with an interpreting angel. Again we see the *The Symbol Replacement Method* being used.

The four winds of heaven churning up the great sea represented the troubled world, the sea of nations. The four great beasts represent four kings and their empires. This is very similar to Nebuchadnezzar's dream although Daniel's dream highlighted the kings' cruelty whereas Nebuchadnezzar's dream emphasised their glory and splendour.

This dream continues the theme of kingdoms introduced in Nebuchadnezzar's two earlier dreams and adds extra information about end time events. There is nothing simple about this dream. Much of it remains hidden until today.

The angel's interpretation was along the lines the four great beasts are four kings that will rise from the earth. But the holy people of the Most High will receive the kingdom and will possess it forever.

This echoes Daniel 2, where we have the depiction of four human kingdoms followed by the establishment of God's eternal kingdom. When Daniel wanted to know more about the fourth beast, the angel said, The fourth beast is a fourth kingdom that will appear on earth. It will be different from all the other kingdoms and will devour the whole earth, trampling it down and crushing it. Daniel was then told,

> The ten horns are ten kings who will come from this kingdom. After them another king will arise, different from the earlier ones; he will subdue three kings. He will speak against the Most High and oppress his holy people and try to change the set times and the laws. The holy people will be delivered into his hands for a time, times and half a time.[7]

But the final outcome will be with God, when the heavenly court sits and the fourth beast's power is taken away and completely destroyed forever. Then the sovereignty, power and greatness of all earthly kingdoms will be handed over to the holy people of the Most High. His kingdom will be an everlasting kingdom, and all rulers will worship and obey him.

The Usual Suspects

∽

God, in the form of Jesus, appears as the Ancient of Days and sits in Judgement. God as the victorious Man Jesus appears in the clouds and receives an everlasting Kingdom. Satan is depicted as waging war against God's covenant people.

Takeaways

∽

In this dream we get a tantalising glimpse of the Divine Council from Psalm 82 in operation. We see thrones being set in place and Jesus taking his seat before thousands of attendants and the gods. Then the whole court was seated and God's books concerning God's plans and purpose were opened.

Perhaps the main thing dream interpreters can learn from this dream is that some dreams, especially apocalyptic dreams, can be extremely difficult if not impossible to correctly interpret and apply.

Once we understand the revelation or the riddle it all seems so simple. Of course we all now know the virgin that will have a baby is Mary. Of course we all now know smoking causes cancer. It's easy to be wise after the event. But before we understand the mystery it's an entirely different matter.

In one sense the interpretation of Daniel's apocalyptic dream is simple enough. The angel explains, The four great beasts are four kings that will rise from the earth. But the holy people of the Most High will receive the kingdom and will possess it forever—yes, for ever and ever.

The real difficulty arises when we try to put names and dates and times to these kings and their kingdoms. Then the real trouble begins and I believe this is because God is keeping some revelation hidden in His own purpose. Or perhaps it's because we're not able to bear it yet.[8]

Lets have a quick glance at some of the opposing positions concerning these four kingdoms. Many Biblical scholars believe this dream is about the same kingdoms mentioned in Nebuchadnezzar's *Large Statue Dream* with some additional facts concerning the antichrist, yet over the centuries there have been many diverse schools of thought on this.

For example Jewish and Christian Historicists, Partial Preterists, Futurists, Dispensationalists, and other futuristic Jewish and Christian hybrids, as well as certain Messianic Jews, typically identify the kingdoms in Daniel as: the Babylonian Empire, the Medo-Persian

Empire, the Greek Empire and the Roman Empire, with other implications to come later. Christian interpreters also tend to read and compare the Book of Daniel alongside The Book of Revelation.

On the other hand, Full Preterists, Idealists, certain Reconstructionists and other non-futurists also believe in the same general sequence, but teach Daniel's prophecies ended with the destruction of the Second Temple of Jerusalem, and have few or no implications beyond that.

Jewish and Christian Futurists, Dispensationalists, and, to some degree, Partial Preterists believe the prophecies of Daniel stopped with the destruction of the Second Temple of Jerusalem; but will resume at some point in the future after a gap in prophecy that accounts for the Church Age.

Other Biblical scholars have imagined the lion with wings might be America and Britain, the bear is perhaps Russia and maybe the leopard is the Arab world while the dragon might be China.

These are all interesting speculations but the fact is when we're not sure and certain about our revelation we dare not become dogmatic about our position.

If the heavily anointed Daniel turned pale and kept the matter to himself I'm also willing to patiently wait for the proper time when the revealer of mysteries chooses to show His hand.

DANIEL'S 'RAM, GOAT AND LITTLE HORN' DREAM

The Dream Setting/Backstory

Daniel received this night vision dream just two years after his *Four Beast's Dream*. Daniel wrote,

> In the third year of King Belshazzar's reign, I, Daniel, had a vision, after the one that had already appeared to me.[1]

His first dream was a night vision and so was this one. It was very similar to the previous dream that Daniel couldn't fully understand. He said, I was appalled by the vision; it was beyond understanding.[2]

The Dream Scripture

Daniel 8:1-27

∿

In the third year of King Belshazzar's reign, I, Daniel, had a vision, after the one that had already appeared to me. In my vision I saw myself in the citadel of Susa in the province of Elam; in the vision I was beside the Ulai Canal. I looked up, and there before me was a ram with two horns, standing beside the canal, and the horns were long. One of the horns was longer than the other but grew up later. I watched the ram as it charged toward the west and the north and the south. No animal could stand against it, and none could rescue from its power. It did as it pleased and became great.

As I was thinking about this, suddenly a goat with a prominent horn between its eyes came from the west, crossing the whole earth without touching the ground. It came toward the two-horned ram I had seen standing beside the canal and charged at it in great rage. I saw it attack the ram furiously, striking the ram and shattering its two horns. The ram was powerless to stand against it; the goat knocked it to the ground and trampled on it, and none could rescue the ram from its power. The goat became very great, but at the height of its power the large horn was broken off, and in its place four prominent horns grew up toward the four winds of heaven.

Out of one of them came another horn, which started small but grew in power to the south and to the east and toward the Beautiful Land. It grew until it reached the host of the heavens, and it threw some of the starry host down to the earth and trampled on them. It set itself up to be as great as the commander of the army of the Lord; it took away the daily sacrifice from the Lord, and his sanctuary was thrown down. Because of rebellion, the Lord's people and the daily sacrifice were given over to it. It prospered in everything it did, and truth was thrown to the ground.

Then I heard a holy one speaking, and another holy one said to him, "How long will it take for the vision to be fulfilled—the vision concerning the daily sacrifice, the rebellion that causes desolation, the surrender of the sanctuary and the trampling underfoot of the Lord's people?"

He said to me, "It will take 2,300 evenings and mornings; then the sanctuary will be reconsecrated."

The Interpretation of the Vision

While I, Daniel, was watching the vision and trying to understand it, there before me stood one who looked like a man. And I heard a man's voice from the Ulai calling, "Gabriel, tell this man the meaning of the vision."

As he came near the place where I was standing, I was terrified and fell prostrate. "Son of man," he said to me, "understand that the vision concerns the time of the end."

While he was speaking to me, I was in a deep sleep, with my face to the ground. Then he touched me and raised me to my feet.

He said: "I am going to tell you what will happen later in the time of wrath, because the vision concerns the appointed time of the end. The two-horned ram that you saw represents the kings of Media and Persia. The shaggy goat is the king of Greece, and the large horn between its eyes is the first king. The four horns that replaced the one that was broken off represent four kingdoms that will emerge from his nation but will not have the same power.

"In the latter part of their reign, when rebels have become completely wicked, a fierce-looking king, a master of intrigue, will arise. He will become very strong, but not by his own power. He will cause astounding devastation and will succeed in whatever he does. He will destroy those who are mighty, the holy people. He will cause deceit to prosper, and he will consider himself superior. When they feel secure, he will destroy many and take his stand against the Prince of princes. Yet he will be destroyed, but not by human power.

"The vision of the evenings and mornings that has been given you is true, but seal up the vision, for it concerns the distant future."

I, Daniel, was worn out. I lay exhausted for several days. Then I got up and went about the king's business. I was appalled by the vision; it was beyond understanding.

The Problem

∼

It's another case of Amos 3:7,

> Surely the Sovereign Lord does nothing without
> revealing his plan to his servants the prophets.

Again Daniel is being shown revelation concerning God's sovereign dominion over coming kingdoms and the last days. Daniel is overwhelmed by it all and feels the revelation is beyond all understanding.

The Dreamer's Metron

∼

Daniel was a major prophet with a worldwide and end time metron. He was gifted in dreams and visions that prophesied world history, including Daniel's people, Israel and all mankind in the latter days. He also received revelation and interpretation from the angel Gabriel.

Daniel served in prominent positions in both Babylonian and Medo-Persian empires under Nebuchadnezzar, Belshazzar, Darius and Cyrus. In the first year of Darius's reign Daniel understood the prophecy of Jeremiah that predicted a 70-year captivity of his people was soon coming to an end.

Daniel often prayed and fasted for his nation's sins and pleaded for God's mercy on himself, his fellow captives and all the inhabitants of Jerusalem. He faithfully prayed three times a day even thought this activity threatened his life.

Ezekiel called him a righteous man alongside Noah and Job. Daniel's fame spread well beyond the borders of Israel. When God granted Daniel the wisdom to interpret the king's dream, it launched Daniel's long career as a political leader, trusted advisor, major prophet and dream interpreter.

God's purpose for Daniel was to impact Babylon through revelation and dream interpretation in order to reveal God's sovereignty to the then most powerful nation on earth.

Through Daniel's influence Israel's God was revealed as the Most High God who raises and removes kings and establishes new world empires. He is the Ancient of Days on the throne and the God of heaven, whose kingdom will never end.

Daniel's dreams and visions showed God's faithfulness and care for His people Israel. God enabled Daniel to prophesy some of God's long-term plans for all nations including the Messiah, the temple, Jerusalem, and a coming kingdom of righteousness.

The Message

Daniel saw a *Games of Thrones*; The Babylonian Empire would be replaced by The Medes and Persian Empire that in turn would be replaced by the Greek Empire.

The Greek Empire would be led by a powerful king who'd die at the height of his success. (We now know this was Alexander the Great). Four Greek kings would arise after Alexander but none would be as powerful as Alexander. From one of the four a king will arise to attack Israel. This king would have supernatural power. He will be an embodiment of Satan and will attempt to be as great as the Messiah.

He will stop the daily sacrifice in the temple in Jerusalem. God will permit him to do this because of the rebellious state of the chosen people towards God.

Finally God will take this king out; he will be destroyed, but not by human power. Daniel was told to seal up the vision, for it concerns the distant future.

God's Purpose

God's purpose was to comfort Daniel and His covenant people with the knowledge that He is the One in control and His plans and purpose are being patiently worked out.

He also gave Daniel some sad revelation. He said the sins of Israel would grow to a point where He would have to pour out His wrath upon them and give them what they deserve.

This is similar to *Abrahams Covenant Dream* when God said His chosen people would have to wait four hundred years to possess Canaan because the iniquity of the Amorites was not yet full.

God was telling Daniel that Israel's cup of sin would be full in the time of the Little Horn King.

And even though the little horn, empowered by Satan would resist God, persecute His saints, and appear to be victorious God wanted Daniel to know it was God who would raise up the little horn to do His bidding and help fulfil His purpose.

Satan's Purpose

∼

Satan is symbolically presented in the person of the 'little horn' that grows to be powerful. At one point in the dream the "little horn" morphs from a human being to an incarnation of Satan himself who grows up to the host of heaven, causing some of the host and some of the stars to fall to earth. This reminds us of Revelation 12:4;

> Then another sign appeared in heaven: an enormous red dragon with seven heads and ten horns and seven crowns on its heads. Its tail swept a third of the stars out of the sky and flung them to the earth.

The ram and the goat had magnified themselves above men while this last king magnifies himself to be equal with the commander of the host. He removes the regular sacrifice from God and throws down the place of His sanctuary. This king opposes God and wants equality with God.

Yet thousands of years before the event God is showing Daniel He has already set a time limit on it all. It will only last for 2,300 evenings and mornings and then the holy place will be restored again.

Both the 'little horn' and Satan have a sell-by date.

Dreamer's Eyes Enlightened

∼

Even though Daniel said the dream was beyond understanding he did know many things. He knew of the future empires that would arise after Babylon. He'd already been told this through previous dreams.

He understood the people of Israel would suffer astounding devastation for their sins under the hands of the 'little horn.' He knew the temple sacrifice would be stopped for a certain time and then restored.

He knew the 'little horn' would be removed by God when his task was accomplished. The certainty of all these things happening to his nation appalled him. He was especially appalled in seeing Satan and his works in the latter days.

Dreamer's Response and Application

Daniel paid a price for this dream. He was exhausted and sick for days after experiencing it. He was appalled at the great suffering laid out for Israel and there was nothing he could do about it because Gabriel said it was certain to take place.

Although Daniel understood much from the dream the enormity and scope of the revelation overwhelmed him. This also happened to Abraham in *Abraham's Covenant Dream*,

> Now when the sun was going down, a deep sleep fell upon Abram; and behold, great terror and great darkness overwhelmed him.[3]

Know God Better

Knowing God is not a simple thing! Today most of us want a good clear interpretation of our dreams made relevant to our situation. After all God has a wonderful plan for our lives. He wants us to be happy, successful and fulfilled.

Not so with the prophets of old. They were often persecuted and killed for their unpopular revelation. Daniel and many other prophets often didn't fully understand their prophetic revelation especially when it concerned the suffering and glory of the Messiah and last day events.

In Romans St Paul takes great pains to explain the nuances of how the salvation of Jews and Gentiles was always a major part of God's eternal plans and purpose. Yet at the end of his intricate explanation he indicates that even when we reflect on fulfilled prophecy it still often seems incomprehensible. He says,

> Oh, the depth of the riches of the wisdom and
> knowledge of God! How unsearchable his
> judgments, and his paths beyond tracing out![4]

If God's wisdom is difficult to understand after it has come to pass then how much more difficult will it be understand God's great plans and purpose in advance?

No wonder Daniel didn't fully understand the prophecy contained in his apocalyptic dream, even after Gabriel's detailed explanation.

The Dream Process

∽

It would be a dozen years before Belshazzar's death heralded the end of Babylonian domination. Yet Daniel's dream takes him to the very city where Nehemiah and Esther will later play their important parts in God's plans and purpose for Israel.

Daniel's dream carried him in time and space to a place called Susa, north of the Persian Gulf, destined in a few years time to become the future capital of the Persian Empire.

There beside Susa's Ulai Canal Daniel discovered the Babylonian empire would be followed in succession by the kingdoms of Medo-Persia and Greece.

This is a complex symbolic dream requiring the help of the angel Gabriel to interpret and even then Daniel feels he understands so little. Again we see *The Symbol Replacement Method* in operation.

Gabriel interprets the ram as being the kings of Medo-Persia with two horns. He said the first horn symbolised Media and the second Persia which came later and was more powerful. The directions in which the ram charged and in which these kings extended their dominion has been confirmed by history.

Then after the Medo-Persian Empire had served God's purpose of returning the Jews to Israel and rebuilding the temple it was replaced by Greece symbolised by the male goat with only one horn.

It is generally believed this one horn represented Alexander the Great who came from the west and defeated the Medo-Persian ram. Then sometime after Alexander's early death at age thirty-three, four kings represented by the four prominent horns arose to take control of his empire.

All the forgoing is simple enough. The complicated part for generations of Bible scholars has been the issue of the 'little horn' that God uses to chastise his people Israel.

Perhaps this part operates on two levels. On one level Gabriel said in the last days of the Greek Empire just before the Messiah arrives a king will arise who will oppose God and oppress His people.

History has shown this was fulfilled under Antiochus Epiphanes, the Seleucid king, who reigned from 175-164 B.C. In 167 BC Antiochus began to carry out all of Daniel's dream predictions when he took Jerusalem by storm and brutally enforced a programme of Greek Hellenization upon the Jews.

On another level this 'little horn' represents an Anti-Christ spirit that has afflicted mankind from time to time and will finally play its hand and bring about great tribulation before Jesus Christ returns.

This seems to be the way Jesus interpreted Daniel's dream. Jesus said,

> "Then you will be handed over to be persecuted and put to death, and you will be hated by all nations because of me. At that time many will turn away from the faith and will betray and hate each other, and many false prophets will appear and deceive many people. Because of the increase of wickedness, the love of most will grow cold, but the one who stands firm to the end will be saved. And this gospel of the kingdom will be preached in the whole world as a testimony to all nations, and then the end will come.
>
> "So when you see standing in the holy place 'the abomination that causes desolation,' spoken of through the prophet Daniel—let the reader understand— then let those who are in Judea flee to the mountains. Let no one on the housetop go down to take anything out of the house. Let no one in the field go back to get their cloak. How dreadful it will be in those days for pregnant women and nursing mothers! Pray that your flight will not take place in winter or on the Sabbath. For then there will be great distress, unequaled from the beginning of the world until now—and never to be equaled again.[5]

The Usual Suspects

~

God is there working His purposes out, rising up kings and putting down kings and administering appropriate justice to all nations including Israel. In Matthew, Jesus calls Daniel a prophet and affirms his dream as being accurate.[6]

Jesus also appears as the Prince of princes in Daniel's dream. Satan is especially seen in the 'little horn' the fierce-looking king, a master of intrigue who will destroy many and take his stand against the Prince of princes.

Takeaways

~

History records when Alexander the Great's army arrived at Jerusalem in 333BC, he was met by Jaddua the Jewish high priest outside the city gates.

Jaddua then unrolled a scroll before Alexander and showed him *Daniel's 'Ram, Goat and Little Horn' Dream* from Daniel chapter 8.

Alexander was so touched his appearing had been prophesied two hundred years before that he decided to spare Jerusalem because of Daniel's dream.

ZECHARIAH'S DREAM OF HORSES

A note on Zechariah's Eight Night Vision Dreams

Twenty years after Daniel interpreted the writing on King Belshazzar's wall, Zechariah recently returned to Israel had a series of eight night vision dreams during the night of February 15, 519 BC. The Book of Zechariah doesn't clearly say whether these revelations were dreams or night visions or both.

But at one point Zechariah does say, Then the angel who was speaking with me returned and woke me, as a man is awakened from his sleep. This means it's entirely possible everything up to this point has been a dream. As I've mentioned elsewhere, as in Job 33:15 and Isaiah 29:7, a dream can be described as a vision of the night. If this is the case here then Zechariah's dream in eight sections would be the longest recorded dream in the Bible.

The Dream Setting/Backstory

In *Solomon's Warning Dream* God said,

> But if indeed you or your sons turn away from following Me and do not keep the commandments and statutes I have set before you, and if you go off to serve and worship other gods, then I will cut off Israel from the land that I have given them, and I will banish from My presence this temple I have sanctified for My Name. Then Israel will become an object of scorn and ridicule among all peoples.[1]

Neither Solomon nor Israel heeded God's warning so God kept His word by handing them over to their enemies. The Assyrians exiled Israel's northern kingdom in 722 BC and the Babylonians exiled the southern kingdom of Judah in 586 BC.

This Babylonian exile ended when as symbolised in *Nebuchadnezzar's Large Tree Dream* the Persian Empire conquered the Babylonian Empire in 539 BC. Afterwards Cyrus the Great allowed the Jews to return to Jerusalem to rebuild their Temple.

In the first year they built an altar of burnt offerings and in the second year they laid the foundation of the temple but it would be another sixteen years before any further building took place because of opposition from their enemies.

God then sent the prophet Haggai who preached four sermons in four months to encourage the Jews to begin rebuilding. Two months later Zechariah began his prophetic ministry of spiritual renewal and encouragement and in five years the temple was completed.

God gave Zechariah eight successive night vision dreams, (or perhaps just one long dream) to inspire the beleaguered returnees.

These eight revelations are like a thumbnail sketch of God's plans and purposes for Israel and all nations.

They are all very symbolic and some have more than one interpretation. They all follow a similar pattern. Introductory words are followed by a description of things seen. Then Zechariah asks the angel for the meaning of his vision followed by the angel's explanation. This is the first night vision dream.

The Dream Scripture
Zechariah 1:4-17

∾

On the twenty-fourth day of the eleventh month, the month of Shebat, in the second year of Darius, the word of the LORD came to the prophet Zechariah son of Berechiah, the son of Iddo. I looked out into the night and saw a man riding on a red horse that stood among the myrtle trees in the hollow. Behind him were red, sorrel, and white horses.

"What are these, my lord?" I asked.

And the angel who was speaking with me replied, "I will show you what they are."

Then the man standing among the myrtle trees explained, "They are the ones the LORD has sent to patrol the earth."

And the riders answered the Angel of the LORD who stood among the myrtle trees, "We have patrolled the earth, and behold, all the earth is at rest and tranquil."

Then the Angel of the LORD said, "How long, O LORD of Hosts, will You withhold mercy from Jerusalem and the cities of Judah, with which You have been angry these seventy years?"

So the LORD spoke kind and comforting words to the angel who was speaking with me. Then the angel who was speaking with me said, "Proclaim this word: This is what the LORD of Hosts says: 'I am very jealous for Jerusalem and Zion, but I am fiercely angry with the nations that are at ease. For I was a little angry, but they have increased the calamity.'

Therefore, this is what the LORD says: 'I will return to Jerusalem with mercy, and there My house will be rebuilt, declares the LORD of Hosts, and a measuring line will be stretched out over Jerusalem.'

Proclaim further: This is what the LORD of Hosts says: 'My cities will again overflow with prosperity; the LORD will again comfort Zion and choose Jerusalem.'"

The Problem

∾

God has punished unfaithful Israel as promised for seventy years. Now His Chosen People are wounded and broken, in need of His mercy, comfort and inspiration in order to rebuild the Temple.

The Dreamer's Metron

∾

Zechariah was both a prophet and a priest born into a Levite family in Babylon. He returned to Jerusalem with the first batch of 50,000 Jews after their seventy-year exile.

He functioned at the same time as the prophet Haggai, the governor Zerubbabel and Joshua the high priest. While Haggai's preaching focused on Israel's sin and selfishness Zechariah's prophecy encouraged the harassed Israelites to rebuild the temple.

His metron was national and international. He prophetically saw the Messiah in both His first and His second comings. Zechariah has the largest number of messianic passages amongst all the Minor Prophets.

The New Testament contains over forty of his references.

The Book of Revelation is greatly influenced by his imagery. Zechariah's main purpose was to assure Judah that although God disciplined them for seventy years in Babylon He is still their covenant keeping God who will bless them as He promised their fathers.

The Message

Although the whole world is at peace Israel isn't. God was angry at unfaithful Israel for seventy years. Now he is angry at the over zealous nations He used to discipline His chosen people. He assures Judah he will keep His covenant promises and will comfort, restore and prosper Israel once again. To this end God's house, the temple, will be rebuilt, and God's cities will again overflow with prosperity.

God's Purpose

God loves Israel and has good plans and purposes for her. Jeremiah had prophesied of the exact period of time when Zechariah had these eight night vision dreams,

> This is what the Lord says: "When seventy years are completed for Babylon, I will come to you and fulfil

my good promise to bring you back to this place.
For I know the plans I have for you," declares
the Lord, "plans to prosper you and not to harm
you, plans to give you hope and a future. Then you
will call on me and come and pray to me, and I will
listen to you. You will seek me and find me when
you seek me with all your heart. I will be found by
you," declares the Lord, "and will bring you
back from captivity. I will gather you from all the
nations and places where I have banished you,"
declares the Lord, "and will bring you back to the
place from which I carried you into exile."[2]

Although God deeply loved Israel He was very angry at her idolatry. He was also angry at the nations He used to discipline her. They'd been too harsh. Isaiah said,

> I became angry with My people and desecrated My
> inheritance; I gave them into your hand, and you
> showed them no mercy, even on the aged, you laid a
> very heavy yoke[3]... Disaster will come upon you,
> and you will not know how to conjure it away. A
> calamity will fall upon you that you cannot ward off
> with a ransom; a catastrophe you cannot foresee
> will suddenly come upon you.[4]

In *Nebuchadnezzar's Large Tree Dream* and in *Daniel's 'Four Beasts' Dreams* we saw various nations God allowed to rule over and discipline Israel for a time. Then these nations were destroyed by God on behalf of Israel.

This theme of God punishing and defending Israel recurs throughout the Bible. Israel and her chosen people play a pivotal part in God's master plan for the Messiah and all nations. Anyone or any nation, who supports Israel in her calling is blessed by God and anyone or any nation who hinders God's purpose concerning Israel is cursed.

God promised as much to His Covenant partner Abraham,

> The Lord said to Abram, Leave your country, your people and your father's household and go to the land I will show you. I will make you into a great nation and I will bless you; I will make your name great, and you will be a blessing. I will bless those who bless you, and whoever curses you I will curse; and all people on earth will be blessed through you.[5]

God's overriding plan and purpose is always to restore Israel and all nations into their right relationship with Him as Sovereign God and with one another. These eight night vision dreams speak into this purpose.

Satan's Purpose

∽

Satan's plans were to completely destroy Israel. Firstly he tempted them into idolatry so God in His justice would have to punish them. Then he incited Babylon and the other nations God used to discipline Israel to be overly cruel and merciless. Satan's plan was always to prevent the coming of the Messiah who would crush his head.

Dreamer's Eyes Enlightened

∼

Zechariah clearly understands the message and is able to pass it on. No doubt Zechariah was also personally encouraged when he realised God was deeply interested in the lives of His people and not only the Temple building.

Dreamer's Response and Application

∼

During the dream Zechariah asks the angel for clarification about the identity of the horses and their riders. He then immediately goes into another dream.

Know God Better

∼

As usual God is seen as a faithful Covenant Keeping God. He is also seen as a God of justice, a good Father who disciplines His children. Hebrews says,

> And have you completely forgotten this word of
> encouragement that addresses you as a father
> addresses his son? It says, "My son, do not make
> light of the Lord's discipline, and do not lose heart
> when he rebukes you, because the Lord disciplines
> the one he loves, and he chastens everyone he
> accepts as his son." Endure hardship as discipline;

> God is treating you as his children. For what
> children are not disciplined by their father?[6]

Here our loving God is also shown as expressing other emotions. He is angry at Israel for their idolatry and angry at Babylon for their excessive cruelty to Israel

The Dream Process

~

All eight of Zechariah's night vision dreams follow a similar pattern. Introductory words are followed by a description of things seen. Then Zechariah asks the angel for the meaning of his vision followed by the angel's explanation. This dream of national and global importance contains symbolism interpreted by an angel. This revelation gives insight and hope to Zechariah and his people.

The Holy Spirit sent the dream and God the Father, Jesus and an angel are present in this dream. Zechariah talked with the angel and the angel explained things as they occurred instead of afterwards as is common in such dreams.

Zechariah also heard the voice of God speaking. We are not told the significance of the colour of the horses. Nor are we told the significance of the myrtle trees. We were told the riders are angels sent by the Lord to patrol the earth. We're also told a measuring line will be stretched out over Jerusalem. This will occur in Zechariah's third dream. We know the Angel of the Lord is Jesus.

The Usual Suspects

~

The Angel of the Lord who stands amongst the myrtle trees and who intercedes for Israel is Jesus. God the Father responds by comforting the interpreting angel and by having the angel declare His plans and purpose for Israel. Satan is evident in the actions of the nations who were excessively cruel to Israel and who God is angry with.

Takeaways

~

This is possibly the longest recorded dream in the Bible; a dream in eight sections. Similar to *Jacob's 'Go Down To Egypt' Night Vision Dream* it's not actually stated Zechariah had a dream. But we do learn in Zechariah 4:1 that the angel who talked with him woke him up. Was he woken up within the dream and did the dream continue or was he woken up out of the dream and did he then receive four open visions?

As I've already mentioned Scripture makes little or no distinction between dreams and visions. Sometimes we don't know whether the revelation has been a dream or a night vision. To the Hebraic mind the main point was the person experienced a supernatural experience and revelation.

Although there are over two hundred scriptural references to dreams and visions Bible writers are not particularly consistent or concerned with precise definitions.

The book of Job says, In a dream in a vision of the night while the book of Daniel uses phrases like, Your dream and the visions of your head, Visions of my dream, and a dream, a vision of the night. Isaiah also talks of a dream of a night vision.

Solomon Asks For Wisdom Dream is a 2 Chronicles retelling of *Solomon's 'Discerning Heart' Dream* from 1 Kings 3. The interesting thing is although this revelation was sent through a dream there is no mention of the word dream in this incident. We are only told, That night God appeared to Solomon, though from reading about this incident in 1 Kings 3 we know it was a dream.

This begs the question about just how many other similar situations are really dreams when we read words like *God appeared* or *God spoke.* On the basis of the above I'm going to treat Zechariah's eight night vision dreams as dreams. When in doubt keep them in.

ZECHARIAH'S DREAM OF HORNS AND CRAFTSMEN.

A note on Zechariah's Eight Night Vision Dreams

Twenty years after Daniel interpreted the writing on King Belshazzar's wall, Zechariah recently returned to Israel had a series of eight night vision dreams during the night of February 15, 519 BC. The Book of Zechariah doesn't clearly say whether these revelations were dreams or night visions or both.

But at one point Zechariah does say, Then the angel who was speaking with me returned and woke me, as a man is awakened from his sleep. This means it's entirely possible everything up to this point has been a dream. As I've mentioned elsewhere, as in Job 33:15 and Isaiah 29:7, a dream can be described as a vision of the night. If this is the case here then Zechariah's dream in eight sections would be the longest recorded dream in the Bible.

The Dream Setting/Backstory

∽

In *Solomon's Warning Dream* God said,

> But if indeed you or your sons turn away from following Me and do not keep the commandments and statutes I have set before you, and if you go off to serve and worship other gods, then I will cut off Israel from the land that I have given them, and I will banish from My presence this temple I have sanctified for My Name. Then Israel will become an object of scorn and ridicule among all peoples.[1]

Neither Solomon nor Israel heeded God's warning so God kept His word by handing them over to their enemies. The Assyrians exiled Israel's northern kingdom in 722 BC and the Babylonians exiled the southern kingdom of Judah in 586 BC. This Babylonian exile ended when as symbolised in *Nebuchadnezzar's Large Tree Dream* the Persian Empire conquered the Babylonian Empire in 539 BC. Afterwards Cyrus the Great allowed the Jews to return to Jerusalem to rebuild their Temple.

In the first year they built an altar of burnt offerings and in the second year they laid the foundation of the temple but it would be another sixteen years before any further building took place because of opposition from their enemies.

God then sent the prophet Haggai who preached four sermons in four months to encourage the Jews to begin rebuilding. Two months later Zechariah began his prophetic ministry of spiritual renewal and encouragement and in five years the Temple was completed.

God gave Zechariah eight successive night vision dreams, (or perhaps just one long dream) to inspire the beleaguered returnees.

These eight revelations are like a thumbnail sketch of God's plans and purposes for Israel and all nations.

They are all very symbolic and some have more than one interpretation. They all follow a similar pattern. Introductory words are followed by a description of things seen. Then Zechariah asks the angel for the meaning of his vision followed by the angel's explanation. This is the second night vision dream.

The Dream Scripture
Zechariah 1:18-21

~

Then I looked up and saw four horns. So I asked the angel who was speaking with me, "What are these?"

And he told me, "These are the horns that scattered Judah, Israel, and Jerusalem."

Then the LORD showed me four craftsmen.

"What are these coming to do?" I asked.

And He replied, "These are the horns that scattered Judah so that no one could raise his head; but the craftsmen have come to terrify them and throw down these horns of the nations that lifted up their horns against the land of Judah to scatter it."

The Problem

~

God has punished unfaithful Israel as promised for seventy years. Now His Chosen People are wounded and broken, in need of His mercy and comfort and inspiration in order to rebuild the Temple.

The Dreamer's Metron

Zechariah was both a prophet and a priest born into a Levite family in Babylon. He returned to Jerusalem with the first batch of 50,000 Jews after their seventy-year exile.

He functioned at the same time as the prophet Haggai, the governor Zerubbabel and Joshua the high priest. While Haggai's preaching focused on Israel's sin and selfishness Zechariah's prophecy encouraged the harassed Israelites to rebuild the temple.

His metron was national and international. He prophetically saw the Messiah in both His first and His second comings. Zechariah has the largest number of messianic passages amongst all the Minor Prophets. The New Testament contains over forty of his references.

The Book of Revelation is greatly influenced by his imagery. Zechariah's main purpose was to assure Judah that although God disciplined them for seventy years in Babylon He is still their Covenant Keeping God who will bless them as He promised their fathers.

The Message

The simple message is God will judge the nations that afflict Israel. He will use other nations to do this.

God's Purpose

God's purpose is to demonstrate His total dominion over all powers and principalities attacking Israel and their seedline. He is well able to cover his Chosen Peoples.

Satan's Purpose

∽

Satan's purpose were to completely destroy and scatter Israel and prevent the coming of The Messiah who would crush his head.

Dreamer's Eyes Enlightened

∽

Zechariah understands the gist of the message and is able to write it down.

Dreamer's Response and Application

∽

During the dream Zechariah asks the angel for clarification about the horns and the craftsmen and writes down his dream and the angel's answer. I'm sure Zechariah and Israel clearly understood who these nations were.

Know God Better

God is able and willing to destroy all earthly and spiritual powers and principalities that come against His Covenant People.

The Dream Process

All of Zechariah's eight dreams follow a similar pattern. Introductory words are followed by a description of things seen. Then Zechariah asks the angel for the meaning of his dream followed by the angel's explanation.

This dream of national and global importance contains symbolism interpreted by an angel. This revelation gives insight and hope to Zechariah and his people.

The Holy Spirit sent the dream and God the Father, Jesus and an angel are present in this dream. Zechariah talked with the angel and the angel explained things as they occurred instead of afterwards as is common in such dreams.

The interpreting angel explains the horns are national powers and nations that scattered Israel and the craftsmen are nations and powers God uses to terrify and deal with the nations who attacked the people of Judah.

The Usual Suspects

God gives this vision through his Holy Spirit and encourages His Covenant People with the promise of help. Satan is shown in the cruel nations that scattered Israel. Jesus as the Angel of the Lord is still standing in the myrtle trees.

Takeaways

∽

Symbols can carry different layers and levels of meaning within a dream or vision. We see this principle at work in many of the prophets. Usually it only operates on a couple of levels like when Jacob wrestled with both God and man.

Similarly in *The Midianite's Dream for Gideon* on one level the barley bread represents Gideon who will destroy the Midianite army while on another level it represents Jesus the Bread of Life who will destroy the works of Satan.

In Isaiah we often also see three layers of meaning and fulfilment in operation. Isaiah's symbols on one level can refer to the return of Israel from captivity, on another level they can foresee the arrival of the Messiah and His kingdom and on a third level they can speak of Jesus' Second Coming and the restoration of all things.

Similarly we see this principle at work in Zechariah's night vision dreams. Zechariah was shown four horns and four craftsmen. We're not told exactly what the horns are and what the craftsmen are but in the Bible, horns usually represent gentile kings and their empires.

We see this in Daniel and Revelation. So these horns represent earthly empires God used to scatter Judah, Israel, and Jerusalem. Many Bible scholars associate these four horns with the four empires of Babylon, Media-Persia, Greece and Rome evident in *Nebuchadnezzar's Large Tree Dream*.

The craftsmen image is more of a challenge. Some Bible scholars suggest the four craftsmen are the four empires of *Nebuchadnezzar's Large Statue Dream* that followed one another and threw down the previous empire. In this interpretation Media-Persia terrified and threw down Babylon, Greece terrified and threw down Media-Persia and Rome terrified and threw down Greece etc.

But there's something in this interpretation that doesn't entirely ring true. In context craftsmen are creators and builders and not destroying armies. Craftsmen are also special to God who Himself is a creator.

In Exodus God filled Bezaleel, Caleb's grandson, the chief craftsman of the Tabernacle with the Holy Spirit in order to accomplish His work.[2]

Proverbs also symbolically speaks of Jesus as a craftsman delighting in His work with God at creation.

In *Nebuchadnezzar's Large Stature Dream* we see a stone uncut by human hands destroying earthly empires. We know this stone symbolically, represents Jesus's kingdom of love.

Jesus didn't fight with natural weapons. He told Pilate,

> My kingdom is not of this world. If it were, my
>> servants would fight to prevent my arrest by the
>> Jewish leaders. But now my kingdom is from
>> another place.[3]

Jesus' power of Love can destroys all men's power. St Paul said believers have powerful spiritual weapons that can destroy powerful kings and rulers. He said,

> The weapons we fight with are not the weapons of the
>> world. On the contrary, they have divine power to
>> demolish strongholds.[4]

What is being referred to here is God's Kingdom of love destroying Satan's heavenly powers and principalities of hate and tearing them down and destroying their earthly kingdoms. Paul said.

> For in him all things were created: things in heaven and on earth, visible and invisible, whether thrones or powers or rulers or authorities; all things have been created through him and for him.[5]

Paul also said,

> Finally, be strong in the Lord and in His mighty power. Put on the full armour of God, so that you can make your stand against the devil's schemes. For our struggle is not against flesh and blood, but against the rulers, against the authorities, against the powers of this world's darkness, and against the spiritual forces of evil in the heavenly realms.[6]

The Talmud has a tradition that says, these four craftsmen are, The Messiah the son of David, The Messiah the son of Joseph, Elijah and the Righteous Priest.

Jesus who destroyed the work of the devil can be called a craftsman because he will rebuild the Temple.[7]

Elijah who also destroyed the works of the devil in his day also built the altar on Mount Carmel[8] and Melchizedek, the Righteous Priest who appeared after Abraham's victory over the four kings, probably built the earliest temple in Jerusalem.[9]

The point here is, the craftsmen were agents of destruction against God's enemies and agents of redemption for God's people.

Perhaps in context this image was meant to encourage the returning Jewish craftsmen who were to complete the building of the temple in Jerusalem. Nehemiah describes the dangerous situation facing these workers,

> Those who carried materials did their work with one hand and held a weapon in the other, and each of the builders wore his sword at his side as he worked.[10]

ZECHARIAH'S DREAM OF THE MEASURING LINE

A note on Zechariah's Eight Night Vision Dreams

Twenty years after Daniel interpreted the writing on King Belshazzar's wall, Zechariah recently returned to Israel had a series of eight night vision dreams during the night of February 15, 519 BC. The Book of Zechariah doesn't clearly say whether these revelations were dreams or night visions or both.

But at one point Zechariah does say, Then the angel who was speaking with me returned and woke me, as a man is awakened from his sleep. This means it's entirely possible everything up to this point has been a dream. As I've mentioned elsewhere, as in Job 33:15 and Isaiah 29:7, a dream can be described as a vision of the night. If this is the case here then Zechariah's dream in eight sections would be the longest recorded dream in the Bible.

The Dream Setting/Backstory

In *Solomon's Warning Dream* God said,

> But if indeed you or your sons turn away from following Me and do not keep the commandments and statutes I have set before you, and if you go off to serve and worship other gods, then I will cut off Israel from the land that I have given them, and I will banish from My presence this temple I have sanctified for My Name. Then Israel will become an object of scorn and ridicule among all peoples.[1]

Neither Solomon nor Israel heeded God's warning so God kept His word by handing them over to their enemies. The Assyrians exiled Israel's northern kingdom in 722 BC and the Babylonians exiled the southern kingdom of Judah in 586 BC. This Babylonian exile ended when as symbolised in *Nebuchadnezzar's Large Tree Dream* the Persian Empire conquered the Babylonian Empire in 539 BC. Afterwards Cyrus the Great allowed the Jews to return to Jerusalem to rebuild their Temple.

In the first year they built an altar of burnt offerings and in the second year they laid the foundation of the temple but it would be another sixteen years before any further building took place because of opposition from their enemies.

God then sent the prophet Haggai who preached four sermons in four months to encourage the Jews to begin rebuilding. Two months later Zechariah began his prophetic ministry of spiritual renewal and encouragement and in five years the Temple was completed.

God gave Zechariah eight successive night vision dreams, (or perhaps just one long dream) to inspire the beleaguered returnees.

These eight revelations are like a thumbnail sketch of God's plans and purposes for Israel and all nations.

They are all very symbolic and some have more than one interpretation. They all follow a similar pattern. Introductory words are followed by a description of things seen. Then Zechariah asks the angel for the meaning of his vision followed by the angel's explanation. This is the third night vision dream.

The Dream Scripture
Zechariah 2:1-13

~

Then I lifted up my eyes and saw a man with a measuring line in his hand.

"Where are you going?" I asked.

"To measure Jerusalem," he replied, "and to determine its width and length."

Then the angel who was speaking with me went out, and another angel came out to meet him and said to him, "Run and tell that young man: 'Jerusalem will be a city without walls because of the multitude of men and livestock within it. For I will be a wall of fire around it, declares the LORD, and I will be the glory within it.'"

"Get up! Get up! Flee from the land of the north," declares the LORD, "for I have scattered you like the four winds of heaven," declares the LORD. "Get up, O Zion! Escape, you who dwell with the Daughter of Babylon."

For this is what the LORD of Hosts says: "After His glory has sent me against the nations that have plundered you—for whoever touches you touches the apple of His eye— I will surely wave My hand over them, so that they will become plunder for their own servants. Then you will know that the LORD of Hosts has sent Me."

"Shout for joy and be glad, O daughter of Zion, for I am coming to dwell among you," declares the LORD. "On that day many nations will join themselves to the LORD, and they will become My people. I will dwell among you, and you will know that the LORD of Hosts has sent Me to you. And the LORD will take possession of Judah as His portion in the Holy Land, and He will once again choose Jerusalem. Be silent before the LORD, all people, for He has roused Himself from His holy dwelling."

The Problem

~

God has punished unfaithful Israel as promised for seventy years. Now His Chosen People are wounded and broken, in need of His mercy and comfort and inspiration to rebuild the Temple.

The Dreamer's Metron

~

Zechariah was both a prophet and a priest born into a Levite family in Babylon. He returned to Jerusalem with the first batch of 50,000 Jews after their seventy-year exile.

He functioned at the same time as the prophet Haggai, the governor Zerubbabel and Joshua the high priest. While Haggai's preaching focused on Israel's sin and selfishness Zechariah's prophecy encouraged the harassed Israelites to rebuild the temple.

His metron was national and international. He prophetically saw the Messiah in both His first and His second comings. Zechariah has the largest number of messianic passages amongst all the Minor Prophets. The New Testament contains over forty of his references.

The Book of Revelation is greatly influenced by his imagery. Zechariah's main purpose was to assure Judah that although God disciplined them for seventy years in Babylon He is still their Covenant Keeping God who will bless them as He promised their fathers.

The Message

This is a message about God returning and blessing, increasing, prospering and protecting his Covenant People. God reminds Zechariah it was He who both scattered and gathered Israel from Babylon.

Now He has roused Himself from His holy dwelling to deal with Judah's enemies. He is also coming to dwell amongst His people and be a wall of fire around them.

He speaks wonderful promises. He pledges, He will be the glory within them and they will be protected like the apple of his eye.

He then gives a Messianic prophecy about a time when many nations will join themselves to Him, and become His people. Then He will take possession of Judah as His portion in the Holy Land, and He will once again choose Jerusalem.

God's Purpose

God loves and encourages His Covenant People. This dream brims over with hope. God is in our midst. Daddy's home and all is okay! He's not angry with us anymore. He remembers His covenant. We are going to increase and prosper. He promises one day the Messiah will rule from Jerusalem.

God also refers to the Gospel mystery of the Gentiles nations coming to know Him.[2] He says, On that day many nations will join themselves to the LORD, and they will become My people.

This is the same Gospel Jesus preached and promised to Abraham.[3]

Satan's Purpose

∽

Satan's hindering purposes pale into insignificance in the light of God's Covenant Promises in this dream. Satan's part becomes irrelevant after being used by God to discipline His people.

Dreamer's Eyes Enlightened

∽

Zechariah is shown the glorious hope of the Covenant Promises in action.

Dreamer's Response and Application

∽

Zechariah writes it all down for the encouragement of the returnees and future generations of Jews and Gentiles.

Know God Better

Once again we see God as a Covenant Keeper and a God of plans and purpose.

The Dream Process

Zechariah dialogues with the man with the measuring line and asks what he is doing. Symbolically the man was measuring Jerusalem to see if it would be big enough for the coming multitudes.

This was encouraging because at the time there were very few people in the city. God was promising He'd bring so many people from the nations that the crowds would overflow the city. But even though they'd overflow the present walls, Zechariah was told not to worry for God Himself would be a wall of fire around it.

These prophecies and declarations functioned on a couple of levels.

On one hand they referred to God blessing the building work under Ezra and Nehemiah. On the other hand they referred to a time thousands of years later when the heavenly Jerusalem would be established under Jesus Christ The Messiah.

I believe the man with the measuring line was an angel. I also believe the 'other angel' who spoke with the 'measuring line' angel was Jesus as the Angel of the Lord.

In this scenario, Jesus told the 'measuring line' angel what to declare to Zechariah. Then Zechariah could pass these encouragements onto God's beleaguered people. It is entirely appropriate that Jesus should be the One speaking the words of God.

The Usual Suspects

∽

God speaks wonderful promises to His people through Jesus as the Angel of the Lord. Satan is being dealt with in the punishment and disempowerment of the nations.

Takeaways

∽

God encourages the exiles to return to Him and promises great blessings to them and their descendants. Sadly most of the exiles were so comfortable in Babylon they had no intention of becoming involved in God's work.

Again, God's call to leave Babylon is both literal and figurative.[4]

ZECHARIAH'S DREAM OF JOSHUA

A note on Zechariah's Eight Night Vision Dreams

Twenty years after Daniel interpreted the writing on King Belshazzar's wall, Zechariah recently returned to Israel had a series of eight night vision dreams during the night of February 15, 519 BC. The Book of Zechariah doesn't clearly say whether these revelations were dreams or night visions or both.

But at one point Zechariah does say, Then the angel who was speaking with me returned and woke me, as a man is awakened from his sleep. This means it's entirely possible everything up to this point has been a dream. As I've mentioned elsewhere, as in Job 33:15 and Isaiah 29:7, a dream can be described as a vision of the night. If this is the case here then Zechariah's dream in eight sections would be the longest recorded dream in the Bible.

The Dream Setting/Backstory

∼

In *Solomon's Warning Dream* God said,

> But if indeed you or your sons turn away from following Me and do not keep the commandments and statutes I have set before you, and if you go off to serve and worship other gods, then I will cut off Israel from the land that I have given them, and I will banish from My presence this temple I have sanctified for My Name. Then Israel will become an object of scorn and ridicule among all peoples.[1]

Neither Solomon nor Israel heeded God's warning so God kept His word by handing them over to their enemies. The Assyrians exiled Israel's northern kingdom in 722 BC and the Babylonians exiled the southern kingdom of Judah in 586 BC. This Babylonian exile ended when as symbolised in *Nebuchadnezzar's Large Tree Dream* the Persian Empire conquered the Babylonian Empire in 539 BC. Afterwards Cyrus the Great allowed the Jews to return to Jerusalem to rebuild their Temple.

In the first year they built an altar of burnt offerings and in the second year they laid the foundation of the temple but it would be another sixteen years before any further building took place because of opposition from their enemies.

God then sent the prophet Haggai who preached four sermons in four months to encourage the Jews to begin rebuilding. Two months later Zechariah began his prophetic ministry of spiritual renewal and encouragement and in five years the Temple was completed.

God gave Zechariah eight successive night vision dreams, (or perhaps just one long dream) to inspire the beleaguered returnees.

These eight revelations are like a thumbnail sketch of God's plans and purposes for Israel and all nations.

They are all very symbolic and some have more than one interpretation. They all follow a similar pattern. Introductory words are followed by a description of things seen. Then Zechariah asks the angel for the meaning of his vision followed by the angel's explanation. This is the fourth night vision dream.

The Dream Scripture
Zechariah 3:1-10

∼

Then the angel showed me Joshua the high priest standing before the Angel of the LORD, with Satan standing at his right hand to accuse him.

And the LORD said to Satan: "The LORD rebukes you, Satan! Indeed, the LORD, who has chosen Jerusalem, rebukes you! Is not this man a firebrand snatched from the fire?"

Now Joshua was dressed in filthy garments as he stood before the Angel. So the Angel of the LORD said to those standing before Him, "Take off his filthy clothes!"

Then He said to Joshua, "See, I have removed your iniquity, and I will clothe you with splendid robes."

Then I said, "Let them put a clean turban on his head." So a clean turban was placed on his head, and they clothed him, as the Angel of the LORD stood by.

Then the Angel of the LORD gave this charge to Joshua: "This is what the LORD of Hosts says: 'If you walk in My ways and keep My instructions, then you will both govern My house and have charge of My courts; and I will give you a place among these standing here.'

'Hear now, O high priest Joshua, you and your companions seated before you, who are indeed a sign. For behold, I am going to bring My servant, the Branch. See the stone I have set before Joshua;

on that one stone are seven eyes. Behold, I will engrave on it an inscription,' declares the LORD of Hosts, 'and I will remove the iniquity of this land in a single day. On that day,' declares the LORD of Hosts, 'each of you will invite his neighbour to sit under his vine and under his fig tree.'"

The Problem

God is returning and flooding the city with His holy presence but this dream flags up an enormous problem: the people who are to live in God's presence have become filthy with sin and guilt. They are unfit to minister before God. They need to be cleansed and restored.

The Dreamer's Metron

Zechariah was both a prophet and a priest born into a Levite family in Babylon. He returned to Jerusalem with the first batch of 50,000 Jews after their seventy-year exile.

He functioned at the same time as the prophet Haggai, the governor Zerubbabel and Joshua the high priest. While Haggai's preaching focused on Israel's sin and selfishness Zechariah's prophecy encouraged the harassed Israelites to rebuild the temple.

His metron was national and international. He prophetically saw the Messiah in both His first and His second comings. Zechariah has the largest number of messianic passages amongst all the Minor Prophets. The New Testament contains over forty of his references.

The Book of Revelation is greatly influenced by his imagery.

Zechariah's main purpose was to assure Judah that although God disciplined them for seventy years in Babylon He is still their Covenant Keeping God who will bless them as He promised their fathers.

The Message

∼

It is God's Sovereign choice that Israel should live a holy life with Him in Jerusalem. And even though Joshua and Israel are presently defiled, God is able to purify and restore them. God says if Joshua is obedient he will rule in the restored Temple and have charge of His heavenly courts and will be given a place in Glory.

God also says Israel's restoration is a sign of His future Messianic Kingdom.

Here we see Jesus' redeeming work in action. He silences the accusations of Satan and He purifies and restores His servant to his proper place. He also uses his servant as a prophetic sign of Christ's redemptive work on Calvary.

God's Purpose

∼

God's purpose is to encourage and enable his Chosen People to live a holy life with him in Jerusalem and for them to be a sign of the coming Messianic Kingdom.

Satan's Purpose

Satan in his role as the accuser of the brethren was resisting Joshua from functioning in his metron as God's High Priest. This was keeping the whole nation from having an access to God.

Dreamer's Eyes Enlightened

Zechariah realises the incredible love and power of God. He understands it is Jesus the Messiah's job to cleanse and restore His servants. He also understands there is a greater spiritual reality in heaven represented by the High Priest, Priesthood, and Temple. It's there the Messiah will do His best work.

Dreamer's Response and Application

After Jesus removed Joshua's iniquity and said He would clothe Joshua with splendid robes Zechariah jumps into the middle of the action and proclaimed, Let them put a clean turban on his head. Here Joshua was functioning together with Jesus in the restoration of Israel. Zechariah writes down and shares this dream with the returnees.

Know God Better

God displays His sovereignty in this dream. The election of these particular people to dwell with Him in Jerusalem is part of His plans and purpose. Jesus as the Angel of the Lord says, The LORD rebuke you, O Satan! The LORD who has chosen Jerusalem rebuke you!

It is God who has chosen Israel and Satan can't stop it. Joshua and his people are in a state of filthiness; the language used refers to human excrement. But God's electing grace and God's plans and purpose are able to transform them into a Holy People fit for God's purpose.

The Dream Process

This is a highly symbolic dream requiring various levels of interpretation using *The Symbol Replacement Method*.

The brand plucked from the fire symbolises escape from God's fiery judgement. The filthy garments represent sin. Isaiah said in God's eyes all our good works are like filthy garments.[2]

The clean garments symbolise the removal of sin and being equipped for God's service. Isaiah mentioned garments of salvation.[3]

The clean turban represents the High Priest's restoration to God's service. The high priest's headgear had a gold plate with *Holiness to the Lord* written on it.

My servant the Branch refers to Jesus the Messiah, the one who accomplishes God's work. In the ancient world some cultures claimed their heroes were branches of their gods. This meant their heroes were carrying out the plans and purposes of their gods. Jesus used the same imagery for His disciples when He said, I am the vine, you are the branches.[4]

The engraved stone with seven eyes also represents Jesus. The

Second Temple corner stone had just been laid but this stone refers to the chief corner stone Jesus the Messiah.

Elsewhere the Messiah is referred to as a stone. In Daniel He is the stone, cut out of the mountain not by human hands, that destroys all earthly empires.[5]

The seven eyes symbolises Jesus as all seeing. This is confirmed in Revelation,

> And I saw between the throne (with the four living creatures) and the elders a Lamb standing, as if slain, having seven horns and seven eyes, which are the seven Spirits of God, sent out into all the earth.[6]

The engraved inscription on the living stone probably represents Jesus Christ as the Word. Early Christians viewed the engravings as the wounds of Jesus. The single day prophetically refers to Christ's death on The Cross, the day that changed the world. Hebrews says,

> Every priest stands daily ministering and offering time after time the same sacrifices, which can never take away sins; but He, having offered one sacrifice for sins for all time, sat down at the right hand of God, waiting from that time onward until His enemies be made a footstool for His feet. For by one offering He has perfected for all time those who are sanctified.[7]

The Usual Suspects

God was the One initiating this encounter. Satan is there in his role as accuser of the brethren. Jesus stands by in His powerful role as Redeemer and equipper of the saints. He is also shown as the future Messiah.

Takeaways

In this dream we get another tantalising mention of the Divine Council from Psalm 82. Joshua is promised a position of influence in this Council when he is told,

> If you walk in My ways and keep My instructions, then you will both govern My house and have charge of My courts; and I will give you a place among these standing here.[8]

One of the great insights from Zechariah's fourth dream is there is another kingdom coming with a better foundation and a greater scope then the one he was engaged in. Paul refers to this,

> So then you are no longer strangers and aliens, but you are fellow citizens with the saints, and are of God's household, having been built on the foundation of the apostles and prophets, Christ Jesus Himself being the corner stone, in whom the whole building, being fitted together, is growing into a holy temple in the Lord, in whom you also are being built together into a dwelling of God in the Spirit.[9]

ZECHARIAH'S DREAM OF LAMPSTAND AND TREES

A note on Zechariah's Eight Night Vision Dreams

Twenty years after Daniel interpreted the writing on King Belshazzar's wall, Zechariah recently returned to Israel had a series of eight night vision dreams during the night of February 15, 519 BC. The Book of Zechariah doesn't clearly say whether these revelations were dreams or night visions or both.

But at one point Zechariah does say, Then the angel who was speaking with me returned and woke me, as a man is awakened from his sleep. This means it's entirely possible everything up to this point has been a dream. As I've mentioned elsewhere, as in Job 33:15 and Isaiah 29:7, a dream can be described as a vision of the night. If this is the case here then Zechariah's dream in eight sections would be the longest recorded dream in the Bible.

The Dream Setting/Backstory

In *Solomon's Warning Dream* God said,

> But if indeed you or your sons turn away from following Me and do not keep the commandments and statutes I have set before you, and if you go off to serve and worship other gods, then I will cut off Israel from the land that I have given them, and I will banish from My presence this temple I have sanctified for My Name. Then Israel will become an object of scorn and ridicule among all peoples.[1]

Neither Solomon nor Israel heeded God's warning so God kept His word by handing them over to their enemies. The Assyrians exiled Israel's northern kingdom in 722 BC and the Babylonians exiled the southern kingdom of Judah in 586 BC. This Babylonian exile ended when as symbolised in *Nebuchadnezzar's Large Tree Dream* the Persian Empire conquered the Babylonian Empire in 539 BC. Afterwards Cyrus the Great allowed the Jews to return to Jerusalem to rebuild their Temple.

In the first year they built an altar of burnt offerings and in the second year they laid the foundation of the temple but it would be another sixteen years before any further building took place because of opposition from their enemies.

God then sent the prophet Haggai who preached four sermons in four months to encourage the Jews to begin rebuilding. Two months later Zechariah began his prophetic ministry of spiritual renewal and encouragement and in five years the Temple was completed.

God gave Zechariah eight successive night vision dreams, (or perhaps just one long dream) to inspire the beleaguered returnees.

These eight revelations are like a thumbnail sketch of God's plans and purposes for Israel and all nations.

They are all very symbolic and some have more than one interpretation. They all follow a similar pattern. Introductory words are followed by a description of things seen. Then Zechariah asks the angel for the meaning of his vision followed by the angel's explanation. This is the fifth night vision dream.

The Dream Scripture
Zechariah 4:1-14

∼

Then the angel who was speaking with me returned and woke me, as a man is awakened from his sleep.

"What do you see?" he asked.

"I see a solid gold lampstand," I replied, "with a bowl at the top and seven lamps on it, with seven spouts to each of the lamps. There are also two olive trees beside it, one on the right of the bowl and the other on its left."

"What are these, my lord?" I asked the angel who was speaking with me.

"Do you not know what they are?" replied the angel.

"No, my lord," I answered.

So he said to me, "This is the word of the LORD to Zerubbabel: Not by might nor by power, but by My Spirit, says the LORD of Hosts. What are you, O great mountain? Before Zerubbabel you will become a plain. Then he will bring forth the capstone accompanied by shouts of 'Grace, grace to it!'"

Then the word of the LORD came to me: "The hands of Zerubbabel have laid the foundation of this house, and his hands will complete it. Then you will know that the LORD of Hosts has sent me to you. For who has despised the day of small things? But these seven eyes of the LORD, which scan the whole earth, will rejoice when they see the plumb line in Zerubbabel's hand."

Then I asked the angel, "What are the two olive trees on the right and left of the lampstand?" And I questioned him further, "What are the two olive branches beside the two gold pipes from which the golden oil pours?"

"Do you not know what these are?" he inquired.

"No, my lord," I replied.

So he said, "These are the two anointed ones who are standing beside the Lord of all the earth."

The Problem

～

The people needed God's help and God's perspective. Jerusalem was in ruins. They had few resources and their enemies continually harassed them. Their task was immense and the temple they were to build would never be as magnificent as Solomon's Temple. It seemed like the *Glory Days* had gone forever.

The Dreamer's Metron

～

Zechariah was both a prophet and a priest born into a Levite family in Babylon. He returned to Jerusalem with the first batch of 50,000 Jews after their seventy-year exile.

He functioned at the same time as the prophet Haggai, the governor Zerubbabel and Joshua the high priest. While Haggai's preaching focused on Israel's sin and selfishness Zechariah's prophecy encouraged the harassed Israelites to rebuild the temple.

His metron was national and international. He prophetically saw the Messiah in both His first and His second comings. Zechariah has the largest number of messianic passages amongst all the Minor Prophets. The New Testament contains over forty of his references.

The Book of Revelation is greatly influenced by his imagery. Zechariah's main purpose was to assure Judah that although God disciplined them for seventy years in Babylon He is still their Covenant Keeping God who will bless them as He promised their fathers.

The Message

God's message was, He would accomplish His work through His Holy Spirit and His anointed ones and not through the strength and resources of men.

God's Purpose

God's purpose was to give them perspective into His kingdom realities. He was more than able to accomplish His own plans and purpose in His own way.

Satan's Purpose

Satan's purpose was to discourage them, rob their vision and make them believe it all depended on them.

Dreamer's Eyes Enlightened

Zechariah realised it was all a work of God. Not by might nor by power. He understood God was saying human sufficiency can never build God's Kingdom. Our hope and confidence must always rest on God's Holy Spirit being well able to accomplish God's purpose.

Dreamer's Response and Application

Zechariah spoke his revelation to the people and wrote it down.

Know God Better

He is again seen as a Covenant Keeping God well able to bring about His own plans and purpose . Not by might nor by power, but by My Spirit, perfectly describes all the plans and purpose of God. His Eternal purpose through His son Jesus Christ does not depend on man's capabilities but on God's Holy Spirit.

The Dream Process

∽

This is another highly symbolic dream requiring various levels of interpretation. It has an application to Zechariah's time and another universal spiritual application. Again we see *The Symbol Replacement Method in operation.*

There are two main images. The first one is of a solid gold lampstand, with a bowl at the top and seven lamps on it, with seven spouts to each of the lamps.

The second image is of two olive trees, one on either side of the lampstand.

There had been ten similar lampstands in Solomon's Temple but only one was in the tabernacle, which stood just outside the veil, opposite the table for the bread of the Presence. Its purpose was to light up the entrance way to the Holy of Holies, where God met with His people. But still the veil remained in place.

God had told the people to bring pure olive oil so His priests could keep the light burning constantly. So on a natural level the image of a lampstand and the olive oil represented the work and responsibilities God had given to His people.

Zechariah's dream on the other hand also speaks of a supernatural lampstand with a supernatural provision of oil. His lampstand has a bowl on top like a large reservoir for the olive oil. It also has forty-nine lights, seven lamps on it, with seven lips on each of the lamps. Each of these lips contained a flame.

Unlike the Temple lampstand Zechariah's lampstand was a superlight with an endless provision of oil. That's why God says, Not by might nor by power, but by My Spirit, says the LORD of Hosts.

Through this dream image God is showing He is super capable of completing the building work. This dream lampstand also symbolises God's people and the abundant oil constantly filling it represents the abundance of God's Spirit filling His people.

The interpreting angel said the two olive branches are the two anointed ones God will use for the task. On one level, in context, these are Joshua and Zerubbabel who God used to bless His people with His Holy Spirit.

The great mountain that will become a plain symbolised the cessation of all opposition to the rebuilding programme under Darius. In Scripture mountains often represent opposition by spiritual powers.

The capstone that will be positioned accompanied by shouts of 'Grace, grace to it' symbolises the final work will be attributed to God and not man.

God also warns the people not to despise the day of small beginnings for everything God initiates for His Kingdom's sake has a plan and purpose.

After sixteen years the poor returned exiles had little to show for their work but God wanted to encourage them that He would use their sacrificial obedience to bless all nations.

Zechariah is basically saying that whatever God's Holy Spirit is doing is worthy of our full support and focus

The seven eyes of the Lord, which scan the whole earth symbolise Jesus the Messiah as mentioned in the previous dream.

The Usual Suspects

God is there speaking and prophesying. Jesus is there joyfully watching Zerubbabel. The Holy Spirit is evident in the abundant oil and Satan who had discouraged the people was being overcome with prophecy.

Takeaways

~

This dream is great example of prophetic words creating faith in the listeners and destroying the work of Satan at the same time.

ZECHARIAH'S DREAM OF THE FLYING SCROLL

A note on Zechariah's Eight Night Vision Dreams

Twenty years after Daniel interpreted the writing on King Belshazzar's wall, Zechariah recently returned to Israel had a series of eight night vision dreams during the night of February 15, 519 BC. The Book of Zechariah doesn't clearly say whether these revelations were dreams or night visions or both.

But at one point Zechariah does say, Then the angel who was speaking with me returned and woke me, as a man is awakened from his sleep. This means it's entirely possible everything up to this point has been a dream. As I've mentioned elsewhere, as in Job 33:15 and Isaiah 29:7, a dream can be described as a vision of the night. If this is the case here then Zechariah's dream in eight sections would be the longest recorded dream in the Bible.

The Dream Setting/Backstory

In *Solomon's Warning Dream* God said,

> But if indeed you or your sons turn away from following Me and do not keep the commandments and statutes I have set before you, and if you go off to serve and worship other gods, then I will cut off Israel from the land that I have given them, and I will banish from My presence this temple I have sanctified for My Name. Then Israel will become an object of scorn and ridicule among all peoples.[1]

Neither Solomon nor Israel heeded God's warning so God kept His word by handing them over to their enemies. The Assyrians exiled Israel's northern kingdom in 722 BC and the Babylonians exiled the southern kingdom of Judah in 586 BC. This Babylonian exile ended when as symbolised in *Nebuchadnezzar's Large Tree Dream* the Persian Empire conquered the Babylonian Empire in 539 BC. Afterwards Cyrus the Great allowed the Jews to return to Jerusalem to rebuild their Temple.

In the first year they built an altar of burnt offerings and in the second year they laid the foundation of the temple but it would be another sixteen years before any further building took place because of opposition from their enemies.

God then sent the prophet Haggai who preached four sermons in four months to encourage the Jews to begin rebuilding. Two months later Zechariah began his prophetic ministry of spiritual renewal and encouragement and in five years the Temple was completed.

God gave Zechariah eight successive night vision dreams, (or perhaps just one long dream) to inspire the beleaguered returnees.

These eight revelations are like a thumbnail sketch of God's plans and purpose for Israel and all nations.

They are all very symbolic and some have more than one interpretation. They all follow a similar pattern. Introductory words are followed by a description of things seen. Then Zechariah asks the angel for the meaning of his vision followed by the angel's explanation. This is the sixth night vision dream.

The Dream Scripture
Zechariah 5:1-4

∽

Again I lifted up my eyes and saw before me a flying scroll.

"What do you see?" asked the angel.

"I see a flying scroll," I replied, "twenty cubits long and ten cubits wide."

Then he told me, "This is the curse that is going out over the face of all the land, for according to one side of the scroll, every thief will be removed; and according to the other side, everyone who swears falsely will be removed. I will send it out, declares the LORD of Hosts, and it will enter the house of the thief and the house of him who swears falsely by My name. It will remain inside his house and destroy it, down to its timbers and its stones."

The Problem

∽

When Holy God dwells amongst His people sin has to leave. The Scripture says, Be holy because I, the LORD your God, am holy.[2]

The Dreamer's Metron

Zechariah was both a prophet and a priest born into a Levite family in Babylon. He returned to Jerusalem with the first batch of 50,000 Jews after their seventy-year exile.

He functioned at the same time as the prophet Haggai, the governor Zerubbabel and Joshua the high priest. While Haggai's preaching focused on Israel's sin and selfishness Zechariah's prophecy encouraged the harassed Israelites to rebuild the temple.

His metron was national and international. He prophetically saw the Messiah in both His first and His second comings. Zechariah has the largest number of messianic passages amongst all the Minor Prophets. The New Testament contains over forty of his references.

The Book of Revelation is greatly influenced by his imagery. Zechariah's main purpose was to assure Judah that although God disciplined them for seventy years in Babylon He is still their Covenant Keeping God who will bless them as He promised their fathers.

The Message

The Law of Moses is still relevant for God's Covenant People so a scroll of cursing has been released from God's presence for all lawbreakers because God's covenant-law contains curses when not obeyed.

God's Purpose

God's purpose is for his people to be a holy people. Before they entered the Promised Land Moses reminded them,

> For you are a people holy to the Lord your God. The Lord your God has chosen you out of all the peoples on the face of the earth to be his people, his treasured possession.[3]

Satan's Purpose

Satan worked hard to get God's people to sin so God would have to judge them.

Dreamer's Eyes Enlightened

Zechariah understands a curse has been sent out from the presence of God.

Dreamer's Response and Application

Zechariah spoke his revelation to the people and wrote it down.

Know God Better

God is holy and God is love. Zechariah's messages until this point have been about God's presence and His merciful blessings. Now we're told God and sin can't coexist.

Jesus would later say the whole Law could be summed up in two areas. We were to love God with all our heart, soul, mind, and strength, and to love our neighbour as ourselves.[4]

The transgressions mentioned by the scroll concern these two offences and symbolise the whole law. The people were sinning against God by swearing falsely in His name and sinning against their neighbour by stealing. Holy God in His love had to deal with this.

The Dream Process

This simple symbolic dream is clearly interpreted by the angel. God has released a curse over all lawbreakers in Israel.

Zechariah's word of knowledge about the scroll's dimensions reminds us of Solomon's temple where God dwelt in the Holy Place above the ark of the covenant. Its vestibule was twenty cubits long and ten cubits deep.

This curse is coming from God on a scroll that applies the Law of Moses to their current situation. Like the Ten Commandments it has writing on both sides.

Three similar scrolls relating to Israel's breaking of the Law of Moses also appear in the Old Testament. Psalm 40 has one.[5] Later

Jeremiah writes a scroll with God's words of judgement against Israel[6] and Ezekiel also receives a vision of a judgement scroll.[7]

The image of God's curse entering homes reminds us of The Exodus and the need for lamb's blood on the doorposts.

This prophetic symbolism looks forward to the time when Jesus will become a curse on The Cross to deliver us from the curse of the law.[8]

The Usual Suspects

God has sent this scroll concerning His law. Satan's work is evident in the actions of the thieves and liars. Jesus is waiting in the wings to redeem us from the curse of The Law.

Takeaways

There is a scroll in heaven with writing on both sides still waiting for the Messiah to open it.[9] There will come a time when God's covenant curse will fall upon all who are not saved by the Lamb. Hebrews says we will all be judged after death.[10] Yet mercifully God's ultimate plan is to save us from our sins. Peter says,

> Concerning this salvation, the prophets, who spoke of the grace that was to come to you, searched intently and with the greatest care, trying to find out the time and circumstances to which the Spirit of Christ in them

was pointing when he predicted the sufferings of the Messiah and the glories that would follow. It was revealed to them that they were not serving themselves but you, when they spoke of the things that have now been told you by those who have preached the gospel to you by the Holy Spirit sent from heaven. Even angels long to look into these things.[11]

The interpreting angel with Zechariah has watched God's plan unfold over thousands of years but still doesn't fully understand it all but he does know about the terrifying state of the lawbreaker. He knows Deuteronomy warns,

All these curses shall come upon you and pursue you
and overtake you till you are destroyed.[12]

He also now knows the only possible hope for the lawbreaker to escape from the curse of God's law is through trusting in Jesus Christ who took the curse upon himself so we could receive the blessing,

For all who rely on works of the law are under a curse; for it is written, "Cursed be everyone who does not abide by all things written in the Book of the Law, and do them." Now it is evident that no one is justified before God by the law, for "The righteous shall live by faith." But the law is not of faith, rather "The one who does them shall live by them." Christ redeemed us from the curse of the law by becoming a curse for us—for it is written, "Cursed is everyone who is hanged on a tree"— so that in Christ Jesus the blessing of Abraham might come to the

Gentiles, so that we might receive the promised Spirit through faith.[13]

God will destroy all lawbreakers with His curse at the end of history. But the good news for everybody who receives Jesus as their Lord and Saviour is that they are freed from the effects of that curse. They can live in the presence of our Holy God forever.

ZECHARIAH'S DREAM OF THE WOMAN IN A BASKET

A note on Zechariah's Eight Night Vision Dreams

Twenty years after Daniel interpreted the writing on King Belshazzar's wall, Zechariah recently returned to Israel had a series of eight night vision dreams during the night of February 15, 519 BC. The Book of Zechariah doesn't clearly say whether these revelations were dreams or night visions or both.

But at one point Zechariah does say, Then the angel who was speaking with me returned and woke me, as a man is awakened from his sleep. This means it's entirely possible everything up to this point has been a dream. As I've mentioned elsewhere, as in Job 33:15 and Isaiah 29:7, a dream can be described as a vision of the night. If this is the case here then Zechariah's dream in eight sections would be the longest recorded dream in the Bible.

The Dream Setting/Backstory

In *Solomon's Warning Dream* God said,

> But if indeed you or your sons turn away from following Me and do not keep the commandments and statutes I have set before you, and if you go off to serve and worship other gods, then I will cut off Israel from the land that I have given them, and I will banish from My presence this temple I have sanctified for My Name. Then Israel will become an object of scorn and ridicule among all peoples.[1]

Neither Solomon nor Israel heeded God's warning so God kept His word by handing them over to their enemies. The Assyrians exiled Israel's northern kingdom in 722 BC and the Babylonians exiled the southern kingdom of Judah in 586 BC. This Babylonian exile ended when as symbolised in *Nebuchadnezzar's Large Tree Dream* the Persian Empire conquered the Babylonian Empire in 539 BC. Afterwards Cyrus the Great allowed the Jews to return to Jerusalem to rebuild their Temple.

In the first year they built an altar of burnt offerings and in the second year they laid the foundation of the temple but it would be another sixteen years before any further building took place because of opposition from their enemies.

God then sent the prophet Haggai who preached four sermons in four months to encourage the Jews to begin rebuilding. Two months later Zechariah began his prophetic ministry of spiritual renewal and encouragement and in five years the Temple was completed.

God gave Zechariah eight successive night vision dreams, (or perhaps just one long dream) to inspire the beleaguered returnees.

These eight revelations are like a thumbnail sketch of God's plans and purposes for Israel and all nations.

They are all very symbolic and some have more than one interpretation. They all follow a similar pattern. Introductory words are followed by a description of things seen. Then Zechariah asks the angel for the meaning of his vision followed by the angel's explanation. This is the seventh night vision dream.

The Dream Scripture
Zechariah 5:5-11

∽

Then the angel who was speaking with me came forward and told me, "Now lift up your eyes and see what is approaching."

"What is it?" I asked.

And he replied, "It is a measuring basket that is approaching." Then he continued, "This is their iniquity in all the land."

And behold, the cover of lead was raised, and there was a woman sitting inside the basket.

"This is Wickedness," he said. And he shoved her down into the basket, pushing down the lead cover over its opening.

Then I lifted up my eyes and saw two women approaching, with the wind in their wings. Their wings were like those of a stork, and they lifted up the basket between heaven and earth.

"Where are they taking the basket?" I asked the angel who was speaking with me.

"To build a house for it in the land of Shinar, " he told me. "And when it is ready, the basket will be set there on its pedestal."

The Problem

∽

God had returned to His people and there was no longer any place in Israel or in God's Chosen People for wickedness and iniquity to exist. Wickedness had to go.

The Dreamer's Metron

Zechariah was both a prophet and a priest born into a Levite family in Babylon. He returned to Jerusalem with the first batch of 50,000 Jews after their seventy-year exile.

He functioned at the same time as the prophet Haggai, the governor Zerubbabel and Joshua the high priest. While Haggai's preaching focused on Israel's sin and selfishness Zechariah's prophecy encouraged the harassed Israelites to rebuild the temple.

His metron was national and international. He prophetically saw the Messiah in both His first and His second comings. Zechariah has the largest number of messianic passages amongst all the Minor Prophets. The New Testament contains over forty of his references.

The Book of Revelation is greatly influenced by his imagery. Zechariah's main purpose was to assure Judah that although God disciplined them for seventy years in Babylon He is still their Covenant Keeping God who will bless them as He promised their fathers.

The Message

God was banishing wickedness from His people and His dwelling place.

God's Purpose

∾

God hates idolatry which He calls wickedness. His purpose was to remove all wicked idolatry from His land and His people. God has always warned His people about wickedness. When He rescued them out of Egypt and brought them into the Promised Land He cautioned them about the evil of the nations and their idols. Deuteronomy says,

> It is not because of your righteousness or your integrity that you are going in to take possession of their land; but on account of the wickedness of these nations, the Lord your God will drive them out before you, to accomplish what he swore to your fathers, to Abraham, Isaac and Jacob.[2]

God also told His people how He would treat idolatry,

> I will destroy your high places, cut down your incense altars and pile your dead bodies on the lifeless forms of your idols, and I will abhor you.[3]

Satan's Purpose

∾

Satan's purpose was to promote idolatry and wickedness in the Holy Land and in the hearts of God's holy people. Then God would have to judge them severely.

Dreamer's Eyes Enlightened

Zechariah understood God was putting wickedness in her place in Babylon.

Dreamer's Response and Application

Zechariah spoke his revelation to the people and wrote it down.

Know God Better

In the past God sent His people into exile in Babylon. Now He is keeping His people close to Him and sending their iniquity back to Babylon.

The Dream Process

This is a complex symbolic dream in which the dreamer dialogues with an angel. It requires interpretation. The three main images are the basket, the woman and the place to where she and the basket are going. It's suitable for the *The Symbol Replacement Method*.

The basket also called an ephah was a measuring device for flour or grain. Its two main purposes were for commerce and worship. People traded grain for their personal use and also for various sin offerings.

God had warned them not to steal from him in worship or from their neighbour in trade with an unjust ephah, which He called an abomination.[4]

So at one level the image of the woman in the basket symbolised false weights and measurements amongst God's people who weren't being descent and honest with one another.

Just before their exile God had sent Amos and Micah to rebuke Israel for using unjust ephahs and thereby serving money rather than God.[5]

So we're back to loving God and loving our neighbour. The basket represents the iniquity of the people in not keeping the Law of God and not dealing righteously and kindly with both God and man.

The woman called Wickedness puts a face on this iniquity which is really idolatry. Wickedness, who is small enough to fit into a basket is likened to an idol because in verse eleven she gets her own temple and base to sit on in Babylon.

Building a house for her means building a temple for her. The leaden lid on the basket represents judgement. Ezekiel said,

> As silver, copper, iron, lead and tin are gathered into a
> furnace to be melted with a fiery blast, so will I
> gather you in my anger and my wrath and put you
> inside the city and melt you.[6]

Time after time God had warned Israel about the wickedness of the nations and their idols since rescuing them from Egypt. They wouldn't listen to Him so God judged them by exile.

The two women with wings like those of a stork who take Wickedness in the basket to Babylon and build a base and a temple for her are enigmatic figures. They have wings like a stork, which is an unclean bird and they build an idol temple and base. Perhaps they are taking care of their own.

The land of Shinar was Nimrod's old stomping ground, part of which became Babel or Babylon. It symbolises man's organised rebellion against God.

Basically this dream is saying God is removing iniquity and wickedness out of His Holy Land and placing it in Babylon where it belongs. In the past God exiled the people who sinned. Now he is exiling their sin of dealing unfairly with one another.

The Usual Suspects

God is sending Wickedness away from His people. Satan is represented by the woman and by the idolatry of Babylon. Jesus is the One who will finally deal with all sin.

Takeaways

This dream offers a change of modus operandi and a new hope for Israel. In the past people were banished from God's presence because of sin. Adam and Eve were put out of the Garden and the rebellious idolatrous nations perished in The Flood. The giants and the nations and the idols of Canaan were expelled and when Israel refused to forsake her idols they were banished to Babylon.

Then came a time when God Himself, in an image that echoes the stork-winged ladies, departed from His city and Temple because of His people's wickedness and idolatry.

But now it's a brand new day. The exile is over, as promised by Jeremiah, and The Lord has returned to His city and Temple with a new vision.

Now instead of the people being banished, God's presence forces wickedness and idolatry to depart.

God got His people out of Babylon and now He's getting Babylon out of his people. This image prophetically points towards the finished work of Jesus on Calvary. Jesus said,

> Anyone who loves me will obey my teaching. My
> Father will love them, and we will come to them
> and make our home with them.[7]

When Jesus and His Father come and live in us we are sanctified day by day and all wickedness and idolatry have to leave us and flee away.

Also, a day will come when that woman in the basket in her temple in Babylon will also be finally dealt with. Revelation says.

> And all her wickedness will be cast into hell forever,
> and her smoke will rise forever and ever.[8]

ZECHARIAH'S DREAM OF THE FOUR CHARIOTS

A note on Zechariah's Eight Night Vision Dreams

Twenty years after Daniel interpreted the writing on King Belshazzar's wall, Zechariah recently returned to Israel had a series of eight night vision dreams during the night of February 15, 519 BC. The Book of Zechariah doesn't clearly say whether these revelations were dreams or night visions or both.

But at one point Zechariah does say, Then the angel who was speaking with me returned and woke me, as a man is awakened from his sleep. This means it's entirely possible everything up to this point has been a dream. As I've mentioned elsewhere, as in Job 33:15 and Isaiah 29:7, a dream can be described as a vision of the night. If this is the case here then Zechariah's dream in eight sections would be the longest recorded dream in the Bible.

The Dream Setting/Backstory

In *Solomon's Warning Dream* God said,

> But if indeed you or your sons turn away from following Me and do not keep the commandments and statutes I have set before you, and if you go off to serve and worship other gods, then I will cut off Israel from the land that I have given them, and I will banish from My presence this temple I have sanctified for My Name. Then Israel will become an object of scorn and ridicule among all peoples.[1]

Neither Solomon nor Israel heeded God's warning so God kept His word by handing them over to their enemies. The Assyrians exiled Israel's northern kingdom in 722 BC and the Babylonians exiled the southern kingdom of Judah in 586 BC. This Babylonian exile ended when as symbolised in *Nebuchadnezzar's Large Tree Dream* the Persian Empire conquered the Babylonian Empire in 539 BC. Afterwards Cyrus the Great allowed the Jews to return to Jerusalem to rebuild their Temple.

In the first year they built an altar of burnt offerings and in the second year they laid the foundation of the temple but it would be another sixteen years before any further building took place because of opposition from their enemies.

God then sent the prophet Haggai who preached four sermons in four months to encourage the Jews to begin rebuilding. Two months later Zechariah began his prophetic ministry of spiritual renewal and encouragement and in five years the Temple was completed.

God gave Zechariah eight successive night vision dreams, (or perhaps just one long dream) to inspire the beleaguered returnees.

These eight revelations are like a thumbnail sketch of God's plans and purposes for Israel and all nations.

They are all very symbolic and some have more than one interpretation. They all follow a similar pattern. Introductory words are followed by a description of things seen. Then Zechariah asks the angel for the meaning of his vision followed by the angel's explanation. This is the eighth and final night vision dream.

The Dream Scripture
Zechariah 6:1-8

∼

And again I lifted up my eyes and saw four chariots coming out from between two mountains—mountains of bronze. The first chariot had red horses, the second black horses, the third white horses, and the fourth dappled horses—all of them strong.

So I inquired of the angel who was speaking with me, "What are these, my lord?"

And the angel told me, "These are the four spirits of heaven, going out from their station before the Lord of all the earth. The one with the black horses is going toward the land of the north, the one with the white horses toward the west, and the one with the dappled horses toward the south."

As the strong horses went out, they were eager to go and patrol the earth; and the LORD said, "Go, patrol the earth." So they patrolled the earth.

Then the LORD summoned me and said, "Behold, those going to the land of the north have given rest to My Spirit in the land of the north."

The Problem

God's Spirit will not rest until He brings judgement upon the nations that have cruelly afflicted Israel.

The Dreamer's Metron

Zechariah was both a prophet and a priest born into a Levite family in Babylon. He returned to Jerusalem with the first batch of 50,000 Jews after their seventy-year exile.

He functioned at the same time as the prophet Haggai, the governor Zerubbabel and Joshua the high priest. While Haggai's preaching focused on Israel's sin and selfishness Zechariah's prophecy encouraged the harassed Israelites to rebuild the temple.

His metron was national and international. He prophetically saw the Messiah in both His first and His second comings. Zechariah has the largest number of messianic passages amongst all the Minor Prophets. The New Testament contains over forty of his references.

The Book of Revelation is greatly influenced by his imagery. Zechariah's main purpose was to assure Judah that although God disciplined them for seventy years in Babylon He is still their Covenant Keeping God who will bless them as He promised their fathers.

The Message

In Zechariah's first dream, the patrolling horses discovered the nations resting in their rebellion. In this eighth and final dream the horses, now war horses, patrol and put an end to these nations' rebellion. The message is, Babylon has been judged and God's Spirit in now at rest.

God's Purpose

∼

God's purpose was to bring heavenly judgement and justice on the Gentile nations through the assignment of these war chariots and God's four spirits.

Satan's Purpose

∼

Satan's purpose was to incite the Gentile nations, especially Babylon, to punish Israel far harsher than God ever intended.

Dreamer's Eyes Enlightened

∼

Zechariah understood God had judged the nations and now His Spirit was at rest.

Dreamer's Response and Application

He shared the dream with the people and he wrote it down.

Know God Better

God's Spirit will not rest until He has brought judgement to His enemies and the enemies of His chosen people. God's kingdom prevails through justice and judgment. Every other kingdom has to dissolve before His righteous judgement.

The Dream Process

This is a complex symbolic dream in which the dreamer dialogues with an angel. It requires interpretation of the chariots, horses, mountains, directions, nations and God speaking, using *The Symbol Replacement Method*.

The four spirits of heaven symbolised by four war chariots are released from the presence of the Lord via two bronze mountains and go to the four corners of Israel and judge the nations.

The chariot with the black horses goes to Babylon and accomplishes an assignment that gives rest to God's Spirit. The basic interpretation is, God's Spirit is now at rest because Babylon has been judged.

In Zechariah's first dream the riders and horses brought back reports. Here the horses are attached to chariots to bring judgement. In Zechariah's day chariots were war machines.

In Scripture the number four often has global implications, the four corners of the earth, north, south, east, and west. So these four chariots symbolise a heavenly army functioning all around the four corners of Israel judging the surrounding nations. Babylon was to the north, Egypt to the south, the Mediterranean Sea to the west and the desert to the east.

Nowhere else in Scripture are two bronze mountains mentioned. Solomon's temple contained two huge bronze pillars at the front of the Holy Place and in Hebrews we're told the earthly temple was a replica of God's Heavenly Temple. So perhaps there actually are two bronze mountains in heaven.

Mountains can be sacred, places of celebration and places of refuge and security. They can also be awful places of military slaughter. Nearly half of all Biblical references concerning bronze mention its use in the temple or tabernacle.

Another large percentage refers to its use in warfare. Goliath's armour and weapons were made of bronze and bronze shackles usually symbolised the punishment of fallen leaders. Perhaps these bronze mountains symbolise God's double portion of Heavenly judgement on the nations.

The Usual Suspects

God sends out the chariots, gives orders and declares His Spirit is at rest. Jesus in the form of the Angel of the Lord is continually supporting Israel. He was probably with the red horses as He was in dream one. Satan is represented by the enemy nations undergoing God's judgement.

Takeaways

All Zechariah's eight dreams speak of how God intends to save His people. They also point towards Jesus the Messiah and His coming Kingdom.

Zechariah's vision of the restoration of the city points towards the New Jerusalem. The temple rebuilt prefigures Jesus Christ raised from the dead and dwelling in His Church.

Joshua the High Priest points towards Jesus our Great High Priest. The flying scroll curse points towards The Cross and The Lake of Fire. The war chariots point towards a time when God will finally judge all His enemies.

NEW TESTAMENT DREAMS

ST. JOSEPH'S 'MARRY MARY' DREAM

But when the set time had fully come, God sent his Son, born of a woman, born under the law, to redeem those under the law, that we might receive adoption to sonship.[1]

Note on Joseph's Four Dreams

St Joseph's four dreams all occur in the Gospel of Matthew and all follow a similar pattern. In each dream Joseph, the legal father of Jesus, is visited by an angel and receives specific instructions and warnings of impending danger. All four dreams come from the period around the Nativity of Jesus and his early life, between the onset of Mary's pregnancy and the family's return from the Flight to Egypt.

The Dream Setting/Backstory

∼

This dream arrives around 444 years after Zechariah's dreams. *Nebuchadnezzar's 'Large Statue' Dream* has come to pass. The Babylonian, the Medo-Persian and the Greek Empires have come and gone and the Roman Empire is now ruling. The rock not cut by human hands is about to be incarnated in Israel. It's now time for the Lamb slain before the foundation of the world to step onto the stage of human history and finally crush Satan's head.

The Dream Scripture
Matthew 1:18-27

∼

This is how the birth of Jesus the Messiah came about: His mother Mary was pledged to be married to Joseph, but before they came together, she was found to be pregnant through the Holy Spirit. Because Joseph her husband was faithful to the law, and yet did not want to expose her to public disgrace, he had in mind to divorce her quietly.

But after he had considered this, an angel of the Lord appeared to him in a dream and said, "Joseph son of David, do not be afraid to take Mary home as your wife, because what is conceived in her is from the Holy Spirit. She will give birth to a son, and you are to give him the name Jesus, because he will save his people from their sins."

All this took place to fulfil what the Lord had said through the prophet: "The virgin will conceive and give birth to a son, and they will call him Immanuel" (which means "God with us"). When Joseph woke up, he did what the angel of the Lord had commanded him and took Mary home as his wife. But he did not consummate their marriage until she gave birth to a son. And he gave him the name Jesus.

The Problem

∽

Joseph has just discovered his fiancé is pregnant. Because he's a righteous person he decides not to expose her to public shame and possible death by stoning as required by the Law of Moses. He's considering divorcing her privately.

The Dreamer's Metron

∽

St Joseph had a unique metron. He was given the powerful assignment of being the legal father of Jesus, who was number one on Satan's hit list. Joseph's mission was to protect and nurture the Messiah until manhood.

St Joseph has been called the patron saint of hidden ones and this aptly describes him. He is given no words to speak in all of Scripture. There are only a few sentences concerning him. The main qualifications for his 'dream job' was being a righteous man from David's line. Joseph was just an ordinary man who fulfilled an extraordinary responsibility.

The Message

The simple literal message was, Joseph son of David, do not be afraid to take Mary home as your wife, because what is conceived in her is from the Holy Spirit. She will give birth to a son, and you are to give him the name Jesus, because he will save his people from their sins.

God's Purpose

This is a pivotal time for God's plans and purpose. God is keeping His promises to His enemy Satan and His friend Abraham. He is sending the Promised Seed who will crush Satan's head and bless all nations. God is fulfilling oceans of prophesies through Jesus, one of which is,

> All this took place to fulfil what the Lord had said through the prophet: "The virgin will conceive and give birth to a son, and they will call him Immanuel" (which means "God with us").[2]

God's primary purpose in this dream was to calm Joseph's fears and to encourage him to marry Mary and look after the Messiah whose name was to be Jesus.

Satan's Purpose

Satan's purpose was to accuse Mary and have her and her baby killed. His secondary purpose was to cause suspicion to land on her.

Dreamer's Eyes Enlightened

This dream not only solves Joseph's present dilemma but also launches him into his destiny and life's ministry.

Dreamer's Response and Application

Joseph was instantly obedient. He didn't pray or talk to his Rabbi about it. He obediently took Mary as his wife and named the child Jesus. I believe Joseph was a prophet. God spoke very serious things to him in dreams. God told Aaron and Mariam,

> When there is a prophet among you, I, the Lord, reveal myself to them in visions, I speak to them in dreams.[3]

Joseph was also a man of strong faith. He clearly heard from God in dreams and immediately took action.

Know God Better

∽

Once again God is seen as a promise and covenant keeper. We also see that God takes incredible risks. A bit like the time when He gave free will to humanity.

Here we see God taking the astonishing risk of giving the Messiah into the care of a couple of poor Jewish teenagers and sending them down to Egypt, a place then full of powers and principalities who would all dearly love to kill the Promised One.

Once again God shows He doesn't require man's power and wealth to bring about His plans and purpose. Instead of kings and queens He chose two Jewish teenagers to be parents to the Messiah. This reminds us of Paul's words to the Corinthians,

> Brothers and sisters, think of what you were when you were called. Not many of you were wise by human standards; not many were influential; not many were of noble birth. But God chose the foolish things of the world to shame the wise; God chose the weak things of the world to shame the strong. God chose the lowly things of this world and the despised things—and the things that are not—to nullify the things that are, so that no one may boast before him.[4]

The Dream Process

∽

There is nothing symbolic about any of Joseph's four dreams. They all contain literal and unambiguous messages that don't require an interpretation. I suspect the angel in all of Joseph's recorded dreams is Gabriel who gave Mary a very similar message,

> You will conceive and give birth to a son, and you are to call him Jesus. He will be great and will be called the Son of the Most High.[5]

Joseph's dreams are of national and international importance.

The Usual Suspects

~

Mary has become pregnant with Jesus by God's Holy Spirit. Satan is trying to get her stoned to death.

Takeaways

~

Matthew wrote for a mainly Jewish audience to prove Jesus was the Messiah. He records Joseph's linage for legal purposes because the Jews of Jesus' day considered Jesus as a son of Joseph. They all knew the Messiah had to be a descendant of David in order to be eligible to sit on David's throne. But there was a problem.

Joseph, the legal father of Jesus, was a descendant of David from Jeconiah's line and Jeconiah's line was cursed. Jeremiah prophesied concerning Jeconiah,

> This is what the LORD says: "Record this man as if childless, a man who will not prosper in his

lifetime, for none of his offspring will prosper, none will sit on the throne of David or rule anymore in Judah.⁶"

The Virgin Mary on the otherhand was a descendant of David through his son Nathan who was not cursed. So the virgin birth was necessary to ensure the sinless character of Jesus and also His right to sit upon David's throne.

So, Jesus received his blood right to David's throne through Mary, and his legal right to David's throne through Joseph.

Jesus could never have sat upon David's throne had Joseph been His natural father.

THE MAGI'S DREAM

The Dream Setting/Backstory

Around a couple of years after Christ's birth, a group of men called *The Magi* appeared in Jerusalem looking for a child who'd been born King of the Jews. They claimed they had seen his star rise and they had come to worship him.

This disturbed King Herod who asked the chief priests and teachers of the law exactly where the Messiah was to be born. They quoted Micah and said the Messiah was to be born in Bethlehem in Judea[1].

Herod spoke privately with *The Magi* and found out the exact time the star had appeared. He then sent them to Bethlehem and told them to search carefully for the child and report to him so he too could go and worship. Herod lied, he wanted to kill the child.

The Dream Scripture
Matthew 1:20-25

After they had heard the king, they went on their way, and the star they had seen when it rose went ahead of them until it stopped over the place where the child was. When they saw the star, they were overjoyed. On coming to the house, they saw the child with his mother Mary, and they bowed down and worshiped him. Then they opened their treasures and presented him with gifts of gold, frankincense and myrrh. And having been warned in a dream not to go back to Herod, they returned to their country by another route.

The Problem

King Herod wanted to kill this new King of the Jews.

The Dreamers' Metrons

The Magi were from Persia. The ancient church father Julius Africanus said they were skilled in astronomy and dream interpretation. Another church father, Origin, claimed they'd read a copy of Balaam's prophecy from Numbers 24 about the star coming out of Jacob. This copy had apparently been gifted to King Cyrus's library.

The Magi were obviously wealthy and influential men that God allowed to gain revelation about the birth of Jesus. God also used them to financially bless the Holy Family with gold. Like Melchizedek they were men of *general revelation* as opposed to the special revelation of Abraham and his descendants.

The Message

It was a simple literal message warning the Magi not to go back to Herod.

God's Purpose

God's purpose was to have the nations beyond Israel recognise and worship Jesus. The true light (*Jesus*) that gives light to every man (*through general revelation*) was coming into the world. God also wanted to protect the life of baby Jesus. He used the Magi to finance Joseph and Mary's stay in Egypt.

Satan's Purpose

Satan's purpose was to have Herod kill baby Jesus and prevent the One who'd crush his head from succeeding in His assignment.

Dreamer's Eyes Enlightened

The Magi clearly understood and knew what to do.

Dreamer's Response and Application

∼

They immediately heeded the dream and obeyed by returning to their country by another way.

Know God Better

∼

God is an all-knowing promise keeper who often intervenes into our realm in order to protect and advance His plans and purpose.

The Dream Process

∼

We're not told anything about the dream process but I suspect the same angel who directed Joseph in his dreams also spoke to the Magi.

The Usual Suspects

∼

God is protecting Jesus who is there in the flesh. Satan's actions are seen in Herod's fear and jealousy and his desire to murder Jesus.

Takeaways

Here we have another example of non-Jews clearly hearing from God in dreams and blessing His people. In this dream God also prevents a king from harming Joseph, Mary and Jesus.

The Magi's quick obedience kept both Jesus and themselves safe. Unfortunately they'd told Herod about the time of the stars first appearance.

Then, when Herod realised he'd been outwitted he gave orders to kill all the boys in Bethlehem and its vicinity who were two years old and under, in accordance with the time he had learned from the Magi. Then what was said through the prophet Jeremiah was fulfilled:

> A voice is heard in Ramah,
> weeping and great mourning,
> Rachel weeping for her children
> and refusing to be comforted,
> because they are no more.[2]

ST. JOSEPH'S 'ESCAPE TO EGYPT' DREAM

The Dream Setting/Backstory

This dream follows immediately on from *The Magi's Dream.* When Herod realised he'd been outwitted he gave orders to kill all the boys in Bethlehem and its vicinity who were two years old and under, in accordance with the time he had learned from the Magi. Jesus' life was under great threat.

The Dream Scripture
Matthew 2:13-15

When they had gone, an angel of the Lord appeared to Joseph in a dream. "Get up," he said, "take the child and his mother and escape to

Egypt. Stay there until I tell you, for Herod is going to search for the child to kill him." So he got up, took the child and his mother during the night and left for Egypt, where he stayed until the death of Herod.

The Problem

∼

Herod sent soldiers to kill Jesus.

The Dreamer's Metron

∼

St Joseph had a unique metron. He was given the powerful assignment of being the legal father of Jesus, who was number one on Satan's hit list. Joseph's mission was to protect and nurture the Messiah until manhood.

St Joseph has been called the patron saint of hidden ones and this aptly describes him. He is given no words to speak in all of Scripture. There are only a few sentences concerning him. The main qualifications for his 'dream job' was being a righteous man from David's line. Joseph was just an ordinary man who fulfilled an extraordinary responsibility.

The Message

∼

This plain and urgent message from the angel was, Get up take the child and his mother and escape to Egypt. Stay there until I tell you, for Herod is going to search for the child to kill him.

God's Purpose

God's purpose was to instruct Joseph in order to support him in his metron of protecting baby Jesus. God, the Eternal Promise Keeper, was also fulfilling His prophecy in Hosea part of which says,

And out of Egypt I called My son.[1]

Satan's Purpose

Satan's purpose was to have Herod kill baby Jesus and prevent the One who'd crush his head from succeeding.

Dreamer's Eyes Enlightened

St Joseph clearly understood exactly what to do.

Dreamer's Response and Application

St Joseph instantly obeyed and immediately put the dream message into operation. He didn't wait until morning.

Know God Better

Sovereign God is an All Knowing Promise Keeper who speaks of things long before they come to pass. We also see God is able and willing to help us with our metrons, our responsibilities.

The Dream Process

This is a literal warning dream with instructions delivered by an angel. There is no symbolism or interpretation required. The angel clearly instructs Joseph what to immediately do and promises to give further instructions when necessary.

The Usual Suspects

God sent the angel with the message. Jesus is being protected and Satan in the guise of Herod is trying to kill Jesus.

Takeaways

∽

Joseph's angel is definitely a guardian Angel. He tells Joseph to remain in Egypt until he will give him further orders from God.

ST. JOSEPH'S 'BACK TO ISRAEL' DREAM

The Dream Setting/Backstory

In the previous dream the angel told Joseph to remain in Egypt until he received further instructions. This third dream contains those new orders.

The Dream Scripture
Matthew 2:19-21

After Herod died, an angel of the Lord appeared in a dream to Joseph in Egypt and said, "Get up, take the child and his mother and go to the land of Israel, for those who were trying to take the child's life are dead." So he got up, took the child and his mother and went to the land of Israel.

The Problem

It is now time for Joseph and his family to return to Israel.

The Dreamer's Metron

Saint Joseph had a unique metron. He was given the powerful assignment of being the legal father of Jesus, who was number one on Satan's hit list. Joseph's mission was to protect and nurture the Messiah until manhood.

St Joseph has been called the patron saint of hidden ones and this aptly describes him. He is given no words to speak in all of Scripture. There are only a few sentences concerning him. The main qualifications for his 'dream job' was being a righteous man from David's line. Joseph was just an ordinary man who fulfilled an extraordinary responsibility.

The Message

This is a simple and clear message that tells Joseph to, Get up, take the child and his mother and go to the land of Israel, for those who were trying to take the child's life are dead.

God's Purpose

∼

God's purpose was to instruct Joseph in order to protect the life of the Messiah. God, the Eternal Promise Keeper, was also fulfilling his prophecy in Hosea, part of which says, Out of Egypt I called my son.[1]

Satan's Purpose

∼

Satan's purpose was still to kill baby Jesus.

Dreamer's Eyes Enlightened

∼

Joseph understood the threat of Herod was over and it was now safe in God's will and timing to return to Israel.

Dreamer's Response and Application

∼

As is usual with Joseph he immediately obeyed and put God's instructions into operation.

Know God Better

Sovereign Promise Keeping God is still helping Joseph in his metron and still advancing His covenantal promises to Abraham. The Messiah is here.

The Dream Process

This again is a literal warning dream with instructions delivered by an angel. There is no symbolism or interpretation required. The dream is of personal, national and international importance.

The Usual Suspects

God sent the dream. Jesus is the baby under protection. Satan doesn't know where Jesus is.

Takeaways

God is ever willing to help us with our metron, our callings and our responsibilities. He is always able to give us up to date information so we can change our position whenever necessary to align ourselves with His perfect plans.

Geography matters to God. Being in the right place at the right time doing the right thing for the right reasons in the right way is alright.

ST. JOSEPH'S 'GO TO NAZARETH' DREAM

The Dream Setting/Backstory

Joseph has obeyed the previous dream that instructed him to return to Israel. Yet he feels concern for the safety of Jesus because Herod's son Archelaus is now reigning in Judea.

The Dream Scripture
Matthew 2:22-23

But when he heard that Archelaus was reigning in Judea in place of his father Herod, he was afraid to go there. Having been warned in a dream, he withdrew to the district of Galilee, and he went and lived in a town called Nazareth.

The Problem

∼

Joseph is concerned about Jesus' safety. He doesn't think Judea is a good place to live because Herod's son Archelaus is reigning there in place of his father.

The Dreamer's Metron

∼

St Joseph had a unique metron. He was given the powerful assignment of being the legal father of Jesus, who was number one on Satan's hit list. Joseph's mission was to protect and nurture the Messiah until manhood.

St Joseph has been called the patron saint of hidden ones and this aptly describes him. He is given no words to speak in all of Scripture. There are only a few sentences concerning him. The main qualifications for his 'dream job' was being a righteous man from David's line. Joseph was just an ordinary man who fulfilled an extraordinary responsibility.

The Message

The angel warned Joseph against going to live in Judea. We don't know exactly what the angel said, but I suspect he told Joseph to go and live in Nazareth, a place beyond Archelaus' jurisdiction. This warning was probably given by the same angel as before though we're not told in Scripture.

God's Purpose

God's purpose was to keep Jesus safe.

Satan's Purpose

Satan would have liked Joseph to move to live under Archelaus' jurisdiction. Apparently Satan was able to influence Archelaus for his own evil purposes just as He had used Herod.

Dreamer's Eyes Enlightened

Joseph's fears were confirmed by the dream.

Dreamer's Response and Application

Joseph was already concerned about Judea before his dream. His response is the same as in his other three dreams, immediate obedience and action.

Know God Better

Again God is shown to be an all knowing promise keeper who speaks of things long before they come to pass. A God who can save us to the uttermost.[1] Here we see Him confirming Joseph's anxieties and helping him with the answer.

The Dream Process

Although we're not specifically told how the warning was given in this dream most likely it was a similar literal warning message delivered by the same angel in the usual manner. It was of personal, national and international significance.

The Usual Suspects

God sends this warning dream to protect baby Jesus. Satan is represented by Herod's son Archelaus who like his father would gladly kill Jesus.

Takeaways

Concerning Jesus, Matthew said,

> He went and lived in a town called Nazareth. So was fulfilled what was said through the prophets, that he would be called a Nazarene.[2]

In this verse Matthew is not quoting from the Old Testament because there is no such prophecy. Bible teachers have suggested three options. The first suggestion is Matthew is citing a prophecy from another source but I think this is unlikely.

Another idea is that Matthew is linking the word Nazarene with the Hebrew word netser, which means branch or sprout. Isaiah used the symbol of a Branch for the Messiah,

> A shoot will come up from the stump of Jesse; from his roots a Branch will bear fruit.[3]

If this was the case then Matthew would be saying that Jesus was sprouting up from an obscure Galilean village. Another suggestion is that Matthew is using the word Nazarene to symbolise someone who is despised and rejected, because Nazareth of Galilee was shunned by mainline Jews. This image would resonate with Isaiah's image,

> He was despised and rejected by mankind, a man of suffering, and familiar with pain. Like one from whom people hide their faces he was despised, and we held him in low esteem.[4]

On another note, I find it interesting that living in certain locations can make us more vulnerable to Satan's influence and attacks. Geography is obviously important to God for He sent Joseph, Mary and Jesus to a place not under Archelaus' metron.

We see something similar happening with the children of Israel in Exodus when God told them,

> Behold, I am sending an angel before you to protect you along the way and to bring you to the place I have prepared.[5]

JESUS' 'TEMPTED BY SATAN' DREAM

The Dream Setting/Backstory

In God's plans and sovereign purpose it was now time for Jesus to begin His ministry. So, God filled Jesus with His Holy Spirit and sent Him into the desert to be tempted by Satan for forty days.

The Bible doesn't explicitly say these temptations happened in a dream but I think it's useful to consider the possibility. I don't believe Satan has either the power or the ability to physically transport Jesus to a high mountain or the highest point on the temple in Jerusalem anytime he wants.

For the second temptation Satan led Jesus up to a high place and showed him in an instant all the kingdoms of the world. This is obviously symbolic for there is no actual physical place on earth from which one can see all the kingdoms of the world. Yet it's the sort of thing one can easily do in a dream.

For the third temptation Satan had Jesus stand on the highest point of the temple at Jerusalem. This again is typically symbolic and is the sort of thing that can easily occur in a dream.

They way Jesus dealt with Satan's temptations can also help us gain the victory when we are similarly tempted in dreams.

The Dream Scripture
Matthew 4:1-11

∽

Jesus, full of the Holy Spirit, left the Jordan and was led by the Spirit into the wilderness, where for forty days he was tempted by the devil. He ate nothing during those days, and at the end of them he was hungry.

The devil said to him, "If you are the Son of God, tell this stone to become bread."

Jesus answered, "It is written: 'Man shall not live on bread alone.'

The devil led him up to a high place and showed him in an instant all the kingdoms of the world. And he said to him, "I will give you all their authority and splendour; it has been given to me, and I can give it to anyone I want to. If you worship me, it will all be yours."

Jesus answered, "It is written: 'Worship the Lord your God and serve him only.'

The devil led him to Jerusalem and had him stand on the highest point of the temple. "If you are the Son of God," he said, "throw yourself down from here. For it is written:

"'He will command his angels concerning you
   to guard you carefully;
they will lift you up in their hands,
   so that you will not strike your foot against a stone.'

Jesus answered, "It is said: 'Do not put the Lord your God to the test.'

When the devil had finished all this tempting, he left him until an opportune time.

Jesus returned to Galilee in the power of the Spirit, and news about him spread through the whole countryside. He was teaching in their synagogues, and everyone praised him.

The Problem

∽

In God's plan Jesus had to be tempted by Satan before He could begin His ministry as Messiah.

The Dreamer's Metron

∽

Scripture says, Jesus is the eternal Word made Flesh[1] and the Image of the Invisible God[2], He is the perfect manifestation of God; the very substance and embodiment of the Creator. He is also the only Mediator between God and man.[3] He is the Son of Man who gave Himself as a ransom for mankind. He is also Head over All Things.[4] His name of Christ refers to His position of highest dignity and honour at the Father's right hand. Scripture also says Jesus is,

- The Light of the World.[5]
- The Anointed One.[6,7]
- The Good Shepherd.[8]
- The Bread of Life.[9]

- Healer and Forgiver.[10]
- The Way, the Truth, the Life.[11]
- The Resurrection and Life.[12]
- He holds the keys of death.[13]
- Son of David.[14]
- The Messiah-King.[15]
- Man of Sorrows.[16]
- Sinless and Holy.[17]
- Lamb of God.[18]
- Prince of Peace.[19]
- The Power and Wisdom of God.[20]

The Message

The three messages Jesus quotes from Scripture are,

- Man shall not live on bread alone, but on every word that comes from the mouth of God.[21]
- Do not put the Lord your God to the test.[22]
- Worship the Lord your God, and serve him only.[23]

God's Purpose

God's purpose was that Jesus would overcome Satan with God's word.

Satan's Purpose

Satan's purpose was to overcome Jesus by temptation.

Dreamer's Eyes Enlightened

Jesus knew the word of God would overcome Satan and He saw it happening in the dream.

Dreamer's Response and Application

Jesus allowed Himself to be attended to by angels. He then returned to Galilee in the power of the Spirit and began teaching in their synagogues.

Know God Better

God is willing to have His only begotten Son tempted by Satan. He knows every true son and daughter of His must all pass temptations by Satan.

The Dream Process

∼

Satan tempted Jesus in three different ways and each time Jesus destroyed Satan's temptations with the written word of God.

The first temptation targeted Jesus's identity and the lust of the flesh. Satan said, If you are the Son of God?

Perhaps Satan wasn't sure who Jesus was. Nevertheless he tempted the hungry Jesus with the enticement to use His God given powers to satisfy His own desires. Jesus counters this temptation by quoting Deuteronomy 8:3.

The second temptation concerns the pride of life and Satan misquotes and twists Psalm 91:11–12, but Jesus again destroys this lure by quoting, Deuteronomy 6:16.

Jesus will not abuse His God given powers just to put on a big impressive show.

The third temptation concerns the lust of the eyes. Here Satan offers a fast track to Jesus becoming the Messiah without having to endure God's painful will for the Cross. Satan essentially offers control over all the kingdoms of the world[24] if only Jesus will pledge allegiance to Him.

Jesus once again destroys Satan's temptation by quoting God's word, You shall worship the Lord your God and serve Him only.[25]

The Usual Suspects

∼

God led Jesus by His Holy Spirit into the desert to be tempted by Satan.

Takeaways

~

Jesus' temptation by Satan is recorded in Matthew,[26] Mark[27] and Luke.[28] In all three accounts the only witnesses to the temptations are the *Usual Suspects*, God, Jesus and Satan.

So where did all three Evangelists get their story from?

Certainty not from a disgraced Satan who failed miserably in his quest. Possibly from God because these scribes wrote as the Holy Spirit carried them along.[29]

But I think it more likely that Jesus himself often recounted this incident to His disciples in order to illustrate and instruct them on how to defeat attacks from Satan.

PILATE'S WIFE'S DREAM

The Dream Setting/Backstory

The chief priests and the teachers of the law were scheming to kill Jesus. They falsely arrested and questioned Jesus and had found Him guilty of blasphemy against their interpretation of the Law of Moses. They then brought Him before Pilate for these offences, which were unlikely to be considered a capital offence by Roman law.

The Dream Scripture
Matthew 27:15-1

Now it was the governor's custom at the festival to release a prisoner chosen by the crowd. At that time they had a well-known prisoner whose name was Jesus Barabbas. So when the crowd had gathered, Pilate asked them, "Which one do you want me to release to you: Jesus Barabbas, or Jesus who is called the Messiah?" For he knew it was out of self-interest that they had handed Jesus over to him.

While Pilate was sitting on the judge's seat, his wife sent him this message: "Don't have anything to do with that innocent man, for I have suffered a great deal today in a dream because of him."

The Problem

∽

Pontius Pilate knew Jesus was innocent. He realised the Jews were falsely accusing Jesus out of self-interest and not because they cared about the Law. Pilate tried to free Jesus by evoking the governor's custom to release a prisoner chosen by the crowd but they chose Barabbas. Pilate was in a predicament. Should he condemn an innocent man?

The Dreamer's Metron

∽

Pilates' wife's status as his spouse gave her access to the ear of her husband who was the governor of the Roman province of Judaea. Because of her metron as his wife she was the one God used to speak to Pilate. Pilate's wife is the only recorded person in Scripture who spoke out against the decision to kill Jesus.

The Message

~

Pilate's wife understood the dream well enough to be able to tell her husband the clear message, Don't have anything to do with that innocent man, for I have suffered a great deal today in a dream because of him.

God's Purpose

~

God's purpose was to inform Pilate and the whole world that Jesus was innocent. He also gave Pilate the opportunity to be a righteous judge.

Satan's Purpose

~

Satan's purpose as always was to kill Jesus. He ignorantly didn't realise he was doing God's will. He had no knowledge of the mysterious and hidden wisdom of God, which was that Jesus should die for the sins of the whole world on a cross. Neither Satan or any of the gods knew this. Paul says,

> None of the rulers of this age understood it. For if they had, they would not have crucified the Lord of glory.[1]

Dreamer's Eyes Enlightened

Pilate's wife clearly understood the dream message. She also experienced the suffering.

Dreamer's Response and Application

Pilate's wife quickly responded to the dream's message and informed her husband who was in a position to apply the dream message and pardon the innocent Jesus.

Know God Better

God is able and willing to speak truth to power. He is able to get His message through to anyone He desires to speak to. He cares about justice and truth.

The Dream Process

This dream was probably a nightmare. It reminds us of Elihu who said God can frighten us through a nightmare,

> in order to turn us from sin; He may speak in their ears and terrify them with warnings, to turn them from wrongdoing and keep them from pride, to preserve them from the pit, their lives from perishing by the sword.[2]

This was a warning dream with revelation. Most likely it was a literal dream but we're not specifically told about the contents. It had personal importance to Pilate and his wife but also was of national and international significance.

The Usual Suspects

God send the dream and declared Jesus to be innocent. Satan working through the Sanhedrin's jealousy succeeded in getting them to murder Jesus.

Takeaways

It looks like Pilate's wife was no novice as regards dreams. The fact she tried to influence her husband in his important role as governor citing a dream tends to indicate they probably both took dreams very seriously.

Pilate displayed a sign above Jesus on the cross that read, *Jesus of Nazareth, The King of the Jews*.

The chief priests complained and said the sign should read Jesus claimed to be King of the Jews.

Pilate refused to accommodate their evil any longer. He dismissed them by saying, What I have written, I have written.

Pilate, the man who refused to listen to his wife's advice, is well remembered by many Christians every Sunday. He is mentioned in both the Apostles and Nicene Creeds.

PETER INTERPRETING PENTECOST

The Incident Setting/Backstory

After his resurrection Jesus appeared to His apostles over a period of forty days and gave them many convincing proofs He was alive. He also spoke about the kingdom of God.

On one occasion He told them to not leave Jerusalem until they received the gift His Father had promised, which was to be baptised in the Holy Spirit. The disciples were more concerned about the issue of when Jesus was going to restore the kingdom to Israel.

Jesus basically said His time to restore the kingdom to Israel was none of their business at present but they would receive power when the Holy Spirit came upon them and they would be His witnesses in Jerusalem, and in all Judea and Samaria, and to the ends of the earth. The Holy Spirit fell on the day of Pentecost and caused an upheaval amongst the people. God chose Peter to interpret what was happening.[1]

The Scripture
Acts 2:14-18

~

Then Peter stood up with the Eleven, raised his voice and addressed the crowd: "Fellow Jews and all of you who live in Jerusalem, let me explain this to you; listen carefully to what I say. These people are not drunk, as you suppose. It's only nine in the morning! No, this is what was spoken by the prophet Joel:

> In the last days, God says,
>   I will pour out my Spirit on all people.
> Your sons and daughters will prophesy,
>   your young men will see visions,
>   your old men will dream dreams.
> Even on my servants, both men and women,
>   I will pour out my Spirit in those days,
>   and they will prophesy.

The Problem

~

The promise of the Father had been released in Jerusalem and God's chosen people were confused.

The Interpreter's Metron

~

Peter was a colourful character, a wholehearted man of action totally committed to Jesus and constantly at the forefront of things. He is always listed first among the Twelve Apostles. He was the first disciple called by Jesus. He was the first to confess Jesus as the Messiah. He was the first to walk upon water. He was the first to perform a miracle. He was the first to enter Jesus' empty tomb. He was the first to explain the baptism of the Holy Spirit.

Along with St Paul, God sovereignly chose Peter to take the Gospel to the whole world. Peter's opinion in the early Church's debate about Gentiles being converted was pivotal and crucial. Two New Testament epistles are attributed to Peter. Peter like Moses not only knew the Acts of God but he knew His Ways.[2]

The Message

The message was, This unusual phenomena occurring in Jerusalem is not due to alcohol but is the fulfilment of a promise made by God through His prophet Joel.

God's Purpose

God's purpose was to keep His promise made to Abraham and Joel. He also is fulfilling Jesus' promise of power to His disciples for the work of His ministry of building His Church.

Satan's Purpose

Satan's purpose was to confuse the people and keep them from receiving God's Promise of the baptism in the Holy Spirit.

Dreamer's Eyes Enlightened

Peter knew exactly what was happening. He knew this was the Promise of the Father. He knew God was releasing power through His Holy Spirit.

Dreamer's Response and Application

Peter was emboldened and immediately began to preach and explain what was occurring. Three thousand men received Jesus as Lord and Saviour through his new bold Holy Spirit anointed preaching.

Know God Better

God is once again seen as a Covenant Keeping Promise Keeper. He is keeping His Promise to Abraham to bless his offspring and through them the whole world. He is also fulfilling Joel's prophecy.

The Incident Process

∽

People were able to connect the experience with the relevant scripture from Joel.

The Usual Suspects

∽

God was keeping His Promise. Satan was confusing the people and getting some of them to mock the work of God. Jesus's sacrifice was working and He was baptising people in the Holy Spirit and with fire just as John the Baptist prophesied.[3]

Takeaways

∽

The Promised Holy Spirit had come and He hadn't only come to the Jews. Peter said the Holy Spirit was being poured out upon all peoples, all levels of society and all nations in tongues, prophecy, visions and dreams.

SAUL'S VISION ON THE ROAD TO DAMASCUS

The Encounter Setting/Backstory

Jesus told His disciples, after they received Holy Spirit power, they should preach the Gospel in Jerusalem, Judea, Samaria and to the ends of the earth.

Five years later they were still holding Holy Spirit meetings in Jerusalem with no thought whatsoever of Samaria when persecution broke out resulting in Stephen being illegally stoned to death by the Sanhedrin.

A young man called Saul, later named Paul looked after the cloaks of the murderers and approved of their evil deed. Afterwards Saul sought to destroy the church by imprisoning all the believers he could lay his hands on.

The Jerusalem church was scattered and Philip ended up in Samaria where he started a revival amongst the people. Finally Samaritans were being saved, delivered, healed and baptised in the Holy Spirit.

The Encounter Scripture
Acts 9:1-9

~

Meanwhile, Saul was still breathing out murderous threats against the Lord's disciples. He went to the high priest and asked him for letters to the synagogues in Damascus, so that if he found any there who belonged to the Way, whether men or women, he might take them as prisoners to Jerusalem. As he neared Damascus on his journey, suddenly a light from heaven flashed around him. He fell to the ground and heard a voice say to him, "Saul, Saul, why do you persecute me?"

"Who are you, Lord?" Saul asked.

"I am Jesus, whom you are persecuting," he replied. "Now get up and go into the city, and you will be told what you must do."

The men traveling with Saul stood there speechless; they heard the sound but did not see anyone. Saul got up from the ground, but when he opened his eyes he could see nothing. So they led him by the hand into Damascus. For three days he was blind, and did not eat or drink anything.

The Problem

~

Jesus had enough of Saul's ignorant persecution of His Church.

Paul's Metron

Paul was a Messianic Jewish-Roman rabbi and writer who'd studied under the revered Pharisee Gamaliel. Paul had a massive metron from God to preach the Gospel of Jesus Christ to all nations.

He was a very bright spark. Peter said, Paul's letters contained some things hard to understand.[1] Paul wrote thirteen of the twenty-seven New Testament books. His life and work takes up half of the book of Acts.

Paul is universally considered to be one of Christianity's most important figures. His influence on Christian thought and practice has been profound and pervasive.

His status as Jewish and a Roman citizen helped him minister to Jewish and Gentile listeners. He was also the founder of various Christian communities in Asia Minor and Europe.

The Message

Jesus' message to Paul was, When you persecute the Church you are really persecuting Me. Now go into the city and await further orders.

God's Purpose

God's purpose was to give Paul revelation of who Jesus really was and to launch Paul into his life's work and destiny.

Satan's Purpose

Satan's purpose was to keep Paul blind to who Jesus was and to use Paul to join him in destroying Jesus' disciples and church.

Dreamer's Eyes Enlightened

There was a quick reversal in Saul's life. His spiritual eyes were enlightened and his physical eyes were blinded.

Dreamer's Response and Application

He instantly obeyed the heavenly voice and went into Damascus.

Know God Better

We see God's sovereignty at work in this incident. It was He who chose Saul to take the Gospel to all nations.

I believe Paul was God's choice of the apostle to replace Judas. In this incident we see Jesus choosing Saul to be an apostle just like He chose the other apostles. I also believe when Peter chose Matthias as the apostle to replace Judas he was exhibiting his old problem of being too hasty.

The Holy Spirit and power had not yet been poured out. We hear nothing more in Scripture about Matthias yet we read in Galatians,

> Paul, an apostle sent not from men nor by a man, but by Jesus Christ and God the Father who raised him from the dead.[2]

The Encounter Process

Saul was using violence against the believers when this violent incident happened. A heavenly light resulted in him being knocked off his horse. He then heard and saw Jesus who identified Himself and told him what to do next.

The men with Saul heard Jesus speaking but didn't see Him. They were struck speechless and Saul was struck blind by this incident. Saul's blindness lasted for three days. Here we have an example of a heavenly event affecting the physical. Paul also neither ate nor drank during his thee days of blindness.

The Usual Suspects

God's power knocks Saul off his horse and strikes him blind. Jesus appears and speaks to Saul. Satan was behind Saul's ignorant and zealous persecution of Jesus' Church.

Takeaways

∼

God is Sovereign.

ANANIAS' VISION ABOUT PAUL

The Dream Setting/Backstory

After Saul's bewildering encounter on the road to Damascus, he asked Jesus, Lord, what do You want me to do?

Jesus told him to go into the city and await further instructions. So, blind Saul obeyed the vision and waited in Damascus for three days praying and fasting. During this time God gave Saul a vision of a man called Ananias who would come and lay hands on him and restore his sight.

The Vision Scripture
Acts 9:10-19

In Damascus there was a disciple named Ananias. The Lord called to him in a vision, "Ananias!"

"Yes, Lord," he answered.

The Lord told him, "Go to the house of Judas on Straight Street and ask for a man from Tarsus named Saul, for he is praying. In a vision he has seen a man named Ananias come and place his hands on him to restore his sight."

"Lord," Ananias answered, "I have heard many reports about this man and all the harm he has done to your holy people in Jerusalem. And he has come here with authority from the chief priests to arrest all who call on your name."

But the Lord said to Ananias, "Go! This man is my chosen instrument to proclaim my name to the Gentiles and their kings and to the people of Israel. I will show him how much he must suffer for my name."

Then Ananias went to the house and entered it. Placing his hands on Saul, he said, "Brother Saul, the Lord—Jesus, who appeared to you on the road as you were coming here—has sent me so that you may see again and be filled with the Holy Spirit." Immediately, something like scales fell from Saul's eyes, and he could see again. He got up and was baptised, and after taking some food, he regained his strength.

The Problem

God had blinded Saul. Then God gave Saul a vision of a man named Ananias coming to lay hands on him to restore his sight.

The Visionary's Metron

Ananias was a disciple of Jesus, a devout man according to the law, having a good report of all the Jews that dwelt in Damascus. He was obviously a friend of God well used to dialoguing with Him in visions.

When God told him to go to Straight Street and ask for a man from Tarsus named Saul, Ananias had no problem reminding God of just how evil Saul was. God then freely shares His plans and purpose with Ananias. He says,

> Go, for he is a chosen vessel of mine to bear My name before Gentiles, kings and the children of Israel. For I will show him how many things he must suffer for My sake.

There was no annoyance or coercion on God's part. Just, God calmly giving His friend Ananias an important task to which Ananias was instantly obedient. We hear no more about Ananias but his obedience to God in what appeared a very dangerous assignment has helped bring a massive harvest into God's kingdom. Good man Ananias!

The Message

God gave Ananias the name and address of the man He wanted healed. He also gave Ananias the reason for and the significance of the assignment; he is a chosen vessel of mine to bear My name before Gentiles, kings and the children of Israel. God also told

Ananias some personal stuff about Saul, For I will show him how much he must suffer for My sake.

God's Purpose

God's purpose was to keep His visionary promise to Saul and heal him. He also wanted to release Saul into the next stage of his very special ministry. God was still keeping Covenant with Abraham about all nations being blessed through his seed line.

Satan's Purpose

Satan's purpose was to cause fear and disobedience in Ananias and thereby hinder God's plans.

Dreamer's Eyes Enlightened

Ananias knew exactly what to do and the importance of the mission.

Dreamer's Response and Application

Ananias dialogued with God and was instantly obedient to God's instructions.

Know God Better

∽

God has friends all over the place who are ever ready to do His will. He had seven thousand prophets in Israel that Elijah knew nothing about.[1] God was so confident of Ananias's relationship that He gave Saul a vision of Ananias coming to heal him before He even mentions this to Ananias.

I suspect Ananias had run other errands for God. Perhaps that's why he had favour with Jews and Gentiles.

The Vision Process

∽

We're not fully sure if this is a day vision or a night vision dream. We do know Jesus appeared to Ananias and dialogues with him. This is similar to other Bible dreams like *King Abimelek's Dream* and *Solomons 'Discerning Heart' Dream.*

Jesus gave Ananias the name and address of Saul and the reason for the assignment. Jesus also added some personal details of what exactly He was going to tell Saul.

This is not like a superior officer giving an order to an inferior officer. Instead they dialogue like two old friends clarifying things with one another. This is very much like a putting into practise of John 15,

> You are my friends if you do what I command. I no longer call you servants, because a servant does not know his master's business. Instead, I have called you friends, for everything that I learned from my Father I have made known to you. You did not choose me, but I chose you and appointed you so that you might go and bear fruit—fruit that will last.[2]

When Jesus tells Ananias about Paul's vision and its contents this is the only time in Scripture anyone mentions another vision to the visionary.

This is a literal vision with no need for interpretation. It is of universal importance for Saul will turn out to be a significant player in God's Kingdom. Ananias' quick obedience definitely bore fruit that will last.

The Usual Suspects

Jesus was dialoguing with Ananias about God's will. Satan was there perhaps in Ananias' initial hesitancy. Satan was going to be head-crushed greatly through Paul's ministry.

Takeaways

Amazingly, as out of nowhere Ananias moved centerstage and played a major pivotal part in God's marvellous plan for the

Gentiles. By freeing Paul into his ministry Ananias was kickstarting the beginning of Paul's ministry which included releasing the great Mystery of the Gentiles. Paul said,

> Although I am less than the least of all the Lord's people, this grace was given me: to preach to the Gentiles the boundless riches of Christ, and to make plain to everyone the administration of this mystery, which for ages past was kept hidden in God, who created all things. His intent was that now, through the church, the manifold wisdom of God should be made known to the rulers and authorities in the heavenly realms, according to his eternal purpose that he accomplished in Christ Jesus our Lord.[3]

Saul's salvation is quick and sudden. It reminds us of the incident at Cornelius' house in Acts 10 when the Holy Spirit fell amongst the Gentiles.

Here we see God taking the initiative and connecting and arranging unwilling participants in order to move His kingdom forward.

No doubt Ananias' worldview would have been like Peter's. There is no way he could have imagined the Gentiles coming into the Kingdom of God, but this didn't stop him from obeying the heavenly vision.

PAUL'S TRANCE

The Trance Setting/Backstory

Paul began preaching Jesus Christ as the Son of God immediately after his conversion but found no favour with his fellow Jews who plotted to kill him. Neither did he find favour with the Jerusalem disciples who doubted his conversion. He then disputed with the Greek Jews who also wanted to kill him.

Mercifully Jesus came to his rescue. This account of the trance is from Paul's defence before the Jewish crowd in Jerusalem in Acts 22.

We also learn a few more facts about *Saul's Vision on the Road to Damascus* from this account.

The Trance Scripture
Acts 22:2-21

Then Paul said: "I am a Jew, born in Tarsus of Cilicia, but brought up in this city. I studied under Gamaliel and was thoroughly trained in the law of our ancestors. I was just as zealous for God as any of you are today. I persecuted the followers of this Way to their death, arresting both men and women and throwing them into prison, as the high priest and all the Council can themselves testify. I even obtained letters from them to their associates in Damascus, and went there to bring these people as prisoners to Jerusalem to be punished.

"About noon as I came near Damascus, suddenly a bright light from heaven flashed around me. I fell to the ground and heard a voice say to me, 'Saul! Saul! Why do you persecute me?'

"'Who are you, Lord?' I asked.

" 'I am Jesus of Nazareth, whom you are persecuting,' he replied. My companions saw the light, but they did not understand the voice of him who was speaking to me.

"'What shall I do, Lord?' I asked.

" 'Get up,' the Lord said, 'and go into Damascus. There you will be told all that you have been assigned to do.' My companions led me by the hand into Damascus, because the brilliance of the light had blinded me.

"A man named Ananias came to see me. He was a devout observer of the law and highly respected by all the Jews living there. He stood beside me and said, 'Brother Saul, receive your sight!' And at that very moment I was able to see him.

"Then he said: 'The God of our ancestors has chosen you to know his will and to see the Righteous One and to hear words from his mouth. You will be his witness to all people of what you have seen and heard. And now what are you waiting for? Get up, be baptised and wash your sins away, calling on his name.'

"When I returned to Jerusalem and was praying at the temple, I fell into a trance and saw the Lord speaking to me. 'Quick!' he said. 'Leave Jerusalem immediately, because the people here will not accept your testimony about me.'

"'Lord,' I replied, 'these people know that I went from one synagogue to another to imprison and beat those who believe in you. And when the blood of your martyr Stephen was shed, I stood there giving my approval and guarding the clothes of those who were killing him.'

"Then the Lord said to me, 'Go; I will send you far away to the Gentiles.'"

The Problem

∽

Paul was in the wrong place at the wrong time doing the wrong thing in the wrong way. His naive zeal nearly got him killed and nearly scuttled God's plans and purpose for his life.

Paul's Metron

∽

Paul was a Messianic Jewish-Roman rabbi and writer who'd studied under the revered Pharisee Gamaliel. Paul had a massive metron from God to preach the Gospel of Jesus Christ to all nations.

He was a very bright spark. Peter said, Paul's letters contained some things hard to understand.[1] Paul wrote thirteen of the twenty-seven New Testament books. His life and work takes up half of the book of Acts.

Paul is universally considered to be one of Christianity's most important figures. His influence on Christian thought and practice has been profound and pervasive.

His status as Jewish and a Roman citizen helped him minister to Jewish and Gentile listeners. He was also the founder of various Christian communities in Asia Minor and Europe.

The Message

Jesus' clear and urgent message was, Quick! Leave Jerusalem immediately, because the people here will not accept your testimony about me. Go; I will send you far away to the Gentiles.

God's Purpose

God's purpose was to save Paul's life and to move him into God's greater plans and purpose in the harvest fields of the Gentiles.

Satan's Purpose

Satan's purpose was to encourage Paul's headstrong self will and have the Jews make a martyr out of him in order to curtail his kingdom effectiveness.

Dreamer's Eyes Enlightened

～

Paul clearly understood. Jesus plainly explained what Paul should do and why he should do it.

Dreamer's Response and Application

～

Paul's initial response was to disagree with Jesus and offer another explanation. But Jesus didn't dialogue with Paul. He just ordered Paul to obey.

Know God Better

～

God is not a one size fits all kind of Person. He is a God of amazing variety. We see this in His choice of Paul and in the unfolding unique calling upon Paul's life.

The Trance Process

～

Jesus plainly tells Paul to leave Jerusalem immediately because the people will not accept Paul's testimony about Jesus. We're not told exactly which people will not accept Paul's testimony but from reading Acts 9 it appears nobody except Barnabas wanted anything to do with Paul. Paul answers Jesus back to defend his position but Jesus is firm in His response. He tells Paul to do what he was told.

The Usual Suspects

God was releasing His plans and purpose for Paul's life through Jesus who is directing Paul and saving him from Satan's plans to cut his life short by him persisting in preaching to the wrong people.

Takeaways

We learn something new about Paul's calling when Ananias prophesies,

> The God of our ancestors has chosen you to know his will and to see the Righteous One and to hear words from his mouth.[2]

God's will for Paul was he would not receive the gospel from any man but by direct revelation from Jesus personally. This is confirmed in Galatians when Paul says,

> I want you to know, brothers and sisters, that the gospel I preached is not of human origin. I did not receive it from any man, nor was I taught it; rather, I received it by revelation from Jesus Christ.[3]

God had very specific plans for Paul. He was not sent out on his life's mission by any man or group. He told the Galatians,

> Paul, an apostle—sent not from men nor by a man, but by Jesus Christ and God the Father, who raised him from the dead.[4]

CORNELIUS' 'SEND FOR PETER' VISION

The Vision Setting/Backstory

Just before Jesus returned to His Father He gave specific instructions to His disciples. He said,

> But you shall receive power when the Holy Spirit has come upon you; and you shall be my witnesses both in Jerusalem, and in all Judea and Samaria, and even to the remotest part of the earth.[1]

The three stages were, the Jews first, the Samaritans/half Jews second and the Gentiles, the rest of the world last. The breakthrough with the Jews occurred in Acts 2 and the Samaritan breakthrough occurred in Acts 8. Now it was time for the Gentiles.

The Vision Scripture

Acts 10:1-7

~

At Caesarea there was a man named Cornelius, a centurion in what was known as the Italian Regiment. He and all his family were devout and God-fearing; he gave generously to those in need and prayed to God regularly. One day at about three in the afternoon he had a vision. He distinctly saw an angel of God, who came to him and said, "Cornelius!"

Cornelius stared at him in fear. "What is it, Lord?" he asked.

The angel answered, "Your prayers and gifts to the poor have come up as a memorial offering before God. Now send men to Joppa to bring back a man named Simon who is called Peter. He is staying with Simon the tanner, whose house is by the sea."

When the angel who spoke to him had gone, Cornelius called two of his servants and a devout soldier who was one of his attendants. He told them everything that had happened and sent them to Joppa.

The Problem

~

It was God's time for the Gentiles to hear the gospel of Jesus Christ but the Jewish disciples were not being obedient to The Great Commission. So God moved things forward.

The Visionary's Metron

~

Cornelius was the first Gentile converted to Christianity. He was a God-fearing leader of men, a centurion in Caesarea, in charge of a hundred Roman soldiers. He was also in charge of his own home, leading his family in prayer, worship, good works and alms giving.

His baptism was a watermark event in the history of the early Christian church. Prior to Cornelius's conversion the Church was Jewish, the males were circumcised and they still observed the Law of Moses.

Cornelius' conversion initiated a debate among the Church leaders in Jerusalem that culminated in the decision that Gentiles could become Christians without having to obey the Jewish requirements for circumcision. Three cheers for Cornelius!

The Message

The angel informed Cornelius his prayers and good works had got God's attention. He was also told to send servants to collect Peter from a certain address in Joppa. Cornelius wasn't told for what purpose he should fetch Peter. Perhaps he'd been praying to get to know God better.

God's Purpose

God was advancing His Kingdom plans and purpose, keeping His promise about blessing all nations through Abraham. God was being proactive in initiating a major worldview change for Jews and Gentiles.

Satan's Purpose

∾

Satan's purpose was to keep God-fearing, charitable Cornelius from hearing the Gospel and from coming to know Jesus and being baptised in the Holy Spirit.

Visionary's Eyes Enlightened

∾

Cornelius' eyes were opened to the fact that God approved of his behaviour and he also knew what to do next.

Visionary's Response and Application

∾

Cornelius is initially fearful but the angel calmed him through revelation and then Cornelius immediately obeyed the angel's instructions and sent for Peter.

Know God Better

∾

God knows our names and addresses, the names of whoever we're with and how we use our money and time. Caring for the poor and needy is a big deal to God. There's a lovely passage in Jeremiah 22 that has God, through Jeremiah, comparing two kings, father and son, Josiah and Jehoiakim.

Jehoiakim was a bad king who ripped off poor people. He's accused of spending his time building cedar houses–cedar being a metaphor for enormous luxury–trying to prove his rank amongst kings. His father Josiah on the other hand was a really good guy. The scripture says King Josiah did what was 'right and just'.

And God says because 'Josiah dispensed justice to the week and the poor it went well with him'. Then God asks, 'Is this not true knowledge of me?' That's an extraordinary comment: knowing God means caring for the poor and the needy.

The passage doesn't say if you know God, you will care for the poor. It doesn't say if you care for the needy you will get to know God. It says caring for the poor and the needy is the act of knowing God.

So, Cornelius like Paul had knowledge of God but now God was bringing salvation through Jesus Christ to him.

The Vision Process

~

This is a literal vision in which an angel dialogues with and instructs Cornelius. It required no interpretation and had enormous significance for Cornelius, his household, Israel and all nations.

The Usual Suspects

~

God speaks to Cornelius through the angel. Jesus is soon to be revealed to Cornelius and Satan's plan to keep God-fearing Cornelius from knowing Jesus and being baptised in His Holy Spirit is thwarted.

Takeaways

~

Men are saved by the foolishness of preaching and not by good works or by supernatural encounters with angels.

Cornelius' prayers and good works got God's attention and opened the door for him to hear the Gospel, the same Gospel rulers and elders of Israel heard in Acts 4 from Peter;

> Jesus is the stone you builders rejected, which has become the cornerstone. Salvation is found in no one else, for there is no other name under heaven given to mankind by which we must be saved.[2]

God is always watching out for good people and will gladly give them the opportunity to hear the gospel concerning Jesus. It's also interesting that salvation didn't just come to Cornelius but to his whole household.

The same thing happened later in Acts with the Philippian jailer who asked Paul and Silas,

> "Sirs, what must I do to be saved?" They replied, "Believe in the Lord Jesus, and you will be saved—you and your household." Then they spoke the word of the Lord to him and to all the others in his house.[3]

God desires household salvation.

It's also interesting God gave both Ananias and Cornelius the address of the people who needed to be contacted. Perhaps we should be more open to this happening more amongst us. It certainly helped the spread of the Gospel.

PETER'S 'KILL AND EAT' TRANCE

The Dream Setting/Backstory

Cornelius' servants were on their way to collect Peter at Simon the Tanner's house as instructed by the angel. It was now God's sovereign time to reveal the ground breaking, world shattering, worldview changing, news of salvation through Jesus Christ to the Gentile nations.

Isaiah had prophesied the Messiah would be a light to the Gentiles.[1] This was always God's will. When Jesus was being circumcised Simeon prophesied God's sovereign will for Jesus' life and ministry. Simeon said,

> Sovereign Lord, as you have promised, you may now dismiss your servant in peace. For my eyes have seen your salvation, which you have prepared in the sight of all nations: a light for revelation to the Gentiles, and the glory of your people Israel.[2]

Jesus' assignment was to bring revelation and salvation to both Jews and Gentiles.

The Trance Scripture
Acts 10:9-23

About noon the following day as they were on their journey and approaching the city, Peter went up on the roof to pray. He became hungry and wanted something to eat, and while the meal was being prepared, he fell into a trance. He saw heaven opened and something like a large sheet being let down to earth by its four corners. It contained all kinds of four-footed animals, as well as reptiles and birds. Then a voice told him, "Get up, Peter. Kill and eat."

"Surely not, Lord!" Peter replied. "I have never eaten anything impure or unclean."

The voice spoke to him a second time, "Do not call anything impure that God has made clean."

This happened three times, and immediately the sheet was taken back to heaven.

While Peter was wondering about the meaning of the vision, the men sent by Cornelius found out where Simon's house was and stopped at the gate. They called out, asking if Simon who was known as Peter was staying there.

While Peter was still thinking about the vision, the Spirit said to him, "Simon, three men are looking for you. So get up and go downstairs. Do not hesitate to go with them, for I have sent them."

Peter went down and said to the men, "I'm the one you're looking for. Why have you come?"

The men replied, "We have come from Cornelius the centurion. He is a righteous and God-fearing man, who is respected by all the Jewish people. A holy angel told him to ask you to come to his house so that he could hear what you have to say." Then Peter invited the men into the house to be his guests.

The Problem

∼

Peter was called to preach to all nations but his theology was hindering him. His racial prejudice and low level revelation were delaying God's plans and purpose.

To Peter and the early believers the notion of Jesus being a light to the Gentiles was an impossible conception. The Gentiles were unclean, even Jesus had called them dogs.[3]

Paul would later say the Gentiles were separate from Christ, excluded from citizenship in Israel and foreigners to the covenants of the promise, without hope and without God in the world.[4]

Peter like many of us had difficulty putting Jesus' instructions into practise. He'd heard Jesus tell His followers to make disciples of all nations but like the rest of the disciples he didn't know how to do this. Like them he thought non-Jews had to be circumcised and practice the Old Testament Law in order to become Jesus' disciples.

Peter's Metron

∼

Peter was a colourful character, a wholehearted man of action totally committed to Jesus and constantly at the forefront of things.

He is always listed first among the Twelve Apostles. He was the first disciple called by Jesus. He was the first to confess Jesus as the Messiah. He was the first to walk upon water. He was the first to perform a miracle. He was the first to enter Jesus' empty tomb. He was the first to explain the baptism of the Holy Spirit.

Along with Paul, God sovereignly chose Peter to take the Gospel to the whole world. Peter's opinion in the early Church's debate about Gentiles being converts was pivotal and crucial. Two New Testament epistles are attributed to Peter. I believe Peter like Moses not only knew the Acts of God but he knew His Ways.[5]

The Message

This vision was given three times. The message was, Do not call anything impure that God has made clean. This referred to non-Jews. The other instruction was, Simon, three men are looking for you. So get up and go downstairs. Do not hesitate to go with them, for I have sent them.

God's Purpose

Around eight years had elapsed since Pentecost and still the disciples were dragging their heels in bringing the Gospel to the Gentiles. So God moved things forward through this vision. Previously God had allowed a persecution and scattering of the Church in Jerusalem so that Philip could go and bring the Gospel to the Samaritans. Through this vision God showed Peter that the dividing wall of partition was now completely broken down between Jew and Gentile.

Satan's Purpose

Satan's purpose was to keep the Apostles locked into low level revelation and thereby hinder them from obeying Jesus' last command. The disciples weren't always able to understand or bear Jesus' revelation. In John 16, Jesus recognising this says,

> I have much more to say to you, more than you can now bear. But when he, the Spirit of truth, comes, he will guide you into all the truth.

Visionary's Eyes Enlightened

Peter's worldview was severely challenged by the angel's rebuke in this vision. Now he was enlightened to the point he knew he should never again call any man common or unclean.

Visionary's Response and Application

Peter wondered about the meaning of some of the vision and obeyed the portion he did understand. He received the men sent from Cornelius and agreed to go with them.

Know God Better

God wants the Gospel preached to all nations. Paul says,

> This is good, and pleases God our Saviour, who wants all people to be saved and to come to a knowledge of the truth. For there is one God and one mediator between God and mankind, the man Christ Jesus, who gave himself as a ransom for all people.[6]

Through this vision God was keeping His covenant promise to Abraham.

The Vision Process

This is a complex symbolic vision interpreted by God through his Holy Spirit using the *Symbol Replacement Method.* The sheet with all kind of animals symbolised Jews, Samaritans and Gentiles. The clean animals represented the Jews and the unclean animals represented the Samaritans and Gentiles. The sheet being let down and pulled up again represented the fact that Jews, Samaritans and Gentiles all come from God and all can return to God through the Gospel of Jesus Christ.

Peter was hungry while the meal was being prepared and just like Jesus with the Samaritan woman at the well there was also an issue of racial prejudice involved. The Samaritan woman said to Jesus,

> You are a Jew and I am a Samaritan woman. How can

you ask me for a drink? For Jews do not associate with Samaritans.[7]

After Jesus ministered to the Samaritan woman his disciples returned and offered him food. Jesus told them, I have food to eat that you know nothing about.[8]

The food Jesus was talking about was the spiritual nourishment received from doing God's will.

When God tells Peter to kill and eat all the animals this similarly symbolises Peter ministering to Jews, Samaritans and Gentiles and receiving the same food Jesus was talking about.

Essentially God was telling Peter it was his duty to preach the Gospel to all people without prejudice. Jews, Samaritans and Gentiles all equally required cleansing from sin.

The Usual Suspects

God is giving Peter more revelation through His Holy Spirit about Jesus while Satan was hindering progress by tying Peter to old racially prejudiced notions.

Takeaways

It's interesting the Scripture identifies the voice speaking to Peter as the Holy Spirit, who has now been poured out.

In Genesis Joseph told Pharaoh,

> The reason the dream was given to Pharaoh in two forms is that the matter has been firmly decided by God, and God will do it soon.[9]

In Peter's trance the vision and the message was given three times which meant God was going to move very soon, which turned out to be the case.

Even though Peter underwent a major worldview change through this vision he'd still continue to struggle with issues of racial discrimination.

When he was in Antioch, he drew back and separated himself from Gentiles because he was afraid of those who belonged to the Jewish circumcision party.[10]

Nevertheless a world-changing breakthrough for God's Kingdom had occurred and the times of the Gentiles had kicked in.

PETER'S REVELATION AT CORNELIUS'S HOUSE

The Setting/Backstory

The Romans then occupying the Promised Land were the fourth beast of *Nebuchadnezzar's Large Statue Dream*. This fact would not have been lost on Peter.

Peter had been called by Jesus to preach the Gospel to all nations but his culture and worldview were hindering him so God gave him a vision that changed his mindset and showed him the next step and the way forward through a Roman soldier's lifestyle and faith.

The Experience Scripture
Acts 10:23-48

The next day Peter started out with them, and some of the believers from Joppa went along. The following day he arrived in Caesarea. Cornelius was expecting them and had called together his relatives and close friends. As Peter entered the house, Cornelius met him and fell at his feet in reverence. But Peter made him get up. "Stand up," he said, "I am only a man myself."

While talking with him, Peter went inside and found a large gathering of people. He said to them: "You are well aware that it is against our law for a Jew to associate with or visit a Gentile. But God has shown me that I should not call anyone impure or unclean. So when I was sent for, I came without raising any objection. May I ask why you sent for me?"

Cornelius answered: "Three days ago I was in my house praying at this hour, at three in the afternoon. Suddenly a man in shining clothes stood before me and said, 'Cornelius, God has heard your prayer and remembered your gifts to the poor. Send to Joppa for Simon who is called Peter. He is a guest in the home of Simon the tanner, who lives by the sea.' So I sent for you immediately, and it was good of you to come. Now we are all here in the presence of God to listen to everything the Lord has commanded you to tell us."

Then Peter began to speak: "I now realise how true it is that God does not show favouritism but accepts from every nation the one who fears him and does what is right. You know the message God sent to the people of Israel, announcing the good news of peace through Jesus Christ, who is Lord of all. You know what has happened throughout the province of Judea, beginning in Galilee after the baptism that John preached— how God anointed Jesus of Nazareth with the Holy Spirit and power, and how he went around doing good and healing all who were under the power of the devil, because God was with him.

"We are witnesses of everything he did in the country of the Jews and in Jerusalem. They killed him by hanging him on a cross, but God raised him from the dead on the third day and caused him to be seen. He was not seen by all the people, but by witnesses whom God had already chosen—by us who ate and drank with him after he rose from the dead. He commanded us to preach to the people and to testify that he is the one whom God appointed as judge of the living and the dead. All the prophets testify about him that everyone who believes in him receives forgiveness of sins through his name."

While Peter was still speaking these words, the Holy Spirit came on all who heard the message. The circumcised believers who had come with Peter were astonished that the gift of the Holy Spirit had been poured out even on Gentiles. For they heard them speaking in tongues and praising God.

Then Peter said, "Surely no one can stand in the way of their being baptised with water. They have received the Holy Spirit just as we have." So he ordered that they be baptised in the name of Jesus Christ. Then they asked Peter to stay with them for a few days.

The Problem

∽

Jesus told His apostles to preach the Gospel to all nations. The problem was, eight years later they were still only preaching to Jews.

Peter's Metron

∽

Peter was a colourful character, a wholehearted man of action totally committed to Jesus and constantly at the forefront of things. He is always listed first among the Twelve Apostles. He was the first disciple called by Jesus. He was the first to confess Jesus as the Messiah. He was the first to walk upon water. He was the first to perform a miracle. He was the first to enter Jesus' empty tomb. He was the first to explain the baptism of the Holy Spirit.

Along with Paul, God sovereignly chose Peter to take the Gospel to the whole world. Peter's opinion in the early Church's debate about Gentiles being converts was pivotal and crucial. Two New Testament epistles are attributed to Peter. I believe Peter like Moses not only knew the Acts of God but he knew His Ways.[1]

The Message

The world changing revelation for Peter and the other Jewish believers was that God was now bringing Gentiles into the kingdom of God through the preaching of the Gospel of Jesus Christ.

God's Purpose

God's promise to Abraham was coming to pass. The nations were being blessed with salvation through Abraham's seed line and the Holy Spirit was being poured out upon all flesh. Habakkuk's prophecy was also coming to pass,

> The earth was being filled with the knowledge of the glory of God as the waters cover the sea.[2]

Satan's Purpose

Satan's purpose was to quarantine the Gospel amongst the Jews and prevent the Gentiles from hearing it.

Peter's Eyes Enlightened

Peter saw and heard the Gentiles receive the Holy Spirit just like he and the other early believers had at Pentecost; they spoke in tongues and prophesied. This experience coupled with his vision of unclean animals forever changed Peter's theology and opened the door for the Gentiles to come to Christ.

Peter's Response and Application

Peter immediately received the Gentile believers as brothers when he heard them speaking in tongues and praising God. He then ordered them to be baptised just as Jesus had said.

Know God Better

God is again seen as a Sovereign Promise Keeper who can change thousands of years of theology in an instant with the use of one vision and one Holy Spirit experience.

The Experience Process

∽

The Jews and the Gentiles were brought together by two visions and an experience. When Peter was finally obedient to Jesus' last command to preach the Gospel to all nations Jesus' immediately kept His promise and baptised them in his Holy Spirit and received them into His Church.

These two visions as the word of God had created faith and expectation in both Peter and Cornelius.

The Usual Suspects

∽

God had shown Peter he should not call anyone impure or unclean. When Jesus was preached as Saviour and the One who destroyed the works of Satan the Holy Spirit fell upon the Gentiles.

Takeaways

∽

God's Eternal Plan that Jesus the Messiah would destroy Satan's work and redeem all humanity was coming to pass and dreams and visions had a part to play in it. In his letter to the Ephesians Paul spoke of a mystery. He said,

> God's hidden mystery was that through the church, the manifold wisdom of God should be made known to the rulers and authorities in the heavenly realms, according to his eternal purpose that he accomplished in Christ Jesus our Lord.[3]

Here Paul is saying that from time immemorial God had predestined Jews and Gentiles who believed in Jesus Christ the Messiah to become the Church, the Body of Christ.

This Bride of Christ would then destroy the works of Satan and take the place vacated by Satan and the fallen angels in the heavenly realms.

PAUL'S 'MAN OF MACEDONIA' NIGHT VISION DREAM

The Setting/Backstory

*J*esus told His disciples to go into all the world and preach the gospel to all creation[1] and Paul is now on his second missionary journey in obedience to Jesus's last command.

But things aren't working out as expected. The Holy Spirit has prevented them from preaching in the province of Asia and Jesus has prevented them from preaching in Bathynia.

The Dream Scripture
Acts 16:6-11

Paul and his companions traveled throughout the region of Phrygia and Galatia, having been kept by the Holy Spirit from preaching the word in the province of Asia. When they came to the border of Mysia, they tried to enter Bithynia, but the Spirit of Jesus would not allow them to. So they passed by Mysia and went down to Troas. During the night Paul had a vision of a man of Macedonia standing and begging him, "Come over to Macedonia and help us." After Paul had seen the vision, we got ready at once to leave for Macedonia, concluding that God had called us to preach the gospel to them.

The Problem

～

The Holy Spirit is enlarging Paul's vision and metron and it's no longer business as usual.

The Dreamer's Metron

～

Paul was a Messianic Jewish-Roman rabbi and writer who'd studied under the revered Pharisee Gamaliel. Paul had a massive metron from God to preach the Gospel of Jesus Christ to all nations.

He was a very bright spark. Peter said, Paul's letters contained some things hard to understand.[2] Paul wrote thirteen of the twenty-seven New Testament books. His life and work takes up half of the book of Acts.

Paul is universally considered to be one of Christianity's most important figures. His influence on Christian thought and practice has been profound and pervasive.

His status as Jewish and a Roman citizen helped him minister to Jewish and Gentile listeners. He was also the founder of various Christian communities in Asia Minor and Europe.

The Message

∼

The message was that Paul should bring his mission over to Macedonia where people needed to hear the Gospel.

God's Purpose

∼

God's purpose was to keep His promise to Abraham to bless all nations, by expanding the Gospel of Jesus Christ to Europe.

Satan's Purpose

∼

Satan's purpose as usual was to limit the Gospel in whatever way he could. Previously he'd managed to keep the Gospel quarantined amongst the Jews for eight years until God moved upon Peter and released it to the Gentiles.

Dreamer's Eyes Enlightened

Paul immediately knew to take the Gospel to Macedonia.

Dreamer's Response and Application

Paul immediately obeyed the revelation.

Know God Better

God was always keeping His promises and advancing His eternal kingdom plans and purpose. He used a night vision dream to do this.

The Dream Process

This is a simple literal dream in which Paul sees a man of Macedonia standing and begging him to come over to Macedonia and help him. It was of great international importance. It meant the Gospel would now explode into Europe.

The Usual Suspects

God moves the Gospel of Jesus forward through His Holy Spirit and no doubt Satan was taking advantage of the initial difficulty over preaching in Asia and Bithynia.

Takeaways

Often when we are experiencing difficulty in knowing how and where to function in ministry it might well be the Holy Spirit directing us into newer and greater fields of opportunity in His eternal purpose. Paul was trying to reach a few cities in his area with the Gospel but God's plan was that he should win an entire continent for Jesus Christ. That is one of the great benefits of dreams. They can give us current up to date instructions and breaking news.

PAUL'S 'FEAR NOT' NIGHT VISION DREAM

The Night Vision Dream Setting/Backstory

God chose Paul to proclaim the Gospel of Jesus Christ to Israel and to the Gentiles and their Kings. To this end, Paul's second missionary journey began in the spring of 49 A.D. Paul had been three years in Antioch when he said to Barnabas, Let us go back and visit the believers in every town where we preached.[1]

This eventually led to a split between Paul and Barnabas resulting in Barnabas and Mark going on a mission to Cyprus and Paul and Silas going their mission through Syria and Cilicia.[2]

During this journey Paul also revisited believers and churches at Derbe in Lycaonia, Lystra in Lycaonia, Iconium in Pisidia and Antioch in Pisidia. From there Paul travelled to Europe and planted churches in Philippi in Macedonia, Thessalonica in Macedonia, Berea in Macedonia and Athens in Greece. Then he came to Corinth where he experienced great opposition.

The Night Vision Dream Scripture
Acts 18:1-11

∼

After this, Paul left Athens and went to Corinth. There he met a Jew named Aquila, a native of Pontus, who had recently come from Italy with his wife Priscilla, because Claudius had ordered all Jews to leave Rome. Paul went to see them, and because he was a tentmaker as they were, he stayed and worked with them. Every Sabbath he reasoned in the synagogue, trying to persuade Jews and Greeks. When Silas and Timothy came from Macedonia, Paul devoted himself exclusively to preaching, testifying to the Jews that Jesus was the Messiah. But when they opposed Paul and became abusive, he shook out his clothes in protest and said to them, "Your blood be on your own heads! I am innocent of it. From now on I will go to the Gentiles." Then Paul left the synagogue and went next door to the house of Titius Justus, a worshiper of God. Crispus, the synagogue leader, and his entire household believed in the Lord; and many of the Corinthians who heard Paul believed and were baptized.

One night the Lord spoke to Paul in a vision: "Do not be afraid; keep on speaking, do not be silent. For I am with you, and no one is going to attack and harm you, because I have many people in this city."

So Paul stayed in Corinth for a year and a half, teaching them the word of God.

The Problem

Just before this night vision Paul was discouraged and in pretty bad shape. Turbulent times in Philippi, small success in Athens, and a general lack of support and friends were taking their toll. Later he would tell the Corinthians, I was with you in weakness and in fear and in much trembling.[3]

The Dreamer's Metron

Paul was a Messianic Jewish-Roman rabbi and writer who'd studied under the revered Pharisee Gamaliel. Paul had a massive metron from God to preach the Gospel of Jesus Christ to all nations.

He was a very bright spark. Peter said, Paul's letters contained some things hard to understand.[4] Paul wrote thirteen of the twenty-seven New Testament books. His life and work takes up half of the book of Acts.

Paul is universally considered to be one of Christianity's most important figures. His influence on Christian thought and practice has been profound and pervasive.

His status as Jewish and a Roman citizen helped him minister to Jewish and Gentile listeners. He was also the founder of various Christian communities in Asia Minor and Europe.

The Message

God told Paul not give way to fear but to keep on preaching. He encouraged Paul by promising to be with him in his ministry. He also revealed Paul would be kept safe because God had many people in Corinth whom Paul wasn't aware of.

God's Purpose

∼

God's purpose was to encourage, protect and strengthen Paul in his ministry and to challenge and expand his vision of the harvest field.

Satan's Purpose

∼

Satan's purpose was to hinder the expansion of the Gospel through fear and discouragement.

Dreamer's Eyes Enlightened

∼

Paul clearly understood God had work for him in Corinth and God would keep him safe and provide for him. Paul was experiencing the reality of Jesus' last words in Matthew,

> All authority in heaven and on earth has been given to me. Therefore go and make disciples of all nations, baptising them in the name of the Father

and of the Son and of the Holy Spirit, and teaching them to obey everything I have commanded you. And surely I am with you always, to the very end of the age.[5]"

Dreamer's Response and Application

∽

Paul obeyed the Lord's instructions. He didn't give way to fear. Rather he stayed in Corinth for a year and a half, teaching the 'many people of God' the word of God. He also wrote 1 and 2 Thessalonians during this fruitful time.

Before this night vision dream Paul was annoyed with the Jews and seemed to be pronouncing desolation upon them. Afterwards he returned to visiting synagogues again. God had opened Paul's heart again to the 'many people.'

Know God Better

∽

Through this incident we're shown God knows what's best in ministry and mission. He's also revealed as being intimately aware of everything happening to His servants. It was God who chose and sent Paul to preach to the Jews and the Gentiles and it is God who is able to keep him on track.

Through this night vision dream we're also shown God is able to guide his ministers to specific people and places for specific amounts of time. God kept Paul in Corinth for a year and a half while he only needed to stay a few days or a few weeks elsewhere. God who knows times and seasons can make us successful in accomplishing His purpose.

The Dream Process

This was a literal night vision dream not requiring an interpretation but requiring obedience. Jesus himself appeared and spoke plainly. The vision had personal, national and international significance.

The Usual Suspects

God sent Jesus to encourage Paul who was being attacked by fear from Satan.

Takeaways

If we carefully listen to and obey God's plans and purpose for our lives and ministries we will be kept safe and on track, ever open to further revelation.

Just before this night vision Paul had rejected Israel but perhaps the night vision helped change his mind. We are reminded of the dejected Elijah in Kings. Elijah like Paul had become battle worn and weary. He had lost perspective. He told God he was the only one left, and now they are trying to kill him too.

God was able to encourage Elijah and instruct him what to do next so God's plans and purpose would go forward. God also explained Elijah was not alone. He revealed there were seven thousand other true believers Elijah had no knowledge of.[6]

Later Paul in his letter to the Romans would write,

> I ask then: Did God reject his people? By no means! I am an Israelite myself, a descendant of Abraham, from the tribe of Benjamin. God did not reject his people, whom he foreknew. Don't you know what Scripture says in the passage about Elijah—how he appealed to God against Israel: "Lord, they have killed your prophets and torn down your altars; I am the only one left, and they are trying to kill me"? And what was God's answer to him? "I have reserved for myself seven thousand who have not bowed the knee to Baal." So too, at the present time there is a remnant chosen by grace.[7]

And there's even better news for Abraham's descendants,

> I do not want you to be ignorant of this mystery, brothers and sisters, so that you may not be conceited: Israel has experienced a hardening in part until the full number of the Gentiles has come in, and in this way all Israel will be saved. As it is written: The deliverer will come from Zion; he will turn godlessness away from Jacob. And this is my covenant with them when I take away their sins.[8]

PAUL'S 'ANGELIC' NIGHT VISION DREAM

The Dream Setting/Backstory

In 62 A.D. Paul and some other prisoners were being taken to Rome on a ship. The Scripture says,

> Much time had been lost, and sailing had already become dangerous because by now it was after the Day of Atonement.[1]

Paul shared a word of knowledge with the leaders; Men, I can see that our voyage is going to be disastrous and bring great loss to ship and cargo, and to our own lives also.[2] But the centurion Julius disregarded Paul's prophecy, set sail and soon found himself in stormy waters.

The Night Vision Dream Scripture

Acts 27:20-25

~

When neither sun nor stars appeared for many days and the storm continued raging, we finally gave up all hope of being saved. After they had gone a long time without food, Paul stood up before them and said: "Men, you should have taken my advice not to sail from Crete; then you would have spared yourselves this damage and loss. But now I urge you to keep up your courage, because not one of you will be lost; only the ship will be destroyed. Last night an angel of the God to whom I belong and whom I serve stood beside me and said, 'Do not be afraid, Paul. You must stand trial before Caesar; and God has graciously given you the lives of all who sail with you.' So keep up your courage, men, for I have faith in God that it will happen just as he told me. Nevertheless, we must run aground on some island."

The Problem

~

The centurion Julius had disregarded God's word through Paul and now God's plans and purpose are under threat.

The Dreamer's Metron

~

Paul was a Messianic Jewish-Roman rabbi and writer who'd studied under the revered Pharisee Gamaliel. Paul had a massive metron from God to preach the Gospel of Jesus Christ to all nations.

He was a very bright spark. Peter said, Paul's letters contained some things hard to understand.[3] Paul wrote thirteen of the twenty-seven New Testament books. His life and work takes up half of the book of Acts.

Paul is universally considered to be one of Christianity's most important figures. His influence on Christian thought and practice has been profound and pervasive.

His status as Jewish and a Roman citizen helped him minister to Jewish and Gentile listeners. He was also the founder of various Christian communities in Asia Minor and Europe.

The Message

God's message to Paul was, Do not be afraid, Paul. You must stand trial before Caesar; and God has graciously given you the lives of all who sail with you.

God's Purpose

God's purpose was to encourage and equip Paul in order to deal with the situation because God still had much work for Paul to do.

Satan's Purpose

Satan's purpose was to kill Paul and stop him from fulfilling his life's calling. He was using an unbelieving leader to do this.

Dreamer's Eyes Enlightened

Paul now knew God would bring him safe to Rome and also spare the other 275 people on board ship.

Dreamer's Response and Application

Paul boldly declared the words from the angel in order to encourage everyone and to instruct Julius in order to prevent the sailors from rebelliously escaping. He was also able to persuade everyone to eat in order to survive the shipwreck.

Know God Better

God was keeping His promises to Paul. He was also willing to bless many others through His servant's obedience. The presence of one listening believer amongst 276 people saved everyone's life.

The Dream Process

∽

This was a literal message for Paul with great personal significance for those travelling with him. It had great international importance for God's Kingdom.

The Usual Suspects

∽

God's prophetic work destroys the work of Satan and allows the Gospel of Jesus Christ to go forward.

Takeaways

∽

Paul was aware he was walking in the midst of God's timing and God's great plans and purpose for humanity. He clearly shows this when he writes to his disciple Timothy,

> So do not be ashamed of the testimony about our Lord or of me his prisoner. Rather, join with me in suffering for the gospel, by the power of God. He has saved us and called us to a holy life—not because of anything we have done but because of his own purpose and grace. This grace was given us in Christ Jesus before the beginning of time, but it has now been revealed through the appearing of

our Saviour, Christ Jesus, who has destroyed death and has brought life and immortality to light through the gospel. And of this gospel I was appointed a herald and an apostle and a teacher. That is why I am suffering as I am. Yet this is no cause for shame, because I know whom I have believed, and am convinced that he is able to guard what I have entrusted to him until that day.[4]

APOCRYPHAL DREAMS

EGYPT'S 'DREADFUL DREAMS'

Note

The Wisdom of Solomon is one of the Apocryphal books, also called Deuterocanonical books of the Bible. Early Judaism treasured the Apocryphal scriptures but didn't accept them into the Hebrew Bible. The early Christian church also cherished these Apocryphal writings, but also believed they shouldn't be in the canon of Scripture.

Although the New Testament quotes from the Old Testament hundreds of times, it never quotes from any of the books of the Apocrypha. The Wisdom of Solomon is accepted as Scripture by the Roman Catholic and Orthodox Church traditions, but rejected in the Protestant Scriptures.

The Dream Setting/Backstory

Pharaoh had stubbornly refused to let the children of Israel leave Egypt and he and his people had suffered much because of this. But now in God's perfect will, as prophesied to Abraham, Israel's 400 years of slavery are finished, and it was time to let God's people go. So, God unleashed the final plague, the death of the Egyptian firstborn.

The Dream Scripture
The Wisdom of Solomon 18:17-19

Then at once apparitions in dreadful dreams greatly troubled them, and unexpected fears assailed them; and one here and another there, hurled down half dead, made known why they were dying; for the dreams that disturbed them forewarned them of this, so that they might not perish without knowing why they suffered.

The Problem

Time after time God had warned Pharaoh to let God's chosen people leave Egypt but time after time Pharaoh refused.

The Dreamers' Metrons

Most Egyptian firstborn sons probably knew nothing about the spiritual battle raging in the heavenly realm and were totally ignorant of why they were being killed. Much like the 1.5 billion children recently lost to abortion in our modern world they hadn't a clue it was because of bad leadership. The scripture says the whole nation was deluded by magic.[1]

The Message

The dream messages explained to each individual why they were suffering death.

God's Purpose

God's primary purpose was to fulfil His covenantal promise to Abraham and further His plans and purpose for Israel and the coming Messiah. He was also telling the Egyptian firstborn sons the reason why they were dying; for the dreams that disturbed them forewarned them of this, so that they might not perish without knowing why they suffered.

Satan's Purpose

Satan's purpose was to keep the chosen people as slaves in Egypt.

Dreamer's Eyes Enlightened

∼

They understood why they were being punished.

Dreamer's Response and Application

∼

It seems there was nothing the dreamers could do. The time for repentance was over. These dreams were for information only.

Know God Better

∼

God is a God of justice. Psalm 98:9 says God is coming to judge everyone on the earth, and he will be honest and fair.

Through these horrible dreams God broke the delusions of the magic of Egypt over the people and explained exactly why they were suffering.

This incident is a type of *The Great White Throne Judgement*[2] at the end of the millennium when unbelievers whose names are not written in the *Lamb's Book of Life* will be judged openly and fairly to correctly determine their degree of punishment in the lake of fire.

The Dream Process

∼

We're not told what the dream process was. We do know they were dreadful, fearful, troubling dreams that explained why they were suffering and dying.

The Usual Suspects

God sent the dreams to explain why they were dying. Satan was evident in the magic that had deluded the whole nation. Jesus was in the seed line of God's people who were being freed.

Takeaways

Chapter seventeen of *The Wisdom of Solomon*[3] describes the awful terror that gripped the Egyptians on the night of the death of their firstborn. Scripture says, They perished in trembling fear, the delusions of their magic art lay humbled, and their boasted wisdom was scornfully rebuked.

Chapter eighteen[4] says the Egyptians are being punished for the multitude of Israeli children they cruelly murdered at Pharaoh's command.

Chapter eighteen[5] also says the Egyptians disbelieved everything because of their magic arts but turned to acknowledge Israel as God's people when they saw their first born children dead.

God further enlightened them by giving the Egyptians dreadful dreams so they might know why they were suffering this dreadful plague.

ESDRAS' EAGLE AND LION' DREAM

The Dream Setting/Backstory

As is typical of apocalyptic literature, the author of 2 Esdras expresses his grief at Israel's distress and the state of the world while he hears from God and encounters an angel.

Esdras' tone reminds us of the weeping prophet Jeremiah and the complaining prophet Habakkuk; How long, Lord, must I call for help, but you do not listen?[1]

Esdras also complains about God's promises to Israel not coming to pass. Throughout the book he questions God's plans and purpose in creation, the choice of Israel and world history in general.

The Dream Scripture
2 Esdras 11 & 12 Common English Bible (CEB)

On the second night I had a dream. I saw an eagle, with twelve feathered wings and three heads, rising up from the sea. As I looked, it spread its wings over the whole earth, and all the winds of heaven blew toward it, and the clouds gathered around it. Out of its wings grew opposing wings. These became small, tiny wings. Its heads were at rest. The middle head was larger than the other heads, but it was also at rest with them.

I kept looking and saw the eagle flying with its wings to rule over the earth and over those who lived on the earth. I saw how everything under heaven was made to submit to it, and no one opposed it, not a single creature that lives on the earth. I looked and saw the eagle rise on its talons and call out to its wings, saying, "Don't all watch together. Let each one sleep in its place and take turns watching, but the heads will be kept for the end." I looked and saw that the voice didn't come from its heads but from the middle of its body. I counted its opposing wings, and there were eight of them.

A wing arose on the right side, and it ruled over the whole earth; and while it was ruling, it came to an end and disappeared so that its place vanished. The next one rose up and ruled, and it held sway a long time. While it was exercising its rule, it came to its end, so that it disappeared like the previous one.

Then a voice rang out, saying to this wing, "Listen, you who have held sway over the earth all this time. I announce this to you before you begin to disappear. No one after you will hold sway as long a time—not even half as long." A third wing raised itself up, and it also exercised rulership like the previous ones, and it too disappeared. And so it happened to each of the wings in turn, to come to power and then never to be seen again. I looked, and indeed the wings that followed on the right side also rose up in time so that they too might rule, but some of those who came to power disappeared immediately, while others of them rose up but didn't succeed in establishing their rule. After all this, I looked again, and the twelve wings and two of the little wings had disappeared. Nothing remained on the body of the eagle except the three heads that were at rest and six little wings.

I looked and noticed that two of the six little wings were set apart and remained under the head on the right side, but four remained in their place. I watched as these little wings plotted to rise up and take power. One was raised up, but it immediately disappeared, and then a second, but this one disappeared more quickly than the previous one. I saw the two that were left plotting among themselves that they too should rule, and while they were making their plans, one of the heads that had been at rest, the one in the middle, woke up. This one was bigger than the other two heads. I saw how it formed a partnership with the two other heads, and then how the head turned with those that were with it, and it ate the two little wings that had planned to rule. Moreover, this head gained power over the whole earth and dominated those who lived on it, inflicting great distress. It had greater power over the whole world than all the wings that had gone before.

After all this, I watched as the middle head, just like the wings, suddenly disappeared. There were two heads left, however, which also ruled over the earth and over those who live on it. I looked and watched as the head on the right side devoured the one on the left. I heard a voice saying to me, "Look in front of you and consider what you see." I looked and saw something like a lion being roused, roaring out of the forest. I heard how he spoke in a human voice and said to the eagle, "Listen, you, and I will speak to you. The Most High says to you, 'Aren't you the last of the four beasts that I made to rule in my world so that I might bring about the end of my times through them? You, the fourth that has come, conquered all the beasts that came before you, ruling over the world with much terror and over the whole world with harsh oppression. You have lived in the world with deceit for so long! You judged the earth, but not in truth, for you have oppressed the meek and injured those who caused no unrest. You hated those who spoke the truth and loved liars. You destroyed the dwellings of those who bore fruit and tore down the walls of those who had done you no harm. Your insolence has ascended to the Most High and your pride to the mighty one. The Most High has reviewed his times. Look! They are finished, and his ages are complete. Therefore, eagle, you must utterly vanish, you and your terrifying wings, your dreadful little wings and your evil heads, and your dreadful talons and all your worthless body. Then the whole earth will be refreshed and restored, set free from your violence, and will hope for the judgment and mercy of him who made it.'"

While the lion was saying these words to the eagle, I looked and saw that the head that had prevailed disappeared, and the two wings that had gone over to it rose up so that they might rule, but their rule was weak and chaotic. I watched as they disappeared, and the whole body of the eagle was burned; the earth was filled with fear.

I woke up because my mind was racing and full of fear. I said to myself, Look, you've brought all this on yourself with your probing into the ways of the Most High. Look here! I'm emotionally exhausted and barely alive. I don't have even a little strength left in me because of the great fear that has shaken me this night. Now, therefore, I will pray to the Most High that he may strengthen me to the end. I said, "Supreme Lord, if you do look upon me favourably, if you consider me to be among the more righteous, and if my prayer has indeed risen into your presence, strengthen me, and show me, your servant, the interpretation and meaning of this terrible vision. Console my soul, since you have thought me worthy to be shown the end of times and the last events of the times."

He said to me, "This is the interpretation of the vision that you saw. The eagle you saw rising from the sea is the fourth kingdom. It appeared in a vision to your brother Daniel, but it wasn't interpreted for him as I now interpret it for you or have shown it to you. Look, the days are coming when a kingdom will rise on earth that will be more terrifying than all the kingdoms that came before it. Twelve kings will rule in it, one after the other. The second one to rule will have a longer time than the rest of the twelve. This then is the interpretation of the twelve wings that you saw. As for the fact that you heard a voice that spoke, coming not from its heads but from the middle of its body, this is the interpretation: In the midst of this kingdom's time, great conflicts will arise. It will be in danger of falling; it won't fall then but will be restored again to its beginning.

"As for the fact that you saw eight little wings clinging to its wings, this is the interpretation: Eight kings will arise in it. Their rules will amount to nothing, and their years will be swift. Two of them will perish when the middle of the time draws near, but four will be reserved until the time approaches for its end. Two will be preserved until the very end.

"As for the fact that you saw three heads at rest, this is the interpretation: In the last period the Most High will raise up three kings, and he will renew many things in it, and they will rule the earth and greatly oppress those who dwell on it, more than all the rest who were before them. Therefore, they are called the heads of the eagle, because they will sum up its acts of impiety and complete its last deeds.

"As for your seeing the biggest head disappear, one of the kings will die on his bed, though in agonies. As to the two who are left, the sword will destroy them. The sword of one of them will destroy the one who is with him, but he too will fall by the sword in the last days.

"As for your seeing the two small wings passing over to the head on the right, this is the interpretation: The Most High is keeping these for the eagle's end. This rule will be weak and full of upheaval, as you saw. The lion whom you saw rousing itself from the forest and roaring and speaking to the eagle and rebuking it for its deeds of injustice, as for all the words that you heard him speaking, this is the anointed one. The Most High has kept him for the end of days. He will arise from the line of David, and he will come and speak to them. He will denounce their wicked acts and indict them for their injustice. He will set before them their despicable deeds. He will put them on trial while they are still alive, and after he has convicted them, he will destroy them. Yet he will mercifully liberate the remaining few from my people who are saved throughout my territory. He will make them joyful until the end comes—the Judgment Day, of which I have spoken to you from the beginning.

"This is the dream that you saw, and this is its interpretation. You alone were counted worthy to know this secret of the Most High. Therefore, write all these things that you saw in a scroll and hide it away. Teach these matters to the wise among your people, whose minds you know can grasp and keep these secrets. But wait here yet another seven days so that you may be shown whatever it pleases the Most High to show you." Then he left me.

When the whole people heard that seven days had passed and I hadn't returned to the city, they all gathered, from the smallest to the biggest. They came and said to me, "How have we sinned against you? What wrong did we do to you that you abandon us and sit in this place? You are the only one of all the prophets left to us, like a cluster of grapes from the vineyard, and like a lamp in a dark place, and like a harbor for a ship saved from a storm. Or are the disasters that have befallen us not enough for us? If you abandon us now, it would have been better for us to have been burned up along with Zion! We are no better than those who died there." They wept with a loud voice.

I answered them: "Have confidence, Israel! Don't be sad, house of Jacob. The Most High keeps you in memory. The mighty one hasn't forgotten you in your struggle. I haven't abandoned you, nor have I gone away from you. I came to this place to pray because of Zion's desolation, in order to seek mercy for the humiliation of your sanctuary. Now go home, each of you, and I will come to you in a few days." So the people went into the city as I told them, but I sat in the field for seven days as he had commanded me, and I ate only the flowers that grew in the field, and plants were my food in those days.

The Problem

∼

The prophet Esdras also know as Ezra is distressed over the destruction of Zion. He asks why evil Babylon prospers while God's chosen people languish. He wants to know when will God's covenant promises to Israel come to pass?

The Dreamer's Metron

∼

Ezra was a priest and a scribe skilled in the law. When he returned from Babylon to help build up Jerusalem he found God's people were generally living in sin and had intermarried with pagan women. He began calling them back to God's written word and the true worship of God. He challenged the mixed marriages and convinced the people to divorce their foreign wives voluntarily.

He then had the people make a solemn covenant before God to

avoid future mixed marriages and to refrain from working on the Sabbath. He also challenged the people in their financial responsibility to the work of God.

Ezra helped make Judaism a religion in which the law was central. This has allowed the Jews to survive as a community over thousands of years of persecution. Because of this Ezra has been called the father of Judaism and later tradition regarded him like a second Moses.

The Message

God has not forgotten His people. At an appointed time the Messiah will arrive on the scene. The rule of the Roman Empire will end and the righteous remnant of God's people will be saved.

God's Purpose

God's purpose was to answer Ezra's questions and bring peace and perspective to the situation. He also wanted Ezra to write all he saw in a scroll, hide it away and teach these matters to those wise and capable of understanding and keeping those secrets.

Satan's Purpose

Satan's purpose was to discourage Ezra and the people of God.

Dreamer's Eyes Enlightened

∼

Ezra was enlightened to realise God hadn't forgotten his chosen people and their struggles. He was also instructed what to do next.

Dreamer's Response and Application

∼

Ezra awoke from his dream fearful and emotionally exhausted. He was anxious he might have been too forward in questioning God. He asked God to strengthen him and give him the dream's interpretation.

After the interpretation Ezra was obedient to God's instructions to wait where he was for seven days. He was also obedient to write the vision and instruct certain capable people. He also encouraged the people by telling them God was still keeping His promises to Abraham and his descendants.

Know God Better

∼

Despite all outward circumstances God is working His plans and purpose out and is totally aware of times and seasons. He rises up kings and sets down kings. He is well aware of the *Game of Thrones* taking place amongst the gods and is still keeping His covenant promises to Abraham.

The Dream Process

This is a complex symbolic dream requiring interpretation. God personally interprets Ezra's dream using *The Symbol Replacement Method* used by Jesus when he interpreted the *Parable of the Sower*. Jesus simply replaced each symbol in the parable with its symbolic meaning.

The sower became the preacher, the seed became the word of God, the birds of the air represented Satan, the stony ground represented a hard heart and so on.

Similarly here, the Eagle represents the Roman Empire; the fourth kingdom of Nebuchadnezzar's 'Large Statue' Dream interpreted by Daniel.

The twelve wings and three heads represent various emperors. The eagle/Roman Empire rules both Gentiles and God's chosen people until a lion, representing the Messiah, arrives and destroys the eagle/Roman Empire.

Then the righteous remnant of God's chosen people are saved through God's mercy. This was the same method of interpretation Mordecai used in his *Two Dragons Dream*. The dream has personal, national and international significance.

The Usual Suspects

God shows Ezra that He is in total control over all the powers and principalities that dare attack His chosen people. Jesus is there in the guise of the lion from the line of David and Satan is the one being judged.

Takeaways

∼

This visionary prediction of historical events culminates in promises of divine intervention, Messianic rule and the final judgment, with vindication for the righteous.

ESDRAS 'MAN FROM THE SEA' DREAM

The Dream Setting/Backstory

After interpreting his *Eagle and Lion Dream,* God told Ezra to stay where he was and await further instructions.

The Dream Scripture
2 Esdras 13:1-57 Common English Bible (CEB)

After seven days, I had a dream during the night. I looked and saw a wind rising from the sea and stirring up all its waves. As I watched, this wind made something like the figure of a man come up out of the heart of the sea. That man was flying among the clouds of heaven. Wherever he turned his face to look, everything that fell under his gaze trembled. Wherever an utterance came from his mouth, all who heard his voice melted as wax melts when it feels the fire.

I kept watching these things, and an innumerable multitude of people came together from the four winds of heaven to fight against the man who had come up from the sea. I watched as he carved a great mountain for himself and flew onto it. I tried to see the region or place from which the mountain was carved, but I couldn't.

After this I looked and I saw that all who had gathered to do battle against him were sorely afraid, yet they dared to fight. When he saw the rush of the multitude coming, he didn't raise his hand or hold a spear or any weapon of war. Rather, I saw something like a wave of fire shoot forth from his mouth, and a breath of flame from his lips, and a storm of sparks from his tongue. All these things—the wave of fire, the breath of flame, and the mighty storm—mixed together and fell upon the crowd that was rushing forward, prepared to fight. It burned them all up so that suddenly nothing was seen of the innumerable mob except the dust of ashes and the smell of smoke. I saw this and was amazed.

After these things I saw the same man coming down from the mountain and calling to himself another crowd—a peaceful one. Many people came to him. Some were rejoicing and some were sad, some were even tied up, while some were bringing other people as an offering.

I woke up in great fear and pleaded with the Most High. I said, "From the beginning you showed your servant these wonders, and you considered me worthy that you should receive my prayer. Now show me also the interpretation of this dream. As I turn it over in my mind, I think: How terrible it will be for those who will be left in those days, and how much worse for those who aren't left! Those who aren't left will be full of sorrow, since they now know what lies in store for the last days, but they won't live to see them. But how terrible it will be also for those who are left, for that very reason! They will see great dangers, and there will be many kinds of distress, as these dreams show. Yet it is better to encounter these things, even incurring danger, than to pass from the world like a cloud and not see what happens at the end.

He answered me, I will tell you the interpretation of the dream as well, and I will explain to you the things you spoke about. As to what you said about those who are left, this is the interpretation: He who brings the danger at that time will himself guard those who fall into danger, who have works and faith in the most mighty one. Know, therefore, that those who are left enjoy greater privilege than those who have died. The interpretations of the vision are as follows:

In that you saw a man going up from the heart of the sea, that is the one whom the Most High has been keeping for many ages. He will liberate God's creation all by himself, and he will put in order those who are left.

In that you saw something like wind and fire and storm go out of his mouth, and that he didn't hold a spear or weapon of war, yet destroyed the rush of that multitude that had come to fight him, here is the interpretation: Look, the days are coming when the Most High will begin to rescue those who are on the earth. Those who live on earth will go out of their minds. They will plan to wage war against each other, city against city, place against place, nation against nation, and kingdom against kingdom. When these things happen, and the signs that I showed you before take place, then my Son will be revealed, whom you saw as a man rising up. When all the nations hear his voice, then each one will leave its own region and will leave off the wars they were waging against each other. An innumerable mob will be gathered together, as you saw, wanting to come and fight against him. But he will take his stand on the summit of Mount Zion. Zion will come and will appear to all, built and ready, as you saw a mountain carved without hands. My Son himself will indict the assembled nations for their impious deeds—these things were indicated by the storm. He will scold them for their evil plans and reveal the torments with which they are about to be tortured. These things correspond to the flame. He will destroy them without effort by the Law, which was indicated by the fire.

As to the fact that you saw him collecting to himself another peaceful multitude, these are the ten tribes that were taken captive from their land in the days of King Hoshea, whom King Shalmaneser of the Assyrians took across the river as a captive. They were taken into another land, but they made this plan for themselves: They would leave the multitude of the nations and go into a more remote region, where the human race had never lived. There they would be able to observe their customs, which they hadn't kept in their own region. They went in through the narrow passages of the Euphrates River. Then the Most High gave them signs and stopped the flow of the river until they had passed. They made a long journey through that region for a year and a half, and that region is called Arzareth. They lived there until the last time, and now they begin again to return. The Most High will once again stop the flow of the river so that they can cross. These people make up the multitude gathered in peace, along with those who are left of your people, who are found within my holy boundaries. Then when he begins to destroy the multitude of the nations that are gathered, he will protect the people who have survived. Then he will show them many more signs.

I said, Supreme Lord, show me why I saw a man rising up from the heart of the sea.

He said to me, Just as no one can seek out or know what is in the depth of the sea, so no one on earth can see my Son or those who are with him, except in that time when his day has come. This is the interpretation of the dream that you saw, which has enlightened you alone of all people. You have abandoned your own affairs and occupied yourself with mine, and you have sought out my Law. You have given your life to wisdom, and have called understanding your mother. Because of this, I have shown you these things, for you have a reward with the Most High. After three days I will tell you more and explain to you weighty and wonderful things.

I went out from there into a large field, glorifying and praising the Most High for the wonders he performed over time, and because he governs the times and all that comes about in its time. I stayed there for three days.

The Problem

~

Ezra, doing what he was told, was patiently awaiting further revelation from God.

The Dreamer's Metron

~

Ezra was a priest and a scribe skilled in the law. When he returned from Babylon to help build up Jerusalem he found God's people were generally living in sin and had intermarried with pagan women. He began calling them back to God's written word and the true worship of God. He challenged the mixed marriages and convinced the people to divorce their foreign wives voluntarily.

He then had the people make a solemn covenant before God to avoid future mixed marriages and to refrain from working on the Sabbath. He also challenged the people in their financial responsibility to the work of God.

Ezra helped make Judaism a religion in which the law was central. This has allowed the Jews to survive as a community over thousands of tears of persecution. Because of this Ezra has been called the father of Judaism and later tradition regarded him like a second Moses.

The Message

The Messiah will come and slay all His enemies with His powerful words. He will gather the ten lost tribes of Israel and a remnant of Israel will be saved.

God's Purpose

God's purpose was to encourage and instruct Ezra and the descendants of Abraham and to calm their fears. Although the Messiah will cause great turmoil;

> He who brings the danger at that time will himself guard those who fall into danger, who have works and faith in the most mighty one.[1]

God also answers Ezra's burning question. He says,

> Know, therefore, that those who are left enjoy greater privilege than those who have died.[2]

Satan's Purpose

Satan's purpose was to discourage Ezra and the people of God.

Dreamer's Eyes Enlightened

God told Ezra only he was enlightened and privileged by the interpretation because he had abandoned his own affairs and occupied himself with God's affairs. Consequently he was shown these things as a reward from God.

Ezra praises God for this revelation as did Daniel after God had revealed Nebuchadnezzar's forgotten dream to him;

> Praise be to the name of God for ever and ever;
> wisdom and power are his. He changes times and seasons; he deposes kings and raises up others. He gives wisdom to the wise and knowledge to the discerning. He reveals deep and hidden things; he knows what lies in darkness, and light dwells with him.[3]

Dreamer's Response and Application

Once again Ezra wakens up fearful and asks God for an interpretation. He ponders the fate of humanity when the Messiah will come and speculates whether it'd be better to be dead or alive by then.

He ended up glorifying and praising God because of his great power and wisdom. Like the Psalmist he realised, It is God who judges: He brings one down, he exalts another.[4]

Ezra also obeyed God and stayed put for three days as instructed.

Know God Better

∽

Again God is seen as a purposeful all knowing God who keeps covenant with Abraham and his descendants. We also see a God who is willing to have a meaningful dialogue with and share revelation with His servant.

The Dream Process

∽

This again is a complex symbolic dream interpreted by God using the *Symbol Replacement Method.* The man from the sea with the clouds of heaven who will liberate God's creation is God's son the Messiah.

The multitudes are the troubled nations who will reject the Messiah. The great mountain carved without hands is Mount Zion from where the Messiah will rule and destroy His enemies.

The peaceful multitude are the ten lost tribes of Israel, lost after Solomon failed to obey God's warning dream. The dream is of personal, national and international importance.

The Usual Suspects

◆

God sends this dream and afterwards answers Ezra's questions. The Man from the heart of the sea is Jesus. Satan is seen in the great multitude who fight against the Messiah.

Takeaways

◆

This dream left Ezra glorifying and praising the Most High. This reminds us of the Virgin Mary's joyful response when she realised she was pregnant with the Messiah. She proclaimed,

> He has performed mighty deeds with his arm; he has scattered those who are proud in their inmost thoughts. He has brought down rulers from their thrones but has lifted up the humble. He has filled the hungry with good things but has sent the rich away empty. He has helped his servant Israel, remembering to be merciful to Abraham and his descendants forever, just as he promised our ancestors.[5]

We also learn revelation is often a reward for those who have set aside their own concerns to be busy about God's plans and purpose.

MORDECAI'S 'TWO GREAT DRAGONS' DREAM

The Dream Setting/Backstory

Mordecai was a Jew from the tribe of Benjamin. His great-grandfather Kish had been taken captive to Babylon under King Nebuchadnezzar. Mordecai now served in the King Ahasuerus court in Persia.

He had an archenemy, an Amalekite, named Haman, who hated God's chosen people. Haman had recently been promoted to the powerful position of prime minister.

Mordecai was also a diligent and loving father figure to his young cousin Esther who had lost both parents. Under his care Esther grew up to be a woman of wisdom, tact, humility and grace, qualities fitting for a queen.

The Dream Scriptures
Esther 11:2-12 & 12:1-6 (Addition A) (NRSVCE)

Esther 10:4-13 (Addition F) (NRSVCE)

In the second year of the reign of Ahasuerus the Great, on the first day of Nisan, Mordecai son of Jair son of Shimei son of Kish, of the tribe of Benjamin, had a dream. He was a Jew living in the city of Susa, a great man, serving in the court of the king. He was one of the captives whom King Nebuchadnezzar of Babylon had brought from Jerusalem with King Jeconiah of Judah. And this was his dream: Noises and confusion, thunders and earthquake, tumult on the earth! Then two great dragons came forward, both ready to fight, and they roared terribly. At their roaring every nation prepared for war, to fight against the righteous nation. It was a day of darkness and gloom, of tribulation and distress, affliction and great tumult on the earth! And the whole righteous nation was troubled; they feared the evils that threatened them, and were ready to perish. Then they cried out to God; and at their outcry, as though from a tiny spring, there came a great river, with abundant water; light came, and the sun rose, and the lowly were exalted and devoured those held in honour.

Mordecai saw in this dream what God had determined to do, and after he awoke he had it on his mind, seeking all day to understand it in every detail.

Now Mordecai took his rest in the courtyard with Bigthan and Teresh, the two eunuchs of the king who kept watch in the courtyard. He overheard their conversation and inquired into their purposes, and learned that they were preparing to lay hands on King Ahasuerus; and he informed the king concerning them. Then the king examined the two eunuchs, and after they had confessed it, they were led away to execution. The king made a permanent record of these things, and Mordecai wrote an account of them. And the king ordered Mordecai to serve in the court, and rewarded him for these things. But Haman son of Hammedatha, the Agagite, who was in great honor with the king, determined to injure Mordecai and his people because of the two eunuchs of the king.

Esther 11:2-12 & 12:1-6 (Addition A) (NRSVCE)

Mordecai's Dream Fulfilled

And Mordecai said, "These things have come from God; for I remember the dream that I had concerning these matters, and none of them has failed to be fulfilled. There was the little spring that became a river, and there was light and sun and abundant water—the river is Esther, whom the king married and made queen. The two dragons are Haman and myself. The nations are those that gathered to destroy the name of the Jews. And my nation, this is Israel, who cried out to God and was saved. The Lord has saved his people; the Lord has rescued us from all these evils; God has done great signs and wonders, wonders that have never happened among the nations. For this purpose he made two lots, one for the people of God and one for all the nations, and these two lots came to the hour and moment and day of decision before God and among all the nations. And God remembered his people and vindicated his inheritance. So they will observe these days in the month of Adar, on the fourteenth and fifteenth of that month, with an assembly and joy and gladness before God, from generation to generation forever among his people Israel."

Esther 10:4-13 (Addition F) (NRSVCE)

The Problem

∼

God's chosen people were under threat of extinction from Haman. This put God's plans and purpose in jeopardy.

The Dreamer's Metron

∼

Mordecai was a God fearing Jew from the tribe of Benjamin who wouldn't bow down to God's enemies. He was also the fatherly guardian of his orphaned cousin Hadassah who under his tutelage and wise counsel became Queen Esther of Persia, the wife of King Ahasuerus.

Mordecai served within the king's gate and in this position managed to expose a plot against Ahasuerus' life. Although his actions were recorded, Mordecai was not initially rewarded.

Mordecai boldly challenged his niece to stand up and fulfil her role in God's plans and purpose and in so doing help save the nation of Israel. He told Esther,

> Do not think that because you are in the king's house you alone of all the Jews will escape. For if you remain silent at this time, relief and deliverance for the Jews will arise from another place, but you and your father's family will perish. And who knows but that you have come to your royal position for such a time as this?[1]

The Message

The basic message was, Because God's people cried out for help God responded and raised Esther up to be their deliverer.

God's Purpose

God's purpose was to warn, instruct and equip Mordecai in order to preserve the Jewish nation.

Satan's Purpose

Satan's purpose was to use Haman to destroy the Jewish nation and so prevent the coming of the Messiah.

Dreamer's Eyes Enlightened

Mordecai knew there was a fierce attack coming against God's people. He also knew the people would pray and God would rise up a deliverer. We don't know if he fully realised the important roles he and Esther would play in the battle. God also put Mordecai into a favourable position with King Ahasuerus.

Dreamer's Response and Application

∼

Mordecai took the dream seriously and diligently remembered it. He also purposefully and prayerfully spent all day seeking to understand every detail of the dream.

Know God Better

∼

The promise keeping God was still keeping His covenant with Abraham. In this dream God once again demonstrated His dominion over the gods who would attack his Covenant People and their seed line.

In fact all three main important purposes for God's Bible dreams are evident in this dream. God demonstrated His sovereign dominion over the powers and principalities attacking His covenant people and their seed line.

He also encouraged and guided His Covenant People with specific direction for their well-being and the safety of their seed line and He also prevented kings and leaders from harming His covenant people and their seed line and He caused them instead to bless His people.

The Dream Process

∼

This is a complex symbolic dream requiring interpretation. Mordecai pondered the dream symbols and realised a fierce attack was being launched against God's people. He also knew God would rise up a deliverer in answer to prayer. We don't know if he initially realised the important roles he and Esther would play.

Afterwards he remembered the dream and realised all the details had been fulfilled. Then it all made sense.

The two dragons were Mordecai and Haman and the two sides were Israel and those who wanted to destroy them. When God's people cried out for help God raised up Esther as a deliverer. She was the little spring that became a river. She was the exalted lowly one raised up to devour those held in honour.

The dream has personal, national and international significance.

The Usual Suspects

∽

God's chosen people and the seed line of Jesus were under threat by Satan symbolised by Haman.

Takeaways

∽

Once more God uses a dream to save his covenant people and preserve the Messiah's bloodline. Mordecai pondered the dream all day and finally understood it's full confirmation afterwards. He appeared to be using *The Symbol Replacement Method* used by Jesus when he interpreted the *Parable of the Sower*. Jesus simply replaced each symbol in the parable with its symbolic meaning. Jesus basically said the *Parable of the Sower* shows us the technique to interpret all parables.

Like Mordecai in this dream Jesus simply replaced each symbol in the parable with its symbolic meaning. The sower became the preacher, the seed became the word of God, the birds of the air represented Satan, the stony ground was a hard heart and so on.

Mordecai uses the same method of interpretation, the little spring that became a river was Queen Esther, the two dragons represented himself and Haman, and the two sides symbolised the Jews and their enemies. The lovely one raised up was Esther.

It's been said there is no mention of God or Jesus in The Book of Esther but I certainly see them there. God sent the dream and arranged the circumstances to advance His plans and purpose.

Jesus was in the seed line under threat and Esther the deliverer was a type of Christ.

At one point like Jesus it looked like she wanted the cup to pass from her but was warned by Mordecai she'd come to the kingdom for such a time as this.[2]

JUDAS MACCABEES' 'GOLDEN SWORD' DREAM

The Dream Setting/Backstory

The prophetic revelation from *Nebuchadnezzar's 'Large Statue' Dream* was coming to pass. Babylon and the Medo-Persian Empire had fallen, the Greeks were now reigning and the Romans were knocking at the door.

For a brief period under the Maccabees the Jews won a measure of independence until Rome gained control. This Jewish Maccabean revolt started around 167 BC when a Greek Seleucid king named Antiochus III began to Hellenize the Jewish culture and religion.

Then in 175 BC, Antiochus IV came to power and passed anti-Jewish laws through Jason, a Jewish high priest and governor, who'd bribed Antiochus IV to gain this position.

Jason's brother Onias was the rightful high priest of Judah chosen by God. Jason's evil actions set in motion a series of events that ended in Onias being murdered.

This and the fact Greek gods were now being worshipped in God's temple in Jerusalem enraged the people of Judah. They responded by forming a small guerrilla army led by the priest Judas Maccabees. Before an important battle Judas decides to encourage his men by telling them a dream he had.

The Dream Scripture
2 Maccabees 15:6-16

∽

While Nicanor, in his unlimited boastfulness and pride, was planning to erect a general trophy with the spoils taken from Judas and his men, Maccabaeus remained firm in his confident conviction that the Lord would stand by him. He urged his men not to be dismayed by the foreigners' attacks but, keeping in mind the help that had come to them from Heaven in the past, to be confident that this time too victory would be theirs with the help of the Almighty. He put fresh heart into them by citing the Law and the Prophets and, by stirring up memories of the battles they had already won, he filled them with new enthusiasm. Having thus aroused their courage, he ended his exhortation by demonstrating the treachery of the foreigners and how they had violated their oaths. Having armed each one of them not so much with the safety given by shield and lance as with that confidence which springs from noble language, he encouraged them all by describing to them a convincing dream - a vision, as it were.

What he had seen was this: Onias, the former high priest, that paragon of men, modest of bearing and gentle of manners, suitably eloquent and trained from boyhood in the practice of every virtue - Onias was stretching out his hands and praying for the whole Jewish community. Next, there appeared a man equally remarkable for his great age and dignity and invested with a marvellous and impressive air of majesty. Onias began to speak: 'This is a man', he said, 'who loves his brothers and prays much for the people and the holy city - Jeremiah, the prophet of God.' Jeremiah then stretched out his right hand and presented Judas with a golden sword, saying as he gave it, 'Take this holy sword as a gift from God; with it you will shatter the enemy.'

The Problem

The enemy was at the city gates.

The Dreamer's Metron

Judas Maccabeus was a Jewish priest and the son of Jewish priest. He is best remembered as a guerrilla leader and a military genius who defended Israel from invasion by the Seleucid king Antiochus IV Epiphanies. He defeated four Seleucid armies in quick succession and stopped the imposition of Hellenism upon Judea and the Jewish religion.

His restoration of the temple of Jerusalem is still yearly celebrated in Hanukkah the Jewish festival of lights.

Although the Seleucids offered the Jews freedom of worship, Judas continued the fight desiring political freedom as well as religious freedom. He was killed two years later but his younger brothers took over the fight and finally secured the independence of Judaea.

The Message

The dream shows the recently murdered rightful high priest Onias and the prophet Jeremiah who'd passed away four hundred years before. The message says Onias and Jeremiah are interceding for and supporting the people of Judah in this battle. Jeremiah also encourages Judas to believe and use the word of God. This is the help from heaven Judas spoke about.

God's Purpose

God's purpose was to affirm and encourage Judas and his small army that He was with them and they were in His will. It was another case of 'Not by might nor by power, but by my Spirit,' says the Lord Almighty.[1]

Satan's Purpose

As usual Satan's purpose was to wipe out the chosen people and destroy their seed line.

Dreamer's Eyes Enlightened

∼

The eyes of the dreamer and the soldiers were enlightened. The golden sword represented the Word and the testimony of God spoken with faith and the power of the Holy Spirit.

Dreamer's Response and Application

∼

The dreamer's response was to believe and receive and share the encouraging dream with his men before the battle with Nicanor.

Know God Better

∼

Again God is revealed as a caring covenant keeping God who responds to the righteous cries of his people.

The Dream Process

∼

This is a symbolic dream requiring interpretation although the basic image itself is encouraging. This is the only dream in scripture where saints who've passed on appear to encourage their people. One is reminded of Elijah and Moses appearing and talking with Jesus on the Mount of Transfiguration.[2]

The golden sword, a gift from God, with which to shatter the enemy represents the Word and testimony of God spoken with faith and power.

This is exactly what Judas was doing by citing the Law and the Prophets and, by stirring up memories of battles already won.

The Usual Suspects

∽

Jeremiah is God's prophet. Jesus the word of God is symbolised by the golden sword and Satan represented by Nicanor was attacking God's people.

Takeaways

∽

The appearance of Onias and Jeremiah in the dream brings to mind Hebrews 12:1,

> Therefore, since we are surrounded by such a great
> cloud of witnesses, let us throw off everything that
> hinders and the sin that so easily entangles. And let
> us run with perseverance the race marked out
> for us.

There is a sense of us playing our part in God's plans and purpose in our day and the former runners cheering us on. After hearing this dream the army became firmly focused on the issue at hand,

Their concern for their wives and children, their brothers and relatives, had shrunk to minute importance; their chief and greatest fear was for the consecrated Temple.[3]

THE PRIMARY FUNCTION OF GOD'S DREAMS

The primary function of God's dreams is so people can hear from God and obey His instructions.

The primary purpose of all God's Bible dreams was to advance His plans and purpose for Jesus Christ the Messiah.

It is the same with all the gifts, endowments and anointings of God. They are never given to promote our own personal agendas. They are never under our control.

They are given from Heaven in order we can become equipped to do God's will. Dreams must always operate under the control of God and his Holy Spirit. They are always sent to advance His plans and purpose, not our plans and purposes.

These holy things are not something that we can use for our own purposes. The emphasis must always be on submitting to God's will and carrying out His plans and purpose.

God's dreams can only be properly understood when the Holy Spirit reveals the true interpretation. This is the same with the gift of speaking in tongues. It also is a gift of revelation that we cannot comprehend without the gift of interpretation from the Holy Spirit.

No one ever becomes an expert at these things.

We are always totally dependent of the kindness of the Holy Spirit for every single gift of revelation in order we that might be able to do God's will and get to know Him better.

Hear God's voice and do God's will.

ACKNOWLEDGMENTS

We all need help with our God given assignments. Thank God for my family and the body of Christ. In Ephesians 4, Paul says,

> Christ himself gave the apostles, the prophets, the evangelists, the pastors and teachers, to equip his people for works of service. He also says the whole body of Christ is joined and held together by every supporting ligament while it grows and builds itself up in love, as each part does its work.

We all have a role to play. Sometimes it's a large part, sometimes a small part but it's all necessary.

So, especial thanks to my wife Angela and our fourteen children, Shann, Brendan, Nora, Aaron, Mary, Hannah, Ruth, John, Patrick, David, Jacob, Isaac, Abraham and Angela and their respective spouses and children for all their love, support and encouragement during the writing process.

I also want to thank Dr Mary McCauley, Judy McGookin and Gerrit Uitterdijk for proofreading and Abraham McCauley for help with the cover. I'd also like to thank a number of friends for their emotional, prayer and financial support during this project.

Faces that pass through my mind in no particular order are, Ernie & Jill Cahoon, Dirk Lakeman, Jackie and Norma McArthur, Laurence & Rosanne McDowell, Harry & Flo Ferguson, Lionel Batke, Matthew & Rachel Cruickshank, Harry & Rema Wilson, Vince & Rachel Owens, Lynne Elliott, Hilary Ferguson, Nigel & Heather Glasgow, John & Lesley Haw, Brendan Osbourne, Gerrit & Nanda Utterdyke, Stephen & Judy Mc Gookin, Donal & Anne Walsh, Caroline Curtis, Kathleen McKee, Peris Bowers, Aine Fuller, Anne Brosnan, John & Leslie Haw, Cindy & Glen Skinner, Shelley McCullough, Michal & Janka Majercin, Stephen Koni Getty and Fr Peter & Petra Jakub.

NOTES

1. GOD'S HOLY SPIRIT INTERPRETS GOD'S DREAMS

1. 2 Corinthians 10-11

BIBLICAL DREAM INTERPRETERS

1. Proverbs 10:22

4. GOD'S ETERNAL PURPOSE FOR DREAMS

1. Ephesians 3:11
2. Ephesians 1:9-11
3. Isaiah 48:28.
4. John 17:24
5. Ephesians 1:4-7
6. 1 Peter 1:17-21
7. Ephesians 3:8-12
8. 1 Peter 1:12
9. 1 Corinthians 2:7-8
10. Ephesians 5:32
11. John 17:20-24
12. Ezekiel 1:12

5. THE DANGER OF INDIVIDUALISM

1. Luke 14:25-27
2. Matthew 28:19-20
3. Ephesians 4:15-16
4. John 5:19-20
5. 2 Timothy 2:15

6. IT'S ALL ABOUT JESUS!

1. Sirach (Ecclesiasticus) 34:1-8 GNBD
2. John 5:39
3. Isaiah 53:11
4. John 5:39
5. Luke 24:25-27
6. Luke 24:27, 31
7. Ephesians 3:11
8. Yehuda Amichai, Poems, 1948-1962
9. Ephesians 1:17
10. Revelation 11:15
11. Ephesians 1:17-19
12. I Corinthians 1:18-25.
13. John 6:38
14. Psalm 127:1-2
15. John 4:34
16. Psalm 119:105
17. Habakkuk 2:14

7. SATAN HATES GOD'S DREAMS

1. Deuteronomy 18:9-11
2. Deuteronomy 18:9-11

8. MY PURPOSE FOR THIS BOOK

1. Proverbs 16:33

9. MY DREAM QUALIFICATIONS

1. Ephesians 1:17-19
2. John 15:14-15
3. Isaiah 43:19
4. Philippians 3:8
5. 2 John 14:15

10. BIBLE DREAMS AND THE GODS

1. Psalm 86:8
2. Psalm 96:4
3. Psalm 135:5
4. Psalm 29:1
5. Psalm 97:7
6. Psalm 95:3
7. Exodus 12:12
8. Numbers 33:4
9. Exodus 20:3
10. Exodus 23:32–33
11. Deuteronomy 4:19-20
12. Deuteronomy 4:27
13. Colossians 1:15-20
14. Daniel 2:20-22
15. Daniel 4:3
16. Daniel 4:34-35
17. Habakkuk 2:14
18. Zechariah 3:7
19. Genesis 6:1–4
20. Deuteronomy 32:8-9
21. Psalm 82:1-8
22. 1 Peter 1:18, Revelation 13:8.
23. Ephesians 3:6
24. Ephesians 3:10-11
25. 1 Corinthians 2:6-8
26. Daniel 2:28
27. Jeremiah 33:3 (CEV)

11. GOD'S GOOD PURPOSES FOR SLEEP AND DREAMS

1. Ephesians 2:1-3
2. Matthew 6:34
3. Proverbs 3:24-25
4. Matthew 5:45
5. Isaiah 57:20-21
6. Isaiah 57:2 (NET Bible)
7. Psalm 4:8
8. Psalm 16:7
9. Psalm 3:5
10. Lamentations 3:22–23

11. Isaiah 50:4-5
12. Isaiah 50:4-5

12. A SHORT HISTORY OF DREAMS

1. Genesis 41:16
2. (469–399 BC)
3. (384–322 BC)
4. Acts 2:17
5. Ecclesiastes. 5:2
6. Genesis 37:5–10
7. Daniel 2:29-31
8. Genesis 41
9. Daniel 2

13. GOD'S SOVEREIGN PURPOSE

1. Ephesians 1:11
2. Romans 8:28
3. Isaiah 46:11
4. 1 Corinthians 13:2 (NLT)
5. Jeremiah 3.33
6. John 5:19
7. Matthew 6:32-34

14. GOD'S ETERNAL PLANS AND PURPOSE

1. 1 John 3:8
2. Psalm 105:17-17 (NASB)
3. 1 Chronicles 21:1; Job 1–2; Zechariah 3:1–2; and 2 Peter 2:4; Jude 6
4. Job 38:4-7
5. Genesis 1:2
6. Genesis 9:7
7. Ephesians 3:8-9
8. Ephesians 3:10-11
9. Ephesians 1:20-23
10. Romans 16:25; Colossians 1:26; Ephesians 3:9-10.
11. Gen. 3:15
12. Revelation 5:13

15. SATAN'S HINDERING PURPOSE

1. Genesis 3:15
2. Genesis 6:1-8
3. Jude 1:6
4. 2 Peter 2:4
5. Genesis 6:9
6. Numbers 13:33 (The Israel Bible™)
7. Genesis 12
8. Genesis 20
9. Exodus 1:15-16
10. Exodus 14
11. 2 Samuel 7:16
12. 2 Chronicles 21:4
13. 2 Chronicles 21:17; 22:1
14. 2 Chronicles 22:10
15. Isaiah 36:1, 38:1
16. Esther 3
17. Matthew 1:18-20
18. Matthew 2
19. Matthew 4
20. Luke 4
21. Luke 8:22, Mark 4:35, Matthew 8;32
22. John 8:58
23. Isaiah 46:10
24. 1 John 5:19
25. Hebrews 2:8
26. Romans 16:20
27. Genesis 1:28
28. Matthew 4:8-10

16. THE ANGEL OF THE LORD

1. Numbers 12:6-8
2. Genesis 15:1
3. Genesis 18:1
4. Numbers 12:6-8
5. Exodus 33:18-20
6. Exodus 33:11
7. Exodus 33:18-20
8. John 1:18
9. John 6:46
10. 1 Timothy 6:16

11. Hebrews 1:3
12. Matthew 11:27
13. John 14:8-11
14. Exodus 3:1-5
15. Joshua 5:14-15
16. Exodus 3:6
17. Exodus 23:20-23
18. Numbers 22:22-35
19. Judges 6
20. Judges 13
21. 1 Chronicles 21:18
22. Exodus 14: Judges 2:1
23. 1 Kings 19:3
24. Mark 1:21-24
25. Psalm 34: 7
26. Psalm 35:4-6
27. Genesis 16:13
28. Genesis 21:17-18
29. Genesis 22:12
30. Genesis 22:15-18
31. Genesis 32:30
32. Hosea 12:4
33. Exodus 3:6
34. Genesis 15:1
35. Genesis 18:1
36. Judges 2:1-2
37. Judges 6:22
38. Judges 13:22

18. GOD AND JESUS IN BIBLE DREAMS

1. John 1:18 (NKJV)
2. 1 Timothy 6:16 (NLT)
3. John 1:18 (NKJV)
4. Exodus 33:20
5. John 1:47-51
6. Judges 7:22

19. DREAM PURPOSE AND PROCESS

1. Genesis 40:8
2. Genesis 40:8 (NLT)
3. Daniel 2:27

4. 1 Corinthians 14:13
5. 2 Corinthians 10-11

21. GOD'S PURPOSE FOR EACH BIBLE DREAM

1. Romans 10:17
2. Genesis 15:13
3. Genesis 15:13
4. Jeremiah 29:13
5. Daniel 10

22. THE IMPORTANCE OF A DREAMER'S METRON

1. 2 Corinthians 10:12-18
2. Matthew 13:12
3. 1 Timothy 3:5

24. GOD'S PURPOSES FOR BELIEVER'S METRONS

1. Deuteronomy 17:17
2. Genesis 22:16-16
3. Genesis 3:15
4. Genesis 28:13-15
5. Job 1:8
6. Ezekiel 14:19
7. James 5:11
8. Daniel 1:17
9. Daniel 10:14
10. Daniel 8:15-17, 9:20-23, 10:5-14
11. Daniel 9:1-2
12. Daniel 9
13. Daniel 6:10-22
14. Daniel 7:9
15. Daniel 2:44
16. Romans 11:4, 1 Kings 19:18
17. John 1:14; 1 Timothy 3:16
18. Colossians 1:15-17; John 1:17
19. 1 Timothy 2:5; 1 Corinthians 8:6
20. Philippians 2:9-11; 1 Corinthians 15:27-28

21. John 1:4-5; 9:5
22. Luke 4:18-19; John 3:34
23. John 10:14
24. John 6:35, 51
25. Luke 5:22-25; Mark 2:5-11
26. John 10:9, 14:6
27. John 11:25-26
28. Revelation 1:17-18
29. Mark 10:47
30. Matthew 21:8-9
31. Isaiah 53:3; Matthew 8:16-17
32. Hebrews 7:26
33. John 1:29
34. Isaiah 9:6
35. 1 Corinthians 1:24; Colossians 2:2-3)
36. Psalm 103:7
37. 2 Peter 3:16

25. GOD'S PURPOSES FOR NON BELIEVER'S METRONS

1. Genesis 21:22–34
2. Genesis 24:29-60
3. Midrash Raba, Gen 24
4. Genesis 15:13
5. Jeremiah 4:7
6. Daniel 2:48
7. Numbers 24:17

26. DEFINITION OF A DREAM

1. Jeremiah 31:26
2. Job 33:15
3. Daniel 4:5
4. Isaiah 29:7 (KJV)
5. Genesis 28:10-22
6. Matthew 17:1-9
7. Matthew 17:5-7
8. Jeremiah 30:3-31:26

27. FOUR KINDS OF BIBLE DREAMS

1. Jeremiah 23:26
2. Jeremiah 29:8
3. Jeremiah 23:32
4. Deuteronomy 13:1-3
5. Jeremiah 23:25-32
6. Jude 1:8
7. Isaiah 29:7-8
8. Ecclesiastes 5:3

28. WHERE DREAMS COME FROM

1. Job 7:11-16
2. Job 4:12-21
3. Matthew 4:1-11
4. 2 Peter 1:20-21
5. Jeremiah 23:18
6. Jeremiah 23:13
7. Jeremiah 23:14
8. Jeremiah 23:14
9. Jeremiah 23:16
10. Jeremiah 23:25-27
11. Jeremiah 23:28-29
12. Hebrews 4:12-13
13. 2 Corinthians 10:3-5 (NKJV)
14. Jeremiah 23:20
15. Jeremiah 23:30-32
16. Isaiah 43:13 (ASV)

32. THE TIMELINE OF BIBLE DREAMS

1. John 21:25
2. Job 4:12-21
3. Job 7:11-16
4. Job 33:14-18
5. Genesis 15:1-21
6. Genesis 20:1-18
7. Genesis 28:10-22
8. Genesis 31:10-13
9. Genesis 31:22-24
10. Genesis 32:1-32

11. Genesis 37:1-11
12. Genesis 37:1-11
13. Genesis 40:1-23
14. Genesis 40:1-23
15. Genesis 41:1-49
16. Genesis 41:1-49
17. Genesis 46:1-7
18. Numbers 12:6-8
19. Numbers 22:8-10
20. Numbers 22:19-20
21. Deuteronomy 13:1-5
22. Judges 7:9-18
23. 1 Samuel 3:1-15
24. I Samuel 28:6 -15)
25. 2 Chronicles 1:7
26. Psalm 26:1
27. 2 Samuel 7:1-29
28. Psalm 17:1-15
29. Psalm 73.20
30. I Kings 3:5-28
31. 2 Chronicles 1:1-17
32. Proverbs 29:18
33. Song of Songs 3:1-5:16
34. I Kings 9:1-9
35. 2 Chronicles 1:1-17
36. Joel 2:28,29
37. Hosea 12:9,10
38. Isaiah 29: 5-12
39. Isaiah 35:5
40. Jeremiah 30:3 -31:26
41. Jeremiah 23:25-40
42. Jeremiah 27:9-11
43. Daniel 1:17
44. Daniel 4:4-37
45. Daniel 2:17-48
46. Daniel 4:4-37
47. Daniel 5:5-30
48. Daniel 7:1-28
49. Daniel 8:1-27
50. Daniel 10:1-12:13
51. Zechariah 1:18 - 4:4:1
52. Zechariah 10:2
53. Zechariah 13:4
54. Matthew 1:20-25
55. Matthew 1:20-25

56. Matthew 2:3-15
57. Matthew 2:19-23
58. Matthew 2:19-23
59. Matthew 27:19
60. Acts 2:17
61. Acts 9:1-9
62. Acts 9:10-19
63. Acts 10:1-7
64. Acts 10:9-22
65. Acts 10:44-48
66. Acts 16:6-11
67. Acts 18:9-11
68. Acts 27:20-25
69. The Wisdom of Solomon 18:17-19
70. 2 Esdras 11 & 12 Common English Bible (CEB)
71. 2 Esdras 13:1-57 Common English Bible (CEB)
72. Esther 10:4-13 (Addition F) (NRSVCE)
73. 2 Maccabees 15:6-16

33. HOW JESUS INTERPRETS DREAMS

1. Mark 4:1-20
2. Daniel 1:17
3. Daniel 2:31-35
4. Daniel 2:38-45
5. Genesis 40:8
6. Daniel 2:27-28
7. Daniel 2:29-30
8. Judges 7:13-14

34. THE MCCAULEY DREAM CHECKLIST

1. Ephesians 1:17-19
2. Psalm 46:1-2
3. Ephesians 3:6
4. Hebrews 1:3
5. Hebrews 1:3
6. Ephesians 3:6
7. Ephesians 3:10
8. John 10:10
9. Luke 22:31
10. 1 Peter 5:8
11. Ephesians 1:17

12. Revelation 11:15
13. Luke 24:13-35

35. GOD'S PURPOSE FOR ABRAHAM

1. Genesis 12:1-3
2. Galatians 3:6-9
3. Acts 26:6
4. Ephesians 2:12
5. Ephesians 2:12-13
6. Romans 15:8
7. Hebrews 11:8
8. 1 Corinthians 14:1
9. Genesis 12:3
10. 1 Kings 9:6-7
11. Mark 16:15
12. Romans 12:26
13. Revelation 20:10
14. Revelation 21:2
15. Genesis 12:1
16. Matthew 28
17. Genesis 17:1-8
18. Genesis 22:15-18
19. Genesis 15:1-7
20. Genesis 15:18
21. James 2:23; 2 Chronicles 20:7; Isaiah 41:8
22. Romans 4:11,16
23. Romans 4:13
24. Romans 4:1-3
25. Galatians 3:6-9
26. Hebrews 6:12-19
27. Hebrews 11:39
28. Romans3:14,22
29. Romans 3:26-29
30. John 8:56
31. Galatians 3:29
32. Genesis 17:6
33. Galatians 3:7-9
34. Galatian 3:13-14

36. ABRAHAM'S COVENANT DREAM

1. Genesis 6:7
2. Genesis 11:1-9
3. Acts 7:2-3
4. Genesis 12:1-3
5. Genesis 13:14-18
6. James. 2:23
7. Hebrews 11:8-9
8. Jeremiah 34:18
9. Galatians 3:8
10. Matthew 16:16-17
11. John 16:12-13
12. Genesis 15:6
13. John 1:18 (NKJV)
14. 1 Timothy 6:16 (NLT)
15. 2 Peter 3:9

37. KING ABIMELEK'S DREAM

1. Genesis 17:19

38. JACOB'S COVENANT DREAM

1. Genesis 25:23
2. Genesis 26:34-35
3. Genesis 25:23
4. Genesis 28:13-15
5. John 1:51 (NLT)
6. Matthew 1:16
7. Hosea 12:4

39. JACOB'S 'GOATS AND GO BACK HOME' DREAM

1. Daniel 2:20-21
2. Genesis 28:13-15
3. Genesis 31:8-9
4. Romans 8:27-28

40. LABAN'S 'DON'T HARM JACOB' DREAM

1. Genesis 15:13

41. JACOB WRESTLES WITH GOD AND MAN

1. Genesis 25:15
2. Genesis 28:13-15
3. Hosea 12:3
4. Genesis 32:12
5. Jeremiah 29:13
6. 1 Corinthians 12:31 (KJV)

43. JOSEPH'S 'SHEAVES OF GRAIN' DREAM

1. Genesis 37:20
2. Romans 8:28
3. 1 Chronicles 5:1-2
4. Psalm 105:17-19
5. Matthew 4:4
6. Romans 10:17

44. JOSEPH'S 'SUN, MOON AND STARS' DREAM

1. Isaiah 51:1
2. Revelation 12:1
3. Genesis 37:20
4. Romans 8:28
5. Deuteronomy 4:19
6. Deuteronomy 4:19-20
7. Isaiah 53:3
8. Zechariah 12:10
9. Luke 1:33

45. PHARAOH'S CUPBEARER'S DREAM

1. Genesis 15:13
2. Romans 8:28
3. Matthew 26:39
4. Luke 22:20

46. PHARAOH'S BAKER'S DREAM

1. Genesis 15:13
2. Romans 8:28
3. Romans 4:4-5
4. Matthew 26:39
5. Isaiah 53:5
6. Galatians 3:13

47. PHARAOH'S TWO SAME 'FAMINE' DREAMS

1. Psalm 105:17-19
2. Genesis 15:13-14
3. 1 Kings 3:16-28
4. Daniel 12:9
5. Exodus 10:13
6. Hosea 13:15

48. JACOB'S 'GO DOWN TO EGYPT' NIGHT VISION DREAM

1. Genesis 45:4-7
2. Genesis 28:13-15
3. 2 Corinthians 12:9
4. Isaiah 61:3
5. Matthew 28:20

49. BALAAM'S 'DON'T CURSE ISRAEL' DREAM

1. Matthew 6:24
2. Proverbs 26:2,
3. Genesis 12:3
4. Numbers 23:8
5. Numbers 24:9 (NASB)

50. BALAAM'S 'IF THEY CALL YOU' DREAM

1. Matthew 6:24
2. Jude 1:11
3. Numbers 22:8

4. Numbers 24:17
5. Numbers 25:1–9; Deuteronomy 23:3–6
6. Joshua 13:22, 24:9, and Nehemiah 13:2
7. Numbers 31:8
8. Numbers 25
9. 2 Peter 2:15
10. Jude 1:11
11. Revelation 2:14

51. THE MIDIANITE'S DREAM FOR GIDEON

1. Deuteronomy 18:9-13
2. Judges 6:7-10
3. Romans 10:17
4. Judges 6:25-26
5. Genesis 18:19
6. Deuteronomy 17:17
7. Judges 8:25–27

52. SAMUEL'S NIGHT VISION DREAM

1. 1 Samuel 2:12-17
2. 1 Samuel 2:12
3. 1 Samuel 2:33
4. Isaiah 29:13
5. Isaiah 29:9-12
6. 1 Samuel 28:15
7. Micah 3:5-9
8. 1 Peter 4:17
9. Malachi 4:6
10. 1 Samuel 8:1-4
11. 1 Samuel 8:7

53. NATHAN'S DREAM FOR KING DAVID

1. 1 Chronicles 29:29
2. 2 Chronicles 9:29
3. 2 Chronicles 29:25
4. 2 Samuel 12:7–14
5. 2 Samuel 12:24–25
6. First Chronicles 3:5
7. 1 Kings 1:8–45

8. 1 Chronicles 22:7-10
9. 2 Samuel 7:13-14

54. DAVID'S BEDTIME PRAYER

1. 1 Samuel 20:32–33
2. 2 Kings 18:5-6
3. 2 Kings 23:25
4. 1 Samuel 10:1
5. 1 Chronicles 5:2
6. Luke 2:4
7. 1 Samuel 13:14
8. Acts 13:22
9. 1 Samuel 10:1–6, 1 Samuel 16:14
10. 2 Samuel 1:19-27
11. 1 Samuel 17:8-11
12. 1 Samuel 18:5
13. Psalm 17:5-6
14. Psalm 17:8-9

55. SOLOMON'S 'DISCERNING HEART' DREAM

1. Deuteronomy 18:16-19
2. Ephesians 3:20-21
3. Nehemiah 13:26
4. Matthew 6:33

56. SOLOMON'S 'THE BRIDE'S' DREAM

1. Jeremiah 29:13
2. Deuteronomy 4:29
3. Psalm 63:1
4. Psalm 42:1
5. Hebrews 10:19
6. Isiah 62:6-7
7. John 17:24
8. Revelation 3:20
9. Matthew 22:37
10. John 14:23-28

57. SOLOMON'S WARNING DREAM

1. 1 Kings 8:21
2. I Kings 8:22-25
3. I Kings 8:25
4. Deuteronomy 17:16
5. 1 Kings 11:1-9
6. Genesis 18:18-19

58. SOLOMON 'ASKS FOR WISDOM' DREAM

1. 1 Kings 3:14
2. Deuteronomy 17:16-20
3. Proverbs 10:22

59. ELIPHAZ'S 'DEMONIC NIGHTMARE' DREAM

1. Matthew 10:29
2. Matthew 6:23
3. Job 42:7-8
4. Job 1:8
5. Isaiah 8:19-20
6. Job 5:13

60. JOB'S SATANIC NIGHTMARES

1. Job 1:8
2. Ezekiel 14:19
3. James 5:11
4. Ephesians 1:17-19
5. Job 19:25

61. ELIHU'S DREAM TALK

1. Job 32:2
2. Daniel 8:27
3. 2 Peter 3:9

62. ISAIAH'S ORACLE ON DREAMS

1. Isaiah 2:1
2. Isaiah 6:3
3. Isaiah 14:12-15
4. Isaiah 1:2; Isaiah 2:11-20; Isaiah 34:1-2; Isaiah 42:25
5. Isaiah 11:16; Isaiah 14:1-2; Isaiah 32:2; Isaiah 41:14-16
6. Isaiah 42:7
7. Isaiah 30:15; Isaiah 55:6-9
8. Isaiah 26:15; Isaiah 43:2-6)
9. Isaiah 40:9
10. Isaiah 11:6-9
11. Romans 11:25
12. Isaiah 42:7, 2 Corinthians 3:14-16
13. Ephesians 3:6
14. John 10:16

63. JEREMIAH'S 'ISRAEL WILL RETURN' DREAM

1. 1 Kings 9:7
2. Jeremiah 30:12-15
3. Jeremiah 30:18
4. Deuteronomy 11:26
5. Galatians 6:7-8
6. Deuteronomy 28:64-65
7. Jeremiah 31:33

64. NEBUCHADNEZZAR'S 'LARGE STATUE' DREAM

1. Jeremiah 4:7
2. Revelation 11:15
3. Job 33:14-18

65. DANIEL'S 'MYSTERY REVEALED' NIGHT VISION DREAM

1. Daniel 2:27-28
2. Daniel 2:23
3. Daniel 2:27

4. Matthew 21:42-44

66. NEBUCHADNEZZAR'S 'LARGE TREE' DREAM

1. Daniel 2:47
2. Jeremiah 4:7
3. Psalm 72:11-14
4. Daniel 4:37
5. 2 Peter 3:9
6. Psalm 35:10
7. Psalm 146:5-9
8. Daniel 4:17
9. Psalm 68:5; Psalm 146:9
10. Ezekiel 29:17-20 (NLT)
11. 2 Peter 3:8-9
12. Daniel 4:35-37

67. DANIEL'S 'FOUR BEASTS' DREAM

1. Daniel 4:17
2. Revelation 19:20
3. Proverbs 25:2
4. Isaiah 46:10
5. John 16:12-13
6. Isaiah 43:13
7. Daniel 7:24-25
8. John 16:12

68. DANIEL'S 'RAM, GOAT AND LITTLE HORN' DREAM

1. Daniel 8:1
2. Daniel 8:27
3. Genesis 15:12 (BSB)
4. Romans 11:33
5. Matthew 24:9-21
6. Matthew 24:15

69. ZECHARIAH'S DREAM OF HORSES

1. 1 Kings 9:6-7
2. Jeremiah 29:10-14
3. Isaiah 47:6
4. Isaiah 47:11
5. Genesis 12:1-3
6. Hebrews 12:5-7

70. ZECHARIAH'S DREAM OF HORNS AND CRAFTSMEN.

1. 1 Kings 9:6-7
2. Exodus 31:1-6
3. John 18:36
4. 2 Corinthians 10:4
5. Colossians 1:16
6. Ephesians 6:10-12
7. Jeremiah 33:18
8. 1 Kings 18:30-32
9. Genesis 14:18
10. Nehemiah 4:17-18

71. ZECHARIAH'S DREAM OF THE MEASURING LINE

1. 1 Kings 9:6-7
2. Ephesians 3:1-6
3. Galatians 3:8
4. Revelation 18:4-5

72. ZECHARIAH'S DREAM OF JOSHUA

1. 1 Kings 9:6-7
2. Isaiah 64:6
3. Isaiah 61:10
4. John 15:5
5. Daniel 2:45
6. Revelation 5:6
7. Hebrews 10:11-15

8. Zechariah 3:7
9. Ephesians 2:19-22

73. ZECHARIAH'S DREAM OF LAMPSTAND AND TREES

1. 1 Kings 9:6-7

74. ZECHARIAH'S DREAM OF THE FLYING SCROLL

1. 1 Kings 9:6-7
2. Leviticus 19:2
3. Deuteronomy 7:6
4. Mark 12:30-31
5. Psalm 40:7
6. Jeremiah 36:2
7. Ezekiel 3:3
8. Galatians 3:13
9. Revelation 5:1-6
10. Hebrews 9:27
11. 1 Peter 10:11-12
12. Deuteronomy 28:45
13. Galatians 3:10-14

75. ZECHARIAH'S DREAM OF THE WOMAN IN A BASKET

1. 1 Kings 9:6-7
2. Deuteronomy 9:5
3. Leviticus 26:30
4. Ezekiel 45:10; Proverbs 20:23
5. Amos 8:4-8; Micah 6:10-13
6. Ezekiel 22:20
7. John 14:23
8. Revelation 19:3

76. ZECHARIAH'S DREAM OF THE FOUR CHARIOTS

1. 1 Kings 9:6-7

77. ST. JOSEPH'S 'MARRY MARY' DREAM

1. Galatians 4:4-5
2. Matthew 1:22-23
3. Numbers 12:6
4. 1 Corinthians 1:26-29
5. Luke 1:31-32
6. Jeremiah 22:30

78. THE MAGI'S DREAM

1. Micah 5:2
2. Jeremiah 31:15

79. ST. JOSEPH'S 'ESCAPE TO EGYPT' DREAM

1. Hosea 11:1 (NKJV)

80. ST. JOSEPH'S 'BACK TO ISRAEL' DREAM

1. Hosea 11:1

81. ST. JOSEPH'S 'GO TO NAZARETH' DREAM

1. Hebrews 7:25
2. Matthew 2:23
3. Isaiah 11:1
4. Isaiah 53:3
5. Exodus 23:20

82. JESUS' 'TEMPTED BY SATAN' DREAM

1. John 1:14; 1 Timothy 3:16
2. Colossians 1:15-17; John 1:17
3. 1 Timothy 2:5; 1 Corinthians 8:6
4. Philippians 2:9-11; 1 Corinthians 15:27-28
5. John 1:4-5; 9:5
6. Luke 4:18-19; John 3:34
7. Mark 10:47
8. John 10:14
9. John 6:35, 51
10. Luke 5:22-25; Mark 2:5-11
11. John 10:9, 14:6
12. John 11:25-26
13. Revelation 1:17-18
14. Mark 10:47
15. Matthew 21:8-9
16. Isaiah 53:3; Matthew 8:16-17
17. Hebrews 7:26
18. John 1:29
19. Isaiah 9:6
20. 1 Corinthians 1:24; Colossians 2:2-3)
21. Deuteronomy 8:3
22. Deuteronomy 6:16
23. Deuteronomy 6:13, I Samuel 7:3
24. Ephesians 2:2
25. Deuteronomy 6:13
26. Matthew 4:1-11
27. Mark 1:12-13
28. Luke 4:1-13
29. 2 Peter 1:21

83. PILATE'S WIFE'S DREAM

1. 1 Corinthians 2:8
2. Job 33:17

84. PETER INTERPRETING PENTECOST

1. Acts 2:1-13
2. Psalm 103:7
3. John 3:11

85. SAUL'S VISION ON THE ROAD TO DAMASCUS

1. 2 Peter 3:6
2. Galatians 1:1

86. ANANIAS' VISION ABOUT PAUL

1. 1 Kings 19:18
2. John 15:14-16
3. Ephesians 3:8-11

87. PAUL'S TRANCE

1. 2 Peter 3:6
2. Acts 2:14
3. Galatians 1:11-12
4. Galatians 1:1

88. CORNELIUS' 'SEND FOR PETER' VISION

1. Acts 1:8
2. Acts 4:11-12
3. Acts 16:30-31

89. PETER'S 'KILL AND EAT' TRANCE

1. Isaiah 42:6
2. Luke 2:29-32
3. Matthew 15:26
4. Ephesians 2:12
5. Psalm 103:7
6. 1 Timothy 2:3-6
7. John 4:9
8. John 4:32
9. Genesis 41:32
10. Galatians 2:12

90. PETER'S REVELATION AT CORNELIUS'S HOUSE

1. Psalm 103:7
2. Habakkuk 2:14
3. Ephesians 3:10-11

91. PAUL'S 'MAN OF MACEDONIA' NIGHT VISION DREAM

1. Mark 16:5
2. 2 Peter 3:6

92. PAUL'S 'FEAR NOT' NIGHT VISION DREAM

1. Acts 15:36
2. Acts 15:36-41
3. 1 Corinthians 2:3
4. 2 Peter 3:6
5. Matthew 28:18-20
6. 1 Kings 19:18
7. Romans 11:1-6
8. Romans 11:25-27

93. PAUL'S 'ANGELIC' NIGHT VISION DREAM

1. Acts 27:9
2. Acts 27:10
3. 2 Peter 3:6
4. 2 Timothy 1:8-12

94. EGYPT'S 'DREADFUL DREAMS'

1. The Wisdom of Solomon 17:7 GNTD
2. Revelation 20:11-15
3. The Wisdom of Solomon
4. The Wisdom of Solomon
5. The Wisdom of Solomon

95. ESDRAS' EAGLE AND LION' DREAM

1. Habakkuk 1:2

96. ESDRAS 'MAN FROM THE SEA' DREAM

1. 2 Esdras 13:23-25 (CEB)
2. 2 Esdras 13:24 (CEB)
3. Daniel 2:20-22
4. Psalm 75:7
5. Luke 1:51-55

97. MORDECAI'S 'TWO GREAT DRAGONS' DREAM

1. Esther 4:13-14
2. Esther 4:14

98. JUDAS MACCABEES' 'GOLDEN SWORD' DREAM

1. Zechariah 4:6
2. Matthew 17:3
3. 2 Maccabees 15:18

Printed in Great Britain
by Amazon